Controversies in Constitutional Law

Collections of Documents and Articles on Major Questions of American Law

General Editor

Paul Finkelman

University of Tulsa School of Law

A Garland Series

Labor and the Constitution

Volume 1
The Constitutionality of Labor Laws and their Relation to Freedom of Religion and Speech

Edited with introductions by

David L. Gregory
St. John's University

GARLAND PUBLISHING, INC.
A MEMBER OF THE TAYLOR & FRANCIS GROUP
New York & London
1999

Library of Congress Cataloging-in-Publication Data

Labor and the constitution / edited with an introduction by David L. Gregory.
p. cm. — (Controversies in constitutional law)
Includes bibliographical references.
Contents: v. 1. The constitutionality of labor laws and their relation to freedom of religion and speech — v. 2. Labor and property, privacy, discrimination, and international relations.
ISBN 0-8153-3389-7 (set : alk. paper)
1. Labor laws and legislation—United States. 2. Civil rights—United States. I. Gregory, David L. II. Series.
KF3321.L33 1999
344.7301—dc21 99-33953
CIP

Printed on acid-free, 250-year-life paper
Manufactured in the United States of America

Contents

vii General Introduction
ix Volume Introduction

The Constitutionality and Purpose of the Federal Labor Laws

1 *National Labor Relations Board* v. *Jones and Laughlin Steel Corp.*
51 A Common Law for Labor Relations: A Critique of the New Deal Labor Legislation
Richard A. Epstein
103 The Common Law, Labor Law, and Reality: A Response to Professor Epstein
Julius G. Getman and Thomas C. Kohler

Labor and Religion

124 *National Labor Relations Board* v. *Catholic Bishop of Chicago*
153 *Trans World Airlines, Inc.* v. *Hardison*
189 Government Regulation of Religion Through Labor and Employment Discrimination Laws
David L. Gregory

Labor and Speech

231 *Communications Workers of America* v. *Beck*
277 *Waters* v. *Churchill*
317 Free Speech and Due Process in the Workplace
Cynthia L. Estlund
369 Acknowledgments

General Introduction

This ongoing series, *Controversies in Constitutional Law,* provides teachers, scholars, and students convenient access to the debates and scholarly literature surrounding major questions of constitutional law. Each set of books—from two to four volumes—consists of four elements: an extended introduction to the issue by the editor; reprints of the significant cases and briefs on the subject; congressional testimony, and other primary documents on the issue; and a selection of the best scholarly articles on the subject. By conveniently gathering all this material in one place, each set of volumes allows users to become familiar quite quickly with the arguments and positions surrounding a particular constitutional controversy.

Scholars and students interested in constitutional law and public policy are often overwhelmed by the sheer amount of material published on controversial subjects. The topics in *Controversies in Constitutional Law* are timely, politically significant, and intellectually compelling. They are the issues that bring the legal academy, courts, politicians, and general public together—although not always in harmony.

Many scholars are barely able to keep up with the material in their own fields. Yet there is a need to learn about issues beyond our own specialties. A new course may require an introduction to a problem; our own research may lead us to a new issue. The series *Controversies in Constitutional Law* is designed to meet these needs, enabling scholars and teachers to come up to speed quickly on the topics in each volume.

This series also serves students at all levels of higher education. Students often encounter controversial topics without the background in how the problem developed. These volumes provide such a background. The important cases are reprinted in full; the introductions provide students with a map to the issues; the briefs, congressional testimony, and scholarly articles give convenient access to the arguments and debates.

The volumes bring together in one place a wide variety of sources and materials that are unlikely to be found in any one library. The primary documents include cases, briefs, testimony from legislative committee hearings, and, on occasion, executive branch publications. Few law libraries, university libraries, or public libraries will have all these materials. The secondary literature comes from the scholarly literature of law, history, political science, economics, criminology, and other relevant fields. Some of the articles also may be from serious nonacademic journals.

The related government publications, briefs, and congressional testimony are particularly important. Too often scholars overlook them. There is a tendency to focus on court opinions—what the Supreme Court said. Obviously this is important for understanding doctrine, but briefs, especially amicus briefs, are also an important source of information about the larger constitutional controversy the case represents. The politics of a case are often more apparent in these briefs than in either the oral agruments or the Court's opinion. Similarly, congressional hearings illustrate the social, philosophical, and political dimensions of these questions.

The goal of limiting each collection—two to four focused volumes—and the occasional inability to secure a reasonable copyright permission fee for some important articles often forces hard and judicious choices. Important articles that are not reprinted here are listed in the further reading sections at the end of the introductions.

The ongoing series *Controversies in Constitutional Law* provides in one single place comprehensive introductions to topics that will satisfy most lawyers, scholars, and students. By combining cases, briefs, legislative debates, and testimony from committee hearings with secondary articles, it is hoped to facilitate access to the issue presented in each set of volumes.

Introduction

In the structure of government in the United States the Constitution, the Bill of Rights and other Amendments — especially the Fourteenth Amendment — are the primary referential points to locate, protect, and enhance our fundamental political freedoms. The intersections between Labor Law and Constitutional Law occasionally synergize, but perhaps more often obviate the tensions among, several fundamental freedoms. This first volume will situate and examine the intersections among labor, religion, and speech, the two latter among our most fundamental First Amendment rights.

Labor management relations in the unionized context, and employment law relations in the larger non-unionized and private sector workplace context, generally operate without direct reference to the Constitution. Because the super majority of the workforce in the United States is situated in the private sector, and thus is not directly employed by the government at the municipal, county, state, or federal level, the Constitution thus does not generally and directly come into play in the labor and employment law regime. Throughout most of the twentieth century, however, commencing especially during the New Deal administration of President Franklin D. Roosevelt, labor management relations in the unionized employment environment in the private sector came increasingly within the oversight supervision of the National Labor Relations Board, the administrative agency created by the Congress to implement, effectuate, and adjudicate labor management relations pursuant to the National Labor Relations Act of 1935, sometimes popularly called the Wagner Act, in honor of its primary sponsor Senator Robert Wagner. In 1937, in *NLRB* v. *Jones and Laughlin Steel Corp.*, the Supreme Court pronounced the National Labor Relations Act constitutional by a narrow 5 to 4 margin. With the Court's pronouncement of the constitutionality of the National Labor Relations Act, previously unfettered ownership prerogatives to manage and utilize private property as ownership saw fit were partially constrained. Employees seeking to unionize and union organizers could, to some carefully calibrated extent, now intrude into the employers' property rights. The legitimacy of ownership of private property has been endorsed by political theoreticians from Aristotle and St. Augustine of Hippo through St. Thomas Aquinas, and was brought into the English common-law by political theoreticians such as Thomas Hobbes and John Locke. In Federalist Paper 10, James Madison, the primary framer of the United States Constitution, again eloquently reiterated the importance of private property as preserving and enhancing liberty. Given this powerful structure of political theory that has endorsed private property ownership for millennia, the critics of labor law have argued that it is diametrically opposed to fundamental principles of the common law, and thus constitutes an anti-capitalist intrusion into the common-law regime of private property and freedom of contract.

These were also among the fundamental philosophical and practical lines of demarcation during the bitter fights in the early 1930s that culminated in the enactment of the National Labor Relations Act. Although it has been an important working part of contemporary labor law for more than sixty years, the fundamental philosophical questions remain. For the better part of the past two decades, labor law scholars have been forced to take into account the brilliant and incisive critique of the NLRA New Deal labor law regime eloquently set forth by Professor Richard Epstein of the University of Chicago Law School. Because his landmark *Yale Law Journal* article in 1983 so astutely reiterates many of the fundamental philosophical and political principles underlying the tensions between private property ownership prerogatives and labor's collective concerns, that dynamic article is an apt beginning to the series of readings. Likewise, perhaps the single most effective response to Professor Epstein comes from Professor Jack Getman of the University of Texas Law School and his former Yale Law School student Thomas C. Kohler, now a professor at the Boston College Law School, in the 1983 *Yale Law Journal*. Thus, *NLRB* v. *Jones and Laughlin Steel Corp.*, situates a critically important philosophical and practical debate with continuing contemporary ramifications. These three initial readings, comprised of the Jones and Laughlin decision and the Epstein and Getman articles, elucidate the fundamental premises and structure which frame the inquiry into the constitutionality and the purposes of contemporary labor law.

Perhaps the most fundamental of all of our freedoms are the freedoms of conscience and of thought, in practical terms perhaps most brought into practice through religious belief and associated observances. In *NLRB* v. *Catholic Bishop of Chicago*, 440 U.S. 490 (1979), Chief Justice Warren Burger, speaking for the majority of the Court, disingenuously dodged First Amendment issues through judicial resort to the anti-establishment principle. The Court thereby vitiated the collective bargaining rights of secular faculty members within the Catholic school system. *Catholic Bishop* especially highlights the more egregious possible tension between Labor Law and the Constitution, with profoundly adverse consequences upon workers who wish to be union-represented and to bargain collectively in the religiously-affiliated educational context. The Roman Catholic hierarchy successfully invoked First Amendment considerations protecting against governmental establishment of religion to effectively preclude the secular courts from embarking upon examination of the personnel practices of the schools operated under the auspices of the Catholic Church. By judicial fiat, through the Court's precipitous invocation of First Amendment establishment clause considerations, the collective bargaining rights and the labor law rights of the teachers in the Catholic schools were dramatically subordinated by the Constitution's First Amendment protection against governmental establishment of religion. Unfortunately, the judicial reasoning was not well developed; due to the short-circuiting of the at best cursory judicial reasoning, many unanswered questions remain.

In 1977, the Supreme Court subordinated employment discrimination law protections for workers to more powerful and structural employer institutional interests. In *TWA, Inc.* v. *Hardison*, 432 U.S 63 (1977), the Court refused to extend protections against employment discrimination in private sector employment to a religiously-observant employee. Hardison, a worker of relatively junior seniority in TWA's 24-hour per day, 7-day per week operations, was a religiously observant Sabbatarian who observed his weekly Sabbath from Friday at sundown through Saturday at sundown. Consequently, given his relatively low seniority, he was relegated to afternoon shift duty that interfered directly with his weekly Sabbath observance. He unsuccessfully invoked Title VII of the Civil Rights Act of 1964, which was purportedly designed to protect somewhat his exercise of religion in his secular employment, at least to the limited extent of being able to adjust his work schedule to avoid working on Friday evening through Saturday evening of his scheduled work week. Despite or because of the considerable corporate institutional power of TWA Airlines, the Supreme Court nevertheless subordinated the statutory protections for Mr. Hardison to TWA's institutional interest for stable union management relations. Because Hardison did not have sufficient seniority pursuant to the collective bargaining agreement between TWA Airlines and its union which represented Hardison, the employer was not required to alter or to supercede the collective bargaining seniority roster in order to accommodate Hardison's request for release from work for his Sabbath observances. Thus, in the arena of labor law and religion, for more than two decades the Supreme Court has rather consistently elucidated the message that it will be loathe to disturb powerful institutional arrangements to vindicate the rights of employees with religiously-affiliated powerful employers (e.g., the Catholic school system) or with powerful secular employers. Thus, both the collective bargaining rights and rights to union representation theoretically protected by the National Labor Relations Act and the Title VII employment discrimination law protections have both been dramatically subordinated to larger structural employer interests.

Perhaps the most salient of all constitutional rights are the First Amendment rights to speech and press. The political initiatives of labor unions are oftentimes closely related to the more immediate collective bargaining concerns of the unions, and their periodic endeavors to obtain improved labor contracts, enhancing the hours, wages, and terms of conditions of employment on behalf of their constituents, the employees of the enterprise. For more than two decades, however, beginning with *Abood* v. *Detroit Board of Education*, the Court dramatically divorced the broader political initiatives and the class prerogatives of organized labor from the utilization of labor union dues to fund those broader political labor agenda items. In a complex series of cases, the Supreme Court has designed an intricate system of internal administrative mechanisms whereby individual labor union members who object to the broader politics and political endorsements by their particular union are protected against any portion of their union dues diverted for such broader purposes and spent on other than the immediate orbit of grievance arbitration and labor contract negotiations. In simple terms, if the individual union member objects to the political agenda and political endorsements of particular candidates made by his or her labor union, that individual worker is entitled not to see any portion of his union dues go to those broader political purposes. One decade after the *Abood* decision, the Supreme Court issued the landmark decision, *Communication*

Workers v. *Beck*, 487 U.S. 735 (1988), and followed Beck with a series of refining decisions.

It is certainly true that the Constitution does not directly protect employees in the private sector. Thus, one might think, largely erroneously, unfortunately, that at least workers in the public sector government workforce have the direct protection of the Constitutional right to free speech in the public sector workplace. This belief would be seductive, dangerous, and, for the most part, wrong. A decision exemplifying the pernicious erosion of First Amendment speech rights in the public sector workplace is *Waters* v. *Churchill*, 511 U.S. 661 (1994). The employer, acting in good faith on the facts as it understood them at the time, could discharge an employee for the adverse consequences flowing from the employee's speech, even if the predicates upon which the employer originally acted were subsequently determined to be without foundation in fact. Thus, as long as the employer acts in good faith, even if subsequently proven to be not factually grounded, the employer may discipline or discharge the public sector worker for otherwise protected First Amendment speech. Even if the employee said nothing detrimental to the employer, as long as the employer believed in good faith that the employee did speak, and even though subsequent facts establish that the employee did not speak, the employer's prior decision to discipline or discharge the employee will not be disturbed! A decade earlier, in *Connick* v. *Myers*, the District Attorney of New Orleans terminated an assistant attorney who proselytized for improved personnel practices in the District Attorney's office and who objected to certain practices, distributing the dissenting Assistant District Attorney's survey and personnel inquiry forms to fellow workers in the District Attorney's office. Because the speech was not sufficiently calibrated to implicate directly the public sector qua public sector, First Amendment Speech and press issues, the Supreme Court decided that it would not serve as a meta-personnel agency. Thus, for the past two decades, there has been precious little free speech, and perhaps even less due process, in the public sector workplace. This fragile situation makes any claim of free speech or due process in the private sector, where the Constitutional protections generally are not directly available, all the more ephemeral and, for all practical purposes, effectively nonexistent.

It is quite paradoxical that constitutional protections in the public sector have been so subordinated to employer interests. The Supreme Court has never fully articulated with any particular cogency why this must necessarily be the operative calculus. In the private sector workplace, the subordination of implicit constitutional rights and collective bargaining and unionization rights to the institutional prerogatives of powerful private employers is perhaps even more dramatic. For the past two decades, consonant with the concurrent proliferation of the power of largely unregulated transnational capital through the international markets, constitutional law and labor law, rather than being in tension, have both been conveniently and dangerously subordinated to the institutional interests of complex transnational bureaucracies. The challenge for the foreseeable future will be the restoration of constitutional law and labor law as regulatory mechanisms to effectuate more fully rights and protections for individuals and collective workers. The continuing subordination of labor law and constitutional law to the prerogatives of complex bureaucratic employers will be increasingly fraught with hazards to any meaningful sense of rights and freedoms.

Further Reading

Cases

Abood v. *Detroit Board of Education*, 431 U.S. 209 (1977) (union members not required to fund political activities of the union, beyond the scope of labor contract negotiation and administration)

Brown v. *Pro Football, Inc.* U.S. (1996) (labor law, rather than federal antitrust law, governs labor management relations in the absence of a current collective bargaining agreement)

Communication Workers v. *Beck*, 487 U.S. 735 (1998) (refines and extends Abood principles)

Jacksonville Bulk Terminals, Inc. v. *Longshoremen's Association*, 457 U.S. 702 (1982) (union liable for damages caused by unlawful secondary boycott activities)

Johnson v. *Transportation Agency of Santa Clara County*, 480 U.S. 616 (1987) (extends affirmative action to promotional opportunities)

Lechmere, Inc. v. *NLRB*, 502 U.S. 527 (1992) (nonemployee union organizers do not have access to the employer's property during union organizational campaign of the workers, absent extraordinary circumstances)

Lehnert v. *Ferris Faculty Ass'n.*, 500 U.S. 507 (1991) (extends the Abood principles)

National Treasury Employees Union v. *von Rabb*, 489 U.S. 656 (1989) (sets standards for drug testing employees without probable cause and without Fourth Amendment search warrants)

NLRB v. *Catholic Bishop of Chicago*, 440 U.S. 490 (1979) (First Amendment precludes application of labor law protection to the faculty of Catholic schools)

NLRB v. *Jones and Laughlin Steel Corp.*, 301 U.S. 1 (1937) (upholds the National Labor Relations Act as constitutional)

San Diego Building Trades v. *Garmon*, 359 U.S. 236 (1959) (federal labor law and the NLRA broadly preempt state law causes of action in labor relations disputes)

Sheet Metal Workers v. *EEOC*, 478 U.S. 501 (1986) (imposes precise affirmative remedy in hiring, to correct long-standing and deliberate intentional race discrimination)

Skinner v. *Railway Labor Executives Association*, U.S. 109 S.Ct. (1989) (upholds drug testing of workers, as companion case with von Rabb, above)

Steele v. *Louisville and Nashville R. Co.*, 323 U.S. 192 (1944) (establishes the union's duty to fairly represent all workers, in a way not "arbitrary, discriminatory, or in bad faith")

Thornhill v. *Alabama*, 310 U.S. 88 (1940) (Alabama law that summarily prohibited labor picketing was unconstitutional)

Trans World Airlines, Inc. v. *Hardison*, 423 U.S. 63 (1977) (employer's duty to reasonably accommodate the religious practices of the employee is nothing more than a de minimis standard)

United Steelworkers of America v. *Sadlowski*, 457 U.S. 102 (1982) (prohibits external funding of labor union officer elections)

United Steelworkers of America v. *Weber*, 443 U.S. 193 (1979) (endorses affirmative action in collective bargaining agreements)

Vegelahn v. *Guntner,* 167 Mass. 92, 44 N.E. 1077 (1896) (prohibits peaceful labor picketing)

Wygant v. *Jackson Board of Education,* 476 U.S. 262 (1986) (affirmative action layoffs unconstitutional)

Books

Stanley Aronowitz, *Labor: Up From the Ashes* (1998).

Stanley Aronowitz (ed.), *Post-Work: Wages of Cybernation* (1998).

James B. Atleson, *Values and Assumptions in American Labor Law* (1982).

Frank Elkouri and Elkouri, *How Arbitration Works* (5th Edition 1996).

William E. Forbath, *Law and the Shaping of the American Labor Movement* (1991).

Richard B. Freeman and James L. Medoff, *What Do Unions Do?* (1984).

William B. Gould, *Agenda for Reform: The Future of Employment Relationships and the Law* (1993).

U.S. Dept. of Labor, *Fact Finding Report/Commission on the Future of Worker-Management Relations* (1994)

Robert Reich, *The Work of Nations* (1991).

Articles

Deborah Ballam. "Affirmative Action: Purveyor of Preferential Treatment of Guarantor of Equal Opportunity? A Call for a 'Revisioning' of Affirmative Action." 18 *Berkeley J. Employment and Lab. L.I.* (1997).

Mary Becker. "How Free is Speech at Work?" 29 *U.C. Davis L. Rev.* 815 (1996).

Leslie S. Blickenstaff. Note. "Don't Tip the Scales! The Actual Malice Standard Unjustifiably Eliminates First Amendment Protection for Public Employees' Recklessly False Statements." 80 *Minn. L. Rev.* 911 (1996).

Thomas D. Brierton. "An Unjustified Hostility Toward Religion in the Workplace." 34 *Cath. Law.* 289 (1991).

James J. Brundney. "Reflections on Group Action and the Law of the Workplace." 74 *Tex. L. Rev.* 1563 (1996).

Steven J. Buchholtz. Note. "Run, Kick, and (Im)passe: Expanding Employers' Ability to Unilaterally Impose Conditions of Employment After Impasses in *Brown* v. *Pro Football.*" 81 *Minn. L. Rev.* 1201 (1997).

Norman L. Cantor. "'Forced Payments' to Service Institutions and Constitutional Interests in Ideological Non-Association." 36 *Rutgers L. Rev.* 3 (1984).

Edward M. Chen, et al. "Common Law Privacy: A Limit on Employer's Power to Test for Drugs." 12 *Geo. Mason U.L. Rev.* 651 (1990).

John J. Coleman. "Muddy Waters: Allis-Chambers and the Federal Policy Favoring Labor Arbitration." 44 *Wash. and Lee L. Rev.* 345 (1987).

William R. Corbett. "The 'Fall' of Summers, the Rise of 'Pretext Plus' and the Escalating Subordination of Federal Employment Discrimination Law to Employment at Will: Lessons From McKennon and Hicks." 30 *Ga. L. Rev.* 305 (1996).

Kiernan M. Corcoran. Note. "When Does the Buzzer Sound?: The Non-Statutory Labor Exemption in Professional Sports." 94 *Colum. L. Rev.* 1045 (1994).

Craig M. Cornish and Donald B. Louria. "Employment Drug Testing, Preventive Searches, and the Future of Privacy." 33 *Wm. and Mary L. Rev.* 95 (1991).

Roberto L. Corrada. "Religious Accommodation and the NLRA." 17 *Berkeley J. Employment and Labor L.* 185 (1996).

Marion Crain. "Expanded Employee Drug-Detection Programs and the Public Good: Big Brother at the Bargaining Table." 64 *N.Y.U. L. Rev.* 1286 (1989).

Barry Cushman. "Twentieth-Century Constitutional History: Rethinking the New Deal Court." 80 *Va. L. Rev.* 201 (1994).

Mary C. Daly. "Some Runs, Some Hits, Some Errors — Keeping Score in the Affirmative Action Ballpark From Weber to Johnson." 30 *B.C. L. Rev.* 1 (1998).

Kenneth G. Dau-Schmidt. "Union Security Agreements Under the National Labor Relations Act: The Statute, The Constitution, and the Courts' Opinion in Beck." 27 *Harv. J. on Legis.* 51 (1990).

Henry H. Drummonds. "The Sister Sovereign States: Preemption and the Second Twentieth Century Revolution in the Law of the American Workplace." 62 *Fordham L. Rev.* 469 (1993).

Karen Engle. "The Persistence of Neutrality: The Failure of the Religious Accommodation Provision to Redeem Title VII." 76 *Tex. L. Rev.* 317 (1997).

Richard A. Epstein. "A Common Law for Labor Relations: A Critique of the New Deal Labor Legislation." 92 *Yale L.J.* 1357 (1983).

Richard A. Epstein. "The Proper Scope of the Commerce Power." 73 *Va. L. Rev.* 1387 (1987).

Richard A. Epstein. "Religious Liberty in the Welfare State." 31 *Wm. and Mary L. Rev.* 375 (1990).

Cynthia L. Estlund. "Speech on Matters of Public Concern: The Perils of an Emerging First Amendment Category." 59 *Geo. Wash. L. Rev.* 1 (1990).

———. "What do Workers Want? Employee Interests, Public Interests, and Freedom of Expression Under the NLRA." 140 *U. Pa. L. Rev.* 921 (1992).

———. "Labor, Property, And Sovereignty After Lechmere." 46 *Stan. L. Rev.* 305 (1994).

Mayer G. Freed, et al. "Unions, Fairness, and the Conundrums of Collective Choice." 56 *S. Cal. L. Rev.* 461 (1983).

Julius Getman. "Labor Law and Free Speech: The Curious Policy of Limited Expression." 43 *Md. L. Rev.* 4 (1984).

Julius G. Getman and Thomas C. Kohler. "The Common Law, Labor Law, and Reality: A Response to Professor Epstein." 92 *Yale L.J.* 1415 (1983).

Michael C. Harper. "Multiemployer Bargaining, Antitrust Law, and Team Sports: The Contingent Choice of a Broad Exemption." 38 *Wm. and Mary L. Rev.* 1663 (1997).

Michael C. Harper and Ira C. Lupu. "Fair Representation as Equal Protection." 98 *Harv. L. Rev.* 1211 (1985).

Charles W. Hemingway. "A Closer Look at *Waters* v. *Churchill* and the *United States* v. *Nat'l Treasury Employees Union*: Constitutional Tensions Between the Government as Employer and the Citizen as Federal Employee." 44 *Am.*

U.L. Rev. 2231 (1995).
Jonathan V. Holtzman. "Applicant Testing for Drug Use: A Policy and Legal Inquiry." 33 *Wm. and Mary L. Rev.* 47 (1991).
Alan Hyde. "Democracy in Collective Bargaining." 93 *Yale L.J.* 793 (1984).
Douglas Laycock. "Towards a General Theory of the Religion Clauses: The Case of Church Labor Relations and the Right to Church Autonomy." 81 *Colum. L. Rev.* 1373 (1981).
Douglas L. Leslie. "*Brown* v. *Pro Football.*" 82 *Va. L. Rev.* 629 (1996).
Ira C. Lupu. "Free Exercise Exception and Religious Institutions: The Case of Employment Discrimination." 67 *B.U.L. Rev.* 391 (1987).
Martin H. Malin. "The Legal Status of Union Security Fee Arbitration After *Chicago Teachers Union* v. *Hudson.*" 29 *B.C. L. Rev.* 857 (1988).
Christina Louise Mell. Note. "Employee Drug Testing: Guilty Until Proven Innocent." 52 *Mo. L. Rev.* 625 (1987).
Glenn Merten. "The Non Statutory Labor Exemption, Collective Bargaining, and Impasses." 64 *Geo. Wash. L. Rev.* 1332 (1996).
Gary Minda. "The Law and Metaphor of Boycott." 41 *Buff. L. Rev.* 807 (1993).
Burt Neuborne. "Blues for the Left Hand: A Critique of Cass Sunstein's Democracy and the Problem of Free Speech." 62 *U. Chi. L. Rev.* 423 (1995).
James Gray Pope. "Labor and the Constitution: From Abolition to Deindustrialization." 65 *Tex. L. Rev.* 1071 (1987).
James M. Sokolowski. "Government Drug Testing: A Question of Reasonableness." 43 *Vand. L. Rev.* 1343 (1990).
Alan Story. "Employer Speech, Union Representation Elections, and the First Amendment." 16 *Berkeley J. Employment and Lab. L.* 356 (1995).

CASES ADJUDGED

IN THE

SUPREME COURT OF THE UNITED STATES

AT

OCTOBER TERM, 1936.

NATIONAL LABOR RELATIONS BOARD *v.* JONES & LAUGHLIN STEEL CORP.*

CERTIORARI TO THE CIRCUIT COURT OF APPEALS FOR THE FIFTH CIRCUIT.

No. 419. Argued February 10, 11, 1937.—Decided April 12, 1937.

1. The distinction between what is national and what is local in the activities of commerce is vital to the maintenance of our federal form of government. P. 29.
2. The validity of provisions which, considered by themselves, are constitutional, *held* not affected by general and ambiguous declarations in the same statute. P. 30.
3. An interpretation which conforms a statute to the Constitution must be preferred to another which would render it unconstitutional or of doubtful validity. P. 30.
4. Acts which directly burden or obstruct interstate or foreign commerce, or its free flow, are within the reach of the congressional

---

* No. 419, *National Labor Relations Board* v. *Jones & Laughlin Steel Corp.*; Nos. 420 and 421, *National Labor Relations Board* v. *Fruehauf Trailer Co., post,* p. 49; Nos. 422 and 423, *National Labor Relations Board* v. *Friedman-Harry Marks Clothing Co., post,* p. 58; No. 365, *Associated Press* v. *National Labor Relations Board, post,* p. 103; and No. 469, *Washington, Virginia & Maryland Coach Co.* v. *National Labor Relations Board, post,* p. 142, which are known as the "Labor Board Cases," were disposed of in five separate opinions. The dissenting opinion, *post,* p. 76, applies to Nos. 419, 420 and 421, and 422 and 423. The dissenting opinion, *post,* p. 133, applies to No. 365. The opinion in No. 469 was unanimous.

power; and this includes acts, having that effect, which grow out of labor disputes. P. 31.

5. Employees in industry have a fundamental right to organize and select representatives of their own choosing for collective bargaining; and discrimination or coercion upon the part of their employer to prevent the free exercise of this right is a proper subject for condemnation by competent legislative authority. P. 33.

6. The congressional authority to protect interstate commerce from burdens and obstructions is not limited to transactions which can be deemed to be an essential part of a "flow" of such commerce. Pp. 34–36.

7. Although activities may be intrastate in character when separately considered, if they have such a close and substantial relation to interstate commerce that their control is essential, or appropriate, to protect that commerce from burdens and obstructions, Congress has the power to exercise that control. P. 37.

8. This power must be considered in the light of our dual system of government and may not be extended so as to embrace effects upon interstate commerce so indirect and remote that to embrace them would, in view of our complex society, effectually obliterate the distinction between what is national and what is local and create a completely centralized government. The question is necessarily one of degree. P. 37.

9. Whatever amounts to more or less constant practice, and threatens to obstruct or unduly to burden the freedom of interstate commerce, is within the regulatory power of Congress under the commerce clause; and it is primarily for Congress to consider and decide the fact of the danger and meet it. P. 37.

10. The close and intimate effect which brings the subject within the reach of federal power may be due to activities in relation to productive industry, although the industry when separately viewed is local. P. 38.

11. The relation to interstate commerce of the manufacturing enterprise involved in this case was such that a stoppage of its operations by industrial strife would have an immediate, direct and paralyzing effect upon interstate commerce. Therefore Congress had constitutional authority, for the protection of interstate commerce, to safeguard the right of the employees in the manufacturing plant to self-organization and free choice of their representatives for collective bargaining. P. 41.

Judicial notice is taken of the facts that the recognition of the right of employees to self-organization and to have representatives of their own choosing for the purpose of collective bargaining is often an essential condition of industrial peace, and that refusal to confer and negotiate has been one of the most prolific causes of strife.

12. The National Labor Relations Act of July 5, 1935, empowers the National Labor Relations Board to prevent any person from engaging in unfair labor practices "affecting commerce"; its definition of "commerce" (aside from commerce within a territory or the District of Columbia) is such as to include only interstate and foreign commerce; and the term "affecting commerce" it defines as meaning "in commerce, or burdening or obstructing commerce or the free flow of commerce, or having led or tending to lead to a labor dispute burdening or obstructing commerce or the free flow of commerce." The "unfair labor practices," as defined by the Act and involved in this case, are restraint or coercion of employees in their rights to self-organization and to bargain collectively through representatives of their own choosing, and discrimination against them in regard to hire or tenure of employment for the purpose of encouraging or discouraging membership in any labor organization. §§ 7 and 8. The Act (§ 9a) declares that representatives, for the purpose of collective bargaining, of the majority of the employees in an appropriate unit shall be the exclusive representatives of all the employees in that unit; but that any individual employee or a group of employees shall have the right at any time to present grievances to their employer. *Held:*

(1) That in safeguarding rights of employees and empowering the Board, the statute, in so far as involved in the present case, confines itself to such control of the industrial relationship as may be constitutionally exercised by Congress to prevent burden or obstruction to interstate or foreign commerce arising from industrial disputes. P. 43.

(2) The Act imposes upon the employer the duty of conferring and negotiating with the authorized representatives of the employees for the purpose of settling a labor dispute; but it does not preclude such individual contracts as the employer may elect to make directly with individual employees. P. 44.

(3) The Act does not compel agreements between employers and employees. Its theory is that free opportunity for negotiation

with accredited representatives of employees is likely to promote industrial peace and may bring about the adjustments and agreements which the Act in itself does not attempt to compel. P. 45.

(4) The Act does not interfere with the normal right of the employer to hire, or with the right of discharge when exercised for other reasons than intimidation and coercion; and what is the true reason in this regard is left the subject of investigation in each case with full opportunity to show the facts. P. 45.

13. A corporation which manufactured iron and steel products in its factories in Pennsylvania from raw materials most of which it brought in from other States, and which shipped 75% of the manufactured products out of Pennsylvania and disposed of them throughout this country and in Canada, was required by orders of the National Labor Relations Board to tender reinstatement to men who had been employed in one of the factories but were discharged because of their union activities and for the purpose of discouraging union membership. The orders further required that the company make good the pay the men had lost through their discharge, and that it desist from discriminating against members of the union, with regard to hire and tenure of employment, and from interfering by coercion with the self-organization of its employees in the plant. *Held* that the orders were authorized by the National Labor Relations Act, and that the Act is constitutional as thus applied to the company. Pp. 30, 32, 34, 41.

14. The right of employers to conduct their own business is not arbitrarily restrained by regulations that merely protect the correlative rights of their employees to organize for the purpose of securing the redress of grievances and of promoting agreements with employers relating to rates of pay and conditions of work. P. 43.

15. The fact that the National Labor Relations Act subjects the employer to supervision and restraint and leaves untouched the abuses for which employees may be responsible, and fails to provide a more comprehensive plan, with better assurance of fairness to both sides and with increased chances of success in bringing about equitable solutions of industrial disputes affecting interstate commerce, does not affect its validity. The question is as to the power of Congress, not as to its policy; and legislative authority, exerted within its proper field, need not embrace all the evils within its reach. P. 46.

16. The National Labor Relations Act establishes standards to which the Board must conform. There must be complaint, notice and hearing. The Board must receive evidence and make findings. These findings as to the facts are to be conclusive, but only if supported by evidence. The order of the Board is subject to review by the designated court; and only when sustained by the court may the order be enforced. Upon that review all questions of the jurisdiction of the Board and the regularity of its proceedings, all questions of constitutional right or statutory authority, are open to examination by the court. These procedural provisions afford adequate opportunity to secure judicial protection against arbitrary action, in accordance with the well-settled rules applicable to administrative agencies set up by Congress to aid in the enforcement of valid legislation. P. 47.
17. The provision of the National Labor Relations Act, § 10 (c), authorizing the Board to require the reinstatement of employees found to have been discharged because of their union activity or for the purpose of discouraging membership in the union, is valid. P. 47.
18. The provision of the Act, § 10 (c), that the Board, in requiring reinstatement, may direct the payment of wages for the time lost by the discharge, less amounts earned by the employee during that period, does not contravene the provisions of the Seventh Amendment with respect to jury trial in suits at common law. P. 48.

83 F. (2d) 998, reversed.

CERTIORARI, 299 U. S. 534, to review a decree of the Circuit Court of Appeals declining to enforce an order of the National Labor Relations Board.

Mr. J. Warren Madden and *Solicitor General Reed*, with whom *Attorney General Cummings* and *Messrs. Charles E. Wyzanski, Jr., Charles A. Horsky, A. H. Feller, Charles Fahy, Robert B. Watts, Philip Levy,* and *Malcolm F. Halliday* were on the brief, for petitioner.*

* Arguments in this case are summarized from the briefs. Extracts from the oral arguments in this and in other Labor Act cases immediately following will appear in an appendix in the bound volume.

The National Labor Relations Act is an exercise of the power of Congress to protect interstate commerce from injuries caused by industrial strife.

Before this statute was enacted experience had shown that industrial strife was a recurrent burden upon the interstate commerce of the nation. Not only in its totality had such strife produced obstructions to commerce, but also in many individual instances such strife eventuated in conspiracies to restrain commerce or imposed such substantial burdens upon it that penalties or injunctions were applied under the Sherman Act. These facts are clearly shown by a survey of the results of individual disputes, the statistics with regard to the total number of such disputes, and repeated federal activities in connection with industrial strife.

Congress, in dealing with this evil of industrial strife, might have approached the problem in either of two ways. It might have enacted a statute designed to remove the burden on interstate commerce after it had evinced itself in a particular case, as the Sherman Act did; or, it might have enacted a statute to deal with the causes of the burden in anticipation of their probable effect, as the Packers and Stockyards Act did. Congressional power to enact this second type of statute (hereinafter called the preventive power) extends at least as far as the power to enact a statute to control the burden after its appearance (hereinafter called the control power). *Stafford* v. *Wallace,* 258 U. S. 495, 525.

The National Labor Relations Act, which is an exercise of this preventive power, does not attempt to eliminate causes of strife in *all* enterprises. The statute and the mandate addressd to the administrative Board are specifically directed to the elimination of the proscribed practices only when they are found to be "affecting commerce." § 10 (a). This phrase "affecting commerce" is defined in § 2 (7) of the statute as "in commerce, or burdening or obstructing commerce or the free flow of commerce, or having led or tending to lead to a labor dispute burdening or obstructing commerce or the free flow of commerce." These words are plainly patterned upon language used in decisions of this Court in cases arising under other statutes enacted by Congress under the commerce power. This jurisdictional limitation is manifestly a direction to the Board to exercise the national power within the limits permitted by the Constitution. In other words, Congress has taken as the ambit of this particular preventive statute the boundaries to which it would be restricted were it exercising to the full its control power under appropriate legislation.

Of course, in eliminating these proscribed practices in situations which are likely to come within the control power of Congress, the application of the Act will upon occasion result in the prohibition of activities which, even if allowed to spend their force, would not result in industrial strife which did in fact come within the federal control power. But, provided that when the practice was indulged in there was a reasonable likelihood that any industrial strife which resulted would be within the control power, the Board may apply the preventive measure. To hold otherwise would deprive Congress of any preventive power, since no one can predict with absolute accuracy, in advance of the complete development of the effects of a cause, exactly what those effects will be. Compare *Stafford* v. *Wallace,* 258 U. S. 495; *Chicago Board of Trade* v. *Olsen,* 262 U. S. 1. This lack of predictability is particularly true of industrial strife. Moreover, in eliminating the cause of an evil within the power of Congress, the Act may on occasion eliminate the cause of purely local evils. Indeed, this is almost inevitable, since a single event has multiple consequences.

Yet plainly the existence of a granted federal power cannot be limited by the collateral consequences of its exercise. *Ashwander* v. *Tennessee Valley Authority,* 297 U. S. 288.

The foregoing epitome of the statutory scheme makes it clear that the question of the validity of a specific application of the statute depends upon whether industrial strife resulting from the practices in the particular enterprise under consideration would be of the character which the federal power could control if it occurred. The question of primary importance therefore is the extent of the federal power of control. Since the language of this statute does not go beyond the ambit of this power, whatever it may be, the statute is clearly constitutional on its face, and the only issue is whether it has been constitutionally applied.

This Court has never had occasion to define the full extent to which industrial strife in the manufacturing, producing, or processing divisions of an enterprise engaged extensively in interstate commerce may be subjected to the exercise of the control power of Congress. It has, however, held that certain situations in these divisions are clearly within the control power, and has further laid down general principles which furnish standards for the proper appreciation of the full scope of that power.

It is well settled that an industrial dispute in such an enterprise involving an intent to affect commerce is within the control power of Congress. *United Mine Workers* v. *Coronado Coal Co.,* 259 U. S. 344; *Bedford Cut Stone Co.* v. *Stone Cutters' Assn.,* 274 U. S. 37; *Duplex Printing Co.* v. *Deering,* 254 U. S. 443; *Loewe* v. *Lawlor,* 208 U. S. 274. Consequently, where the situation in a particular enterprise presents a reasonable likelihood that industrial strife, if it occurred, would involve an intent to affect commerce, the Board can apply the statute to that enterprise.

This Court has also recognized the principle that an industrial dispute having the necessary effect of substantially burdening commerce would be within the control power of Congress. *Industrial Association* v. *United States,* 268 U. S. 64, 81; *United Mine Workers* v. *Coronado Coal Co.,* 259 U. S. 344, 410–411. Hence, the statute is applicable to an enterprise which is shown by evidence before the Board to be of such a character that strife, if it occurred, would have such a necessary effect. The proper application of the statute to such situations depends, of course, on the precise scope of the "necessary effect" principle. Although the Court has recognized the principle it has not heretofore had occasion to define it.

Lastly, the scope of the control power extends to recurring evils which in their totality constitute a burden on interstate commerce. This Court has stated that such recurrent evils may, after appropriate findings, be subjected by Congress to national supervision and restraint. *Stafford* v. *Wallace,* 258 U. S. 495; *Chicago Board of Trade* v. *Olsen,* 262 U. S. 1. This principle extends to industrial strife in enterprises which receive a substantial part of their raw material from, or ship a substantial part of their products in, interstate commerce. *United Mine Workers* v. *Coronado Coal Co.,* 259 U. S. 344, 408; *United Leather Workers* v. *Herkert & Meisel Trunk Co.,* 265 U. S. 457, 469; *Texas & New Orleans R. Co.* v. *Brotherhood of Railway Clerks,* 281 U. S. 548. Here Congress has found, and experience shows, that industrial strife in such enterprises constitutes such a recurring evil. Under this view of the control power the statute may be applied to the individual instances of this recurring burden—that is, to any enterprise which receives a substantial part of its materials from, or ships a substantial part of its products in, interstate commerce, and is dependent upon such commerce for the successful conduct of its business.

We believe that the instant case falls within each of these three situations in which the control power of Congress may be exercised.

The reasonable likelihood of a controversy with the intent to affect commerce might be demonstrated in either of two ways: First, evidence might be presented to the Board that in a particular situation the intent already exists; or second, evidence might be presented to the Board that the situation was comparable to, and of the same general type as, others out of which in the past there had evolved controversies with intent to affect commerce, or that in the particular situation confronting the Board, such definite intention might reasonably be expected to develop. In the case at bar it is not claimed that there is evidence of the first sort; but there is abundant evidence that the situation is fraught with the risk that after strife developed it would involve the purpose to curtail the movement of goods in commerce.

As previously stated, the Court has not yet determined the exact scope of the phrase "necessary effect of substantially burdening commerce." It undeniably includes situations in which the participants cannot be charged with a conscious specific desire to interrupt commerce. *United States* v. *Patten,* 226 U. S. 525. The statements of this Court make it clear that the application of this principle may depend upon the magnitude of the effect on commerce. The possible use of such a standard is entirely consistent with *Carter* v. *Carter Coal Co.,* 298 U. S. 238. Three possible definitions of the scope of the "necessary effect" principle may be advanced: (1) a necessary effect on commerce results from industrial strife occurring in an enterprise which lies within a well-defined stream or flow of commerce, or (2) a necessary effect on commerce results from industrial strife which restrains a substantial part of all the commerce in a particular commodity, or (3) a necessary effect on commerce results from industrial strife which restrains the movement of a substantial volume of goods which would otherwise move in interstate commerce. The instant case falls within all three of these aspects of the principle, but this brief addresses particular attention to the first and second.

Neither *Schechter Corp.* v. *United States,* 295 U. S. 495, nor *Carter* v. *Carter Coal Co.,* 298 U. S. 238, is here applicable. In the *Schechter* case it was urged that wages and hours in local industry bore a relation to interstate commerce by reason of an intricate chain of economic causes and effects. An effect on commerce which occurred in such a manner the Court characterized as indirect. The Act involved in the *Carter* case had as its purpose the "stabilizing" of the bituminous coal industry through regulation of prices and wages. The effect of wage cutting on interstate commerce was held to be indirect on the basis of the *Schechter* case. The collective bargaining provisions of that Act were, as is clear from the face of the statute and from the opinion of the Court, ancillary to the wage fixing provisions and furnished the means through which regulations with respect to wages having the force of law were to be arrived at. On the other hand, the National Labor Relations Act is designed solely to eliminate the burden on interstate commerce caused by industrial strife. Such strife constitutes an interruption to commerce operating directly without "an efficient intervening agency or condition." Thus it deals with matters closely connected with commerce, does not go beyond what is necessary for the protection of commerce, and does not attempt "a broad regulation of industry within the State."

Mr. Earl F. Reed, with whom *Messrs. Charles Rosen* and *W. D. Evans* were on the brief, for respondent.

The respondent contends that the National Labor Relations Act is, in reality, a regulation of labor relations, and not of interstate commerce, and that, as a consequence, it is not within the power of Congress to enact. Even if it should be considered a true regulation of interstate commerce, it still has no application to the respondent's relations with its production employees, because they are not subject to regulation by the Federal Government. In addition, the provisions of the Act which the petitioner seeks to apply in the present cases are invalid, because they violate § 2 of Art. III of the Constitution, as well as the Fifth and Seventh Amendments.

The respondent is a corporation engaged in the manufacture of iron and steel products. In this connection, it owns and operates a large steel plant at Aliquippa, Pennsylvania, in which are employed approximately ten thousand men. The present case is, in reality, a controversy between ten individuals who were formerly employed by the respondent in production work at this plant, and the respondent. These individuals, with three others, filed a complaint with the petitioner, the National Labor Relations Board, charging that they had been discharged or demoted by the respondent because of union affiliations. The respondent objected to the jurisdiction of the petitioner, but its motion to dismiss was overruled and the petitioner, after hearing, determined that the complainants had been wrongfully discharged and ordered their immediate restoration, with compensation for lost pay.

The petitioner has endeavored to justify its assumption of jurisdiction over the respondent's employment relations, by making a finding that the respondent has engaged in unfair labor practices "affecting commerce" within the definition of the National Labor Relations Act. The respondent insists that the facts upon which this "finding" pretends to be based are, in law, insufficient to justify any such conclusion, and that this Court is entitled to reëxamine the facts for the purpose of determining the jurisdictional issue. *Crowell* v. *Benson,* 285 U. S. 22; *St. Joseph Stock Yards* v. *United States,* 298 U. S. 38.

The National Labor Relations Act is not a true regulation of interstate commerce.

The power of Congress is clearly defined by the commerce clause of the Constitution, and considerations of political expediency have no weight in fixing the dividing line between the powers of Congress and the reserved powers of the several States. The argument of the petitioner is, in the last analysis, a plea that, from an economic standpoint, Congress should have power to apply its legislation to the respondent's employment relations. This, we submit, is entirely beside the point if the exercise of such power would run counter to the Constitution.

The jurisdiction of Congress under the commerce clause includes the power to regulate, restrict and protect interstate commerce; but not the right to use such jurisdiction as a pretext for legislation which interferes with the local sovereignty of the separate States. *Gibbons* v. *Ogden,* 9 Wheat. 1. The use of an admitted power of Congress as a pretext to interfere with local activities which are not subject to its jurisdiction, is to be condemned. The commerce clause will not serve as an excuse for legislating with respect to labor relations, which do not constitute a part of interstate commerce. *Schechter Poultry Corp.* v. *United States,* 295 U. S. 495; *Railroad Retirement Board* v. *Alton R. Co.,* 295 U. S. 330; *United States* v. *Butler,* 297 U. S. 1.

The legislative history of the National Labor Relations Act and its substantive provisions are sufficient to demonstrate that the Act, although disguised as a regulation of interstate commerce, is, in actuality, a regulation of labor. The terms of the statute apply to almost every employer and every employee (§ 2), although the jurisdiction of the petitioner to enforce it is somewhat circumscribed.

The provisions of the statute, if carefully analyzed, will indicate that Congress is primarily concerned with the protection and establishment of labor organizations. The provisions condemning plant unions and sanctioning "closed shop" agreements, bear no reasonable relation to interstate commerce. Similarly, the express preservation of the right to strike indicates that Congress was not interested in preventing interruptions to the movement of commerce. The interference with the employer's discretion to hire and fire is another reason for believing that efficiency in the shipment of products in interstate commerce has not been the object of the statute.

Congress has endeavored to save the statute from the taint of invalidity by confining its enforcement to transactions "affecting commerce," which the Act defines as transactions which burden commerce or lead or tend to lead to a labor dispute which burdens commerce. § 2. Despite this limitation on the enforcement of the Act, the substantive provisions make no such exception and are, in fact, broad enough to cover almost every employment relation.

The petitioner has followed the same involved line of reasoning in endeavoring to "find" that the respondent's operations "affect commerce." Like Congress, it has found itself faced with the task of piling premise upon premise and hypothesis upon hypothesis to reach the conclusion that the discharge of a few production employees at the respondent's plant has a vital bearing upon the movement of interstate commerce. We submit that the ultimate fact remains that Congress has enacted a labor law, and not a regulation of commerce, and it does not help to sustain the pretext that there may be an indirect connection between the two. *Carter* v. *Carter Coal Co.,* 298 U. S. 238.

The National Labor Relations Act can have no application to the respondent's relations with its production employees.

Although the respondent purchases raw materials, which have a point of origin in other States, and ships a large portion of its finished products across state lines, its production activities, including its employment relations, are not thereby subjected to the jurisdiction of Congress. *Howard* v. *Illinois Central R. Co.,* 207 U. S. 463. There is no logical or legal connection between the respondent's limited participation in interstate commerce and the union affiliations of its production employees. *Adair* v. *United States,* 208 U. S. 161; *Hammer* v. *Dagenhart,* 247 U. S. 251; *Railroad Retirement Board* v. *Alton R. Co.,* 295 U. S. 330.

The principle which impeaches the validity of the National Labor Relations Act, viz., that federal power over interstate commerce must be confined to *bona fide* regulation of the movements of commerce, likewise prevents the application of the statute in the present case. An unbroken line of decisions under the commerce clause has established that manufacturing and production activities are not in or a part of interstate commerce, even though they may be preceded or followed by the movement of materials between States. *Kidd* v. *Pearson,* 128 U. S. 1; *Arkadelphia Milling Co.* v. *St. Louis Southwestern Ry. Co.,* 249 U. S. 134; *Oliver Iron Co.* v. *Lord,* 262 U. S. 172; *Utah Light & Power Co.* v. *Pfost,* 286 U. S. 165; *Chas-*

saniol v. *Greenwood,* 291 U. S. 584; *Industrial Association* v. *United States,* 268 U. S. 64. Although most of the decisions have dealt with the police or taxing powers of the States, they are based upon the fundamental principle that manufacturing activities are subject to the exclusive jursdiction of the separate States. *Bacon* v. *Illinois,* 227 U. S. 504; *Susquehanna Coal Co.* v. *South Amboy,* 228 U. S. 665; *Packer Corp.* v. *Utah,* 285 U. S. 105; *Nashville, C. & St. L. Ry.* v. *Wallace,* 288 U. S. 249; *Edelman* v. *Boeing Air Transport,* 289 U. S. 249; *Minnesota* v. *Blasius,* 290 U. S. 1; *Federal Compress Co.* v. *McLean,* 291 U. S. 17; *Cornell* v. *Coyne,* 192 U. S. 418; *Crescent Cotton Oil Co.* v. *Mississippi,* 251 U. S. 129; *Heisler* v. *Thomas Colliery Co.,* 260 U. S. 245; *Oliver Iron Co.* v. *Lord,* 262 U. S. 172; *Champlin Refining Co.* v. *Corporation Commission,* 286 U. S. 210; *United Mine Workers* v. *Coronado Coal Co.,* 259 U. S. 344; *United Leather Workers* v. *Herkert & Meisel Trunk Co.,* 265 U. S. 457; *Delaware, L. & W. R. Co.* v. *Yurkonis,* 238 U. S. 439.

The distinction between the local manufacturing activities of a business and its subsequent or precedent participation in interstate commerce has been maintained in the field of labor relations. *Hammer* v. *Dagenhart,* 247 U. S. 251; *Industrial Accident Comm'n* v. *Davis,* 259 U. S. 182. Even though an employee may be employed in directly assisting the movement of products in interstate commerce, his relationship to his employer is a status existing wholly within the State, whose incidents, such as wages, hours of labor and the like, are purely domestic in character. *Carter* v. *Carter Coal Co.,* 298 U. S. 238.

Congressional regulation of the labor relations of interstate carriers furnishes no precedent for the present Act. Because interstate carriers are instrumentalities of the movement of commerce, and because they are public utilities, Congress has subjected them to an exhaustive scheme of regulation, of which the labor legislation is merely an incident. As a result, the decision in *Texas & N. O. R. Co.* v. *Railway Clerks,* 281 U. S. 548, is not controlling.

Decisions such as *Stafford* v. *Wallace,* 258 U. S. 495, and *Chicago Board of Trade* v. *Olsen,* 262 U. S. 1, which sustain federal regulation of stockyards and grain exchanges, have no application to the present case. Grain exchanges and stockyards are instrumentalities of interstate commerce in much the same sense as the actual carriers of interstate commerce. They are focal points through which the stream of commerce in grains and cattle sweeps on its way from producer to the ultimate consumer. The activities which were regulated in both cases were activities in the stream of commerce and exerted a direct effect upon its flow. Neither case sanctions the extension of the doctrine to production activities which may indirectly affect the stream of commerce. *Carter* v. *Carter Coal Co.,* 298 U. S. 238. Cf. *Swift & Co.* v. *United States,* 196 U. S. 376; *Hill* v. *Wallace,* 259 U. S. 44; *Tagg Bros. & Moorhead* v. *United States,* 280 U. S. 420; *Tyson & Bro.* v. *Banton,* 273 U. S. 418.

The petitioner relies upon decisions which have upheld the application of the Anti-Trust Laws to industrial conspiracies, such as *Coronado Coal Co.* v. *United Mine Workers,* 268 U. S. 295. These were cases involving conspiracies to restrain interstate commerce by means of local combinations. The element of an intentional interference with the movement of interstate commerce was essential in these cases, not only because an intent to restrain commerce was a part of the proscribed offense, but also because the existence of such an intent made the effect on interstate commerce necessarily direct. This is shown by a comparison of the first *Coronado* case, 259

146212°—37——2

U. S. 344, where there was no intent, with the second *Coronado* case, 268 U. S. 295, where there was both direct and inferential evidence of intent. Cf. *United Leather Workers* v. *Herkert & Meisel Trunk Co.,* 265 U. S. 457.

The petitioner's efforts to show an intended restraint in the present case are futile. Even if a strike should occur at the respondent's plant, the respondent could not be held responsible for the voluntary intervening act of outside agencies. The suggestion that the respondent might be charged with an implied intent to destroy interstate trade, if a labor dispute should occur, is obviously unsound.

The conspiracy cases, such as *United Mine Workers* v. *Coronado Coal Co.,* 259 U. S. 344, and *Local 167* v. *United States,* 291 U. S. 293, although primarily concerned with the application of the Anti-Trust Laws, prove the fallacy of the petitioner's argument, because they establish that Congress cannot regulate local transactions or relations unless they exert a direct effect on interstate commerce. The definition of "affecting commerce" in the National Labor Relations Act is a confession of the indirectness of the connection between the respondent's labor relations and the movement of interstate commerce. See *Schechter Corp.* v. *United States,* 295 U. S. 495; *Industrial Association* v. *United States,* 268 U. S. 64. The petitioner calls attention to the fact that strikes may and frequently do produce an inhibitory effect on the movement of interstate trade to and from the affected area. This is the fundamental error in the petitioner's argument, in that it assumes that it need only establish the connection between strikes and the stoppage of commerce. There has been no strike or labor dispute in the present case. In actuality, the petitioner means that the respondent's discharge of ten employees might have led to dissatisfaction, which might have led to a labor dispute, which might have led to a strike and a consequent interruption of interstate commerce.

The findings of Congress that discriminatory discharges may lead to an interruption of commerce, are unavailing. A declaration by Congress of the need of regulation will not automatically justify its action, where its legislative findings run counter to established rules of construction, which hold that there is no necessary and direct connection between the relations of an employer and his employees and the movement of interstate commerce. In this respect, the present case is clearly controlled by the decision in *Carter* v. *Carter Coal Co.,* 298 U. S. 238.

There are dangerous implications in the petitioner's argument. If it be accepted, there would be no reason why Congress should not use its power over interstate commerce as a pretext to stifle the sovereignty of the States. We therefore believe that the Court will not suffer the powers of the States to be whittled away by a statute which piles speculation upon speculation to attain its ends. *United States* v. *Butler,* 297 U. S. 1; *Schechter Corp.* v. *United States,* 295 U. S. 495.

The National Labor Relations Act confers upon the petitioner exclusive original jurisdiction over controversies between an employee and his employer as to the propriety of the employee's discharge, and the Board is authorized to render affirmative relief to the employee, including the restoration of his employment and compensation for lost wages. The findings of fact of the Board are conclusive and only objections made before the Board will be heard. The Act does not make any provision for a trial *de novo* in the constitutional courts on constitutional or jurisdictional issues.

We submit that the Act is invalid because it authorizes the Board to award a money judgment, depriving the employer of his right to trial by jury in cases involving more than twenty dollars. If, as the petitioner contends, the action of the Board should be considered in the nature of a suit in equity, with authority in the Board to award a mandatory injunction restoring employment, with incidental damages for back pay, then the Act violates the provision of Art. III of the Constitution, for it deprives the constitutional courts of their authority to try constitutional and jurisdictional issues.

The present case presents a controversy between employees and the respondent, in which the petitioner has directed the restoration to employment of the complaining employees, with back pay. This being the case, it is a controversy between private citizens, enforcing private rights. The failure to provide means for a trial *de novo* of jurisdictional issues in such a case is fatal. *Crowell* v. *Benson,* 285 U. S. 22.

The proceedings of the Board are not comparable to those of the Federal Trade Commission.

The petitioner's order constitutes an unlawful interference with the right of the respondent to manage its own business.

The law has always been hesitant to interfere in questions of employer-employee relationships. From the standpoint of the employee, the law has recognized that he should not be forced into a relationship which may be distasteful, and from the employer's viewpoint, the courts have held that the right to judge the capabilities of employees is absolutely essential to the efficient management of the employer's business. The question of retaining or discharging an employee involves delicate considerations of discretion which the law is loath to attempt to weigh. The facts of the present case show the dangers of bureaucratic interference, in that each discharge involved some admitted fault on the part of the complaining employee, but the petitioner determined that it was better qualified to decide and that the respondent's action had been too drastic. This is clearly an interference with the normal right of the respondent to manage its own business, because it is a dictatorial usurpation of the respondent's discretion to determine the capabilities of its employees.

Another dangerous implication of the law and of the petitioner's decision is that it confers a kind of civil service status upon union employees, which will inevitably encourage laziness, insolence, and inefficiency. This is confirmed by a notice which the petitioner, in its decision, has ordered the respondent to post in its plants, to the effect that it will not discharge members of the union. It would be the equivalent of informing the employees that if they become affiliated with the union, they will be thenceforth immune from discharge.

We submit that the underlying philosophy of the National Labor Relations Act is a constant threat to the respondent's normal right to manage its own business. Not only does the Act provide, in effect, that an unqualified bureau will sit as a higher court over the respondent's employment office, but it also ordains that the respondent must deal with whatever union may be selected by a majority of its employees and refuse to negotiate with other employees or their representatives. The power which it delegates to a majority of the employees to bind the minority is arbitrary and unfair and will necessarily lead to the suffocation of minorities and to the closed shop, forcing the employer to herd his employees into an organization which is not of their own choice. This will in turn seriously disturb the discipline and morale of the respondent's employees, with obvious injury to them and to the respondent. Cf. *Carter* v. *Carter Coal Co.*, 298 U. S. 238.

MR. CHIEF JUSTICE HUGHES delivered the opinion of the Court.

In a proceeding under the National Labor Relations Act of 1935,[1] the National Labor Relations Board found that the respondent, Jones & Laughlin Steel Corporation, had violated the Act by engaging in unfair labor practices affecting commerce. The proceeding was instituted by the Beaver Valley Lodge No. 200, affiliated with the Amalgamated Association of Iron, Steel and Tin Workers of America, a labor organization. The unfair labor practices charged were that the corporation was discriminating against members of the union with regard to hire and tenure of employment, and was coercing and intimidating its employees in order to interfere with their self-organization. The discriminatory and coercive action alleged was the discharge of certain employees.

The National Labor Relations Board, sustaining the charge, ordered the corporation to cease and desist from such discrimination and coercion, to offer reinstatement to ten of the employees named, to make good their losses in pay, and to post for thirty days notices that the corporation would not discharge or discriminate against members, or those desiring to become members, of the labor union. As the corporation failed to comply, the Board petitioned the Circuit Court of Appeals to enforce the order. The court denied the petition, holding that the order lay beyond the range of federal power. 83 F. (2d) 998. We granted certiorari.

The scheme of the National Labor Relations Act—which is too long to be quoted in full—may be briefly stated. The first section sets forth findings with respect to the injury to commerce resulting from the denial by employers of the right of employees to organize and from the refusal of employers to accept the procedure of col-

[1] Act of July 5, 1935, 49 Stat. 449, 29 U. S. C. 151.

lective bargaining. There follows a declaration that it is the policy of the United States to eliminate these causes of obstruction to the free flow of commerce.[2] The Act

---

[2] This section is as follows:

"Section 1. The denial by employers of the right of employees to organize and the refusal by employers to accept the procedure of collective bargaining lead to strikes and other forms of industrial strife or unrest, which have the intent or the necessary effect of burdening or obstructing commerce by (a) impairing the efficiency, safety, or operation of the instrumentalities of commerce; (b) occurring in the current of commerce; (c) materially affecting, restraining, or controlling the flow of raw materials or manufactured or processed goods from or into the channels of commerce, or the prices of such materials or goods in commerce; or (d) causing diminution of employment and wages in such volume as substantially to impair or disrupt the market for goods flowing from or into the channels of commerce.

"The inequality of bargaining power between employees who do not possess full freedom of association or actual liberty of contract, and employers who are organized in the corporate or other forms of ownership association substantially burdens and affects the flow of commerce, and tends to aggravate recurrent business depressions, by depressing wage rates and the purchasing power of wage earners in industry and by preventing the stabilization of competitive wage rates and working conditions within and between industries.

"Experience has proved that protection by law of the right of employees to organize and bargain collectively safeguards commerce from injury, impairment, or interruption, and promotes the flow of commerce by removing certain recognized sources of industrial strife and unrest, by encouraging practices fundamental to the friendly adjustment of industrial disputes arising out of differences as to wages, hours, or other working conditions, and by restoring equality of bargaining power between employers and employees.

"It is hereby declared to be the policy of the United States to eliminate the causes of certain substantial obstructions to the free flow of commerce and to mitigate and eliminate these obstructions when they have occurred by encouraging the practice and procedure of collective bargaining and by protecting the exercise by workers of full freedom of association, self-organization, and designation of representatives of their own choosing, for the purpose of negotiating the terms and conditions of their employment or other mutual aid or protection."

then defines the terms it uses, including the terms "commerce" and "affecting commerce." § 2. It creates the National Labor Relations Board and prescribes its organization. §§ 3-6. It sets forth the right of employees to self-organization and to bargain collectively through representatives of their own choosing. § 7. It defines "unfair labor practices." § 8. It lays down rules as to the representation of employees for the purpose of collective bargaining. § 9. The Board is empowered to prevent the described unfair labor practices affecting commerce and the Act prescribes the procedure to that end. The Board is authorized to petition designated courts to secure the enforcement of its orders. The findings of the Board as to the facts, if supported by evidence, are to be conclusive. If either party on application to the court shows that additional evidence is material and that there were reasonable grounds for the failure to adduce such evidence in the hearings before the Board, the court may order the additional evidence to be taken. Any person aggrieved by a final order of the Board may obtain a review in the designated courts with the same procedure as in the case of an application by the Board for the enforcement of its order. § 10. The Board has broad powers of investigation. § 11. Interference with members of the Board or its agents in the performance of their duties is punishable by fine and imprisonment. § 12. Nothing in the Act is to be construed to interfere with the right to strike. § 13. There is a separability clause to the effect that if any provision of the Act or its application to any person or circumstances shall be held invalid, the remainder of the Act or its application to other persons or circumstances shall not be affected. § 15. The particular provisions which are involved in the instant case will be considered more in detail in the course of the discussion.

The procedure in the instant case followed the statute. The labor union filed with the Board its verified charge.

The Board thereupon issued its complaint against the respondent alleging that its action in discharging the employees in question constituted unfair labor practices affecting commerce within the meaning of § 8, subdivisions (1) and (3), and § 2, subdivisions (6) and (7) of the Act. Respondent, appearing specially for the purpose of objecting to the jurisdiction of the Board, filed its answer. Respondent admitted the discharges, but alleged that they were made because of inefficiency or violation of rules or for other good reasons and were not ascribable to union membership or activities. As an affirmative defense respondent challenged the constitutional validity of the statute and its applicability in the instant case. Notice of hearing was given and respondent appeared by counsel. The Board first took up the issue of jurisdiction and evidence was presented by both the Board and the respondent. Respondent then moved to dismiss the complaint for lack of jurisdiction; and, on denial of that motion, respondent in accordance with its special appearance withdrew from further participation in the hearing. The Board received evidence upon the merits and at its close made its findings and order.

Contesting the ruling of the Board, the respondent argues (1) that the Act is in reality a regulation of labor relations and not of interstate commerce; (2) that the Act can have no application to the respondent's relations with its production employees because they are not subject to regulation by the federal government; and (3) that the provisions of the Act violate § 2 of Article III and the Fifth and Seventh Amendments of the Constitution of the United States.

The facts as to the nature and scope of the business of the Jones & Laughlin Steel Corporation have been found by the Labor Board and, so far as they are essential to the determination of this controversy, they are not in dispute. The Labor Board has found: The corporation is organized under the laws of Pennsylvania and has its principal office at Pittsburgh. It is engaged in the business of manufacturing iron and steel in plants situated in Pittsburgh and nearby Aliquippa, Pennsylvania. It manufactures and distributes a widely diversified line of steel and pig iron, being the fourth largest producer of steel in the United States. With its subsidiaries—nineteen in number—it is a completely integrated enterprise, owning and operating ore, coal and limestone properties, lake and river transportation facilities and terminal railroads located at its manufacturing plants. It owns or controls mines in Michigan and Minnesota. It operates four ore steamships on the Great Lakes, used in the transportation of ore to its factories. It owns coal mines in Pennsylvania. It operates towboats and steam barges used in carrying coal to its factories. It owns limestone properties in various places in Pennsylvania and West Virginia. It owns the Monongahela connecting railroad which connects the plants of the Pittsburgh works and forms an interconnection with the Pennsylvania, New York Central and Baltimore and Ohio Railroad systems. It owns the Aliquippa and Southern Railroad Company which connects the Aliquippa works with the Pittsburgh and Lake Erie, part of the New York Central system. Much of its product is shipped to its warehouses in Chicago, Detroit, Cincinnati and Memphis,—to the last two places by means of its own barges and transportation equipment. In Long Island City, New York, and in New Orleans it operates structural steel fabricating shops in connection with the warehousing of semi-finished materials sent from its works. Through one of its wholly-owned subsidiaries it owns, leases and operates stores, warehouses and yards for the distribution of equipment and supplies for drilling and operating oil and gas wells and for pipe lines, refineries and pumping stations. It has sales offices in twenty cities in the United States and a wholly-owned subsidiary which is devoted exclusively to distributing its product in Canada. Approximately 75 per cent. of its product is shipped out of Pennsylvania.

Summarizing these operations, the Labor Board concluded that the works in Pittsburgh and Aliquippa "might be likened to the heart of a self-contained, highly integrated body. They draw in the raw materials from Michigan, Minnesota, West Virginia, Pennsylvania in part through arteries and by means controlled by the respondent; they transform the materials and then pump them out to all parts of the nation through the vast mechanism which the respondent has elaborated."

To carry on the activities of the entire steel industry, 33,000 men mine ore, 44,000 men mine coal, 4,000 men quarry limestone, 16,000 men manufacture coke, 343,000 men manufacture steel, and 83,000 men transport its product. Respondent has about 10,000 employees in its Aliquippa plant, which is located in a community of about 30,000 persons.

Respondent points to evidence that the Aliquippa plant, in which the discharged men were employed, contains complete facilities for the production of finished and semi-finished iron and steel products from raw materials; that its works consist primarily of a by-product coke plant for the production of coke; blast furnaces for the production of pig iron; open hearth furnaces and Bessemer converters for the production of steel; blooming mills for the reduction of steel ingots into smaller shapes; and a number of finishing mills such as structural mills, rod mills, wire mills and the like. In addition there are other buildings, structures and equipment, storage yards, docks and an intra-plant storage system. Respondent's operations at these works are carried on in two distinct stages, the first being the conversion of raw materials into pig iron and the second being the manufacture of semi-finished and finished iron and steel products; and in both cases the operations result in substantially changing the character, utility and value of the materials wrought upon, which is apparent from the nature and extent of the processes to which they are subjected and which respondent fully describes. Respondent also directs attention to the fact that the iron ore which is procured from mines in Minnesota and Michigan and transported to respondent's plant is stored in stock piles for future use, the amount of ore in storage varying with the season but usually being enough to maintain operations from nine to ten months; that the coal which is procured from the mines of a subsidiary located in Pennsylvania and taken to the plant at Aliquippa is there, like ore, stored for future use, approximately two to three months' supply of coal being always on hand; and that the limestone which is obtained in Pennsylvania and West Virginia is also stored in amounts usually adequate to run the blast furnaces for a few weeks. Various details of operation, transportation, and distribution are also mentioned which for the present purpose it is not necessary to detail.

Practically all the factual evidence in the case, except that which dealt with the nature of respondent's business, concerned its relations with the employees in the Aliquippa plant whose discharge was the subject of the complaint. These employees were active leaders in the labor union. Several were officers and others were leaders of particular groups. Two of the employees were motor inspectors; one was a tractor driver; three were crane operators; one was a washer in the coke plant; and three were laborers. Three other employees were mentioned in the complaint but it was withdrawn as to one of them and no evidence was heard on the action taken with respect to the other two.

While respondent criticises the evidence and the attitude of the Board, which is described as being hostile toward employers and particularly toward those who insisted upon their constitutional rights, respondent did not take advantage of its opportunity to present evidence to refute that which was offered to show discrimination and coercion. In this situation, the record presents no ground for setting aside the order of the Board so far as the facts pertaining to the circumstances and purpose of the discharge of the employees are concerned. Upon that point it is sufficient to say that the evidence supports the findings of the Board that respondent discharged these men "because of their union activity and for the purpose of discouraging membership in the union." We turn to the questions of law which respondent urges in contesting the validity and application of the Act.

First. The scope of the Act.—The Act is challenged in its entirety as an attempt to regulate all industry, thus invading the reserved powers of the States over their local concerns. It is asserted that the references in the Act to interstate and foreign commerce are colorable at best; that the Act is not a true regulation of such commerce or of matters which directly affect it but on the contrary has the fundamental object of placing under the compulsory supervision of the federal government all industrial labor relations within the nation. The argument seeks support in the broad words of the preamble (section one [3]) and in the sweep of the provisions of the Act, and it is further insisted that its legislative history shows an essential universal purpose in the light of which its scope cannot be limited by either construction or by the application of the separability clause.

If this conception of terms, intent and consequent inseparability were sound, the Act would necessarily fall

[3] See Note 2, *supra*, p. 23.

by reason of the limitation upon the federal power which inheres in the constitutional grant, as well as because of the explicit reservation of the Tenth Amendment. *Schechter Corp.* v. *United States,* 295 U. S. 495, 549, 550, 554. The authority of the federal government may not be pushed to such an extreme as to destroy the distinction, which the commerce clause itself establishes, between commerce "among the several States" and the internal concerns of a State. That distinction between what is national and what is local in the activities of commerce is vital to the maintenance of our federal system. *Id.*

But we are not at liberty to deny effect to specific provisions, which Congress has constitutional power to enact, by superimposing upon them inferences from general legislative declarations of an ambiguous character, even if found in the same statute. The cardinal principle of statutory construction is to save and not to destroy. We have repeatedly held that as between two possible interpretations of a statute, by one of which it would be unconstitutional and by the other valid, our plain duty is to adopt that which will save the act. Even to avoid a serious doubt the rule is the same. *Federal Trade Comm'n* v. *American Tobacco Co.,* 264 U. S. 298, 307; *Panama R. Co.* v. *Johnson,* 264 U. S. 375, 390; *Missouri Pacific R. Co.* v. *Boone,* 270 U. S. 466, 472; *Blodgett* v. *Holden,* 275 U. S. 142, 148; *Richmond Screw Anchor Co.* v. *United States,* 275 U. S. 331, 346.

We think it clear that the National Labor Relations Act may be construed so as to operate within the sphere of constitutional authority. The jurisdiction conferred upon the Board, and invoked in this instance, is found in § 10 (a), which provides:

"SEC. 10 (a). The Board is empowered, as hereinafter provided, to prevent any person from engaging in any unfair labor practice (listed in section 8) affecting commerce."

The critical words of this provision, prescribing the limits of the Board's authority in dealing with the labor practices, are "affecting commerce." The Act specifically defines the "commerce" to which it refers (§ 2 (6)):

"The term 'commerce' means trade, traffic, commerce, transportation, or communication among the several States, or between the District of Columbia or any Territory of the United States and any State or other Territory, or between any foreign country and any State, Territory, or the District of Columbia, or within the District of Columbia or any Territory, or between points in the same State but through any other State or any Territory or the District of Columbia or any foreign country."

There can be no question that the commerce thus contemplated by the Act (aside from that within a Territory or the District of Columbia) is interstate and foreign commerce in the constitutional sense. The Act also defines the term "affecting commerce" (§ 2 (7)):

"The term 'affecting commerce' means in commerce, or burdening or obstructing commerce or the free flow of commerce, or having led or tending to lead to a labor dispute burdening or obstructing commerce or the free flow of commerce."

This definition is one of exclusion as well as inclusion. The grant of authority to the Board does not purport to extend to the relationship between all industrial employees and employers. Its terms do not impose collective bargaining upon all industry regardless of effects upon interstate or foreign commerce. It purports to reach only what may be deemed to burden or obstruct that commerce and, thus qualified, it must be construed as contemplating the exercise of control within constitutional bounds. It is a familiar principle that acts which directly burden or obstruct interstate or foreign commerce, or its free flow, are within the reach of the congressional power. Acts having that effect are not rendered immune because they grow out of labor disputes. See *Texas & N. O. R . Co.* v. *Railway Clerks,* 281 U. S. 548, 570; *Schechter Corp.* v. *United States, supra,* pp. 544, 545; *Virginian Railway* v. *System Federation, No. 40,* 300 U. S. 515. It is the effect upon commerce, not the source of the injury, which is the criterion. *Second Employers' Liability Cases,* 223 U. S. 1, 51. Whether or not particular action does affect commerce in such a close and intimate fashion as to be subject to federal control, and hence to lie within the authority conferred upon the Board, is left by the statute to be determined as individual cases arise. We are thus to inquire whether in the instant case the constitutional boundary has been passed.

Second. The unfair labor practices in question.—The unfair labor practices found by the Board are those defined in § 8, subdivisions (1) and (3). These provide:

Sec. 8. It shall be an unfair labor practice for an employer—

"(1) To interfere with, restrain, or coerce employees in the exercise of the rights guaranteed in section 7."

"(3) By discrimination in regard to hire or tenure of employment or any term or condition of employment to encourage or discourage membership in any labor organization: . . ."[4]

[4] What is quoted above is followed by this proviso—not here involved—"*Provided,* That nothing in this Act, or in the National Industrial Recovery Act (U. S. C., Supp. VII, title 15, secs. 701–712), as amended from time to time, or in any code or agreement approved or prescribed thereunder, or in any other statute of the United States, shall preclude an employer from making an agreement with a labor organization (not established, maintained, or assisted by any action defined in this Act as an unfair labor practice) to require as a condition of employment membership therein, if such labor organization is the representative of the employees as provided in section 9 (a), in the appropriate collective bargaining unit covered by such agreement when made."

Section 8, subdivision (1), refers to § 7, which is as follows:

"Sec. 7. Employees shall have the right to self-organization, to form, join, or assist labor organizations, to bargain collectively through representatives of their own choosing, and to engage in concerted activities, for the purpose of collective bargaining or other mutual aid or protection."

Thus, in its present application, the statute goes no further than to safeguard the right of employees to self-organization and to select representatives of their own choosing for collective bargaining or other mutual protection without restraint or coercion by their employer.

That is a fundamental right. Employees have as clear a right to organize and select their representatives for lawful purposes as the respondent has to organize its business and select its own officers and agents. Discrimination and coercion to prevent the free exercise of the right of employees to self-organization and representation is a proper subject for condemnation by competent legislative authority. Long ago we stated the reason for labor organizations. We said that they were organized out of the necessities of the situation; that a single employee was helpless in dealing with an employer; that he was dependent ordinarily on his daily wage for the maintenance of himself and family; that if the employer refused to pay him the wages that he thought fair, he was nevertheless unable to leave the employ and resist arbitrary and unfair treatment; that union was essential to give laborers opportunity to deal on an equality with their employer. *American Steel Foundries* v. *Tri-City Central Trades Council,* 257 U. S. 184, 209. We reiterated these views when we had under consideration the Railway Labor Act of 1926. Fully recognizing the legality of collective action on the part of employees in

146212°—37——3

order to safeguard their proper interests, we said that Congress was not required to ignore this right but could safeguard it. Congress could seek to make appropriate collective action of employees an instrument of peace rather than of strife. We said that such collective action would be a mockery if representation were made futile by interference with freedom of choice. Hence the prohibition by Congress of interference with the selection of representatives for the purpose of negotiation and conference between employers and employees, "instead of being an invasion of the constitutional right of either, was based on the recognition of the rights of both." *Texas & N. O. R. Co.* v. *Railway Clerks, supra.* We have reasserted the same principle in sustaining the application of the Railway Labor Act as amended in 1934. *Virginian Railway Co.* v. *System Federation, No. 40, supra.*

Third. The application of the Act to employees engaged in production.—The principle involved.—Respondent says that whatever may be said of employees engaged in interstate commerce, the industrial relations and activities in the manufacturing department of respondent's enterprise are not subject to federal regulation. The argument rests upon the proposition that manufacturing in itself is not commerce. *Kidd* v. *Pearson,* 128 U. S. 1, 20, 21; *United Mine Workers* v. *Coronado Coal Co.,* 259 U. S. 344, 407, 408; *Oliver Iron Co.* v. *Lord,* 262 U. S. 172, 178; *United Leather Workers* v. *Herkert & Meisel Trunk Co.,* 265 U. S. 457, 465; *Industrial Association* v. *United States,* 268 U. S. 64, 82; *Coronado Coal Co.* v. *United Mine Workers,* 268 U. S. 295, 310; *Schechter Corp.* v. *United States, supra,* p. 547; *Carter* v. *Carter Coal Co.,* 298 U. S. 238, 304, 317, 327.

The Government distinguishes these cases. The various parts of respondent's enterprise are described as interdependent and as thus involving "a great movement of iron ore, coal and limestone along well-defined paths to the steel mills, thence through them, and thence in the form of steel products into the consuming centers of the country—a definite and well-understood course of business." It is urged that these activities constitute a "stream" or "flow" of commerce, of which the Aliquippa manufacturing plant is the focal point, and that industrial strife at that point would cripple the entire movement. Reference is made to our decision sustaining the Packers and Stockyards Act.[5] *Stafford* v. *Wallace,* 258 U. S. 495. The Court found that the stockyards were but a "throat" through which the current of commerce flowed and the transactions which there occurred could not be separated from that movement. Hence the sales at the stockyards were not regarded as merely local transactions, for while they created "a local change of title" they did not "stop the flow," but merely changed the private interests in the subject of the current. Distinguishing the cases which upheld the power of the State to impose a non-discriminatory tax upon property which the owner intended to transport to another State, but which was not in actual transit and was held within the State subject to the disposition of the owner, the Court remarked: "The question, it should be observed, is not with respect to the extent of the power of Congress to regulate interstate commerce, but whether a particular exercise of state power in view of its nature and operation must be deemed to be in conflict with this paramount authority." *Id.,* p. 526. See *Minnesota* v. *Blasius,* 290 U. S. 1, 8. Applying the doctrine of *Stafford* v. *Wallace, supra,* the Court sustained the Grain Futures Act of 1922[6] with respect to transactions on the Chicago Board of Trade, although these transactions were "not in and of themselves interstate commerce." Congress had found

[5] 42 Stat. 159.

[6] 42 Stat. 998.

that they had become "a constantly recurring burden and obstruction to that commerce." *Chicago Board of Trade* v. *Olsen,* 262 U. S. 1, 32; compare *Hill* v. *Wallace,* 259 U. S. 44, 69. See, also, *Tagg Bros. & Moorhead* v. *United States,* 280 U. S. 420.

Respondent contends that the instant case presents material distinctions. Respondent says that the Aliquippa plant is extensive in size and represents a large investment in buildings, machinery and equipment. The raw materials which are brought to the plant are delayed for long periods and, after being subjected to manufacturing processes, "are changed substantially as to character, utility and value." The finished products which emerge "are to a large extent manufactured without reference to pre-existing orders and contracts and are entirely different from the raw materials which enter at the other end." Hence respondent argues that "If importation and exportation in interstate commerce do not singly transfer purely local activities into the field of congressional regulation, it should follow that their combination would not alter the local situation." *Arkadelphia Milling Co.* v. *St. Louis Southwestern Ry. Co.,* 249 U. S. 134, 151; *Oliver Iron Co.* v. *Lord, supra.*

We do not find it necessary to determine whether these features of defendant's business dispose of the asserted analogy to the "stream of commerce" cases. The instances in which that metaphor has been used are but particular, and not exclusive, illustrations of the protective power which the Government invokes in support of the present Act. The congressional authority to protect interstate commerce from burdens and obstructions is not limited to transactions which can be deemed to be an essential part of a "flow" of interstate or foreign commerce. Burdens and obstructions may be due to injurious action springing from other sources. The fundamental principle is that the power to regulate commerce is the power to enact "all appropriate legislation" for "its protection and advancement" (*The Daniel Ball,* 10 Wall. 557, 564); to adopt measures "to promote its growth and insure its safety" (*Mobile County* v. *Kimball,* 102 U. S. 691, 696, 697); "to foster, protect, control and restrain." *Second Employers' Liability Cases, supra,* p. 47. See *Texas & N. O. R. Co.* v. *Railway Clerks, supra.* That power is plenary and may be exerted to protect interstate commerce "no matter what the source of the dangers which threaten it." *Second Employers' Liability Cases,* p. 51; *Schechter Corp.* v. *United States, supra.* Although activities may be intrastate in character when separately considered, if they have such a close and substantial relation to interstate commerce that their control is essential or appropriate to protect that commerce from burdens and obstructions, Congress cannot be denied the power to exercise that control. *Schechter Corp.* v. *United States, supra.* Undoubtedly the scope of this power must be considered in the light of our dual system of government and may not be extended so as to embrace effects upon interstate commerce so indirect and remote that to embrace them, in view of our complex society, would effectually obliterate the distinction between what is national and what is local and create a completely centralized government. *Id.* The question is necessarily one of degree. As the Court said in *Chicago Board of Trade* v. *Olsen, supra,* p. 37, repeating what had been said in *Stafford* v. *Wallace, supra*: "Whatever amounts to more or less constant practice, and threatens to obstruct or unduly to burden the freedom of interstate commerce is within the regulatory power of Congress under the commerce clause and it is primarily for Congress to consider and decide the fact of the danger and meet it."

That intrastate activities, by reason of close and intimate relation to interstate commerce, may fall within federal control is demonstrated in the case of carriers who are engaged in both interstate and intrastate transportation. There federal control has been found essential to secure the freedom of interstate traffic from interference or unjust discrimination and to promote the efficiency of the interstate service. *Shreveport Case,* 234 U. S. 342, 351, 352; *Wisconsin Railroad Comm'n* v. *Chicago, B. & Q. R. Co.,* 257 U. S. 563, 588. It is manifest that intrastate rates deal *primarily* with a local activity. But in rate-making they bear such a close relation to interstate rates that effective control of the one must embrace some control over the other. *Id.* Under the Transportation Act, 1920,[7] Congress went so far as to authorize the Interstate Commerce Commission to establish a state-wide level of intrastate rates in order to prevent an unjust discrimination against interstate commerce. *Wisconsin Railroad Comm'n* v. *Chicago, B. & Q. R. Co., supra; Florida* v. *United States,* 282 U. S. 194, 210, 211. Other illustrations are found in the broad requirements of the Safety Appliance Act and the Hours of Service Act. *Southern Railway Co.* v. *United States,* 222 U. S. 20; *Baltimore & Ohio R. Co.* v. *Interstate Commerce Comm'n,* 221 U. S. 612. It is said that this exercise of federal power has relation to the maintenance of adequate instrumentalities of interstate commerce. But the agency is not superior to the commerce which uses it. The protective power extends to the former because it exists as to the latter.

The close and intimate effect which brings the subject within the reach of federal power may be due to activities in relation to productive industry although the industry when separately viewed is local. This has been abundantly illustrated in the application of the federal Anti-Trust Act. In the *Standard Oil* and *American Tobacco* cases, 221 U. S. 1, 106, that statute was applied to combinations of employers engaged in productive industry.

---

[7] §§ 416, 422, 41 Stat. 484, 488; Interstate Commerce Act, § 13 (4).

Counsel for the offending corporations strongly urged that the Sherman Act had no application because the acts complained of were not acts of interstate or foreign commerce, nor direct and immediate in their effect on interstate or foreign commerce, but primarily affected manufacturing and not commerce. 221 U. S. pp. 5, 125. Counsel relied upon the decision in *United States* v. *Knight Co.,* 156 U. S. 1. The Court stated their contention as follows: "That the act, even if the averments of the bill be true, cannot be constitutionally applied, because to do so would extend the power of Congress to subjects *dehors* the reach of its authority to regulate commerce, by enabling that body to deal with mere questions of production of commodities within the States." And the Court summarily dismissed the contention in these words: "But all the structure upon which this argument proceeds is based upon the decision in *United States* v. *E. C. Knight Co.,* 156 U. S. 1. The view, however, which the argument takes of that case and the arguments based upon that view have been so repeatedly pressed upon this court in connection with the interpretation and enforcement of the Anti-trust Act, and have been so necessarily and expressly decided to be unsound as to cause the contentions to be plainly foreclosed and to require no express notice" (citing cases). 221 U. S. pp. 68, 69.

Upon the same principle, the Anti-Trust Act has been applied to the conduct of employees engaged in production. *Loewe* v. *Lawlor,* 208 U. S. 274; *Coronado Coal Co.* v. *United Mine Workers, supra; Bedford Cut Stone Co.* v. *Stone Cutters' Assn.,* 274 U. S. 37. See, also, *Local 167* v. *United States,* 291 U. S. 293, 397; *Schechter Corp.* v. *United States, supra.* The decisions dealing with the question of that application illustrate both the principle and its limitation. Thus, in the first *Coronado* case, the Court held that mining was not interstate commerce, that the power of Congress did not extend to its regulation as such, and that it had not been shown that the activities there involved—a local strike—brought them within the provisions of the Anti-Trust Act, notwithstanding the broad terms of that statute. A similar conclusion was reached in *United Leather Workers* v. *Herkert & Meisel Trunk Co., supra, Industrial Association* v. *United States, supra,* and *Levering & Garrigues Co.* v. *Morrin,* 289 U. S. 103, 107. But in the first *Coronado* case the Court also said that "if Congress deems certain recurring practices, though not really part of interstate commerce, likely to obstruct, restrain or burden it, it has the power to subject them to national supervision and restraint." 259 U. S. p. 408. And in the second *Coronado* case the Court ruled that while the mere reduction in the supply of an article to be shipped in interstate commerce by the illegal or tortious prevention of its manufacture or production is ordinarily an indirect and remote obstruction to that commerce, nevertheless when the "intent of those unlawfully preventing the manufacture or production is shown to be to restrain or control the supply entering and moving in interstate commerce, or the price of it in interstate markets, their action is a direct violation of the Anti-Trust Act." 268 U. S. p. 310. And the existence of that intent may be a necessary inference from proof of the direct and substantial effect produced by the employees' conduct. *Industrial Association* v. *United States,* 268 U. S. p. 81. What was absent from the evidence in the first *Coronado* case appeared in the second and the Act was accordingly applied to the mining employees.

It is thus apparent that the fact that the employees here concerned were engaged in production is not determinative. The question remains as to the effect upon interstate commerce of the labor practice involved. In the *Schechter* case, *supra,* we found that the effect there was so remote as to be beyond the federal power. To find "immediacy or directness" there was to find it "almost everywhere," a result inconsistent with the maintenance of our federal system. In the *Carter* case, *supra,* the Court was of the opinion that the provisions of the statute relating to production were invalid upon several grounds,—that there was improper delegation of legislative power, and that the requirements not only went beyond any sustainable measure of protection of interstate commerce but were also inconsistent with due process. These cases are not controlling here.

Fourth. Effects of the unfair labor practice in respondent's enterprise.—Giving full weight to respondent's contention with respect to a break in the complete continuity of the "stream of commerce" by reason of respondent's manufacturing operations, the fact remains that the stoppage of those operations by industrial strife would have a most serious effect upon interstate commerce. In view of respondent's far-flung activities, it is idle to say that the effect would be indirect or remote. It is obvious that it would be immediate and might be catastrophic. We are asked to shut our eyes to the plainest facts of our national life and to deal with the question of direct and indirect effects in an intellectual vacuum. Because there may be but indirect and remote effects upon interstate commerce in connection with a host of local enterprises throughout the country, it does not follow that other industrial activities do not have such a close and intimate relation to interstate commerce as to make the presence of industrial strife a matter of the most urgent national concern. When industries organize themselves on a national scale, making their relation to interstate commerce the dominant factor in their activities, how can it be maintained that their industrial labor relations constitute a forbidden field into which Congress may not enter when it is necessary to protect interstate commerce from the paralyzing consequences of industrial war? We have often said that interstate commerce itself is a practical conception. It is equally true that interferences with that commerce must be appraised by a judgment that does not ignore actual experience.

Experience has abundantly demonstrated that the recognition of the right of employees to self-organization and to have representatives of their own choosing for the purpose of collective bargaining is often an essential condition of industrial peace. Refusal to confer and negotiate has been one of the most prolific causes of strife. This is such an outstanding fact in the history of labor disturbances that it is a proper subject of judicial notice and requires no citation of instances. The opinion in the case of *Virginian Railway Co.* v. *System Federation, No. 40, supra,* points out that, in the case of carriers, experience has shown that before the amendment, of 1934, of the Railway Labor Act "when there was no dispute as to the organizations authorized to represent the employees and when there was a willingness of the employer to meet such representative for a discussion of their grievances, amicable adjustment of differences had generally followed and strikes had been avoided." That, on the other hand, "a prolific source of dispute had been the maintenance by the railroad of company unions and the denial by railway management of the authority of representatives chosen by their employees." The opinion in that case also points to the large measure of success of the labor policy embodied in the Railway Labor Act. But with respect to the appropriateness of the recognition of self-organization and representation in the promotion of peace, the question is not essentially different in the case of employees in industries of such a character that interstate commerce is put in jeopardy from the case of employees of transportation companies. And of what avail is it to protect the facility of transportation, if interstate commerce is throttled with respect to the commodities to be transported!

These questions have frequently engaged the attention of Congress and have been the subject of many inquiries.[8] The steel industry is one of the great basic industries of the United States, with ramifying activities affecting interstate commerce at every point. The Government aptly refers to the steel strike of 1919–1920 with its far-reaching consequences.[9] The fact that there appears to have been no major disturbance in that industry in the more recent period did not dispose of the possibilities of future and like dangers to interstate commerce which Congress was entitled to foresee and to exercise its protective power to forestall. It is not necessary again to detail the facts as to respondent's enterprise. Instead of being beyond the pale, we think that it presents in a most striking way the close and intimate relation which a manufacturing industry may have to interstate commerce and we have no doubt that Congress had constitutional authority to safeguard the right of respondent's employees to self-organization and freedom in the choice of representatives for collective bargaining.

Fifth. The means which the Act employs.—Questions under the due process clause and other constitutional restrictions.—Respondent asserts its right to conduct its business in an orderly manner without being subjected to arbitrary restraints. What we have said points to the fallacy in the argument. Employees have their correlative

[8] See, for example, Final Report of the Industrial Commission (1902), vol. 19, p. 844; Report of the Anthracite Coal Strike Commission (1902), Sen. Doc. No. 6, 58th Cong., spec. sess.; Final Report of Commission on Industrial Relations (1916), Sen. Doc. No. 415, 64th Cong., 1st sess., vol. I; National War Labor Board, Principles and Rules of Procedure (1919), p. 4; Bureau of Labor Statistics, Bulletin No. 287 (1921), pp. 52–64; History of the Shipbuilding Labor Adjustment Board, U. S. Bureau of Labor Statistics, Bulletin No. 283.

[9] See Investigating Strike in Steel Industries, Sen. Rep. No. 289, 66th Cong., 1st sess.

right to organize for the purpose of securing the redress of grievances and to promote agreements with employers relating to rates of pay and conditions of work. *Texas & N. O. R. Co.* v. *Railway Clerks, supra; Virginian Railway Co.* v. *System Federation, No. 40.* Restraint for the purpose of preventing an unjust interference with that right cannot be considered arbitrary or capricious. The provision of § 9 (a)[10] that representatives, for the purpose of collective bargaining, of the majority of the employees in an appropriate unit shall be the exclusive representatives of all the employees in that unit, imposes upon the respondent only the duty of conferring and negotiating with the authorized representatives of its employees for the purpose of settling a labor dispute. This provision has its analogue in § 2, Ninth, of the Railway Labor Act which was under consideration in *Virginian Railway Co.* v. *System Federation, No. 40, supra.* The decree which we affirmed in that case required the Railway Company to treat with the representative chosen by the employees and also to refrain from entering into collective labor agreements with anyone other than their true representative as ascertained in accordance with the provisions of the Act. We said that the obligation to treat with the true representative was exclusive and hence imposed the negative duty to treat with no other. We also pointed out that, as conceded by the Government,[11] the injunc-

[10] The provision is as follows: "SEC. 9 (a) Representatives designated or selected for the purposes of collective bargaining by the majority of the employees in a unit appropriate for such purposes, shall be the exclusive representatives of all the employees in such unit for the purposes of collective bargaining in respect to rates of pay, wages, hours of employment, or other conditions of employment: *Provided,* That any individual employee or a group of employees shall have the right at any time to present grievances to their employer."

[11] See *Virginian Railway Co.* v. *System Federation, No. 40,* 300 U. S. 515.

tion against the Company's entering into any contract concerning rules, rates of pay and working conditions except with a chosen representative was "designed only to prevent collective bargaining with anyone purporting to represent employees" other than the representative they had selected. It was taken "to prohibit the negotiation of labor contracts generally applicable to employees" in the described unit with any other representative than the one so chosen, "but not as precluding such individual contracts" as the Company might "elect to make directly with individual employees." We think this construction also applies to § 9 (a) of the National Labor Relations Act.

The Act does not compel agreements between employers and employees. It does not compel any agreement whatever. It does not prevent the employer "from refusing to make a collective contract and hiring individuals on whatever terms" the employer "may by unilateral action determine."[12] The Act expressly provides in § 9 (a) that any individual employee or a group of employees shall have the right at any time to present grievances to their employer. The theory of the Act is that free opportunity for negotiation with accredited representatives of employees is likely to promote industrial peace and may bring about the adjustments and agreements which the Act in itself does not attempt to compel. As we said in *Texas & N. O. R. Co.* v. *Railway Clerks, supra,* and repeated in *Virginian Railway Co.* v. *System Federation, No. 40, supra,* the cases of *Adair* v. *United States,* 208 U. S. 161, and *Coppage* v. *Kansas,* 236 U. S. 1, are inapplicable to legislation of this character. The Act does not interfere with the normal exercise of the right of the employer to select its employees or to discharge them. The employer may not, under cover of that right, intimidate or coerce its employees with respect to their

[12] See Note 11.

self-organization and representation, and, on the other hand, the Board is not entitled to make its authority a pretext for interference with the right of discharge when that right is exercised for other reasons than such intimidation and coercion. The true purpose is the subject of investigation with full opportunity to show the facts. It would seem that when employers freely recognize the right of their employees to their own organizations and their unrestricted right of representation there will be much less occasion for controversy in respect to the free and appropriate exercise of the right of selection and discharge.

The Act has been criticised as one-sided in its application; that it subjects the employer to supervision and restraint and leaves untouched the abuses for which employees may be responsible; that it fails to provide a more comprehensive plan,—with better assurances of fairness to both sides and with increased chances of success in bringing about, if not compelling, equitable solutions of industrial disputes affecting interstate commerce. But we are dealing with the power of Congress, not with a particular policy or with the extent to which policy should go. We have frequently said that the legislative authority, exerted within its proper field, need not embrace all the evils within its reach. The Constitution does not forbid "cautious advance, step by step," in dealing with the evils which are exhibited in activities within the range of legislative power. *Carroll* v. *Greenwich Insurance Co.,* 199 U. S. 401, 411; *Keokee Coke Co.* v. *Taylor,* 234 U. S. 224, 227; *Miller* v. *Wilson,* 236 U. S. 373, 384; *Sproles* v. *Binford,* 286 U. S. 374, 396. The question in such cases is whether the legislature, in what it does prescribe, has gone beyond constitutional limits.

The procedural provisions of the Act are assailed. But these provisions, as we construe them, do not offend against the constitutional requirements governing the creation and action of administrative bodies. See *Interstate Commerce Comm'n* v. *Louisville & Nashville R. Co.,* 227 U. S. 88, 91. The Act establishes standards to which the Board must conform. There must be complaint, notice and hearing. The Board must receive evidence and make findings. The findings as to the facts are to be conclusive, but only if supported by evidence. The order of the Board is subject to review by the designated court, and only when sustained by the court may the order be enforced. Upon that review all questions of the jurisdiction of the Board and the regularity of its proceedings, all questions of constitutional right or statutory authority, are open to examination by the court. We construe the procedural provisions as affording adequate opportunity to secure judicial protection against arbitrary action in accordance with the well-settled rules applicable to administrative agencies set up by Congress to aid in the enforcement of valid legislation. It is not necessary to repeat these rules which have frequently been declared. None of them appears to have been transgressed in the instant case. Respondent was notified and heard. It had opportunity to meet the charge of unfair labor practices upon the merits, and by withdrawing from the hearing it declined to avail itself of that opportunity. The facts found by the Board support its order and the evidence supports the findings. Respondent has no just ground for complaint on this score.

The order of the Board required the reinstatement of the employees who were found to have been discharged because of their "union activity" and for the purpose of "discouraging membership in the union." That requirement was authorized by the Act. § 10 (c). In *Texas & N. O. R. Co.* v. *Railway Clerks, supra,* a similar order for restoration to service was made by the court in contempt proceedings for the violation of an injunction issued by the court to restrain an interference with the right of employees as guaranteed by the Railway Labor Act of 1926. The requirement of restoration to service, of employees discharged in violation of the provisions of that Act, was thus a sanction imposed in the enforcement of a judicial decree. We do not doubt that Congress could impose a like sanction for the enforcement of its valid regulation. The fact that in the one case it was a judicial sanction, and in the other a legislative one, is not an essential difference in determining its propriety.

Respondent complains that the Board not only ordered reinstatement but directed the payment of wages for the time lost by the discharge, less amounts earned by the employee during that period. This part of the order was also authorized by the Act. § 10 (c). It is argued that the requirement is equivalent to a money judgment and hence contravenes the Seventh Amendment with respect to trial by jury. The Seventh Amendment provides that "In suits at common law, where the value in controversy shall exceed twenty dollars, the right of trial by jury shall be preserved." The Amendment thus preserves the right which existed under the common law when the Amendment was adopted. *Shields* v. *Thomas,* 18 How. 253, 262; *In re Wood,* 210 U. S. 246, 258; *Dimick* v. *Schiedt,* 293 U. S. 474, 476; *Baltimore & Carolina Line* v. *Redman,* 295 U. S. 654, 657. Thus it has no application to cases where recovery of money damages is an incident to equitable relief even though damages might have been recovered in an action at law. *Clark* v. *Wooster,* 119 U. S. 322, 325; *Pease* v. *Rathbun-Jones Engineering Co.,* 243 U. S. 273, 279. It does not apply where the proceeding is not in the nature of a suit at common law. *Guthrie National Bank* v. *Guthrie,* 173 U. S. 528, 537.

The instant case is not a suit at common law or in the nature of such a suit. The proceeding is one unknown to the common law. It is a statutory proceeding. Reinstatement of the employee and payment for time lost are

1

requirements imposed for violation of the statute and are remedies appropriate to its enforcement. The contention under the Seventh Amendment is without merit.

Our conclusion is that the order of the Board was within its competency and that the Act is valid as here applied. The judgment of the Circuit Court of Appeals is reversed and the cause is remanded for further proceedings in conformity with this opinion.

Reversed.

The Yale Law Journal
Volume 92, Number 8, July 1983

A Common Law for Labor Relations: A Critique of the New Deal Labor Legislation

Richard A. Epstein†

During the nineteenth century, the area of labor relations was governed by a set of legal rules that spanned the law of property, contract, tort, and procedure. There was no special set of rules for labor cases as such. Since the advent of the New Deal, these common law principles have largely given way to a complex body of statutory and administrative law that treats labor law as a separate and self-contained subject. The central question in this paper is whether there is any warrant for the special treatment that labor law receives today. I shall concentrate upon the Norris-LaGuardia Act of 1932,[1] and the Wagner Act of 1935,[2] the latter a New Deal statute and the former nearly so. My conclusion is that this (for ease of expression) New Deal legislation is in large measure a mistake that, if possible, should be scrapped in favor of the adoption of a sensible common law regime relying heavily upon tort and contract law. The tort principles protect all individuals against the use or threat of force, and—of great relevance here—against the deliberate inducement of breach of contract. The contract principles allow individuals within this

† James Parker Hall Professor of Law, University of Chicago. I would like to thank Dennis Carlton, Frank Easterbrook, Bernard Meltzer, and Cass Sunstein for their valuable comments on an earlier draft of this Article. Ross Green provided valuable research assistance. I have also benefited from the comments made both at the Yale Law Journal Symposium in February, 1983, and at a faculty workshop at the University of Michigan in April, 1983.

1. 18 U.S.C. § 3692, 29 U.S.C. §§ 101-115 (1982).
2. 29 U.S.C. §§ 151-169 (1982).

social framework of entitlements to make whatever bargains they please with whomever they please.

At the outset it is important to note several important caveats about my analysis. In making these arguments I seek to analyze and evaluate labor law, not to construct a practical program or propose political reform. My operating premise is simple: No set of institutions should be exempt from serious criticism and review. The point is especially important in labor relations, where most modern legal scholarship is confined to the analysis of cases and practices within the current statutory framework. What is needed is an analysis of the statutory framework itself. Much of the critical writing on the subject dates from the 1930's and earlier,[3] before the recent advances both in general legal theory and in law and economics. The fiftieth anniversary of the New Deal is an appropriate occasion for renewed critical scrutiny, as well as for celebration.

The outline of this paper is as follows. In the first section, I argue that common law rules provide an appropriate benchmark against which to measure the modern statutory developments. In the second section, I show how a coherent theory of private law, with well developed principles of contract and tort, can govern labor relations. Section III shows the substantial convergence of libertarian and utilitarian principles as they apply to labor relations. In Section IV, I shall look at the way in which the New Deal reforms handled the tort and contract issues, particularly the soundness of a statutory list of "unfair labor practices" of employers and of its system of exclusive collective bargaining. Section V then examines and criticizes the broader justifications of industrial peace and industrial democracy used to justify the New Deal labor statutes. In dealing with the basic institutional structures, I shall look at both their inherent desirability and their dependence upon a large administrative apparatus. No constitutional questions are assayed. After the basic examination, I shall conclude with a brief discussion about the relationship between the New Deal legislation and the ends it seeks to advance.

I. The Common Law Benchmark

In conducting this investigation, one might ask, why look at common law rules? The answer is that traditional common law principles provide a benchmark, both theoretical and historical, against which the modern statutory schemes can be measured. The actual common law, however, is often highly unruly. Judges themselves often have profound disagreements

3. *See, e.g.*, F. FRANKFURTER & N. GREENE, THE LABOR INJUNCTION (1930); Magruder, *A Half Century of Legal Influence Upon the Development of Collective Bargaining*, 50 HARV. L. REV. 1071 (1937); Powell, *Collective Bargaining Before the Supreme Court*, 33 POL. SCI. Q. 396 (1918).

as to the first premises in the legal debate, and in any event the number of decisions is simply too great to allow harmony to reign here, just as it is (a fortiori) with administrative actions pursuant to complex legislative schemes. In speaking of "the" common law, therefore, I am referring to the best set of private-law rules that can be devised to handle the problems of labor relations. The rules themselves, however, cannot be judged sufficient simply because they give the ideal responses suitable to an ideal world. To the contrary, these rules, like all others, must be judged as well by the way in which they handle problems of uncertainty, error, and enforcement.

As a substantive matter, the defense of a common law system is not an assertion that the "market" can handle every social problem. The law of property and the law of torts are strictly required in order to establish the framework of original rights in which voluntary transactions can take place. Nonetheless, the reference to common law solutions throughout this article does reflect a basic intellectual orientation in favor of limited government and the maximization of private autonomy. This premise is not, of course, an endorsement of anarchy. It accepts—indeed insists—that the state is entitled to prevent the private use of force and violence and to enforce promises, except when those promises are induced by duress or misrepresentation, or made by persons of manifest incompetence such as infants and insane persons.[4]

One virtue of this basic set of rules is that it is capable of sustained application. The qualifications of the basic principle (misrepresentation, duress, and incompetence) are not, as has been suggested,[5] so infinitely expandable that they may be invoked almost as a matter of course to defeat every commercial or employment transaction, whenever either party has regrets after the fact. Misrepresentation may be expanded to cover cases of "a nod or a wink";[6] duress may include duress of goods;[7] and incompetence (or at least necessity) may reach bargains entered into by persons in imminent peril of their lives.[8] But taken together, only a tiny percentage of transactions will be caught by these escape clauses, even recognizing their central role in the theoretical structure of contract. In

4. *See* Epstein, *Unconscionability: A Critical Reappraisal,* 18 J.L. & ECON. 293 (1975), where I defend this basic position. Much of this paper is an extended application of that theory to labor relations.

5. Kennedy, *Distributive and Paternalist Motives in Contract and Tort Law, With Special Reference to Compulsory Terms and Unequal Bargaining Power,* 41 MD. L. REV. 563, 582 (1982).

6. Walters v. Morgan, 3 DeG. F. & J. 718, 724, 45 Eng. Rep. 1056, 1059 (Ch. App. 1861).

7. Duress of goods includes cases in which a party who has promised to supply goods at a given price will do so only if some higher price is paid. *See, e.g.,* Sistrom v. Anderson, 51 Cal. App. 2d 213, 124 P.2d 372 (1942). For discussions, see Dawson, *Economic Duress—An Essay in Perspective,* 45 MICH. L. REV. 253 (1947); Epstein, *supra* note 4.

8. *See, e.g.,* Post v. Jones, 60 U.S. (19 How.) 150 (1857).

any event, these grounds are generally inapposite in employment cases, a point tacitly conceded by the well-nigh universal insistence that such transactions should be set aside on a still broader ground—the "inequality of bargaining power." This principle, of course, is wholly incompatible with the liberal ideal that most contracts are for the mutual benefit of both sides, regardless of their original endowments of wealth.[9]

The strength of the common law's premises is also revealed by considering the alternatives. As a positive matter, Dean Verkuil is correct in noting that modern common law judges could develop rules for the contract of employment that are far worse than those created by the statute.[10] But the criticism is wide of the mark in this context, as the question is whether it is possible to develop a competing normative view of the subject. The program of "substantive justice" in contracting, although oft proposed, is as far from realization today as it has ever been.[11] Nor is that

9. Kennedy makes an effective critique of the usual arguments about standard form contracts, only to urge more fundamental measures to reshape the structure of American business institutions. *See* Kennedy, *supra* note 5, at 615-20.

More generally, one possible test of "inequality of bargaining power" asks us to imagine a perfect bilateral monopoly in which, for example, the issue was the division of $100 between A and B, where it was understood that neither party would get anything unless both agreed to the split. Inequality of bargaining power in this context refers to the situation in which one person is expected to receive more than $50. Yet even if this account is viable, it is very difficult to imagine what set of workable institutions could restore the even split without upsetting the balance in the other direction. In any event, the best way to handle the problem is to undermine the institutional structures that perpetuate these rigid bilateral monopolies, as by facilitating freedom of entry into various markets. *See infra* p. 1396. (discussion of bilateral monopolies).

10. *See* Verkuil, *Whose Common Law for Labor Relations*? 92 Yale L.J. 1409 (1983).

11. The work of Zweigert and Kotz is representative of the dominant tradition:

> We now realize that true freedom of contract cannot exist unless the parties to the contract are economically and socially equal.
>
> > Judge Pitney made this point brilliantly in *Coppage v. Kansas*, 236 U.S. 1, 17 (1915): "It is impossible to uphold the freedom of contract and the right of private property without at the same time recognizing as legitimate those inequalities of fortune that are the necessary result of the exercise of those rights . . . . Indeed, a little reflection will show that whenever the right of private property and the right of free contract co-exist, each party, when contracting, is inevitably more or less influenced by the question whether he has much property or little or none: for the contract is made to the very end that each may gain something he needs or desires more urgently than that which he proposes to give in exchange."
>
> Thus true freedom of contract could only operate in a Utopia, in a society in which businesses were independent, economically equal and fully automated, with neither labour nor management. If the parties are not socially and economically equal, only the stronger party is free to determine whether and how to form a contract. Such a society of equals does not exist anywhere, even in socialist countries, and probably never will, since it is a dream, freedom of contract in its pure form is itself a chimera, a fantasy and not in any way a reality. In the vast majority of the contracts which are concluded in modern society there is no freedom of contract, for the suppliers have fixed the conditions which the consumer can do nothing to alter. Freedom of contract exists only in contracts between large undertakings over atypical objects, and possibly in the area of labour law in the wage scale contracts produced by modern collective bargaining. Legal scholars must give up the habit of proclaiming that freedom of contract is a principle and then listing the exceptions to it. The main task is to discover criteria and procedures for the development of *contractual justice*, which the absence of freedom of contract makes it all the more necessary to promote.

program supplied by an insistence that the public interest or "public values"[12] forms an essential part of sound legal doctrine. Basically, this approach views regulation in all its aspects "to be not a matter of counting economic costs and benefits, or of defending private entitlements, but part of a continuing process of deciding what sort of a society we shall be."[13] One problem with this approach is that it defines the scope of public values residually: Public values cover only that ground not incorporated by theories of individual entitlement or social production. Yet this theory cannot, in and of itself, establish where matters of private right end and matters of public dominance begin; the things which can count as public values are so wide and varied that virtually any manifestation of the collective legislative power is in principle sufficient to displace private rights. This public-interest view of legal doctrine is very different from the view of government that regards protection of private rights—of rich and poor alike—as the chief justification for the use of force. Likewise the public-interest view is very different from a system that permits in some instances the taking of private property upon payment of just compensation. The eminent-domain vision of the world abandons any idea that an original set of property rights is immutable within the social order. But it still insists that these original property rights be respected even if they are abrogated to advance the social good, by making the state pay for what it takes by force.[14] By contrast, a public-interest view of the subject abandons any conception of private entitlements as its starting point, and thereby allows far greater latitude for government action.

To be sure, the common law theory developed here finds no place for the redistribution of wealth from rich to poor so characteristic of the modern state. Theories of redistribution are always difficult to construct: Welfare payments are never a matter of a legal entitlement of the recipients, but only an expression of collective benevolence by the transferors.[15] No

> The achievement of such contractual justice is no easy matter, and much further thought will have to be given to its answer.

2 K. ZWEIGERT & H. KOTZ, AN INTRODUCTION TO COMPARATIVE LAW: THE INSTITUTIONS OF PRIVATE LAW 8-9 (1977). The last sentence gives away the game. The entire passage is further flawed: It neglects the possibility that, even with economic inequality, the institution of contract still allows the weaker party to be left better off by the exchange.

12. Stewart & Sunstein, *Public Programs and Private Rights*, 95 HARV. L. REV. 1195, 1238 (1982).

13. *Id.*

14. For an elaboration, see Epstein, *Taxation, Regulation, Confiscation*, 20 OSGOODE HALL L.J. 433 (1982).

15. The point is often lost sight of in the modern terminological shifts in the welfare area. Originally welfare payments were called "handouts" or the "dole," which inescapably captured the precarious position of the transferee. The word "welfare" tends to obscure the nature of the legal relation and to emphasize the end for which the payments are made. The modern emphasis upon "human services" (as in the shift from the Department of Health, Education and Welfare to the (reconstituted) Department of Health and Human Services) makes it appear that the payments are obligatory on the

principle limits the power of a private party to choose who shall receive favors, and in what amounts; no private cause of action for want of benevolence forms the basis of the analogous public right, as does, for example, the law of nuisance for environmental protection. Private individuals find it difficult to identify who shall receive their bounty and to what extent. The problems are only compounded when these same matters are made the subject of collective decisions.

Nonetheless the indelible mark that the condition of the poor leaves on people of all political persuasions is enough to force any comprehensive theory of government to address the question.[16] That examination could still conclude that compulsory redistribution is out of bounds as a matter of principle; if it did, it would strengthen the argument here by showing that there is no additional feature of the basic situation that could require a reexamination of the positions taken thus far. The critique of current labor laws stands, however, even if redistribution from rich to poor is accepted: There is no solid moral case for treating union members, as such, as the favored class of wealth redistribution. To make union members wealthier is to make poorer not only employers (whose shareholders are often workers whose pension funds have been invested in the corporation) but also the nonunion workforce and the poorer members of the general population. Redistributions from rich to poor have far greater appeal than redistributions, for example, from a nonunionized worker to a unionized worker of initially comparable economic status. Desired redistributions (if any) are best accomplished by general tax measures. The possibility of factional or class legislation is thereby reduced, as is the likelihood that the process of redistribution itself will hamper the creation of wealth.[17]

transferor.

16. One commentator has asserted:

> My point is rather that this principle—that basic material needs be guaranteed by government to those who cannot meet them through their own efforts—has come to have an entrenched status as one of the fixed moral imperatives governing our political life . . . . No working American politician would, for instance, advocate the libertarian doctrine advanced in *Anarchy, State, and Utopia*, with its principled rejection of all income security programs. Our Reagans and Goldwaters argue that there is waste and fraud in our welfare programs, that people are receiving welfare who should support themselves, that benefit levels are too high. Those all are arguments within the terms of the principle of basic needs as I have stated it, and presuppose acceptance of the principle itself.

Grey, *Property and Need: The Welfare State and Theories of Distributive Justice*, 28 STAN. L. REV. 877, 901 (1976) [hereinafter cited as *Property and Need*]; *see also* Grey, *The First Virtue* (Book Review), 25 STAN. L. REV. 286, 323-25 (1973).

17. The difference between special labor legislation and general taxation best explain the constitutional response of the Supreme Court to various forms of social legislation in the period before the New Deal. The Court struck down, on constitutional grounds, both federal and state statutes prohibiting yellow dog contracts in employment. *See* Adair v. United States, 208 U.S. 161 (1908) (federal); Coppage v. Kansas, 236 U.S. 1 (1915) (state). Yet at the same time the Court allowed, without so much as a note of protest, forms of taxation which did have, and were intended to have, general

The weakness of overt redistributive arguments in the labor context is further revealed by the rhetoric used to justify both the Norris-LaGuardia and the Wagner Acts. While income redistribution to union employees from (amongst others) their employers was one apparent consequence of both these statutes, their passage was not overtly justified in these terms. Instead, it was said that the statutes were not designed to repudiate the market or to confiscate employer wealth. The statutes were said to be designed to cure the present system of its imperfections, if only to save capitalism from its own excesses. It seems therefore appropriate to put aside the question of income distribution as such, and to ask how any system of labor relations can be squared with a sound theory of individual entitlements and their social protection.

One further element is put aside in this analysis—the particular conditions of labor unrest both in the 1930's and before. It is often said that the massive social and economic dislocations of the Depression made it quite impossible to rest content with incremental adjustments to common law doctrine.[18] Many New Deal reforms perished during and after the Depression, however,[19] and there is no reason to hold modern labor law sacrosanct because it gained its maturity in the 1930's. Indeed, a sense of quiet desperation may well have led to the passage of labor statutes which in calmer times would have been rejected as destructive of both personal liberty and economic wealth for both society as a whole and most (but never all) individuals within it.

redistributive consequences. *See, e.g.*, Brushaber v. Union Pac. R.R., 240 U.S. 1 (1916) (rejecting challenges to a progressive income tax while upholding the 1913 federal income tax law); Knowlton v. Moore, 178 U.S. 41 (1900) (upholding the federal inheritance tax); Magoun v. Illinois Trust & Sav. Bank, 170 U.S. 283 (1898) (upholding the Illinois inheritance tax). *See generally* Blum & Kalven, *The Uneasy Case for Progressive Taxation*, 19 U. CHI. L. REV. 417, 424 n.21 (1952) ("The cases are not helpful on the merits of the principle of progression.").

18. For judicial expression of the sentiment, see Home Bldg. & Loan Ass'n v. Blaisdell, 290 U.S. 398, 442-48 (1934) (referring to emergency conditions that justified state mortgage moratoria against contract clause challenges).

The connection between social dislocations and labor law is a very different question, as no coherent theory links the common law of labor relations (unlike, for example, the management of the money supply) with bringing on the Depression, or shows that the legislation produced in the Depression contributed in any sensible way to economic recovery. There is certainly no explanation of why the common law of labor relations should be charged with the problems of the 1930's instead of being credited with the economic successes of earlier and better times.

19. *See, e.g.*, United States v. Butler, 297 U.S. 1 (1936) (striking down Agricultural Adjustment Act); Schechter Poultry Corp. v. United States, 295 U.S. 495 (1935) (striking down § 3 of National Industrial Recovery Act). Note too, that some programs have passed political muster, as with the deregulation of the airline industry, see Levine, *Revisionism Revised? Airline Deregulation and Public Interest*, 44 LAW & CONTEMP. PROBS. 179 (1981).

II. The Common Law of Labor Organization

In turning to our normative account of labor relations, it is proper to stress that common law rules in their ideal form make legal entitlements among strangers without reference to personal status. Legal rules do not refer to flesh-and-blood individuals, but to those lifeless abstractions, *A* and *B*, about whom nothing else is known or—more to the point—is relevant. It may well be that certain individuals will in the end assume certain well-specified roles, but if so there is no reason to have legal institutions either subsidize or penalize their efforts: Individuals should not have to sacrifice their rights against the rest of the world because they become an employer of *A* or an employee of *B*. Stating propositions in general form is, moreover, a powerful antidote to abuse and favoritism, even if standing alone it cannot guarantee a just set of rules or outcomes.[20] To use Rawls' popular phrase, generalizations place people behind the veil of ignorance, depriving them of the knowledge of whether their application will help or hurt themselves or their friends.[21] What, we ask, might these general rules look like in the context of labor organization?

We must begin with the original position: What are the rights and duties between strangers? We start first with the account offered under a theory of individual liberty, which can then be qualified by considerations of overall utility.[22] Here the common law (except for its unfortunate early flirtation with the law of criminal conspiracy)[23] took the sound position:[24] Every person owns his own person and can possess, use and dispose of his labor on whatever terms he sees fit.[25] To state otherwise is to say either

20. On the importance of generalization as protection against class intrigue, see Epstein, *The Social Consequences of Common Law Rules*, 95 HARV. L. REV. 1717 (1982).

21. *See* J. RAWLS, A THEORY OF JUSTICE 136-42 (1971).

22. For my own views on how these two areas might be reconciled, see Epstein, *Nuisance Law: Corrective Justice and its Utilitarian Constraints*, 8 J. LEGAL STUD. 49 (1979); Epstein, *Private Property and the Public Domain: The Case of Antitrust*, 24 NOMOS 48 (1982) [hereinafter cited as *Private Property and the Public Domain*].

23. *See, e.g.*, Commonwealth v. Pullis (Phila. Mayor's Ct. 1806) (the Philadelphia Cordwainer's case), *reprinted in* 3 J. COMMONS & E. GILMORE, A DOCUMENTARY HISTORY OF AMERICAN INDUSTRIAL SOCIETY 59-248 (1958). The turning point is often taken to be Shaw's opinion in Commonwealth v. Hunt, 45 Mass. (4 Met.) 111 (1842), but there were occasional strong anti-union sentiments thereafter. *See, e.g.*, State v. Donaldson, 32 N.J.L. 151 (Sup. Ct. 1867) (indictable conspiracy exists when several employees combine and notify their employer that unless he discharges certain enumerated persons, they will quit in a body).

24. *See* Witte, *Early American Labor Cases*, 35 YALE L.J. 825 (1926). Witte's central conclusion was as follows:

> It was never the law in the United States that labor unions are illegal per se, or that all strikes are unlawful. The unreported cases of the early nineteenth century did not turn upon the legality of the unions per se, but on the methods which they employed to gain their ends. Nor were the views expressed in these early cases as to the methods which might lawfully be employed less liberal than those now generally held by the courts.

Id. at 825-26.

25.

> Every person has a right under the law, as between him and his fellow subjects, to full

that the labor cannot be used or that someone else is entitled to direct its use. At the same time, the common law position also blocks off the institution of slavery—a constant theme in the debates over labor legislation[26]—at the outset.

Of the three rights in the original ownership bundle, ambiguity in the labor context attaches only to the right of disposition. In this context it could mean that a person has a right to dispose of his labor on his own terms, so that if I wished to dispose of my labor for $10 per hour, some other person would be required to acquire it at that price. Such a system of rights cannot be applied to all individuals, however,[27] for it would allow me to deny others the very liberties that I claim for myself: What could I say if someone wanted me to hire him for $1000 per hour? To be universal in application, the right of disposition must be understood to include only the right to offer one's services on whatever terms and conditions one sees fit. In good Hobbesian fashion, the appetite of every person determines the appropriate terms of exchange. The system can now specify the correlative obligations of the right to offer one's labor unhindered—without interference by force or fraud—which can be held simultaneously by all individuals.[28]

Over time, the original distribution of wealth is likely to change as labor is exchanged for labor or for capital. Within the liberty-based framework, no limitation is placed upon the voluntary recombination of entitle-

> freedom in disposing of his own labor or his own capital according to his own will. It follows that every other person is subject to the correlative duty arising therefrom, and is prohibited from any obstruction to the fullest exercise of this right which can be made compatible with the exercise of similar rights by others. Every act causing an obstruction to another in the exercise of the right comprised within this description—done, not in the exercise of the actor's own right, but for the purpose of obstruction—would, if damage should be caused thereby to the party obstructed, be a violation of this prohibition . . . .

W. ERLE, THE LAW RELATING TO TRADE UNIONS 12 (1869) (emphasis deleted). The passage is clearly correct when it notes that the articulation of the basic right is incomplete without the specification of the correlative duty. But it nowhere indicates why the "purpose of the obstruction" should be decisive instead of the means used to achieve it. And it hardly suffices to include a statement of the "actor's own right" in a description of the correlative duties.

26. The theme of the "wage slave" is evident enough in political theory. The provisions of the Clayton Act which stipulate that labor should not be regarded as an article of commerce also reflect that view. *See* Clayton Act, § 6, 15 U.S.C. § 17 (1982).

27. For an extended treatment of this theme, see Epstein, *Intentional Harms*, 4 J. LEGAL STUD. 391, 425-27 (1975).

28. The constraints upon a generalized system of entitlements reveal the intrinsic weakness of the view, advanced by Grey among many others, that all individuals are entitled to receive some minimum standard of support when they are unable to support themselves. *See Property and Need*, *supra* note 16, at 897-901. This standard must define the minimum level of support, and show how the system itself can generate sufficient wealth to meet its minimum obligations. It must also explain which individuals bear the correlative duties necessary to furnish the wealth in question. I am skeptical that these tasks can be discharged in a persuasive way, but for these purposes the central point is that this conception of entitlement is of no use in labor cases, where the redistributions will almost always be capricious, whatever its critical relevance to the question of welfare legislation.

ments by their holders, original or derivative.[29] Any set of moves is as good as another, so long as the moves themselves do not violate the rights of third parties and do not involve the use of prohibited means between competent parties. Becoming an employer or an employee is strictly a private act in which one person decides to offer his own capital in exchange for the services of another individual, or vice versa, on whatever terms the parties to the exchange see fit. The parties' decision to enter into a contractual agreement does not increase or decrease the sum of rights that they have against the rest of the world, or that the rest of the world has against them. The creation of voluntary arrangements is therefore never an occasion for increased state regulation of private transactions apart from the faithful enforcement of their agreement, be it in employment relations or anything else.

As the identities of the contracting parties and the terms on which they contract are of no special concern to the state, a contract between an employer and an employee is indistinguishable from one between two prospective employees. The protection of labor unions from doctrines of criminal conspiracy, therefore, should not depend upon any elaborate affirmative social justification for their use. If *A* could enter into a contract with a prospective employer, then there is no reason he cannot enter into a contract with his potential rival, *B*, to present a united front against the employer.[30] Similarly, the voluntary formation of labor unions need involve neither the use of force and fraud nor the inducement of breach of contract. There is therefore no need to appeal to special justification to account for the legality of labor unions, as it is already accounted for by a general theory of entitlements. To be sure, there are profound differences in the worth of the original set of endowments held by individuals (and by the firms or organizations that they create), but these have only descriptive significance in predicting what moves the parties will make within the rules. The refusal (or inability) to predict which arrangements will emerge in no way amounts to a defect of the theory. Prediction is within the province of economics and sociology. The function of a system of enti-

29. The position was well enunciated in the classical statement of libertarian principles in Coppage v. Kansas, 236 U.S. 1, 17 (1915). *Coppage* was, however, overruled sub silentio in Virginian Ry. v. System Fed'n No. 40, 300 U.S. 515 (1937), and expressly in Phelps Dodge Corp. v. NLRB, 313 U.S. 177, 187 (1941). The approach of *Coppage* has found modern philosophical support in R. NOZICK, ANARCHY, STATE, AND UTOPIA (1974).

30. The parallel between antitrust law and labor law is evident: There is no autonomy-based theory that accounts for antitrust law as applied to industry or for antitrust law as applied to labor law. I have explored this point in greater detail in *Private Property and the Public Domain*, *supra* note 22. The late nineteenth-century cases on economic harms show the close relationship between the two problems by treating both antitrust and labor cases within a single framework. *See, e.g.*, Mogul S.S. Co. v. McGregor Gow, & Co., [1889] 23 Q.B.D. 598, *aff'd*, 1892 A.C. 25; Allen v. Flood, 1898 A.C. 1; Quinn v. Leathem, 1901 A.C. 495; *see also* Mayor of Bradford v. Pickles, 1895 A.C. 587 (same analysis applied to nuisance cases).

tlements is only to determine after the fact whether the patterns that have emerged fall within the proper rules of the game. The law of contracts is no more designed to predict the terms contained in particular contracts than the rules of chess are designed to determine the soundness of the Ruy Lopez.

The strength of the theory is revealed by its treatment of three recurrent problems in the law of labor relations. The first problem is the role of "malice" and combination in labor disputes; the second concerns the place of the so-called "yellow dog" contract in employment relationships; and the last is the question of picketing.

A. *Malice and combination*

Malice and combination were at the heart of the great labor cases of the late nineteenth century in both England and the United States. One position, chiefly associated with the majority view in *Allen v. Flood*,[31] treated both malice and combination as wholly immaterial to the question of liability. When, therefore, one group of workers announced through their union leaders that they would not continue in the employ of a third party unless he dismissed the members of a rival union working under contracts at will, this conduct was held in *Allen* not to be tortious, even if actuated by malice.[32] The majority relied heavily on its earlier decision in *Mogul v. McGregor*,[33] which held that a combination of shippers could act to exclude rivals by predatory pricing even though their intention was to inflict economic harm in order to secure their own self-advancement.

Three years later, however, the House of Lords adopted a very different view of labor disputes in *Quinn v. Leathem*,[34] holding that a second-

31. For an interpretation of *Allen v. Flood* that stresses the factual argument that Allen was no more than a messenger for the iron-men in his union who did not induce the dismissal at all, see Petro, *Unions and the Southern Courts: Part III—The Conspiracy and Tort Foundations of the Labor Injunction*, 60 N.C.L. REV. 543, 558-67 (1982). Support for his view of the facts is found, for example, in the careful opinion of Lord Macnaghten, 1898 A.C. at 143-150. But Macnaghten also said: "Even if I am wrong in my view of the evidence and the verdict, if the verdict amounts to a finding that Allen's conduct was malicious in every sense of the word, and that he procured the dismissal of Flood and Taylor, that is, that it was his act and conduct alone which caused their dismissal, . . . I should still be of the opinion that judgment was wrongly entered for the respondents." *Id.* at 151. In addition, his view was sharply contested in other opinions, including that of Lord Morris, which found that Allen "proceeded to threaten the employers with the withdrawal of the boilermakers which would be most injurious to the employers, unless the plaintiffs were dismissed at once." *Id.* at 159. In any event, it is only on the point of principle—the rule of malice—that the case has any theoretical interest. It is quite incomprehensible why it should attract any attention if it turned on a simple question of fact. Note that Lord Herschell concluded his long opinion by saying "that I regard the decision under appeal as one absolutely novel, and which can only be supported by affirming propositions far-reaching in their consequences and in my opinion dangerous and unsound." *Id.* at 143.

32. 1898 A.C. at 1.

33. 23 Q.B.D. 598 (1889), *aff'd*, 1892 A.C. 25.

34. 1901 A.C. 495.

ary boycott by a labor union, which sought both to unionize the defendant's shop and to replace his current employees with union members, was actionable, given the conspiracy of the union members and their asserted malice toward the plaintiff. The decision has been rightly attacked as wholly inconsistent with the general principles of *Allen*, which itself could be transformed easily into a conspiracy case given that the defendant Allen represented a union, all of whose members were prepared to strike over the work issue.[35] In addition, *Quinn* seems difficult to reconcile with *Mogul* given that the union's actions were well calculated to serve the self-interest of its members, both by placing current members in high paying jobs and by choking off the powerful economic competition from nonunion shops.

The irreconcilable differences amongst these three English cases is warning enough of the difficulty of maintaining a harmonious set of common law rules. It should not be surprising therefore that these same doctrinal conflicts manifested themselves in the American cases, which in this particular instance rested very heavily upon the English decisions. *Plant v. Wood*,[36] strongly reminiscent of *Quinn*, held that liability turned on matters of intent when employees acted in concert—in this case, an effort to force nonunion workers to join a union shop.[37] The court in *Plant* took the general, if vague, position that workers who combined together to injure another engaged in wrongful conduct, whereas those who combined together to benefit themselves did not. The determination as to which ends were consonant with "legitimate" self-interest required courts to develop shadowy and unsatisfactory ways to distinguish between different brands of egoism: Should there be one response where the collective refusal to deal was intended to force other workers to join the striking union, and another where the goal was higher wages for union members? *Plant* and *Quinn* are clearly less consistent with a liberty-based theory than is *Allen*. That they impose greater restrictions upon labor unions is quite beside the point.

A closer analysis of the legal conception of malice helps clarify the proper rules of union liability. Malice in its pure form means more than an intention to inflict some temporal injury. All competition, and most economic activity, will do that. Instead it refers to actions done out of spite or ill will, whereby someone is prepared to impose costs upon himself solely to make someone else worse off. So defined, malice does not offer a viable route to either survival or advancement; indeed it is negated by the

35. *See* C. GREGORY, LABOR AND THE LAW 46-51 (2d ed. 1958).
36. 176 Mass. 492, 57 N.E. 1011 (1900).
37. *Id.* For a contrast to the majority view of *Plant*, see National Protective Ass'n v. Cumming, 170 N.Y. 315, 63 N.E. 369 (1902), which followed the argument of Holmes' classic dissent in *Plant*.

economic self-interest found in both *Quinn* and *Plant*. Any prohibition against malicious conduct, therefore, at most reaches only the fringes of individual and union behavior. *Allen* neatly avoids the problem of inquiring into motives for collective action entirely. But, by fastening exclusively on the means used, *Allen* did not reduce the law to conclusionary assertions about lawful and unlawful acts.

Under *Allen*, however, it is possible to supply an independent account of what constitutes unlawful means: force, fraud, and inducement of breach of contract. As long as workers, either alone or in combination, do no more than withhold or threaten to withhold labor that they are not bound by contract to supply, they have not trenched upon the rights of the rival workers, even if rival workers suffer as a consequence. The third-party employer could resist the demands of the defendants and continue to employ the plaintiffs, as did the employer in *Quinn*. Alternatively, the plaintiffs could agree to reduced wages or to different work in order to keep their previous positions. The targeted employer may even capitulate to the demands of the rival union. The autonomy-based theory does not predict outcome, but accepts whichever outcome emerges as the voluntary recombination of entitlements within the framework of the tort law.[38]

Unless, therefore, one wants to take the position that unions by their nature must engage in such illegal acts, they and a wide range of their activities remain protected under a strong theory of entitlements that contains not a whisper of special status or privilege. Labor unions should not be considered criminal conspiracies not because they do not operate in restraint of trade—many do—but because restraint of trade itself should not be illegal. The vacillation between *Allen* and *Quinn* has been attacked as a double standard of the private law—with harsher rules for labor than for business.[39] Whether this overall condemnation is justified is an open question. What is beyond dispute is the proposition that (at least in the libertarian view) legislation that secures the rules of *Allen* is appropriate, even if more massive labor legislation is not.

38. It remains true that if malice and combination are found in cases in which there is the threat or use of force, or an inducement of contractual breach, matters are worsened by the combination. Mobs are more dangerous than isolated individuals. But even here the important point is as before: The nature of the conduct must first be shown to be a violation of right before questions of motive and combination can be introduced by way of aggravation. The matter became quite cloudy in English law. *See, e.g.*, Crofter Hand Woven Harris Tweed Co. v. Veitch, 1942 A.C. 435; Sorrell v. Smith, 1925 A.C. 700. For discussion, see W. ROGERS, WINFIELD & JOLOWICZ ON TORT 461-67 (10th ed. 1975).

39. *See* C. GREGORY, *supra*, note 35, at 46-51. Note that the equivocation on the central point in both the American and the English cases makes it very difficult to draw any clear inferences of judicial bias from the legal decisions. If the judges had been so biased in the first instance, there would be no way to explain *Allen*.

B. *Yellow Dog Contracts*

The strong theories of individual entitlement applicable to labor unions apply with equal force to the "yellow dog" contract. In such contracts, a worker agrees as a condition of employment that he will not become a member of a labor organization. These contracts are today forbidden by explicit statutory command[40] and have been uniformly condemned by academic writers as being self-evidently unjust—even, as Calvert Magruder said, a "curse."[41] Their status as a matter of strict autonomy-based theory is, however, quite different: They should be accorded the same respect as any other voluntary agreement. Thus, in order to invalidate such an arrangement, one must show that it involves the use or the threat of force against a third party. To the extent that it requires only that a worker steer clear of unions in order to obtain or keep a job it does nothing of the sort.[42] To be sure, the yellow dog contract is improper if it requires an individual worker to breach a membership contract with his union. If the current statutory prohibition were directed only to that situation, it would be fully justified as a protection of vested rights. But no one thinks that the problem with yellow dog contracts is inducement of breach of intra-union contracts by employers. The opposition always takes the position that the yellow dog contract is against public policy in all its manifestations.[43] The support for the prohibition came from labor unions, its chief beneficiaries, who wanted to overcome any obstacles to unionization these contracts posed. Yet no attention was paid to the mode of that frustration, which by the general theory of entitlements is the one question that matters.[44]

In defense of the current prohibition of the yellow dog contract it is sometimes said that "[t]he Norris-LaGuardia Act introduced the only per-

40. National Labor Relations Act, 29 U.S.C. § 158(a)(3) (1982).

41. Magruder, *supra* note 3, at 1083. The relevant passage reads as follows:

> The *Adair* case was carried further in *Coppage v. Kansas*, where by a six-to-three vote the Supreme Court held invalid under the Fourteenth Amendment a state statute making it criminal for an employer to exact a yellow dog contract as a condition of employment. The curse has finally been taken from these cases by the recent decision upholding the National Labor Relations Act.

It seems an easy inference (especially from the tenor of the paper) to assume that *Adair* and *Coppage* were curses because the yellow dog contract was a curse. No argument is offered, however, to explain its social evil.

For similar sentiments, see A. COX, LAW AND THE NATIONAL LABOR POLICY (1960), where it is assumed that the errors in *Hitchman* are self-evident: "Decisions like the *Hitchman* case seemed to display either prejudice or a lack of elementary economics." Id. at 7. The only economic analysis offered here, however, consists of a theoretical and inaccurate assertion urging: "The *Hitchman* injunction thwarted the United Mine Workers but did not improve the lot of the coal miners." *Id.*

42. Justice Brandeis took the view that coercion should be very narrowly defined in labor cases. Hitchman Coal & Coke Co. v. Mitchell, 245 U.S. 229, 271-72 (1917) (Brandeis, J., dissenting).

43. F. FRANKFURTER & N. GREENE, *supra* note 3; A. COX, *supra* note 41.

44. A. COX, *supra* note 41, at 8.

iod of unqualified laissez faire in labor relations."[45] But the proposition is based upon a misapprehension of what laissez faire demands of government. To be sure, the Norris-LaGuardia Act (like the Wagner Act) did not involve government dictation of the terms and conditions of individual or collective agreements.[46] Yet the insistence, as revealed in the Norris-LaGuardia Act's exhortation, that workers obtain "acceptable terms and conditions of employment,"[47] hardly speaks to the process of contractual formation, much less to the glory of "the competitive struggle of life," that is central to the theory of laissez faire. To the contrary, the statute looks to the outcome of the process and demands a theory of just dessert that is incompatible with laissez faire principles.

Nor does the absence of any administrative structure convert the Norris-LaGuardia Act into a safeguard for laissez faire principles. For laissez faire, the ultimate question is *not* whether, given the established legal framework, the parties are entitled to bargain to whatever terms and conditions they see fit. It is whether the legal constraints within which the negotiation takes place are consistent with a rigorous theory of individual entitlements. Individuals can bargain with kidnappers without the benefit of state mediation on the amount of the ransom needed to secure release, but the prior question is, by what warrant must a person purchase the release of another individual when that individual ought already to be free as a matter of right? If we have learned anything from the law of the duress of goods,[48] it is that the existence of choice, without more, is not a sufficient condition for contractual freedom. The issue remains one of entitlements: Is the choice between something one owns and something one wants, or is it between two things one owns? In the former context we can speak of bargains worthy of respect. In the latter, by analogy to duress of goods, we can speak only of bargains under coercion.

These insights apply with undiminished force to the labor context. Why limit freedom of contract between employer and employee? It is often said that choices left to the worker under the common law are "illusory," in that without statutory protection the worker has no choice but to succumb

45. *Id.*

46. "The basic theory of the law [i.e., the Wagner Act] in its original form, as today, was that the arrangement of the substantive terms and conditions of employment is a private responsibility." *Id.* at 11. The position is endorsed in many judicial decisions. *See, e.g.*, H.K. Porter Co. v. NLRB, 397 U.S. 99 (1970). There is no question that the government is well advised to stay out of these matters. But it is quite a different proposition to treat massive structural interferences with voluntary transactions as though there were no interferences at all.

47. 29 U.S.C. § 102 (1982). The section also refers to the workers' right of "full freedom of association" as a justification for the limitation of the yellow dog contract, but does not address the question of how the statutory prohibition preserves the similar "full freedom of association" for both employers and workers who wish to sign yellow dog agreements.

48. *See supra* note 7.

to the employer's pressure. One factual objection to the theory is that it can neither account for the fact that the workers received positive wages for their employment before the adoption of the modern labor legislation, nor for the equally obvious fact that there were wage differentials between workers in different trades and with different skills. If inequality of bargaining power had any descriptive power as a model, then why did employers not use their power to reduce wages to the vanishing point, or refuse to accept unionization before the passage of either the Norris-LaGuardia or Wagner Acts? As a matter of principle, the liberal theory of contract draws a very powerful distinction between the duress which is imposed by the threat of force by one party against the other, and the duress, so-called, attributable to economic and personal pressures to which all parties are subjected by the inevitable considerations of scarcity. To adopt the modern language of "unconscionability,"[49] it is a meaningful choice to refuse employment altogether; no one would count it the loss of a meaningless choice if employers were given the right to conscript employees into service. To insist, therefore, that there be economic equality before there can be contract is to destroy the usefulness of contract by imposing a set of exacting conditions that can never be satisfied or even approached. To confuse economic inequality with duress is to say that no bargains are ever free from duress, and to swallow up freedom of contract by an unprincipled expansion of the principled limitations upon the basic rule. It is quite enough that the contracts leave the parties better off than they were before. It is too much to ask of any system of rules that it correct whatever asserted social imbalances exist before the contract formation.

The weakness of the arguments of economic duress can be demonstrated in yet another fashion. It is not coercive for a party to choose not to go into business at all, even though that exercise of rights reduces the options available to any prospective employee. It cannot therefore be an abuse to increase the options available to any person by giving him an opportunity to work that he cannot claim as of right and, in fact, would not have otherwise. A yellow dog agreement could be coercive only if prospective employees had a precontractual right to demand both union membership and employment. But it is unclear how any principled account of individual rights could generate that set of uneven entitlements. So long as the worker owns his labor, and the employer his capital, then the liberal theory of contract is neutral with respect both to the identity of contracting parties and to the terms of the agreement. No law prohibits two business partners from demanding exclusive loyalty from each other, nor

49. Williams v. Walker-Thomas Furniture Co., 350 F.2d 445, 449-50 (D.C. Cir. 1965).

is there any reason why such loyalty cannot be demanded of an employee by his employer, or of an employer by the employee (as in the promise not to hire nonunion labor). The Norris-LaGuardia Act can be regarded as compatible with laissez faire only if the sole permissible sequence of agreements dictates that agreements among workers precede those between workers in combination with employers. This is no more sensible than saying that sound industrial policy demands that cartelization amongst sellers should necessarily precede sales to customers.

In principle, there remains one other way to argue that public policy should prohibit the yellow dog contract. That is to show that the contracts themselves are of necessity entered into by processes (to wit, force and fraud) that themselves negate any true consent. There is a clear hint of this theme in the language of the Norris-LaGuardia Act, which states without elaboration that "the individual unorganized worker is commonly helpless to exercise actual liberty of contract and to protect his freedom of labor, and thereby to obtain acceptable terms and conditions of employment."[50] The source of the helplessness is left unspecified, but there is no indication that it is anything more than the difference between the two sides, command over resources, itself a factor immaterial to an entitlement theory of contract. And it is surely odd that a yellow dog contract should not count as an exercise in liberty of contract as much as a decision to cast one's lot with other workers.

The theory of laissez faire, then, is unambiguous in its support of the legality of the yellow dog contract. This was recognized by the believers in constitutionally based laissez faire when they struck down statutory prohibitions against the arrangements in *Adair v. United States.*[51] The strength of *Adair*'s conclusion is further supported by an examination of *Hitchman Coal & Coke Co. v. Mitchell,*[52] the key case upholding the legality of the yellow dog contract in the pre-New Deal era.

In *Hitchman*, the plaintiff coal mine had struggled through a protracted dispute with the United Mine Workers. On several occasions, management agreed to accept a closed union shop, but the arrangements always collapsed when up for renewal, producing a series of strikes that depleted the resources of both the firm and the union. During one of these strikes, several miners came to the employer offering to work on a nonunion basis for the prevailing union wages. It was agreed that the company would no longer recognize the United Mine Workers, and that no employee of the

50. 29 U.S.C. § 102 (1982).

51. 208 U.S. 161 (1908). Holmes' dissent, *id.* at 190, went not so much to the status of the agreement under the general common law theory, but to the separate and difficult question of the extent to which that theory has been incorporated into the Constitution. *Id.* at 191.

52. 245 U.S. 229 (1917).

firm could be a member of the union. These were contracts at will, so the workers were free to leave the employ of the company at any time and join the union. The agreement in question was accepted by all employees of the mine. Representatives of the United Mine Workers later attempted to secure workers' promises to go out on strike as members of the union when requested to do so. The organizers did not use force or misrepresentation against the employees to achieve their goals. The organizers did, however, request employees who agreed to join the union to remain on their jobs, fearing that the company could easily secure replacements if dissatisfied workers left on a gradual basis. When the company discovered the activities of the key union personnel, it sought to enjoin those activities on the ground that they constituted an inducement of breach of contract. In an analysis consistent with the general liberal theory of contract developed here, the Supreme Court held that the injunction was warranted, although overbroad in some of its particulars. There was no question that the contract of employment was valid as between the parties. As the arrangement was at will, the company could have dismissed individual workers on the spot if it discovered their affiliation with the union. More to the point, it could have argued that the employees were in breach of a material condition and therefore could have made a powerful claim to withhold (or perhaps recover) the wages paid to the workers during the period of their union affiliation. These conclusions could not be upset on the ground that the contract infringed the rights of third persons to be free, among other things, from force and fraud.

The only way to argue against an injunction was therefore to show that the tort of inducement of breach of contract did not apply to ordinary labor disputes. *Lumley v. Gye*,[53] the basic decision in the area, had granted the plaintiff impresario an injunction against a defendant who had knowingly induced a famous opera singer to breach her contract with the plaintiff. Thereafter, both the English and American courts extended *Lumley* to ordinary labor contracts, finding the use of the injunction uncontroversial.[54]

The application of *Lumley* to *Hitchman* is clear enough. So long as the current contract had any positive value to the promisee, the tort action is appropriate. As it was clear to all concerned that covert union membership (aside from being a fraud against the employer) weakened the employer's economic position against the employee, the common law tort applied to the case in a perfectly straightforward manner. The only question that remained was whether an injunction against the third party provided

53. 2 E. & B. 216, 118 Eng. Rep. 749 (1853).

54. *See* Walker v. Cronin, 107 Mass. 555 (1871); Bowen v. Hall, 6 Q.B.D. 333 (1881).

the proper remedy. Here the ongoing commission of the tort and the difficulty in estimating the damages that could flow from a sudden disruption of services brought about by a strike make such a remedy proper under the ordinary equitable principles governing injunctions.

In its own way, Brandeis's dissent is even more instructive than Pitney's admirable majority opinion. Brandeis utters not a single word against the common law conceptual framework that Justice Pitney used to analyze the case. The crux of Brandeis's argument follows:

> The contract created an employment at will: and the employee was free to leave at any time. The contract did not bind the employee *not* to join the union; and he was free to join it at any time. The contract merely bound him to withdraw from plaintiff's employ, if he joined the union. There is evidence of an attempt to induce plaintiff's employees to *agree* to join the union; but none whatever of any attempt to induce them to violate their contract. Until an employee actually joined the union he was not, under the contract, called upon to leave the plaintiff's employ. There consequently would be no breach of contract until the employee both joined the union *and* failed to withdraw from plaintiff's employ.[55]

At best this is an argument only of contract construction, and a very bad argument at that. As Pitney points out,[56] there is nothing of substance to distinguish joining the union from agreeing to join the union at some future time. The arrangement between the employer and the workers was that the workers' sole loyalty was to the employer. There is no question that dual and inconsistent loyalties are created even if a worker takes the neat precaution of not signing a membership card while remaining on the job at the behest of the union. If this had been a case in which one impresario had bid for the services of an opera star already under contract to a rival, a demonstration of the breach and its inducement would have been trivial matters. Pitney was clearly correct in observing that, as courts of equity had long looked "to the substance and essence of things and disregarded matters of form and technical nicety, it is sufficient to say that to induce men to *agree* to join is but a mode of inducing them to join. . . ."[57]

C. *Picketing*

It remains here only to consider the proper treatment of picketing within the libertarian framework. Here the point of departure is that the prohibition against the use of force reaches the threat of force. If killing is

55. 245 U.S. at 272.
56. *Id.* at 255 (italics in original).
57. *Id.*

illegal, then so too must be armed robbery, even if the gun is not fired. Wholly apart from the labor context, there has never been a difficulty in accepting the general proposition. But what are the limits of the rule? Blackstone's definition of assault was restrictive: It included an "attempt or offer to beat another, without touching him; as if one lifts up his cane, or his fist in a threatening manner at another."[58] Under this account the defendant must have both the capability and the immediate opportunity to inflict the harm in question, an overly restrictive view of liability, even for a common lawyer. Today the general view is that an action lies "when it is shown that one, in the absence of any privilege, intentionally subjects another to the mental suffering incident to serious threats to his physical well-being, whether or not the threats are made under such circumstances as to constitute a technical assault."[59] The creation of, as it were, an action on the case for an indirect assault lengthens the causal chain and complicates the manner of proof, but these difficulties do not preclude liability on theoretical grounds.

For our purposes the general rules of assault form the framework with which to analyze picketing. The first inquiry is whether "picketing" constitutes a threat of force against persons who cross the picket line. The question is difficult to answer because there are enormous variations in the form and style of "picketing." The presence of an isolated picketer etches in the mind of the observer the futility of the picketer's cause, while a group of angry men may well convey a different, if unmistakable, message. In principle, it is possible to wait until the damage manifests itself, allowing only individual actions of assault by aggrieved customers. That course of action, however, is tantamount to leaving a wrong wholly unredressed. Individual citizens at the picket line can cut their losses simply by not crossing the line. In any event, they will not be induced to maintain a cause of action that promises only small rewards after arduous litigation. The real victim is the proprietor deprived of customers. The only effective means of social control, therefore, is to grant an action to the proprietor of the picketed establishment. This action itself requires no innovation in principle, even if it may call for some novelty in application. The old schoolmaster's case[60] and *Tarleton v. McGawley*[61] both granted

58. 3 W. BLACKSTONE, COMMENTARIES 120 (1790).

59. State Rubbish Collectors Ass'n v. Siliznoff, 38 Cal.2d 330, 336, 240 P.2d 282, 284-85 (1952). *See* W. PROSSER, HANDBOOK OF THE LAW OF TORTS 59 (4th ed. 1971).

60. This case is referred to in Keeble v. Hickeringill, 11 East 574, 576, 103 Eng. Rep. 1127, 1128 (K.B. 1809): "But suppose Mr. Hickeringill should lie in the way with his guns, and fright the boys from going to school, and their parents would not let them go thither, sure that schoolmaster might have an action for the loss of his scholars."

61. 170 Eng. Rep. 153 (K.B. 1793).

actions for the (if it matters here, the deliberate) interference with prospective advantage by the threat or use of force.

To state the problem in this fashion is only to give some hint as to the problems that follow. Does picketing itself constitute a threat of force, or is it only an effort to convey information so that customers make an informed choice not to do business with the picketed establishment? In the celebrated case of *Vegelahn v. Guntner*,[62] the court was forced to confront this very question in passing on the scope of an injunction awarded against two trade unions and their members. In making his preliminary determination, Justice Holmes noted that the defendants had engaged in two separate types of activities, the first involving the use of "persuasion and social pressure," and the second "threats of personal injury or unlawful harm," that were often conveyed in a disguised manner.[63] The first of these he rightly treated as legal, and the second as illegal. The difficulty in the case was that the two patterns of behavior could be intertwined. Holmes tailored his original injunction to stop the second type of activity but to permit the first. In his dissent to the decision of the court, he justified his position by noting that if during the continuation of their picketing the defendants did use or threaten force, their conduct would fall under the injunction that he had granted so that the defendants would be "liable to summary punishment."[64] The court in turn ordered a broader injunction that forbade the defendants from interfering with the plaintiff's business "by any scheme . . . organized for the purpose of . . . preventing any person or persons who now are or may hereafter be . . . desirous of entering [the plaintiff's employment] from entering it."[65] The court's position is widely rejected today,[66] and is open to condemnation as an excessive use of the injunctive power. Nonetheless, the court's judgment is not subject to any categorical denunciation, even if wrong. Thus, the broader injunction can be defended by pointing to the weaknesses of the finely tuned injunction that Holmes had adopted. Leaving the pickets in place by the plaintiff's business invites, or at least increases the likelihood of, the threat or use of force, which will go unredressed because the summary remedies available in principle are imperfect in practice. Case-by-case determinations are expensive to make, and are subject to very high error rates, especially where disguised threats are a substantial possibility.

62. 167 Mass. 92, 44 N.E. 1077 (1896).

63. 167 Mass. at 95-96. The passage is not reproduced in 44 N.E.

64. *Id.* at 104, 44 N.E. at 1080 (Holmes, J., dissenting).

65. *Id.*

66. *See, e.g.*, Music Hall Theater v. Moving Picture Mach. Operators Local 165, 249 Ky. 639, 61 S.W.2d 283 (1933); People v. Nixson, 248 N.Y. 182, 161 N.E. 463 (1928). *Vegelahn* itself continued to enjoy some support. *See* Pierce v. Stablemen's Union, Local No. 8,760, 156 Cal. 70, 103 P. 324 (1909).

In some cases at least, the best solution may give too much protection instead of too little.

The case for the majority position in *Vegelahn* becomes more plausible in light of the very powerful regulation of police behavior done today on constitutional grounds. At its root, *Miranda v. Arizona*[67] rests upon the preference for broad over narrow injunctions, given that the simple appearance of a police officer can be so "inherently coercive" that constitutional rules of notice and right to counsel are necessary to help insure the "voluntariness" of a confession. The displaced rule—a case-by-case examination of the voluntariness of individual confessions—was rejected because it offered insufficient protection against official abuse. Picketing frequently constitutes an implicit threat of the use of force that may take the form of jostling or immediate contact. It may carry with it the implicit threat of the future infliction of harm: Who would not hesitate to cross a picket line if he saw a picketer filming persons crossing the line? To be sure, the picketers are not vested with the power of the state; but at the same time they are uncontrolled by any form of state power. The picketers can assert a weighty interest in freedom of speech,[68] but this is matched by the interests in freedom of property, contract, and association on the other side.

The question is in the end a close call. To be sure, there are some easy rules that dispose of some challenges to picketing: One cannot, for example, prohibit picketing solely because of the content of its message—a proposition which no one denies. But when the easy cases have been set to one side, a broad class of situations remain in which the sound discretion of the trial judge will be necessary to determine whether an injunction should issue, and if so on what terms. The factually dense nature of the question, moreover, makes this type of determination inescapable whether we deal with a judge guided only by the general principles of equity, by an administrative officer trying to enforce the provisions of a coherent picketing control statute, or by the Supreme Court trying to determine the appropriate limits of the First Amendment guarantees of freedom of speech. There is simply no general form of words that will determine the appropriateness of or proper terms for an injunction. In some cases, it might suffice to reduce the number of pickets, or to limit the places where they may go. In others, the threat of force may be more severe, and the correct response far greater.

With this said, the limits of the libertarian theory should be evident. It

67. 384 U.S. 436 (1966).

68. *See* Thornhill v. Alabama, 310 U.S. 88 (1940). The subsequent course of doctrine has not been smooth. *See, e.g.*, Hudgens v. NLRB, 424 U.S. 507 (1976); International Bhd. of Teamsters, Local 695 v. Vogt, Inc., 354 U.S. 284 (1957).

only goes so far as to establish two propositions: (i) to condemn the use of force, and (ii) to mandate that injunctions be tailored to minimize the sum of the errors of over- and under-inclusion. Matters of future uncertainty cannot be handled neatly by any normative theory—including those which rely on general legislation. The wide range of considerations identified here must be taken into account in the treatment of picketing under the first amendment or under the New Deal legislation. It is not my task here to reconcile the decided cases, nor to defend the record of the pre-New Deal courts in labor injunction cases.[69] Given the degrees of freedom and uncertainty, no final indisputable reconciliation is ever possible. The law of injunctions here is if anything more difficult than the analogous problem in the law of nuisances. The best one can demand is to understand the nature of the end—the restriction of the use or threat of force—and choose the means most likely to achieve it. The very meaning of the phrase "sound discretion" is that there is an irreducible class of cases in which honest disagreements over proper disposition cannot be resolved in a conceptually rigorous manner. The great strength of the libertarian theory is that it identifies why picketing is a problem. But unlike the treatment of conspiracy or yellow dog contracts, picketing is a problem to which neither it nor any other theory provides a clean conceptual answer.

III. Utilitarian Arguments

The questions of malice, combination, yellow dog contracts, and picketing have thus far been considered solely from the vantage point of a strong theory of entitlements that (with the possible exception of picketing) in no way depends upon explicit utilitarian concerns. While much can be said to support the view that this general theory dispenses with the need to develop any alternative framework of analysis, the soundness of the conclusions urged above does not stand or fall on this single set of premises. The rival tradition of utilitarian thought is very powerful in the Anglo-American philosophical and legal traditions.[70] It can be fairly asked whether its explicit consideration calls for any modification of the conclusions already advanced.

In making this inquiry, one should note at the outset that in historical terms the utilitarian issues arise more in the interpretation of statutes than in the development of common law principles. Combination in restraint of trade is often seen today to invite a utilitarian analysis, but the common

69. For such a defense, see Petro, *Injunctions and Labor Disputes: 1880-1932, Part I: What the Courts Actually Did—And Why*, 14 WAKE FOREST L. REV. 341 (1978).

70. For a recent defense of the wealth maximization variant of utilitarianism, see Posner, *Utilitarianism, Economics, and Legal Theory*, 8 J. LEGAL STUD. 103 (1979).

law cases that considered the legal status of unions never, either expressly or by implication, viewed the problem in a utilitarian light:[71] The social welfare function was not the idiom of common law judges. The central inquiry in the cases was the proper delineation of individual freedom and the proper account of the "coercion" directed against the immediate parties to the dispute, usually rival unions or employers caught in the middle of picketing or jurisdictional disputes. The concept of the private damage action as a rough surrogate for social losses[72] never surfaced in the cases.

The unwillingness of the common law to address the systemic economic issues meant that questions of social welfare were addressed, if at all, only in the great debate on whether labor unions should be subject to the sanctions of the Sherman Act, and later the Clayton Act, as combinations in restraint of trade.[73] On its face, the language of the Sherman Act applies to labor unions as it does to any other aggregation of individuals.[74] While the statutory construction and legislative history of the Sherman Act are complex,[75] for our purposes the critical question is again normative: How should utilitarian considerations, in particular the antitrust laws, apply to labor unions?

One point of considerable importance is that the liberal and utilitarian traditions of analysis differ only in unimportant respects in their treatment of the enforcement of contractual arrangements between the parties to them. Thus the libertarian account will stress that the content of the obligation is no business of the courts, and will decline to look further at the matter unless fraud or misrepresentation or incompetence is present. The utilitarian will generally assume that contracts move resources to more valued uses, so that both parties to the agreement are better off under the agreement than without it. Duress, misrepresentation, and undue influence become relevant to identify those conditions in which the general proposition may not hold because one party has been prevented by the other from soundly assessing the desirability of his agreement.

The key difference between the liberal and the utilitarian approaches

71. Petro, *supra* note 31; Petro, *supra* note 69, at 436-46.

72. *Cf.* Easterbrook, *Predatory Strategies and Counterstrategies*, 48 U. CHI. L. REV. 263 (1981) (suits by victims of predatory pricing protect consumers at large).

73. The statute reads:

> The labor of a human being is not a commodity or article of commerce. Nothing contained in the antitrust laws shall be construed to forbid the existence and operation of labor . . . organizations . . . or to forbid or restrain individual members of such organizations from lawfully carrying out the legitimate objects thereof; nor shall such organizations, or the members thereof, be held or construed to be illegal combinations or conspiracies in restraint of trade, under the antitrust laws.

15 U.S.C. § 17 (1982).

74. *See* Loewe v. Lawlor, 208 U.S. 274 (1908).

75. *See* Winter, *Collective Bargaining and Competition: The Application of Antitrust Standards to Union Activities*, 73 YALE L.J. 14 (1963).

lies in their evaluation of third-party effects. The liberal approach ignores shifts of wealth which are not preceded by a wrongful act such as the use of force or misrepresentation.[76] The utilitarian theory, in contrast, attempts to take these pure economic externalities into account in order to counter perceived economic dislocations that cannot be rectified by agreement because of high transaction costs. In principle, the utilitarian limits contractual freedom whenever the loss of utility to third parties exceeds the gains to the parties to the original transaction. The analysis is complicated, since the transfer of any resource from *A* to *B* will as a matter of course alter the prospects, and hence the utilities, of *C* through *Z*. In most situations, variations in the fortunes of third parties are regarded as random and offsetting, or as excessively costly to determine, and so they are rarely taken into account. The antitrust law—in particular the law of horizontal restraints of trade—is an effort to carve out a set of cases in which the systematic losses to society at large (measured by the failure to produce goods to the point where social marginal revenue equals social marginal cost) justify some restraint on freedom of contract.

It remains to see whether this general utilitarian approach requires us to revise the conclusions reached with respect to the four problems addressed above: malice, combination, yellow dog contracts, and picketing.

A. *Malice*

The structure of the utilitarian inquiry does not change the prior conclusion that malice is essentially an irrelevant factor in dealing with the legality of combinations of labor.[77] Malice could be regarded as a type of satisfaction, equal to other satisfactions. Malice in its unalloyed form, however, is not an important element in situations dominated by economic self-interest and thus deserves little consideration, given the high costs of its isolation and punishment. Ignoring malice per se is especially untroublesome since many cases of malice will be caught by the prohibitions against duress and misrepresentation.

B. *Combination*

The question of combination raises very different concerns. The legality of organizing across industries may allow unions to obtain a degree of market power that, in the absence of their antitrust exemption, would trigger the application of the antitrust laws. The matter becomes particularly pressing once it is recognized that prohibitions against horizontal

76. This is the doctrine of *damnum absque injuria*—harm without legal injury. *See generally* Epstein, *supra* note 27, at 432-33.
77. *See supra* pp. 367-69.

arrangements between firms will be less effective if unions remain free to capture monopoly profits in the form of higher wages. One can argue that entry from nonunion firms will discipline the behavior of the unions, but under antitrust law the absence of legal barriers to entry need not be regarded as any more decisive in labor than in ordinary product markets.[78] One could therefore extend the analysis quite naturally to argue that unions should be allowed to organize individual firms, but that no single union should be able to represent the workers of rival firms where a combination between those firms qua firms would represent impermissible market power. This compromise solution would permit unions to improve relationships between management and workers within the plant by handling personnel and public relation problems,[79] but it would blunt their monopoly power.[80] The effort to subject unions to antitrust laws therefore is supported by a coherent (if controversial) normative theory, even if the checkered history of the union exemption from antitrust laws itself defies rationalization.

C. *Yellow dog contracts*

The yellow dog contract is justifiable under the utilitarian as well as the libertarian analysis. Although it is commonly maintained that the yellow dog contract is unfair to the individual worker because of his weak economic position,[81] there is no reason why this should be so. Allowing employers to demand that their workers not join a union is very different from banning unions themselves. Any worker who accepts a yellow dog contract will demand some compensation for giving up the possibility of the gains of union membership. One has to assume an enormous degree of incompetence or ignorance by workers to ban the yellow dog contract on paternalistic grounds.[82]

The analysis here is borne out by looking again at the terms of the yellow dog contract sanctioned by the Supreme Court in *Hitchman*. The wages, it will be recalled, were set at union scale. Indeed, the agreement

78. *See supra* note 73.

79. For an account of unions that emphasizes this function, see Freeman & Medoff, *The Two Faces of Unionism*, THE PUBLIC INTEREST, Fall 1979, at 69.

80. Efforts to gain monopoly power are clearly central to unionization. A desire only to smooth relationships between the management and the worker would not require the elimination of competition from nonunion plants, be it by the device of coercion or by secondary boycotts. Yet these techniques were and remain commonplace in labor relations. See C. GREGORY, *supra* note 35, at 217 (by the 1920's all nationally affiliated unions were committed to closed shop in every industry).

81. *See* Powell, *supra* note 3, at 403-05.

82. Kennedy addresses the "distributive" and "paternalistic" justifications for the prohibition against yellow dog contracts in a discussion which seems to rest on the implicit assumption that the contract should be banned, apparently on the ground that such a ban enforces the solidarity among workers. *See* Kennedy, *supra* note 5, at 574-75. The question whether the interest of the workers in the plant should be equated with the social interest, however, is not addressed.

provided for a retroactive wage increase if union wages increased after the start of the agreement, but for unchanged wages if union wages fell.[83] "Union" wages implicitly understate the net wages to the nonunion workers, as union membership always imposes some obligations (dues, services) upon workers, wholly apart from the increased likelihood of substantial individual losses through strikes.

We must also take into account the duration of the contract, which was only at the will of both parties. The employer was not able to bind the workers for a fixed term, much less extract a promise from them not to join a union after they terminated their employment. This permitted workers who signed to keep the threat advantage of union membership without having to join one. They also gained an effective counterweight against any employer strategy of divide and conquer. By not signing a long-term employment contract, the workers preserved the option of joining a union at some subsequent time. Nor was the union precluded from organizing the workers while the yellow dog contracts were in effect. The ability retained by workers to quit and to join the union provided a valuable deterrent against the opportunistic behavior of the employer.[84] Had circumstances changed so as to make unionization more attractive, the workers would have been free to switch their allegiance. No worker who signs an employment contract today is disadvantaged in comparison to another employee who withholds his labor, for there is always an opportunity to reassess the basic situation. Indeed, a yellow dog contract does not even prevent the workers from quitting en masse and joining an existing union. The at-will feature of the yellow dog contract in *Hitchman* gave substantial protection to the workers, because the threat of unionization was always there.

The overall examination of the situation only confirms the general proposition that most contracts are in the mutual interest of the parties who sign them. The worker who signs a yellow dog contract may well be better off than one who does not. Certainly the terms of the arrangement in *Hitchman* cannot be explained by any theory under which an employer "dictates" terms to prospective workers. It is difficult to conclude therefore that these contracts, if reached, are necessarily the result of individual error and confusion, let alone desperation. The standard economic presumption of individual and rational self-interest better explains this case than theories of economic duress.

Our analysis of the yellow dog contract within the utilitarian framework is still not complete, however, because we have yet to take into ac-

83. 245 U.S. at 238.

84. On the problems of opportunism in contractual situations, see Muris, *Opportunistic Behavior and the Law of Contracts*, 65 MINN. L. REV. 521 (1981).

count the third-party effects of agreements. The complaint is that union members must bear all the costs of the increased wage structure while the nonunion workers capture the same, if not greater, benefits. This claim seems inconsistent with a concern for the supposed incompetence of nonunion workers, since now nonunion workers are viewed less as the victims of the employers and more as the coexploiters of their union rivals. Nonetheless, as a factual matter there is much truth to this account, though it fails to take into account the ability of unions, especially if unconstrained by a duty of "fair" representation, to exclude outsiders from the benefits of membership. In the extreme case, exclusion takes the form of a closed union shop. Indeed, if unions improved productivity, employers would be willing to forgo yellow dog contracts and share the gains of unionization under a collective bargaining agreement that left both sides better off. Similarly, if yellow dog contracts caused employee demoralization and a resulting drop in productivity, the yellow dog contract would be unattractive. There is therefore no reason for legislative fiat if unionized firms can outperform their nonunionized rivals. If, however, union firms are less efficient than their nonunion rivals, why protect them by imposing legal restrictions upon their competition?

It seems clear that unions have some ways in which they can respond to the efforts of nonunion workers to free ride on union activities. On the other hand, any private responses undertaken by unions will be more costly to them than a legislative ban on the yellow dog contract. But the critical point is that the relevant class of third-party effects embraces all the society at large, not just unions. Suppose a group of producers asked the legislature to prevent rival firms who refused to join their cartel from selling in the market place. The short response is that combination amongst producers is the very thing that the antitrust laws are designed to prevent, so that the nonjoiners are beneficial in undermining monopoly control. Under our principle of neutrality, the nonunion worker is entitled to a similar place of honor, for the yellow dog contract helps constrain the monopolistic practices of unions and thereby reduces the need for direct government control over the unions by the antitrust laws.

Yet it may be said that there is really no social concern with the yellow dog contract at all, at least in those industries with competitive product markets. The union, the argument will run, simply will not be able to extract a monopoly profit because none is to be found. At best, this argument makes the libertarian case in favor of allowing the yellow dog contract decisive. But even if taken on its own terms, the argument is wrong because it ignores the struggle over economic rents[85] that can coexist with

85. "The amount that a factor must earn in its present use to prevent it from transferring to

competitive market structures. To revert to *Hitchman*, all coal deposits are not of equal value, as some are more difficult to extract than others, while some are farther removed from their natural markets. In a competitive system, the low-cost coal will be developed first. But in virtually all markets the aggregate demand will be satisfied only if some more expensive coal is sold as well. The very need to market the expensive coal now is incorporated into the increased capital value of the better situated deposits as economic rents. When a union organizes a mine, it obtains wages or other concessions that appropriate to its membership some portion of the economic rents attributable to the coal without forcing the price of the coal above the competitive level. The firm will of course respond to the threat by taking steps to resist unionization. The struggles over economic rents between mineowners and workers thus follow the familiar pattern, as real resources are expended only to obtain transfer payments, thereby causing substantial efficiency losses even in fully competitive product markets. The yellow dog contract is one low cost device that helps reduce the level of expropriation of rents by hindering union organization. The struggle over rents depends upon the formation of a bilateral monopoly, which is countered whenever employers can adopt contracting strategies that help maintain competitive employment markets.[86] The great irony of *Hitchman*, then is that the location and immobility of the firm's key resource are the source of the economic rents that make the firm more vulnerable to individual exploitation than the individual workers.[87] Workers, to be sure, do not have perfect mobility. Moving away from their homes can disrupt family and personal ties; changing occupations requires them to write off large investments in human capital. But the mass migration of workers through the early part of this century shows that labor has greater mobility than coal buried in the ground.

another use is called its *transfer earnings*; any excess that it earns over this amount is called its *economic rent*." R. LIPSEY & P. STEINER, ECONOMICS 395 (2d ed. 1969).

86. *See* Klein, Crawford & Alchian, *Vertical Integration, Appropriable Rents, and the Competitive Contracting Process*, 21 J.L. & ECON. 297 (1978). The authors identify the quasi-rent value of an asset as "the excess of its value over its salvage value, that is, its value in its next best *use* to another renter." *Id.* at 298. They then note that these quasi-rents can occur in a competitive market, be it in situations in which efforts are made by opportunistic individuals to expropriate gains after two parties have entered into a long-term contract, or in the case closer to that in labor markets, where there is a contest for rents during the precontractual period. *Id.* at 300.

87. The fixed nature of the assets also explains why the firm cannot move to other locations where the labor markets are better, as in the case of the so-called "runaway" plants in textile and other industries. Note too that even where this mobility exists before a plant is opened, it is sharply reduced once a plant is placed in operation.

D. *Picketing*

Picketing is the last practice to be examined under the utilitarian perspective. The analysis is simple enough. To the utilitarian, the general libertarian prohibition against the use of force is granted on the belief that gainful output will be reduced to the inconvenience of all whenever the producer is forced to share his gain with a stranger.[88] Picketing that involves the use of force interferes with transactions that are otherwise beneficial, and it should thus be illegal. With the basic right established, the only question that remains is that of remedy. And here the utilitarian characterization of the problem is made explicit in the desire to reduce the sum of the errors of over- and under-enforcement. The two primary orientations thus yield the same outcome, with the same indeterminacies.

IV. Unfair Labor Practices

The theoretical discussion of the common law rules provides a useful backdrop against which to analyze the major provisions of the Wagner Act.[89] The basic protection to workers under the Act is contained in Section 7, which in its original form guaranteed that "[e]mployees shall have the right to self-organization, to form, join, or assist labor organizations, to bargain collectively through representatives of their own choosing, and to engage in concerted activities, for the purpose of collective bargaining or other mutual aid or protection."[90] Section 8 then sets out a group of five "unfair labor practices"—yet another instance of persuasive definition—that still lie at the heart of American labor legislation.[91] Section 9(a) sets forth the basic structure of labor dynamics as bargaining in "good faith" between the employer and a union, the exclusive representative of the relevant employees:

> Representatives designated or selected for the purposes of collective bargaining by the majority of the employees in a unit appropriate for such purposes, shall be the exclusive representatives of all the em-

88. *See* R. POSNER, ECONOMIC ANALYSIS OF LAW 121-22 (2d ed. 1977).

89. All citations here are to original act, *e.g.*, § 8(1). The modern form of citation, *e.g.*, § 8(a)(1), was introduced when the unfair labor practices by unions were added to the statute under § 8(b).

90. Wagner Act, ch. 372, § 7, 49 Stat. 449, 452 (1935) (codified as amended at 29 U.S.C. § 157 (1982)). The act was subsequently amended to provide that employees "shall also have the right to refrain from any or all of such activities except to the extent that such right may be affected by an agreement requiring membership in a labor organization as a condition of employment as authorized in section 8(a)(3)." Labor Management Relations Act, ch. 120, § 101, 61 Stat. 136, 140 (1947).

91. Ch. 372, § 8, 49 Stat. 449, 452-53 (1935) (codified as amended at 29 U.S.C. § 158 (1982)). Amendments under Taft-Hartley established a similar set of unfair labor practices for unions. Labor Management Relations Act, 61 Stat. 136 (1947), amended, 73 Stat. 519 (1959), 87 Stat. 314 (1973), 88 Stat. 395 (1974) (codified as amended at 29 U.S.C. § 158(a) (1982)). In my view the elaborate provisions of Taft-Hartley were in some measure a union victory, because they kept the original structure of the statute, making it more difficult to return to common law rules.

> ployees in such unit for the purposes of collective bargaining in respect to rates of pay, wages, hours of employment, or other conditions of employment: *Provided*, That any individual employee or a group of employees shall have the right at any time to present grievances to their employer . . . .[92]

It is not possible here to comment at any length on the enormous amount of litigation generated by the statute.[93] What is important, however, is to give some sense of how the structure of the statute has altered the dynamics and the outcomes of labor negotiations. Several questions help mold the general inquiry: (i) How does the statute answer to both the liberty-based and utility-based visions of the law?; (ii) Can any special justification for the statute be found in the necessities of labor relationships?; and (iii) What is the relationship between the substantive rules and the emergence of the modern administrative state?

A. *Section 8(1): Coercion, Interference and Restraint*

Section 8(1) of the original Wagner Act made it an unfair labor practice "to interfere with, restrain, or coerce employees in the exercise of the rights guaranteed in Section 7."[94] On its face, Section 8(1) does not appear to work much of a departure from the previous common law rules. There is no question that the use of force by employers to prevent unionization by workers was both tortious and criminal at common law, and suits for interference with prospective advantage should be available to a union on exactly the same terms and conditions as they are available to the employer. If the statute had confined its operation to the traditional categories, its chief effect would have been to shift jurisdiction of labor disputes from the courts to the National Labor Relations Board. Nonetheless, the Wagner Act was drafted not to enshrine common law principles in the statute, but to throw a larger mantle of protection over unions and union activities, so that as a matter of statutory construction "coercion, restraint and interference" all assumed the broader meaning implicit in

92. 29 U.S.C. § 159(a) (1982).

93. Much of it is collected in B. MELTZER, LABOR LAW: CASES, MATERIALS AND PROBLEMS (2d ed. 1977); R. SMITH, L. MERRIFIELD, & T. ST. ANTOINE, LABOR RELATIONS LAW (6th ed. 1979). For a hornbook treatment of the resulting law, see R. GORMAN, BASIC TEXT ON LABOR LAW, UNIONIZATION AND COLLECTIVE BARGAINING (1976).

94. Ch. 372, § 8, 49 Stat. 449, 452 (1935) (codified as amended at 29 U.S.C. § 158(a)(1) (1982)). This language tracks that of the Norris-LaGuardia Act, 29 U.S.C. § 102 (1982): "[I]t is necessary . . . that [the worker] shall be free from the interference, restraint, or coercion of employers of labor . . . " Norris-LaGuardia merely limits the scope of federal jurisdiction in injunction cases, however, while the Wagner Act creates substantive rights between the parties, *see supra* p. 1386. The constitutional doubts about the original Wagner Act were put to rest in Jones-Laughlin Steel Co. v. NLRB, 301 U.S. 1 (1937). The substantive challenges to the statute were never addressed, as *Adair* and *Coppage* were ignored, not refuted.

the parallel provisions of the Norris-LaGuardia Act.[95] The correlative duties imposed upon employers are therefore far more extensive than the common law, notwithstanding the section's ironic appeal to common law language.[96] In the context of 8(1) this broader construction has affected two types of behavior: attempts by the employer to keep his premises free both from organizational activities of the union and from employer speech.

At common law, the employer, like everyone else, was entitled to the exclusive possession and use of his own property. Persons who wanted to enter[97] or remain upon[98] property could do so only with the owner's consent and under the terms and conditions that he saw fit.

These rules could have been carried over to labor disputes. Nonetheless, in a manner consistent with the general philosophy of the Act, the cases have consistently held that any restriction or prohibition of union activity on company property constitutes an "interference" with Section 7 rights, which must therefore be justified by showing that some competing interest of the employer outweighs the rights of employees under Section 7 of the Act. Within this balancing framework the decisions exhibit a commendable logic. Thus the cases have generally curtailed union activity on the workshop floor during working hours, especially when it may be carried on elsewhere with little disruption, as in the employees' lunchrooms during mealtimes and work breaks.[99] Similarly, the cases have granted the employer a greater right to exclude outside organizers from his premises than to exclude workers already on the premises.[100] And, more questionably perhaps, the cases have given far greater rights to unions seeking economic advantage compared to those who want political influence.[101]

My concern here, however, is not with the reasonableness of the decisions under the statute, but with the soundness of the statute itself. The

95. *See also supra* note 94 (parallel provisions of Norris-La Guardia).

96. *See Hitchman*, 245 U.S. at 263 (Brandeis, J., dissenting).

97. The only exception to the rule was for the rare cases of personal necessity, which applied only to persons in imminent peril of life or limb, and then only on very restrictive terms: The passing of the necessity terminated the privilege, and compensation was required for any damage caused by the entrance. *See, e.g.*, Vincent v. Lake Erie Transp. Co., 109 Minn. 456, 124 N.W. 221 (1910); RESTATEMENT (SECOND) OF TORTS § 263 (1965). *See generally* Bohlen, *Incomplete Privilege to Inflict Intentional Invasions of Interests of Property and Personality*, 39 HARV. L. REV. 307 (1926).

98. *See* W. PROSSER, *supra* note 59, at 73-74: "The trespass may also be committed by remaining on the land after a right of entry has terminated. Thus it is a trespass to refuse to leave after a license to remain has been revoked, or to fail to remove property at the end of an agreed period."

99. Beth Israel Hosp. v. NLRB, 437 U.S. 483 (1978); Republic Aviation Corp. v. NLRB, 324 U.S. 793 (1945). The reach of *Republic Aviation* is shown by the Court's quick rejection of the argument that the anti-solicitation rule could not be an unfair labor practice because it was introduced long before the passage of the statute, 320 U.S. at 804-05, and applied to all solicitations, whether or not labor related, *id.* at 805. Both those points are relevant to the question of employer motive, which is in the balancing process displaced by considerations of the effect of the restriction upon activity.

100. NLRB v. Babcock & Wilcox Co., 351 U.S. 105 (1956).

101. See Hyde, *Economic Labor Law v. Political Labor Relations: Dilemmas for Liberal Legalism*, 60 TEX. L. REV. 1 (1981).

central mistake of the statute as construed is that it introduces any balancing test at all. Any balancing under the Act, however reasonable, quite clearly cuts back upon the absolute power to exclude that is the hallmark of any system of private property.[102] It is wholly incorrect to treat as coercive any action by an employer that works to the economic detriment of union members. The real question is whether a firm should be required to provide an in-kind subsidy to a union regarded as antithetical to its prosperity, and perhaps to its survival. Employers need not make cash contributions to unions; why must they make contributions in kind? If it is argued that access to the property may be critical to an organization drive, then the answer is that denial of access is equally critical to the employer. Here as elsewhere the relative needs of the parties do not in any sense determine the proper set of initial entitlements, but only the subsequent business question whether they will strike some bargain that works to their mutual advantage. There are many ways in which a union could use its own resources to advance its cause, *e.g.*, meetings, leaflets, or campaigns. There is no principled reason why a union should be able to impress a lien upon the property of the employer for its own advantage.

A similar analysis applies to the question of employer speech. In its early decisions, the Labor Board found that any speech by an employer designed to induce its employees to stay out of the union was coercive and improper.[103] In particular, special and vigorous condemnation was found for speeches in which the employer stated that he would bargain hard against the union, close his shop and move elsewhere, or eliminate some of the benefits to which his employees had grown accustomed. As a matter of principle, however, it is hard to imagine how suppression of truthful information could serve the interest of employees faced with deciding where to cast their lot. To be sure, one can understand why a prohibition against employer fraud might be required. But antifraud devices are notoriously difficult to apply to the bluffing that always goes on in hard contractual negotiations, where complex matters of fact are involved. Indeed, if any deviation from the common law rules were to be required, the rules against fraud might be relaxed; the likelihood of a prompt union response is a credible deterrent against fraud, which although imperfect suffers from none of the complexities of the common law action.

Nonetheless, the labor rules go quite beyond that limited objective of the prevention of fraud, attempting to assure something akin to employer

102. The constitutional status of the statute is not the concern here, since the tangled web of cases on the protection afforded possession under the eminent domain clause defies coherent exposition. *See, e.g.*, Loretto v. Teleprompter Manhattan CATV Corp., 458 U.S. 419 (1982); Pruneyard Shopping Center v. Robins, 447 U.S. 74 (1980); Kaiser Aetna v. United States, 444 U.S. 164 (1979).
103. *See* R. GORMAN, *supra* note 93, at 148-49.

neutrality on the question of unionization.[104] The point, however, is hardly one on which employers should be expected to be neutral, given their enormous self-interest in the question of firm organization. Putting to one side the serious constitutional questions, there is no independent account of coercion (or fraud) that can justify in principle the statutory restrictions of the rights of employers to bargain hard and to speak their piece. Speech itself is a proper subject for regulation when it threatens coercive action, but, as before, coercive action must be confined to reach only the threat or use of force or the breach of promise. Speech cannot be redefined as coercive simply by expanding through legislation the list of activities that are prohibited by law. As with the rules of company property, however, the statute appeals to traditional liberal fears of coercion and restraint, but uses them to justify the government control that any sound legal order should condemn.

Section 8(c) of the Taft-Hartley Act[105] reveals the extent to which the rules governing employer speech depart from those required by the principles of defamation and misrepresentation:

> The expressing of any views, argument, or opinion, or the dissemination thereof, whether in written, printed, graphic, or visual form, shall not constitute or be evidence of an unfair labor practice under any of the provisions of this Act, if such expression contains no threat of reprisal or force or promise of benefit.[106]

The section makes perfectly good sense—save for the final "if such expression" clause, which is in truth all that matters. The statute is clearly overbroad in its operation, for it does not ask whether there are less restrictive means to achieve the legitimate end of public control against truly coercive behavior. The "reprisal" language is also prey to all the criticisms of the statutory use of "interference, coercion and restraint" under Section 8(1). The far broader language of "promise of benefit" further compounds the original difficulty: The promise of a benefit is simply not the equal of the threat of force, even if it contains the implicit (but lawful) threat to withhold the benefit if the union is recognized. The current case

104. *See* NLRB v. Federbush Co., 121 F.2d 954, 957 (2d Cir. 1941) (Learned Hand, J.): Arguments by an employer directed to his employees have such an ambivalent character; they are legitimate enough as such, and pro tanto the privilege of "free speech" protects them; but, so far as they also disclose his wishes, as they generally do, they have a force independent of persuasion. The Board is vested with power to measure these two factors against each other, a power whose exercise does not trench upon the First Amendment . . . . What to an outsider will be no more than the vigorous presentation of a conviction, to an employee may be the manifestation of a determination which it is not safe to thwart. The Board must decide how far the second aspect obliterates the first.

105. 29 U.S.C. § 158 (1982).

106. *Id.* § 158(c).

law on the question recognizes that an employer is entitled to say something in opposition to a union. That case law insists, however, that under the statute "an employer is free only to tell 'what he reasonably believes will be the likely economic consequences of unionization that are outside his control'" and is not free to make "threats of economic reprisal to be taken solely on his own volition."[107] One can quarrel with this formulation on the ground that it reduces the law of employer speech to a discourse on grammar, style, and nuance that emphasizes the hidden virtues of the passive voice. But if in fact the basic structure of rights under the NLRA is correct, then this distinction, however murky, is about as serviceable as any that might be adopted. The structure of the NLRA is defective, however, and accordingly the decisive objection to the test is that it fails to explain why economic reprisals short of the use of force can be condemned. If the employer is entitled to close down his plant, or to hire non-union labor, then how can he be prevented from threatening what he has a right to do?[108]

B. *Section 8(2): Company unions*

Section 8(2) makes it illegal "to dominate or interfere with the formation or administration of any labor organization or contribute financial or other support to it."[109] There is little need to dwell at length on its oddities and difficulties. The prohibition against company support and contribution to a union was justified on the ground that company unions make a "sham" of the process of collective bargaining[110] by placing the employer on both sides of the bargaining table. This characterization misstates the nature of the bargaining process: The employers must still bargain with workers to hire and retain them. If the company union imposes costs upon the workers, then the employer will have to make appropriate adjustments elsewhere to maintain the quality of his workforce. Given a company union, the adversity of interest between the parties simply manifests itself before the worker joins the union instead of afterwards, while the protection against opportunism is provided by the at-will feature of the employment agreement. In any case, it is difficult to see why Congress should prohibit by law certain forms of labor organization. In a nation that treasures diversity, why is it so unreasonable for certain workers to decide that they wish to join a company-sponsored union? As with

107. NRLB v. Gissel Packing Co., 395 U.S. 575, 619 (1969) (citing NLRB v. River Togs, Inc., 382 F.2d 198, 202 (2d Cir. 1967)).

108. For an expression of the view that generally one ought to have a right to threaten to do that which one has a right to do, see Epstein, *Blackmail, Inc.*, 50 U. CHI. L. REV. 553 (1983).

109. 29 U.S.C. § 158(a)(2) (1982).

110. *See, e.g.*, 78 CONG. REC. 3443 (1934) (statement of Senator Wagner).

yellow dog contracts, workers will not surrender their rights to remain out of the company's orbit for nothing, and they may well gain substantial benefits from the internal procedures that prevent individual grievances from becoming the source of major employee discontent.

Making employer sponsorship of worker participation an unfair labor practice protects not the workers in the plant, but rather the unions that might want to organize the workers. Yet even here the irony is clear, for the prohibition against company "contributions" complicates negotiations for unions that have gained representation rights under the statute. Every union must obtain funds from its members, funds which typically come out of wages. The union and the employer may well wish to negotiate a direct payment from the firm to the union if that is agreeable to both.[111] As this is prohibited by the statute,[112] however, the union must collect the dues from its members. It is generally cheapest for the union to do so through a dues check-off system with the employer. This dues check-off is allowed under the statute, but cannot be imposed over the objection of the employer.[113] From the union point of view, however, a dues check-off is inferior to direct payment because it does not permit the charges to be levied against non-member workers within the bargaining unit. Here as before, the entire structure of the Act depends upon its perverse limitation of freedom of contract, which necessarily requires the substitution of a regime of complicated arrangements for simpler ones.

C. *Section 8(3): Dismissal Motivated by Union Affiliation*

Section 8(3) forbids the employer "by discrimination in regard to hire or tenure of employment or any term or condition of employment to encourage or discourage membership in any labor organization."[114] This language makes it an unfair labor practice for an employer to hire only workers who agree not to join any union. The limitations under Section 8(3) are far greater than the simple legislative prohibition of the yellow dog contract. No employer needs a yellow dog contract to fire workers who decide to organize or join a union. A contract at will is quite sufficient for that purpose; at common law, the explicit contractual provision

111. The employer might not want to provide a service which costs the union little and contributes materially to its strength. The real cost to the employer is the enhanced power conferred upon the union, not the tiny administrative expenses; yet to speak of them without sufficient justification is to invite charges of unfair labor practices under § 8(5) of the Act. Again, therefore, candor yields to a discussion of irrelevant points of detail. But then the sensible response is to allow the employer to refuse to provide either dues check-offs or direct payments unless he agrees to do so by contract.

112. 29 U.S.C. § 158(a)(2) (1982).

113. H. K. Porter Co. v. NLRB, 397 U.S. 99 (1970).

114. 29 U.S.C. § 158(a)(3) (1982).

was critical against third-party inducement, as in *Hitchman*.[115] The arguments against the anti-yellow dog provisions of Norris-LaGuardia apply a fortiori to the far more intrusive restrictions of the Wagner Act. The employer must continue to employ individuals whose loyalties are known to clash with their duties toward the employer, even though the success of the operation of the firm may well depend upon complete loyalty. Nor can it be said that the issue is a minor affair, though Holmes characterized it as such in his dissent in *Adair*. Membership in a union may be only one feature of a contract that contains a vast number of terms, but it is the one term that skews all the rest. Unions fought hard for Section 8(3) because they perceived it as critical to their success; one can easily imagine their response to its possible repeal.

It may be urged nonetheless that Section 8(3) is needed to protect workers not against the employer as such, but against foremen who engage in various capricious actions against the employee, including demands for favors and kickbacks.[116] The remedy for this ill, if it exists, is not the passage of Section 8(3) or any other labor statute. The problem is one of conflict of interest between principal and agent, often discussed under the heading of "agency costs."[117] Any abuse by the foreman diverts income from the employer and reduces the profitability of his operations, for while kickbacks may come out of the pockets of employees, the economic effect is indistinguishable from a direct payment of part of the workers' wages by the firm to the foreman. Since the workers care about their net salary, they will demand higher wages to compensate for the loss. The firm therefore has a strong financial incentive to monitor the behavior of its supervisory personnel wholly apart from Section 8(3).

The institutional structures established by Section 8(3) impose additional costs as well. The preferences of firms for non-union labor will not disappear with the passage of a statute. Indeed, since the statute increases the costs of unionization to the employer, unions will be less welcome after the Act than before it. As such, we should expect that employers will take elaborate measures to avoid unionization when they are barred from resorting to the simple contractual expedient. Efforts (often surreptitious) may be made to screen prospective employees for their past union affilia-

115. Adair v. United States, 208 U.S. 161, 191 (1908) (Holmes, J., dissenting). The definition of "employer" contained in § 2(3) was modified to exclude "any individual employer as a supervisor." On the origins of this important structural provision, see R. GORMAN, *supra* note 93, at 34-35. This definitional exception places a very powerful roadblock against union power, and the balance under the statute would be very different without it. It is one of the features that helps keep the balance of power under the Act.

116. *See* Winter, *supra* note 75, at 24-25.

117. *See generally* Jensen & Meckling, *Theory of the Firm: Managerial Behavior, Agency Costs and Ownership Structure*, 3 J. FIN. ECON. 305 (1976) (discussing conflicts of interests that pervade principal-agent relationships).

tions or present union sympathies. The organization, practices, and layout of a plant may be restructured to make it difficult for a union to know what workers do or where they live. These counterstrategies may constitute unfair labor practices under the statute, but the risk of their being identified as such will be treated in part as one of the costs that the firm is prepared to bear in order to escape the union. Whether the stratagems succeed or fail, it is quite clear that the statute channels resources into anti-unionization efforts—including the ubiquitous employer consultants. These same resources could be spent on the production of real goods and services if employers were allowed to use contractual measures to meet their objectives, which are, it must be stressed, legitimate under any normative overview of the question.

D. *Bargaining in "Good Faith"*

There is still a need to consider the last of the key unfair labor practices, that of an employer's refusal to bargain—judicially construed to mean bargaining in "good faith"—with the union, a mandate closely and necessarily linked to the exclusive representation provisions of Section 9. The question itself requires an examination of the relationships between the employer and the union and between the union and its members.

1. *Conflicts Between Employer and Union*

In order to understand the dramatic impact that the Wagner Act has had on employer-union relations, it is necessary to recall that the common law imposed no regulatory obstacles upon any collective bargaining agreement. Such agreements did occur before the passage of the Wagner Act, and their provisions were rightly held to bind employers as well as employees.[118] Yet here, as with individual contracts of employment, a court's sole function was to enforce agreements already made. It did not have to coerce the agreement itself; nor was it required to police the environment in which an agreement was being negotiated, beyond applying the usual rules of fraud and duress.

118. *See* Schlesinger v. Quinto, 201 A.D. 487, 498 (1922). There can of course be difficulties in enforcing these collective bargaining agreements. The union may be treated as an unincorporated association that has no legal status, *see, e.g.*, Karges Furniture Co. v. Amalgamated Woodworkers' Local Union No. 131, 165 Ind. 421, 75 N.E. 877 (1905); Pickett v. Walsh, 192 Mass. 572, 589, 78 N.E. 753, 760 (1906), which therefore could not sue or be sued in its own name. Other problems may stem from the fact that a collective bargaining agreement is not the same as an individual contract for employment, but only creates "a trade agreement" which forms the basis for individual employment contracts. *See* J.I. Case Co. v. NLRB, 321 U.S. 332, 335 (1944). These difficulties could have been resolved in ways that eliminate the obstacles against contractual freedom, however, rather than ways that override it. The judgment of Justice Jackson in *J.I. Case* contains the clearest possible acceptance (if not to say endorsement) of the principle that individual vested rights under a contract must yield to the collective good in order to implement the statutory scheme of the labor acts.

The passage of the Act, however, radically changed the nature of labor negotiations. In the previous situation, any refusal to make an agreement meant only that there was no agreement. Breaches of the duty to bargain in "good faith" were generally confined largely to matters of fraud in the inducement of contract. Otherwise the duty of good faith was confined to the infrequent cases in which there was some (non-negligent) precontractual "justifiable" reliance by the other party.[119] Limited in this way, the principle of "good faith" clearly has no bite in the area of labor relations, as employers easily can avoid the twin pitfalls of pre-contractual reliance and misrepresentation. One alternative is simply to refuse to negotiate with a union at all. Still another is explicitly to inform the union as a precondition to negotiation that it will have to bear its own costs in the event that some agreement is not reached.

The statute changes the legal environment, however, by imposing an affirmative duty to bargain. It demands therefore a theory of good faith consistent with the expanded duties that it imposes. Such a theory is not easy to develop. To be sure, one can begin to solve the problem by making the obvious point that the obligations require parties to comply with elaborate procedural requirements about the times and conditions of negotiations. Nonetheless one may also wish to honor the statute's ostensible support of freedom of contract by insisting (as did the Taft-Hartley provisions) that the obligation to bargain collectively in good faith "does not compel either party to agree to a proposal or require the making of a concession."[120] Yet there is an enormous gulf between a statute that rules out the obvious extremes and a workable rule for the many cases in which negotiations do not end in agreement. The case law on the question is an exercise in futility.[121]

The difficulties with the duty to bargain in good faith under the labor statute are perhaps clarified by a comparison with the issue of settlement in both the civil and the criminal law. In the civil case, litigation is settled

119. "[The law] has to provide for the restoration of the *status quo* by giving the injured party his negative interest or reliance damages. The careless promissor has only himself to blame when he has created for the other party the false appearance of a binding obligation. This is the meaning of *culpa in contrahendo.*" Kessler & Fine, Culpa in Contrahendo, *Bargaining in Good Faith, and Freedom of Contract: A Comparative Study*, 77 HARV. L. REV. 401, 402 (1964).

Kessler and Fine then give other instances in which the doctrine of *culpa in contrahendo* has been applied: incomplete agreements, informal agreements, silence, and want of an intention to contract. *Id.* at 412-20. None of these impose restrictions of any institutional importance for labor-management relations.

120. *See* National Labor Relations Act, § 8(d), 29 U.S.C. § 158(d) (1982), which was added to the Act in 1947.

121. For examples of the types of problems courts encounter in defining "good faith," *see, e.g.*, NLRB v. General Elec. Co., 418 F.2d 736 (2d Cir. 1969), *cert. denied* 397 U.S. 965 (1970); NLRB v. Katz, 369 U.S. 736 (1962); NLRB v. Insurance Agents' Int'l Union, 361 U.S. 477 (1960); NLRB v. Truitt Mfg. Co., 351 U.S. 149 (1956); NLRB v. American Nat'l Ins. Co., 343 U.S. 395 (1952).

with each party acting under the threat of coercion from the other side.[122] In contrast to most markets, neither party can go elsewhere if he does not like the offer received from the opposing side. The same is true about plea bargaining in the criminal context; the accused does not go free if he cannot strike a deal with the prosecutor.[123] With the duty to bargain in good faith, the labor situation is transformed from the market case to the litigation case. Protracted negotiations can take place to determine the ultimate outcome of what is, when all is said and done, a legally created bilateral monopoly. No nascent standard of good faith effectively constrains these negotiations, any more than it does for civil settlement or plea bargaining. The most that good faith can demand is that the parties not press claims or defenses known by them to be groundless. But this constraint is of virtually no relevance in the labor context, where the matters in dispute are economic demands, rather than the soundness of legal theories.

In civil litigation a bilateral monopoly results whenever voluntary transactions fail. Because there is no competition between borrowers in the collection market, resort to state-controlled coercion is indispensable. Likewise, the monopoly control of the state over criminal enforcement makes it quite impossible to avoid the bilateral monopoly problem under any system of criminal prosecution, with either public or private enforcement. Yet employment negotiations provide no comparable necessity for the creation of a complex institutional structure at contract formation. On matters of money and conditions of employment, the very notion of good faith has no internal intellectual coherence because there is no theory of the just contractual outcome to which it can be tied. All that can be done is to penalize individuals for candor (as with Boulwarism)[124] or inexperience, and to inject an element of public oversight that can only complicate any real negotiation.

Even without the passage of the Wagner Act, one can expect some very difficult negotiations between employers and workers over the division of the pie. Yet the statute, by making the union the exclusive bargaining representative, increases both the costs of negotiations and the likelihood that no effective agreement will be reached. The parties will play "non-cooperative" games with each other; their bluff and bluster will increase the chances of a strike, even if both sides would have been better off with

122. *See* Cook v. Wright, 1 B. & S. 559, 568-69, 121 Eng. Rep. 822, 826 (Q.B. 1861).

123. For a discussion of the difficult bilateral monopoly problems in plea bargaining, see Easterbrook, *Criminal Justice as a Market System*, 12 J. LEGAL STUD. 289, 291 (1983).

124. The practice involved the decision of the employer to make one "fair, firm offer" to the union which it treated as inflexible. The offer was also accompanied by a barrage of publicity designed to persuade the workers that the union demands were astronomical. *See* NLRB v. General Elec. Co., 418 F.2d 736, 756-62 (2d Cir. 1969) (practice violates § 8(a)(5)).

some agreement sparing them the extensive costs of strikes.[125] Matters only become more complicated when the response to unionization includes the possibility of industry-wide bargaining, or the concentration of economic pressure on some firms in the industry, perhaps after a quick settlement with others.[126] The increased frequency of impasse in turn gives greater scope to the Act's unfair labor provisions, which are sufficiently elastic to allow a colorable claim to be filed with the Board whether or not some agreement is reached. The creation of exclusive rights of representation coupled with duties to bargain shows the want of wisdom in replacing simple institutional arrangements with very complex ones.

The bargaining structure under the Act also increases third-party costs, as other individuals and firms are forced to reorganize their own affairs to respond to increased costs and lower reliability of the current labor structure.[127] Tracing the consequences through a chain of customers and suppliers raises administrative complexities sufficient to daunt the spirit of any common law court, which largely explains the common law's unwillingness to give much protection for interference with prospective advantage.[128] The preferred solution is to eliminate the structures that cause these dislocations. As political pressures have prevented the repeal of the Wagner Act, the response to the unfortunate status quo ante has been further government intervention to restore some balance to the system. The insistence upon "good faith" negotiations is one such effort. "Cooling off" periods and special congressional mandates to suspend or limit particular strikes are another;[129] federal limitations on secondary boycotts are yet a third;[130] and federal mediation services a fourth.[131] Yet since no one

125. The 1982 strike by the National Football League Players is a good example of such a situation. For an account of the strike, see *The NFL Players Run Out of Time*, BUS. WEEK, Nov. 29, 1982, at 35-36.

126. For the modern case law, see American Shipbuilding Co. v. NLRB, 380 U.S. 300 (1965); NLRB v. Brown, 380 U.S. 278 (1965).

127. These costs should obviously be taken into account under a utilitarian analysis. They must be considered under a libertarian perspective as well, for these dislocations are the product of improper statutory restrictions upon the freedom of the employer's right to negotiate at will with whomever he pleases.

128. *See, e.g.*, Robins Dry Dock & Repair Co. v. Flint, 275 U.S. 303, 308 (1927); Byrd v. English, 117 Ga. 191, 194, 43 S.E. 419, 420-21 (1903). *See generally* Rizzo, *The Theory of Economic Loss in the Law of Torts*, 11 J. LEGAL STUD. 281, 291-96 (1982) (limited recovery for loss of prospective advantage designed to "channel" suits through limited number of plaintiffs).

129. *See* Labor Management Relations Act, §§ 201, 206-210, 29 U.S.C. §§ 171, 176-180 (1982). Section 201 states the problems under the old order. Sections 206 to 210 address the mandatory powers of the President in emergency situations, and include the powers to enjoin both strikes and lockouts.

130. *See* National Labor Relations Act, §§ 8(b)(4) to 8(b)(7), 29 U.S.C. §§ 158(b)(4)-158(b)(7) (1982).

131. Section 202 of the Labor Management Relations Act, 29 U.S.C. § 172 (1982), creates the Federal Mediation and Conciliation Service, whose powers are defined in § 203 of the Act, 29 U.S.C. § 173 (1982).

can fine tune so complicated a mechanism, every effort at adjustment itself imposes additional tensions upon the system. The elimination of the basic structure is necessary, not the further embellishment of the regulatory pyramid.

2. *Conflicts Between Employees*

Sections 8(5) and 9(a) are also troublesome from the perspective of the employee as well as the employer. When the statute says that employers may not enter into direct negotiations with individual employees over the terms and conditions of employment, it imposes restrictions upon employees and employers alike. The justification offered for this exclusive right of negotiation is that without it the employer will skim off the best workers and discriminate against union supporters, thereby depriving the union of its strength. The discussion of this issue in connection with the yellow dog contract is sufficient to show that, while the factual assertion may be true, the asserted equation of the union with the social interest is not.

The problem here goes to the root of representative government. Under the older common law system, in the original position, each individual worker had a clear and well-defined set of rights good against the world. He was therefore entitled to bargain those rights away to either the union or the employer for whatever consideration he saw fit. The determination of rights under the system of collective bargaining creates far greater stress. Now no party derives its rights by agreement from a clear original position. Instead, a majority of the workers within an appropriate unit may choose the union as the bargaining representative of that unit. Thereafter the union represents both its supporters and its opponents within the unit, whether or not they are union members. The original entitlements are very much in doubt. The "union" interest itself is no unitary whole, but instead a complex amalgam of the individual interests of the many actors who play on the expanded stage. It is no accident that extensive administrative procedures are needed to determine the contours of an "appropriate bargaining unit" and to enforce fiduciary duties for the protection of minority interests.

In defining bargaining units, no vote can determine who is eligible to vote, nor can any simple principle, like territoriality or citizenship, serve that function. Voluntary arrangements are excluded by the very structure of the Act, for even if the union and the employer agree on the definition of the unit, and their determination is accepted by the Board, that determination is made in a legal environment where the employer is subject to statutory obligations that effectively limit his domain of choice. With negotiation from a set of original entitlements precluded, only a complex but formless weighing of "relevant factors" remains. Does one establish units by plant, by firm, or by craft? Is an agreement between the union and the company sufficient on the question? Or must the interests of anti-union workers or rival unions be taken into account? What about potential employees? The various shifts in preference between large trade unions and small craft unions reflect not only the powerful political divisions on the Board[132] but the utter impossibility of finding any neutral principle of coerced organization to replace the consensual formation of unions.[133] In addition, a host of tactical questions arise within a regulatory framework where an employer cannot simply walk away from a demand for unionization. Should the employer agree to a union for some fraction of its work force, hoping to stave off the unionization of its entire operation? Does a union have sufficient strength in certain core areas to risk seeking a plant-wide unit? What position, if any, should an employer take when it fears one of two rival unions more than another? Any system that allows unionization will have to bear some costs of organization. But at least the principle of selection in a voluntary system is clear enough. Those who agree to join are members, and none else. The statutory scheme imposes a much more complicated regime. Its costs are evident enough. Where are the benefits?

The problem of protecting the interests of a minority within a union is equally complex. One might allow the union to parcel out the benefits of unionization within the unit in any way it chooses, subject only to the constraint of continuing to command the support of a majority of the unit. This constraint is not as trivial as it sounds: If the union pushes too hard on some minority group within it, it risks the loss of that minority's support or even possible decertification if the minority was previously the block whose support allowed the union to command a majority. The possible gains from unionization can be distributed in countless ways without running afoul of these constraints. So too where the industry is in decline, although the distribution of losses in wages and benefits raises even more acute problems.

What additional legal constraints might limit the powers of unions to distribute the pie in whatever manner they see fit? There is the obvious fear that a union (or its dominant coalition) will discriminate on the basis of race, sex, religion, or national origin to benefit some members at the expense of others. Indeed, the duty of "fair representation," read into the

132. On the impact of politics on the composition of the Board, see F. McCulloch & T. Bornstein, The National Labor Relations Board 60-62, 107-09, 112-14 (1974).

133. For examples of the issues involved in certifying a bargaining unit under the NLRA, *see, e.g.*, Local 1325, Retail Clerks Int'l Ass'n v. NLRB, 414 F.2d 1194 (D.C. Cir. 1969); Mallinckrodt Chem. Works, 162 N.L.R.B. 387 (1966).

Wagner Act as a counterweight to union power, addressed these forms of discrimination even before the passage of the modern anti-discrimination laws.[134] This restraint, however, covers only a tiny fraction of the possible situations. Within a single unit, for example, the majority of unskilled workers may capture much of the surplus created by unionization for themselves by reducing the wage differentials between skilled and unskilled workers. The same problem may occur with the merger of separate seniority lists arising from the merger of separate plants or firms.[135] In the extreme case, individual workers may be required to give up benefits they secured under contract before the recognition of the union.[136] Yet even if some prohibition were placed upon tampering with vested rights, there is little to prevent the dominant coalition within the union from undercutting their value by reducing the future share of the common pool for the protected workers.[137]

As the problem itself arises from the unconstrained operation of majority will, the only bulwark against these abuses must depend upon some rule of "fairness" for the distribution of the surplus among all possible claimants. This theory of fairness cannot emerge from a consistent view of individual rights to liberty and property, for that theory flatly condemns the system of coerced collective bargaining on which labor law rests. The required vision of fairness therefore must come from a theory of forced exchanges. That theory, which lies at the root of a theory of eminent domain, in turn requires that those whose rights are taken receive in exchange rights that leave them at least as well off as before.[138] Unfortunately, difficulties block the application of this theory in the labor context.

First, the baseline against which the subsequent benefits should be measured must be determined. In principle this baseline could be the position that an individual worker would have achieved under the common law system; however, this is the one baseline which the labor law, with its insistence upon "full" freedom of contract, has rejected. The common law baseline could bar certain distributions reached under collective agreements, including any in which some workers receive less under collective

134. The first important case was Steele v. Louisville & Nashville R.R. 323 U.S. 192 (1944), which held that the Railway Labor Act imposed on a labor organization representing a craft or class of employees, the duty not to discriminate on the basis of race in the course of representation. Although *Steele* was decided under the Railway Labor Act, the same principles have been carried over to the National Labor Relations Act. Miranda Fuel Co., 140 N.L.R.B. 181 (1962) (employee right to fair and impartial treatment under the NLRA).

135. *See generally* Freed, Polsby & Spitzer, *Unions, Fairness, and the Conundrums of Collective Choice*, 56 S. CAL. L. REV. 462 (1982).

136. *See generally id.* at 484-87 (noting possibility of prospective wage adjustments).

137. *See* J.I. Case Co. v. NLRB, 321 U.S. 332, 338-39 (1944).

138. *See* Michelman, *Property, Utility, and Fairness: Comments on the Ethical Foundations of "Just Compensation" Law*, 80 HARV. L. REV. 1165 (1967).

bargaining than they did before unionization. These workers may not currently be willing to leave the union because their alternative sources of employment may be still less attractive: The restrictive practices of unions may make it difficult to find employment elsewhere within the industry and the aggrieved employees may be unable to transfer their acquired skills and contracts—their specific human capital—to a new line of work. It is difficult to guess the frequency with which this might happen, but as to the possibility there can be no doubt; the labor cases make it clear that the existing contract rights of workers do not survive the institution of collective bargaining.[139]

Let us suppose, however, that we can get over the baseline difficulty. There remains the problem of distributing the surplus. In the classical eminent domain situation, the surplus takes the form of a public good which by virtue of its non-exclusive nature is necessarily shared by the individuals taxed or otherwise charged with the cost of the taking. The subsequent distribution by the state is therefore unproblematic.[140] Unionization, by contrast, creates no nonappropriable public good, but only a complex network of institutions to distribute the cash or in-kind benefits to its members. As to the distribution of this surplus, the theory of eminent domain provides no clue.

The implications should be clear. Within the framework of individual rights, it is proper to accept Hobbes's injunction that the determinants of contractual fairness lie in the "appetites of the contracting parties." No one need undertake the impossible task of forming a theory of substantive justice in exchange, sufficient to cover all exchanges. The complex structures under the labor statute increase the need for a substantive theory but decrease the likelihood of finding it. State-protected unions mirror the problems of collective governance in the larger political context. While the political process is governed by an elaborate constitutional mechanism designed to curtail the excesses of majoritarianism with a finely honed catalogue of individual rights and limitations on state power, collective bargaining does not confront the parallel issues of public governance that it raises. To quarrel with how courts resolve individual cases is, again, to miss the central point. Their "deference" in these matters can be traced not only to a basic sympathy to the underlying Act, but also to the impossibility of developing a coherent theory of fairness for collective choice

139. *See supra* note 118.
140. The original insight that the regulation should leave those who are burdened by it better off in the long run than they were before dates from Michelman, *supra* note 138, at 1214–24. For my own reformulation of the position, see Epstein, *supra* note 14. For its application in the private law context, see Epstein, *Nuisance Law: Corrective Justice and its Utilitarian Constraints*, 8 J. LEGAL STUD. 49 (1979).

within the union context sufficiently powerful to override union determinations to the contrary.

The basic structure of the Wagner Act also precludes its effective justification on utilitarian grounds. As any surplus (or deficit) obtained by the union is not uniquely appropriated, the statute has in effect created a "common pool" of assets for members of the union, with the well-known attendant difficulties.[141] Resources are dissipated, if not by overfishing, then by political action undertaken to increase shares while simultaneously shrinking the total size. The battle will often be intense because a union protected by government order will be able to appropriate economic rents from firm-specific resources[142] and perhaps monopoly profits from industry-wide cartelization. Any worker who leaves the union will not be able to share in those profits. For this reason, the "exit" rights that are so important, for example, in disciplining capital markets, are far less reliable in the labor context, as workers are reluctant to shift jobs and abandon their share of the collective surplus. To avoid these problems, sensible legislation removes resources from common pools. The labor statutes place them there.

The conflicts brought on by the New Deal legislation also send out false signals to other product and labor markets. Thus where the union collapses the wage differential between skilled and unskilled workers, it reduces the incentives for individual workers to acquire those skills. Likewise, the presentation to the employer of a wage scale that does not accurately reflect the marginal levels of productivity will lead him at the margin to substitute, for example, capital improvements for high-priced unskilled workers.[143] The ultimate consequences of these distortions are beyond the power of lawyers (and perhaps economists) to measure, but there is no reason to believe that on balance they bring about an increase in levels of output, be it by worker or firm, industry or nation. The declining success of heavily unionized industries—steel, textiles, automobiles—is not some unfortunate coincidence unrelated to the central structures of American labor law. It is far more likely that it is the necessary outgrowth of a system that shrinks the pie for the benefit of those workers (typically those employees protected by seniority) and those offi-

141. *See generally* Sweeney, Tollison & Willett, *Market Failure, the Common-Pool Problem, and Ocean Resource Exploitation*, 17 J.L. & ECON. 179 (1974).

142. See the earlier discussion on the same point for yellow dog contracts, *supra* pp. 1370-75.

143. The distributional questions within unions are also relevant to one possible explanation of union behavior, which is that unions have to prevent outsiders from freeloading upon the wage scales that they develop at positive cost in their negotiations with employees. Assuming this concern to be valid, the union can control for the issue by trying to limit the circulation of the scale, which may in fact be very difficult to do. Nonetheless it is doubtful that any employer would want to rely upon the union differentials in setting his own standards because the internal union conflicts make it a very bad measuring rod for wage differentials in a nonunion setting where these problems are less acute.

cials who gain from the short-term maintenance of a supra-competitive wage structure.

V. The New Deal in Context

Having looked at its basic structure, we are now in a position to evaluate the Wagner Act in its relationship to the New Deal and the rise of the administrative state. The central theme concerns the relationship between substantive rules and the administrative structures that are necessary to enforce them. The simpler the rules, the easier it is to implement them by ordinary common law procedures; in part the simplicity of the common law rules, and their substance, are a reflection of the administrative limitations of courts. A collective rule that recognizes the individual right to exclude others from the property one owns, for example, transfers the balancing of interests to private parties, leaving the role of the state to enforce the private determinations so made. A rule that requires balancing of two types of rights—private property and rights of organization under Section 7, for example—demands a far greater level of public supervision. There is little need for the NLRB under a sensible version of common law rules, for the one thing that courts know well is the law of contract, property, and torts. And as we have seen, from these simple tools, one could fashion virtually all of the rules of labor relations. The labor statute, in contrast, breeds a need for administrative expertise. If ordinary judges cannot be expected to understand the intricacies of the tax code, how can they be expected to do better under the labor code? The need for administrative control is also critically shaped by the substantive rights and duties created under the statute. What court could determine the boundaries of a proper bargaining unit? And what court could supervise an election to see that it is not conducted in an "unfair" manner, as that term is defined by the statute? There are too many possibilities and too many parties to handle the question in ordinary litigation. Indeed, as there is no obvious plaintiff or defendant, adversary litigation will not do. We have no system of rights but an elaborate balancing of interests that invites and lends justification to the administrative process.

The same theme emerges from the structure of the unfair labor practices. As virtually every labor disagreement becomes the source of a possible legal dispute, it is very difficult to place upon the courts the enormous burden of sifting through these cases. An administrative board to relieve the stress gains an obvious sort of appeal, if only as a filter for unmeritorious claims. In the same vein, the remedial aspirations of the labor statutes are far greater than those of the common law. The common law spared itself massive complications when it enforced contracts at will. Within the administrative framework, damages and injunctions are only part of the picture. There are also elaborate rules for reinstatement of individual workers and complex rules for *post hoc* changes in union elections that go beyond the powers of courts of equity, which balked at any form of specific performance in labor contracts. The basic structure of the Wagner Act thus forges a powerful commitment to an administrative government to which courts will be required to give great deference.

Why should anyone want to adopt this structure? We are told that it is done in the name of industrial peace and industrial democracy. As regards the first we can assume the end is a good, but question whether the statute is the means to achieve it. Mandatory bargaining by exclusive representatives increases the likelihood of bilateral monopolies that reduce the likelihood of agreement.[144]

There remains the question of violence. In principle the response should be clear: Violence should be punished no matter who is responsible. But it is mistaken to ignore the heavy social costs that may be associated with its suppression, especially if there is widespread political support for those who have committed it. Here, therefore, it may be suggested that the purpose of the statute is to defuse violence that might otherwise occur by offering some improved chances of unionization. Yet support for the statute on this ground is itself fraught with peril. It is simply a pragmatic argument which says that sometimes it is better to surrender to the threat of illegal force than it is to resist it. What is lost is any prudential argument that these structures ought to be preserved as of right even in a world without violence. It therefore becomes a purely tactical question of whether the rest of society is better off with the adoption of the New Deal labor legislation or with the punishment of violence when it occurs.

Indeed, those prudential grounds could be used in ways inimical to the legitimate interests of unions. What, for example, could be said against those who support making unions illegal (as criminal conspiracies no less) on the ground that they are a breeding ground for violence which can only be controlled by powerful and draconian measures? One answer rests on the empirical assertion that these measures will be overbroad, but a complete answer must recognize that overbreadth exists only in relationship to some permitted end, which in turn rests upon some prior and independent conception of entitlement. That point in turn depends upon the further acceptance of the proposition (skirting the antitrust difficulty) that the voluntary combined activities of workers for their common good are themselves lawful if pursued by proper means. But it is this same independent sense of entitlement that supports the case of the employer to control the use and operation of his business by the same means, even when faced by

144. *See supra* p. 1396.

the threat of violence. To leap too quickly to the question of social costs is to ignore the question of entitlements altogether. To protect voluntary associations from violence from without, however, is itself a neutral principle that should be applied to both unions and employers.

An analogy to the issue of freedom of speech is appropriate. In certain cases it is said that speakers should not be allowed to air their views because others may respond with violence. Yet the general answer is that no one should (save in very extreme situations) be allowed to suppress the rights of another by committing or threatening a wrong. The speech should be protected and the violence punished or prevented if or when it occurs. If anticipatory measures are needed, they should be narrowly tailored to the evil at hand.[145]

Another analogy comes from the law of self-defense. There, a defendant who does not use excessive force may inflict harm upon a plaintiff that exceeds the harm which he expects to suffer—again on the principle that those in the right need not yield as a matter of course to those in the wrong. These same principles can be extended to labor disputes. If an employer wants to employ only non-union labor, his right (and it is a right) should be abridged only as a last resort when those opposed to his decision might take to the streets. There are, of course, problems in the administration of justice and in the control of the police, but initially these are best handled by direct reform of criminal and safety procedures and not by the introduction of an elaborate scheme of labor relations ill-tailored to the evil to be avoided.

It is also said that participation in democracy is essential to industrial stability. Here again the implicit analogy is to the general structure of government which in this country rightly takes democratic lines. The analogy is nonetheless flawed. The basic problem in general political theory is the question of political obligation: Why is it that any individual owes obedience to the commands of the state? Since Locke, the extensive efforts to account for the state have frequently appealed to notions of consent, however attenuated. The argument against this line is that the attenuated forms are often or wholly fictional, so that the obligation to the state in the end rests upon an uneasy mixture of consent and necessity: Given any vision of individual rights, some limited form of collective control is better than the anarchy that it replaces. By this version, democracy is required because voluntary transactions, however numerous and complex, fail to generate a single group of individuals vested with a monopoly of force within the jurisdiction.[146] Yet in the labor context, voluntary agree-

145. On picketing, see *supra* p. 1376-79.

146. Indeed, it is the inability by voluntary agreement for a single protective association to obtain a monopoly of force within a jurisdiction which explains why libertarian accounts of a state as a

ments by contract are a perfectly viable mechanism for social organization: The state with its monopoly of force is already in place. In the political context, we appeal to democracy because the building blocks of contract, property, and tort fail, singly and in combination, to account for any monopoly of force within the jurisdiction. Yet once the basic political order is assured, there is no reason to take the second-best alternative in labor relations when the best is still available. Those workers who want to form voluntary organizations should be allowed to do so. It is not part of a tradition of voluntarism or democracy to grant workers the power to conscript the employer and dissenting workers into the service of their cause.

It may be said that workers will be alienated from their jobs without the protection of the union. This argument cannot explain the fraction of workers who would rather deal with the employer directly. In no event can it justify the basic structural decision of the Wagner Act that forbids employers to negotiate contracts of employment directly with workers without union intercession, even with regard to their individual grievances under the collective agreement.[147] To repeat the central point, an argument against the Norris-LaGuardia Act and the Wagner Act is not an argument against unions as such. It is an argument against the special privileges and immunities that these statutes confer upon them. Where unions are necessary to foster communication, they can emerge in any voluntary situation, in a form less formal and less adversarial than it is today. The frequently cited goals of labor organization do not justify the essential features of the modern law.

Calvert Magruder wrote of the Wagner Act shortly after its passage:

> We seem to be moving slowly toward a more rational relationship between capital and labor. For the greater part of the past half century, the law tended, on the whole, to retard this consummation. In the latter years its influence, decisively, has been in the right direction. Such progress as we have made has been at needless cost of blood and tears, and economic wastage. If employers would accept with right good will the principles of the National Labor Relations Act, as the carriers generally have accepted its sister Act, it would mean: Away with yellow dogs, company unions, blacklists, deputy sheriffs in the pay of employers, barricades, tear gas, machine guns,

purely voluntary organization must fail. For an effort to overcome the difficulty by positing a set of "visible hand" explanations, see R. NOZICK, *supra* note 29, at 10-25. These explanations do not, however, eliminate the need to develop a good theory of forced exchanges.

147. *See* Vaca v. Sipes, 386 U.S. 171 (1967) (good faith judgment of a union not to take an individual claim to arbitration does not violate duty of fair representation); Feller, *A General Theory of the Collective Bargaining Agreement*, 61 CALIF. L. REV. 663 (1973); Summers, *The Individual Employee's Rights Under the Collective Agreement: What Constitutes Fair Representation*, 126 U. PA. L. REV. 251 (1977).

> vigilante outrages, espionage, and all that miserable brood of union-smashing detective agencies. Can anyone doubt the cordial response labor would make to such a gesture? The old ways will not work, could not work, really. It is time for an act of faith.[148]

No one can quarrel with the power of Magruder's prose. The strength of his arguments, both positive and normative, is quite another matter. In particular, there is no theory of behavior which can explain why labor will give a "cordial" response under the labor acts. While a theory of individual self-interest may not unlock all the secrets of family behavior or religious belief, it is by far the best predictor of behavior between strangers in an economic setting. That theory predicts that unions and their members (like employers) will press for their maximum advantage after the passage of the Act as well as before. There is a theory of "sunk benefits" as well as a theory of sunk costs. That theory of self-interest predicts that unions will never make voluntary concessions tomorrow because of an indefeasible benefit they have received today. On the normative level, too, Magruder's list of grievances against the old order is fatally flawed because of his willingness to condemn contractual practices such as the yellow dog contract and the company union in the same breath that he condemns the use of force in all its manifestations. And he never asks the hard question whether the use of force by employers was justified by the threats of violence by workers.[149]

The course of labor relations under the New Deal statutes has been far rockier and more complex than Magruder foresaw. Unions (except those in the public sector, where their monopoly power is greatest) have continued to lose ground notwithstanding their special legal advantages, a phenomenon best explained by the simple observation that they do not provide their membership with benefits that exceed their costs. It is also fair to say that the intellectual difficulties with the statutes have been far greater than Magruder realized, or could have realized. Increasing disenchantment with organized labor in this country is now a force to be reckoned with in the political arena. Much of that concern is with personalities and the subject matter of particular disputes. What is needed is a greater concern with the institutional structures in which these personali-

148. Magruder, *supra* note 3, at 117.

149. *Compare* F. FRANKFURTER & N. GREENE, *supra* note 3, at 132-33 *with* Petro, *supra* note 69, at 429, 434-35, 446-70. In my view Petro has much the better of the historical argument. The chief flaw of the Frankfurter and Greene study is, as Petro points out, that it never asks the question of whether the issuance of the labor injunction was a use or an abuse of power. Where there is the threat of force by workers, it is the failure to grant the injunction that is the abuse of discretion, not its issuance. Petro, *supra* note 69, at 436. And as Petro rightly points out, *id.* at 377-83, the application of the injunction to labor cases did not involve any departure from the well established equitable principle that injunctions are an appropriate response to threats of irreparable harm.

ties operate and these disputes take place. At present, there may be little prospect for the repeal of basic labor legislation, and there is none for its constitutional overthrow. The possibilities of incremental changes, however, are always present, and the opportunity for a major rehauling might even follow an intensive reexamination of the subject. The New Deal brought forth major labor law legislation, but as a normative and intellectual matter it did not conclude the debate on the nature and function of labor law.

The Common Law, Labor Law, and Reality: A Response to Professor Epstein

Julius G. Getman† and Thomas C. Kohler††

Professor Epstein claims to have undertaken serious criticism and review of the American system of labor relations as it has been structured by two pieces of New Deal era legislation, the Norris-LaGuardia Act and the National Labor Relations Act.[1] Such a work by a scholar of Epstein's stature could be of great value to such diverse disciplines as law, economics, sociology, industrial relations, political science, and psychology. To be worthy of its subject, such a study would involve an inquiry of tremendous empirical scope and raise the most difficult of methodological problems. How should one evaluate a process that has undergone incremental but constant change over the past forty-five years? By what standards should the efficacy of current labor laws be judged? Are basic democratic principles applicable to the workplace, and if so, to what extent should workers be afforded a voice in "managerial" determinations? Should models of worker participation in decisionmaking other than that sanctioned by the National Labor Relations Act be permitted, and if so, of what type?[2] These are important, interesting and difficult questions. Professor Epstein, however, avoids them entirely by a breathtakingly simple device: He takes the "common law" (in its late nineteenth-century form) as the appropriate "benchmark" against which to judge "modern statutory schemes."[3] Thus, he never answers the questions a genuine critical evaluation would have to address, i.e., how have the labor laws worked? Have they helped or hindered American workers and the economy, and in what ways? Have they promoted productivity and industrial peace? Are they consistent with the democratic principles that form the framework of our system of government? What conclusions can be drawn and applied from the extensive transnational research that has already been conducted? In-

† William K. Townsend Professor, Yale Law School.
†† Assistant Professor of Law, Boston College Law School.

1. Epstein, *A Common Law for Labor Relations: A Critique of the New Deal Labor Legislation,* 92 YALE L.J. 1357, 1357 (1983).

2. For two *empirical* studies of the effects of unionization, see R. FREEMAN & J. MEDOFF, WHAT DO UNIONS DO? (1984); S. SLICHTER, J. HEALY & E. LIVERNASH, THE IMPACT OF COLLECTIVE BARGAINING ON MANAGEMENT (1967). For an analysis of alternative schemes of worker participation in management, see Kohler, *Models of Worker Participation: The Uncertain Significance of Section 8(a) (2)* (forthcoming).

3. Epstein, *supra* note 1, at 1359.

stead, he comes to the not very remarkable conclusion that statutes avowedly designed to replace the common law, limit the market and do away with the use of contract by employers as a device to prevent worker self-organization are not consistent with the libertarian political theories, laissez-faire economics, and common law doctrines concerning the employment relationship and property rights that they replaced. In short, Professor Epstein's work does not contribute in any way to our existing store of knowledge about labor law. It sheds no light on the reality of labor relations, nor does it contribute anything to our understanding of the impact of labor law on society. Given the antiquated nature of his methodology, it is not surprising that Professor Epstein reiterates many of the same propositions, syllogisms and rationalizations of those who opposed the enactment of the NLRA and the Norris-LaGuardia Act in the first place, and without any newer evidence.[4] As such, Professor Epstein's Article is representative of a growing but lamentable tendency in the legal literature to comment critically on areas in which the author has no expertise, using as a measure axioms formulated *in vacuo* and without regard to observed actualities.

Given his argument's anachronistic ring, it is interesting that Professor Epstein claims to have analyzed his topic in light of "recent advances both in general legal theory and in law and economics."[5] Prominent among the recent sources thus cited are several of his own earlier writings making similar forays into other fields of law, or analyzing rights from a libertarian perspective. His discussion of the common law governing the employment relationship relies heavily on English cases and commentaries that are no more recent than the eighteenth and nineteenth century. There is only one citation to modern industrial relations research and none to the findings of labor economists. Similarly absent is any discussion of the ac-

4. *See* NATIONAL LAWYERS COMMITTEE OF THE AMERICAN LIBERTY LEAGUE, REPORT ON THE CONSTITUTIONALITY OF THE NATIONAL LABOR RELATIONS ACT (1935). The noted labor historian, Irving Bernstein, has written that

> The du Ponts, with Sloan [Alfred P., Jr., the President of General Motors] . . . had been the principal founders and bankrollers of the American Liberty League, the voice of political and economic reaction in the mid-thirties. Its publications, "lavishly printed and widely circulated," as Arthur M. Schlesinger, Jr. has written, "depicted the United States on the verge of socialism, bankruptcy, and tyranny."

I. BERNSTEIN, TURBULENT YEARS: A HISTORY OF THE AMERICAN WORKER, 1933-1941, at 515 (1970).

Professor Epstein's precursors, however, are much older than the Liberty League. For example, in 1835, Dr. Andrew Ure condemned combinations of workers which he stated interfered with the freedom of workers to offer their services to employers. A. URE, PHILOSOPHY OF MANUFACTURERS (London 1835). (Ure contended that organizations of workers were the product of agitators, who incited workers to violence and crime). Ure was an early apologist for the conditions brought about by industrialization. One of the goals of Ure's work was to demonstrate that child labor was not the cruel and inhumane thing reformers argued it to be. *See* R. BENDIX, WORK AND AUTHORITY IN INDUSTRY 89-91 (1956).

5. Epstein, *supra* note 1, at 1358.

tual state of the common law at the time of the passage of the NLRA or the Norris-LaGuardia Act, or citation to empirical studies investigating the impact of law on reality. Discussion of or reference to the work of scholars in other disciplines concerning the impact of collective bargaining and employee self-organization on society is also wanting. Indeed, Professor Epstein abjures the need to discuss reality at all and at base rests his "investigation"[6] on contractarian notions of rights in a mythic world of actors in the "original position"[7] (whose trades, evidently, are supposed to bind us still).

It is not surprising that Professor Epstein would have us return to the legal order for labor relations that existed a half-century and more ago since he shares the values of those who established and maintained it. What does surprise is his apparent belief that the common law ordering of industrial relations was adequate at the time, or that it would prove efficacious in any manner today.

Common law notions about the employment relationship grew out of the law of domestic relations,[8] and revealingly, leading commentators continued to treat the law governing employment relations (i.e., master and servant) as a part of that field until the early years of the twentieth century.[9] Treatises on the law of domestic relations thus continued to be the chief repository of commentary on employment law until well after the century's turn. As late as 1889, for example, one leading treatise on domestic relations law, in its treatment of the master-servant relationship (which comprises roughly one-third of the treatise's content), defined servant as

> persons commonly known in popular speech as workmen or employees. . . . In this class are included day laborers, factory operatives, miners, colliers, and numerous others, of whom nothing more definite can be said than that they are hired to perform services of a somewhat unambitious character.[10]

That modern forms of industrial organization had, by the last quarter of the nineteenth century, long outstripped the almost feudal premises of a

6. *Id.* at 1358.
7. *Id.* at 1364.
8. In his analytic scheme of the common law, Blackstone grouped master and servant, husband and wife, and parent and child under The Law of Persons, characterizing these as "[t]he three great relations in private life." 1 W. BLACKSTONE, COMMENTARIES 410 (1979).
9. *See, e.g.*, I. BROWNE, ELEMENTS OF THE LAW OF DOMESTIC RELATIONS AND OF EMPLOYER AND EMPLOYED (2d ed. 1890); E. PECK, THE LAW OF PERSONS OR DOMESTIC RELATIONS (1913); J. SCHOULER, A TREATISE ON THE LAW OF THE DOMESTIC RELATIONS: EMBRACING HUSBAND AND WIFE, PARENT AND CHILD, GUARDIAN AND WARD, INFANCY, AND MASTER AND SERVANT (4th ed. 1889).
10. J. SCHOULER, *supra* note 9, at 691–92.

personal and ongoing relationship between the employer and employee on which the common law model rested was clear. The sudden appearance of the employment-at-will doctrine in the last quarter of the nineteenth century reflected the legal response to the growth of industrialization. Previously, the common law of employment in England and the United States had two well-established features: Employment was presumed to be for a period certain, the length of which was fixed by custom, and the employment relationship was terminable only for "reasonable cause" and upon the deliverance of customary and reasonable notice.[11] In contrast, the new rule presumed that employment of no fixed duration was freely terminable at the will of either party. The new rule's appearance, of course, was concomitant with the phenomenal growth of the large industrial organization which so affected and characterized this era.[12] Unlike the small, owner-operated shops and factories it displaced, the new industrial organization was not dependent on the skilled artisan for its successful and continued existence. Mass production techniques increasingly made skills obsolete and workers fungible. Industry now depended upon the availability of a large pool of workers who could be hired and discharged according to the demand for production. The at-will doctrine more accurately mirrored and fit the needs and behavior of industry; hence, it quickly came to replace the prior common law rules governing the employment relationship.

The at-will doctrine thus began to shift employment law away from the law of domestic relations and to shift the intellectual framework within which the relationship was conceptualized from one based on a relationship status to one structured by contract doctrine. Not surprisingly, this change occurred at the height of the success of formalized notions of contract in the courts, which ironically enough coincided with the beginnings of public and legislative rejection of the premises of a laissez-faire market society.[13] These contract notions justified the at-will doctrine on the basis

11. M. GLENDON, THE NEW FAMILY AND THE NEW PROPERTY 148-49 (1981). Professor Glendon also observes that the law of France, Germany and Sweden during this period was similar. *Id.* Blackstone notes that, unless otherwise agreed, a quarter's notice was required before discharging a servant, and that a general hiring was presumed to be for the period of one year. 1 W. BLACKSTONE, *supra* note 8, at 413-14.

12. Some figures help remind one how great this growth was, and how fast it developed. For example, from 252,000 in 1869, the number of manufacturing establishments in the U.S. increased to 512,000 in 1899; the number of factory wage earners from 2.1 to 5.3 million, and the value product of manufacturers from $3.4 to $13.0 billion. M. DERBER, THE AMERICAN IDEA OF INDUSTRIAL DEMOCRACY, 1865-1965, at 30-31 (1970).

13. *See* L. FRIEDMAN, CONTRACT LAW IN AMERICA: A SOCIAL AND ECONOMIC CASE STUDY 17-26 (1965); M. GLENDON, *supra* note 11, at 148-49; J. HURST, LAW AND THE CONDITIONS OF FREEDOM IN THE NINETEENTH-CENTURY UNITED STATES 71-78 (1975).

Interestingly, as Professor Glendon points out, the at-will doctrine "appeared almost simultaneously, as if written by an invisible hand, in the master-servant law of England, France, Germany, Sweden and the United States." M. GLENDON, *supra* note 11, at 148. In the United States, the

of mutuality, i.e., that workers were as free as employers to terminate the relationship.[14] As one noted commentator has observed, this shift in the conceptualization of the relationship exchanged "the older notions of protection and loyalty for a new legitimating fiction—freedom of contract."[15] As is true of most common law doctrines in the process of evolution, however, the law governing the employment relationship continued to carry with it some vestiges of the domestic relations concepts from which it had grown. The most significant of these was the idea of a personal relationship between the employer and employee. This notion was seized upon by the courts as they tried to fit the employment relationship into the intellectual framework that they had worked out for contract law over the preceding fifty or so years. The idea of a personal relationship was a handy one, for it fit well the notions of bargaining, a meeting of the minds, and voluntary association that the contractual elements of offer, acceptance and assent encapsulate. Another notion that was carried over from the domestic relations framework was the employee's duty of loyalty to the employer. Significantly, however, the employer's reciprocal duty of protection that the law once imposed was lost in the process of the new rule's evolution.[16]

It is important to remember in considering Professor Epstein's arguments and the development of the common law ordering of the employment relationship that the most significant developments in the fields of contract law and theory occurred during roughly the first half of the nineteenth century. As Lawrence Friedman has observed, as late as the publication of the *Commentaries* in the latter half of the eighteenth century, Blackstone devoted but a few pages to contract law. In contrast, the law of property occupied nearly an entire volume of the four-volume work.[17]

doctrine was initially announced by H.G. Wood in his treatise on Master-Servant Law, published in 1877. Significantly, this was the first treatise in the United States to be devoted entirely to the subject. Wood noted in the Preface that the topic had previously been treated as part of domestic relations law. Although Wood stated that in the U.S., the at-will rule was "inflexible" and universal, the cases he cited are inapposite. H. WOOD, A TREATISE ON THE LAW OF MASTER AND SERVANT §§ 134, 272 (1877). Nevertheless, Wood's rule was quickly accepted by the courts.

14. *See* Adair v. United States, 208 U.S. 161, 174–75 (1908) ("[T]he right of the employee to quit the service of the employer, for whatever reason, is the same as the right of the employer, for whatever reason, to dispense with the services of such employé.").

15. M. GLENDON, *supra* note 11, at 150.

16. *See id.* at 143–50. There are many examples of the erosion of this duty, from the cessation of a master's obligation to oversee the moral and physical well-being of his servants, to the growth of tort doctrines such as assumption of risk and the fellow servant rule that had the effect of isolating employers from liability for workplace accidents. *See* Green, *Assumed Risk as a Defense*, 22 LA. L. REV. 77, 83–84 (1961).

These developments were all part of a larger trend toward the formulation of new ideologies tailored to fit the rise of industrialization and an entrepreneurial group. *See* R. BENDIX, *supra* note 4, at 73–117.

17. *See, e.g.*, L. FRIEDMAN, A HISTORY OF AMERICAN LAW 244 (1973); L. FRIEDMAN, *supra* note 13, at 17–18.

The growth of contract law was, of course, coeval with the disintegration of a relationally ordered society and the appearance and growth of an entrepreneurial, market-centered economy. Contract, unlike other developed areas of the law, such as property and domestic relations, provided a ready vehicle for arranging private, impersonal market relationships. The elements of contract theory—that parties are individual economic actors who enjoy complete freedom of mobility and decision[18]—were congenial to the people of an era who, as J. Willard Hurst has said, desired the legal order to "protect and promote the release of individual creative energy to the greatest extent compatible with the broad sharing of opportunity for such expression."[19]

The growth of large industrial and financial organizations in the latter half of the nineteenth century, along with the appearance and growth of a subsidiary *rentier* interest, reflected the substantial change in capital distribution that had occurred since the start of the century. "This distribution," Professor Hurst has observed, "concentrated unprecedented power of decision in private hands, first in the railroads, then in heavy industry and in investment banking houses and life insurance companies."[20] Further, the law's provision of "a range of flexible contract and association devices, notably the corporation and the procedures of large-scale finance" resulted in:

> the enormous expansion of practical compulsion imposed on strangers to contracts or associations, as commercial and industrial corporations and investment bankers reached out to occupy the multi-state markets whose availability the law had guaranteed. Economic growth tied the lives of an increasing proportion of people to the market and the division of labor; they were either wage or salary earners, or small producers or traders in specialized ranges of goods or services. Theoretically buyers consent to the practical compulsions of the market in which they buy; if they do not consent, they stay out. But men who find their whole livelihood in the market are too vulnerable to stay out.[21]

The upshot of these developments was a restriction of the breadth of practical choices and equality of opportunity that had once been available to individuals. The resulting sense of personal helplessness and inability to control events, Hurst observes, led to the preoccupation with methods to redress the balance of power that so marked the last quarter of the cen-

18. L. FRIEDMAN, *supra* note 13, at 21.
19. J. HURST, *supra* note 13, at 6.
20. *Id.* at 78.
21. *Id.* at 75.

tury. The release of energy theme now came to be expressed through associations. The unprecedented formation of disciplined groups organized around specific programs, such as the Farmers' Alliance, the Knights of Labor, and the American Federation of Labor were part of this response.[22] Contract, which had earlier served as the vehicle for the release of individual energy, proved "inherently too limited an institution to serve this need" in a society increasingly dominated by large industrial and financial organizations.[23]

It was in this milieu that the "new" common law model of employment was launched. With attributes from both domestic relations and contracts, the model of the employment relationship was precariously and uncomfortably perched between two conceptual frameworks, both of which themselves were becoming anachronistic. The general social and industrial unrest, strikes, demonstrations calling for the legal recognition of workers' rights to organize, and the rapid growth of unions and other organizations devoted to furthering workers' interests that attended the last quarter of the nineteenth and the early decades of the twentieth centuries were all symptomatic of the incapacity of the common law to deal with patterns of modern social organization. By the 1880's, the search for a new model by which to order the employment relationship had become a societal preoccupation and would remain one until the advent of the New Deal era. Detailing the course of this search and the development of the various schemes put forward as alternatives far exceeds the scope of this Comment.[24] It is sufficient for present purposes to note that by the end of the nineteenth century, collective bargaining had surpassed contending models such as producer cooperatives, utopian communities, "industrial partnership plans" (based on various profit-sharing arrangements) and calls for the reformation of government along socialist lines as the predominant alternative scheme for the ordering of the employment relationship.

That the collective bargaining model prevailed over its rivals is predominantly attributable to its congruence with the values and patterns of life in American society. Unions were organized as a response to the organization of capital and employers that had been made possible through the pliable contract and association devices the law had devel-

22. *Id.* at 85. Other such groups mentioned by Professor Hurst include the Grange, the Grand Army of the Republic, the American Woman Suffrage Association and the National Woman Suffrage Association, the Women's Christian Temperance Union, the Anti-Saloon League, and the National Civil Service Reform League. Trade associations and business lobby groups, Hurst notes, also took more formal shape in these years. Among those formed during this period were the National Potters Association, the Stove Founders National Defense Association, and the National Association of Manufacturers. *Id.*

23. *Id.* at 75-76.

24. An admirable study of this search is contained in M. DERBER, *supra* note 12; *see also* Kohler, *supra* note 2.

oped. Like other program groups, the goal of unions was to redress an imbalance of power; here, the imbalance that exists between an individual employee and the entity for which he or she works. In this respect, unions mirrored the industrial organizations that employed their members. As the latter assembled to take advantage of the amplified power that the combination of capital and other resources provided, so workers sought, through association, to obtain bargaining strength in settling the terms and conditions of their employment. The idea of the collective agreement was also consistent with the contract notions that had been developed over the course of the century. The terms of the employment agreement would continue to be privately set. Reflecting the reality of the time, however, they would be set through negotiation between two organized entities, and not between an individual and an organization (which, of course, usually results in no bargaining whatever because the latter can most often state the terms on a take-it-or-leave-it basis). Further, unlike many of its rivals, the collective bargaining model entailed no change in social structure. Unions sought neither to reorganize the economy nor to displace management in the operation of industry.[25] As Mine Workers' president John Mitchell stated in 1903, unionism "stands for the liberty of workingmen to arrange their own lives and to contract jointly for the manner in which they shall be spent in mine or factory."[26] Unions, then, like the other program groups that emerged contemporaneously with them, became the vehicles through which, in Hurst's words, one would "mobilize group power in behalf of individual status"[27] in a society where, in the market and elsewhere, power was increasingly passing away from individuals to organizations.

The deficiency in the common law as it emerged was that it provided the employer techniques for rejecting unions regardless of the wishes of the employees. Under this system, an employer could discipline or blacklist union supporters, refuse to bargain without regard to employee senti-

25.

> Collective bargaining in industry does not imply that wage earners shall assume control of industry, or resonsibility for financial management. It proposes that the employees shall have the right to organize and to deal with the employer through selected representatives as to wages and working conditions.
>
> Among the matters that properly come within the scope of collective bargaining are wages, hours of labor, conditions and relations of employment, the sanitary conditions of the plant, safety and comfort regulations and such other factors as would add to the health, safety and comfort of the employees, resulting in the mutual advantage of both employers and employees. But there is no belief held in the trades unions that its [sic] members shall control the plant or usurp the rights of the owners.

S. GOMPERS, LABOR AND THE EMPLOYER 286 (1920), *quoted in* M. DERBER, *supra* note 12, at 127. For a further elucidation of the role of unions as conceived of by the AFL, see Gompers, *What I Should Do If I Were An Employer*, 27 AMERICAN FEDERATIONALIST 351 (1920).

26. J. MITCHELL, ORGANIZED LABOR (1903), *quoted in* M. DERBER, *supra* note 12, at 123-24.

27. J. HURST, *supra* note 13, at 86.

ment, and obtain court injunctions against union organizing if some of his employees were subject to yellow dog clauses. Much of Professor Epstein's article is devoted to a defense of the yellow dog device. This defense is supported in part by an indirect attack on unions and collective bargaining, and in part by the contention that such contracts should be seen not as employer coercion but rather as an expression of the employee's freedom of contract; a technique by which employees, for an economic premium, exchange their right to join a union. The latter argument ignores the fact that if employees want to trade their right to bargain collectively (and many do), they are in a much stronger position when they have a legal right to secure union representation if they are dissatisfied with what the employer has provided or what they believe the employer will provide. As long as employees have the right to unionize, non-union employers are motivated to pay union scale or above, and employees are in a position to monitor the indirect promises which are a regular feature of union organizing campaigns. What the combination of the yellow dog device and the injunction did was to make it possible for an employer to get the same degree of assurance against unionization for little or nothing. Thus the yellow dog device, like much of the common law scheme that Epstein urges, makes good policy only if one is in favor of allowing employers the legal option of operating on a non-union basis if they feel strongly enough about it to either battle with or pay their employees a small premium for the privilege. During the period in which employers had this choice they exercised it so fiercely and were met by such determined extra-legal resistance that almost no one was satisfied with the law to which Professor Epstein would have us return.

Recognition among policymakers of the inadequacies of the common law ordering of the employment relationship as it stood in the last quarter of the nineteenth century was not long in coming. Within five years of the end of the Civil War, both houses of Congress had established Committees on Labor,[28] and in 1878 the first full-scale congressional inquiry into labor relations was undertaken through a Select Committee of the House.[29] Continuing unrest and disputes led to other inquiries by various House and Senate committees,[30] the creation of the Bureau of Labor (1884),[31]

28. The House Committee on Education and Labor was established in 1867; the Senate Committee on Education and Labor was established in 1870. U.S. DEP'T. OF LABOR, THE ANVIL AND THE PLOW: A HISTORY OF THE UNITED STATES DEPARTMENT OF LABOR 275 (1963).

29. M. DERBER, *supra* note 12, at 83.

30. *See, e.g.*, SELECT COMMITTEE ON EXISTING LABOR PROBLEMS, INVESTIGATION OF LABOR TROUBLES IN MISSOURI, ARKANSAS, KANSAS, TEXAS, AND ILLINOIS, H.R. Rep. No. 4174, 49th Cong., 2d Sess. (1887); SENATE COMMITTEE ON EDUCATION AND LABOR, REPORT OF THE COMMITTEE OF THE SENATE UPON THE RELATIONS BETWEEN LABOR AND CAPITAL AND TESTIMONY TAKEN BY THE COMMITTEE, 48th Cong. (1883).

31. Act of June 27, 1884, ch. 127, 23 Stat. 60. The Bureau was established as a division of the

whose tasks included the collection of information about labor relations and disputes, and the appointment by President Cleveland in 1894 of the U.S. Strike Commission,[32] which was charged with investigating the causes of, and formulating solutions to, labor relation problems on the railroads. Interestingly, among other things, the Commission recommended federal legislation to outlaw the yellow dog device (noting that such legislation had already been enacted in several states) and it urged employers to recognize the labor organizations to which their employees belonged.[33] The work and thoughts of these earlier bodies was capped by the creation of the U.S. Industrial Commission in 1898.[34] The Commission's eighteen members were jointly appointed by President McKinley and Congress, and their investigation was the most extensive of any yet conducted. The Commission heard testimony from nearly seven hundred witnesses, and collected extensive documentary and statistical information.[35] It was assisted in its work by a large staff that included such noted economists as John R. Commons. The Commission recommended the enactment and extension of a variety of legislative reforms that would promote the practice of collective bargaining. "[E]very facility," the Commission stated, "should be given labor to organize if it desires. . . ."[36] The chief advantage to be obtained from collective bargaining, the Committee opined, was that through its practice, "each side obtains a better understanding of the actual state of the industry, of the conditions which confront the other side, and of the motives which influence it."[37] "Most strikes and lockouts would not occur," stated the Committee, "if each party understood exactly the position of the other."[38] The Committee also

Department of the Interior; in 1888, legislation was passed that gave it independent status as the Department of Labor. The Department was under the direction of a commissioner who lacked cabinet status, but who reported directly to the President. Act of June 13, 1888, ch. 389, 25 Stat. 182. The Department gained cabinet status with the enactment of the Sulzer bill in 1913, which President Taft signed on his last day in office.

32. The Commission was appointed by President Cleveland as a result of the Pullman Strike of 1894, under authority of an Act permitting the President to appoint such a body for the purpose of inquiring into and settling labor disputes on the railroads. Act of October 1, 1888, ch. 1063, § 6, 25 Stat. 501. For a brief description of the events surrounding Pullman, see P. TAFT, ORGANIZED LABOR IN AMERICAN HISTORY 147-58 (1964). *See also* W. CARWARDINE, THE PULLMAN STRIKE (1894) (a contemporary account); A. LINDSEY, THE PULLMAN STRIKE (1942); THE PULLMAN BOYCOTT OF 1894: THE PROBLEMS OF FEDERAL INTERVENTION (E. Warne ed. 1955).

33. UNITED STATES STRIKE COMMISSION, REPORT ON THE CHICAGO STRIKE OF JUNE-JULY, 1894 LIV, S. EXEC. DOC. NO. 7, 53d Cong., 3d Sess. (1895).

34. Act of June 18, 1898, ch. 466, 30 Stat. 476.

35. The testimony before, findings of, and special studies conducted by the Commission are contained in nineteen volumes; the Commission pursued its work from 1898 to 1902.

36. U.S. INDUSTRIAL COMMISSION, 5 REPORT OF THE INDUSTRIAL COMMISSION ON LABOR LEGISLATION 8, H.R. DOC. NO. 95, 56th Cong., 1st Sess. (1900).

37. U.S. INDUSTRIAL COMMISSION, FINAL REPORT OF THE INDUSTRIAL COMMISSION 844, H.R. DOC. NO. 380, 57th Cong., 1st Sess. (1902).

38. *Id.*

observed that bargaining would remove "the occasions of minor misunderstandings" and would facilitate their correction. "A large proportion of labor disputes," the Committee reminded, "originate in very unimportant matters." "In the absence of the machinery and the attitude of peaceful discussion," noted the Committee, "misunderstanding grows into bitterness, and too often" a strike or lockout results.[39] The third advantage bargaining offered, stated the Committee, was that its successes were cumulative. "The practice of meeting together," the Committee commented, "constantly increased mutual understanding and mutual respect, between employers and employees."[40] Fifteen years later, the members of the U.S. Commission on Industrial Relations, who had been appointed by Congress to study "the underlying causes of dissatisfaction in the industrial situation,"[41] again recommended extensive reformations of the law governing relations between workers and employers, and endorsed the concept of collective bargaining.[42]

Significantly, participants in the search for a new model by which to order the employment relationship were not limited to social reformers, union activists, academics, and members of congressional panels, but included management itself. Management's objectives in this endeavor were twofold.[43] The first was to discover new methods of group dealing that would improve communication with employees, thereby reducing friction between management and workers and in turn, securing both the willing cooperation of the latter with management's directives and identity with its goals. The second was to develop a model that could compete successfully with collective bargaining;[44] ironically, after the turn of the century, and into the 1920's, union membership continued to grow despite the legal obstacles placed in its way by the courts.[45] Tellingly, of the various schemes with which management experimented, so-called employee representation plans, or company unions, became the dominant employer alternative. As their sobriquet implies, these plans shared many similarities with collective bargaining. They provided employees with a means of having their voices heard concerning company policies and they often provided for grievance machinery, albeit of a much more limited scope than

39. *Id.*

40. *Id.*

41. Act of Aug. 23, 1912, ch. 351, 37 Stat. 415.

42. *See* U.S. COMMISSION ON INDUSTRIAL RELATIONS, FINAL REPORT OF THE COMMISSION ON INDUSTRIAL RELATIONS (1915).

43. For a study of the unfolding ideology of American management in this period, see R. BENDIX, *supra* note 4, at 254–87.

44. Concerning the development of these alternative plans, see Kohler, *supra* note 2, and sources cited therein.

45. In 1897 (at the close of a sharp depression) unions had under 500,000 members; by 1920, over 5 million workers were union members. M. DERBER, *supra* note 12, at 173.

that usually furnished through collective bargaining. The chief and crucial difference between collective bargaining and the employers' alternative, not surprisingly, was the degree of control the employer exercised over the "representation plan" and the limitation of the plan's coverage to the workers of one employer.[46] For purposes of the present discussion, however, the key thing to be noticed is that management, like other sectors of society, had increasingly found the common law ordering of the employment relationship unworkable and unsatisfactory and that, by the 1920's, the leading substitute model that management had come to employ bore a striking similarity to collective bargaining. Significantly, both the growth in union membership and the use of "representation plans" occurred in spite of the fact that management was legally protected from any duty to bargain with employees or their bargaining representatives.

By the eve of the New Deal era, then, the model of the employment relationship that the common law had devised nearly fifty years before had become almost irrelevant. The actions and practices of both employees and employers had grown around and over it, much as a tree surrounds barbed wire stretched about its trunk. The model's chief use was to provide the courts with an intellectual framework for the denial of the associational rights to employees that the law had guaranteed to employers as a fundamental right.

Not surprisingly, the common law of the employment relationship of fifty years ago no more describes current management practices of large businesses than it reflected those of the 1930's. Contemporary management theory and practice emphasizes the involvement of workers in managerial decisionmaking. Like the pre-NLRA era, the management-oriented alternatives to collective bargaining have adopted many of the latter's features; their chief distinction, as in the past, lies in the control management retains over participation schemes in an unorganized setting. More significant, perhaps, is the fact that the common law governing the employment relationship has itself undergone great changes over the last decade, and bears only slight resemblance to the model for which Professor Epstein longs. It now affords workers at least some of the substantive protection once available only through self-organization, and the trend is decidedly in the direction of broadening the protections of employees' interests in the employment relationship.[47] Professor Epstein would reverse all of this development without empirical investigation, and return to an order which had largely been dismissed by all sides because that order conforms more closely to his theoretical preferences.

46. A thorough study of various representation plans is contained in TWENTIETH CENTURY FUND, INC., LABOR AND THE GOVERNMENT (1935). *See also supra* note 44.
47. *See* M. GLENDON, *supra* note 11, at 143-205.

In light of this development, then, Professor Epstein's assertion that "traditional common law principles provide a benchmark, both theoretical and historical" against which to judge the Norris-LaGuardia Act and the National Labor Relations Act is a curious one. Common law rules, Blackstone said, derive their weight and authority from their usage from a "time whereof the memory of man runneth not to the contrary."[48] As the foregoing discussion indicates, contrary to what Professor Epstein suggests, the ordering of the employment relationship along the lines of contractual theory is not practice "used time out of mind," but is instead a fairly recent innovation. Until the late 1870's, employment was treated as a status relationship, and, as Mary Ann Glendon has shown,[49] the common law has since come full circle and is once again according to the relationship many elements of a status. Hence, from an historical standpoint, the common law ordering of employment of the late nineteenth century can be regarded as a fairly short-lived anomaly rather than a longstanding and tested method of ordering.

Professor Epstein, of course, has additionally asserted that the late nineteenth century ordering of employment provides a proper theoretical touchstone against which to judge "modern statutory schemes," because they favor "limited government" and allow "the maximization of private autonomy." These, too, are curious claims.

The reign of the common law model favored by Professor Epstein was hardly one marked by a lack of governmental intervention, as names like Coeur d'Alene, Pullman, and McKeesport recall. Further, the use of the injunction as a device to break strikes, and after the *Hitchman Coal*[50] decision, as a tool to enforce yellow dog clauses entailed extensive involvement of the judiciary in labor relations matters. In his well-known study, *The Government in Labor Disputes*, Edwin Witte found that in the half-century between 1880 and 1930, state and federal courts issued 1,845 injunctions on employer's applications in labor disputes.[51] Interestingly, Witte finds that prior to 1880, American courts issued no injunctions in matters involving labor relations, but that the number of such orders increased steadily with each decade thereafter.[52] Thus, Witte's research revealed the issuance of 28 such orders between 1880 and 1890. In contrast, he found that 921 labor injunctions were granted in the decade 1920–1930.[53] Of these injunctions, sixty were to enforce yellow dog agree-

48. 1 W. BLACKSTONE, *supra* note 8, at 67.
49. M. GLENDON, *supra* note 11.
50. For a meticulous dissection and criticism of the majority's opinion in the *Hitchman* decision, see Cook, *Privileges of Labor Unions in the Struggle for Life*, 27 YALE L.J. 779 (1918).
51. E. WITTE, THE GOVERNMENT IN LABOR DISPUTES 84 (1969).
52. *Id.* at 83–84.
53. As Professor Irving Bernstein has observed, this figure assumes "added meaning when viewed

ments.[54] Indeed, the judiciary's involvement in labor matters through the use of its equity powers became so extensive that calls for the limitation of the courts' authority to issue injunctions in such disputes came not only from labor and academics, but also from leaders of the bar and conservative political figures.[55] Among such persons were S.S. Gregory,[56] a president of the American Bar Association, and Senator George Wharton Pepper of Pennsylvania.[57] Much of these commentators' concern centered on the proper role of the courts in such disputes, where the outcome could largely depend on the decision of an unelected official. "Must we not," asked Pepper, "confine the courts to the sphere in which the creators of our constitutional system intended them to live . . . ?"[58] Interestingly then, the rise of court intervention parallels the growth of large industrial organizations. As the common law model became more inadequate, the resort to state intervention became more frequent.

It should be recalled in discussing nineteenth century notions of contractual freedom that this method of public ordering places great state power in private hands. The role of government in a regime of "freedom of contract" is to enforce private agreements at the instance of a promisee.[59] As Max Weber so early pointed out, the phrase "freedom of contract," though evocative, is misleading to the extent that it suggests an individual is free from domination by others. Its essential feature is not that persons are left unregulated to make agreements as they please, but rather, Weber observed, that their agreements will be enforced by the state, in favor of the promisee.[60] This method of ordering thus does more than lend official backing to private transactions that have no necessary

against the fact that employers faced very few strikes" during this decade. I. BERNSTEIN, THE LEAN YEARS: A HISTORY OF THE AMERICAN WORKER, 1920-1933, at 200-01 (1960).

54. The latter figure, Witte points out, should not be undervalued. While injunctions to enforce yellow dog contracts comprised "less than 10 percent of the total injunctions during this period," Witte notes:

> several of these writs were taken out by a large number of employers acting jointly. These, moreover, have been the most extensive of all injunctions in their provisions and remain in effect so long as the complainants continue to use individual non-union agreements. [After the *Hitchman* decision] [i]njunctions based on yellow-dog contracts now block all attempts to organize the coal miners throughout West Virginia; and there are a considerable number of scattered mines and manufacturing plants elsewhere which are protected against efforts at organization by injunctions issued some years since, now dormant, but likely to be revived should organizers put in an appearance.

E. WITTE, *supra* note 51, at 224 (footnote omitted).

55. For an excellent summary of labors' treatment by the courts during the period 1920-33, see I. BERNSTEIN, *supra* note 53, at 190-243.

56. *See* S. Gregory, Address of the President, Annual Meeting of the American Bar Ass'n, 37 REP. OF THE A.B.A. 255, 264-71 (1912).

57. Pepper, *Injunctions in Labor Disputes*, 44 REP. OF THE A.B.A. 174 (1924).

58. *Id.* at 179.

59. M. WEBER, ECONOMY AND SOCIETY 668-69 (1968); Rheinstein, *Introduction* to MAX WEBER ON LAW IN ECONOMY AND SOCIETY, at lx-lxi (1954).

60. M. WEBER, *supra* note 59, at 99-100.

connection with an individual's freedom from domination; it acts, as Weber pointed out, to strengthen the positions of those who already have economic power over others.[61]

The model for which Epstein argues, as history shows, brought about the results Weber described. It did not, nor would it, afford in Hurst's words, the "release of individual creative energy to the greatest extent compatible with the broad sharing of opportunity for such expression."[62] Indeed, as we have seen, it was when financial and industrial organizations became so dominant that they restricted the equality of opportunity available to individuals that program groups like unions began widespread formation.

Professor Epstein tacitly admits that his model would yield the results delineated by Weber.[63] Hence, it is especially peculiar, given his goal of

61. *Id.* at 729–31. Thus, as Weber states:

> The formal right of a worker to enter into any contract whatsoever with any employer whatsoever does not in practice represent for the employment seeker even the slightest freedom in the determination of his own conditions of work, and it does not guarantee him any influence on this process. It rather means, at least primarily, that the more powerful party in the market, i.e., normally the employer, has the possibility to set the terms, to offer the job "take it or leave it," and, given the normally more pressing economic need of the worker, to impose his terms upon him. The result of contractual freedom, then, is in the first place the opening of the opportunity to use, by the clever utilization of property ownership in the market, these resources without legal restraints as a means for the achievement of power over others. The parties interested in power in the market thus are also interested in such a legal order. Their interest is served particularly by the establishment of "legal empowerment rules." This type of rule does no more than create the framework for valid agreements which, under conditions of formal freedom, are officially available to all. Actually, however, they are accessible only to the owners of property and thus in effect support their very autonomy and power positions.

Id. at 729–30 (footnote omitted).

62. J. HURST, *supra* note 13, at 6.

63. Professor Epstein's only defense to this is an *ipse dixit*: "[T]hat most contracts are for the mutual benefit of both parties, regardless of their original endowments of wealth." Epstein, *supra* note 1, at 1360. Weber, however, pointed out that:

> The increasing significance of freedom of contract and, particularly, of enabling laws which leave everything to "free" agreement, implies a relative reduction of that kind of coercion which results from the threat of mandatory and prohibitory norms. Formally it represents, of course, a decrease of coercion. But it is also obvious how advantageous this state of affairs is to those who are economically in the position to make use of the empowerments. The exact extent to which the total amount of "freedom" within a given legal community is actually increased depends entirely upon the concrete economic order and especially upon the property distribution. In no case can it be simply deduced from the content of the law . . . . [c]oercion is exercised to a considerable extent by the private owners of the means of production and acquisition, to whom the law guarantees their property and whose power can thus manifest itself in the competitive struggle of the market. In this type of coercion the statement "*coactus voluit*"[103] applies with peculiar force just because of the careful avoidance of the use of authoritarian forms. In the labor market, it is left to the "free" discretion of the parties to accept the conditions imposed by those who are economically stronger by virtue of the legal guaranty of their property.
>
> ---
>
> [103]"Coactus voluit" (it is his wish, although coerced)—Romanist phrase to describe the situation of an individual who has engaged in a legal transaction under the influence of coercion, in contrast to the situation in which a person is used as the mere physical tool of another, for instance, where the latter forcibly grabs the former's hand and moves it so as to go through the

maximizing personal autonomy, that he would put into employers' hands, through the legalization of the yellow dog device, the power effectively to determine whether employees should enjoy the same associational rights the law affords employers. It is perhaps at this point that the degree of state authority transferred to private hands under a "freedom of contract" regime is made most clear.

The appearance and extent of power that would be held by large industrial and financial organizations could hardly have been foreseen at the time that liberal economic theories first developed. Yet, even in 1776, Adam Smith observed that

> We rarely hear . . . of the combinations of masters, though frequently of those of workmen. But whoever imagines, upon this account, that masters rarely combine, is as ignorant of the world as of the subject. Masters are always and every where in a sort of tacit, but constant and uniform combination, not to raise the wages of labour above their actual rate. To violate this combination is every where a most unpopular action, and a sort of reproach to a master among his neighbors and equals.[64]

Smith noted, however, that when their employees organize themselves: "The masters upon these occasions . . . never cease to call aloud for the assistance of the civil magistrate, and the vigorous execution of those laws which have been enacted with so much severity against the combinations of servants, labourers, and journeymen."[65]

In summary, if the maximization of personal autonomy is his goal, it is difficult to perceive why Professor Epstein champions a return to the legal order of more than a half-century ago. As Weber recognized,[66] such an order does not lead to greater autonomy, but rather to an ever-increasing restriction upon the freedom of individual action.[67] This proclivity would

physical motions of writing a signature.

M. WEBER, *supra* note 59, at 730-31, 752.

64. A. SMITH, AN INQUIRY INTO THE NATURE AND CAUSES OF THE WEALTH OF NATIONS 75 (U. of Chicago Press ed. 1976). Concerning the appropriation and "misuse" of Smith's thought by apologists for capitalism as it developed in the nineteenth century, see A. LINDEMANN, A HISTORY OF EUROPEAN SOCIALISM 31-33 (1983).

It is interesting to compare the excerpt from Smith above with the following from the report of the U.S. Strike Commission, *supra* note 33, at xlvii:

> We also have employers who obstruct progress by perverting and misapplying the law of supply and demand, and who, while insisting upon individualism for workmen, demand that they shall be let alone to combine as they please and that society and all its forces shall protect them in their resulting contentions.

65. *Id.* at 75-76.

66. Weber's sudden and untimely death occurred in 1920. The first portions of *Economy and Society* appeared in 1921.

67. As Weber stated:

> The private enterprise system transforms into objects of "labor market transactions" even those

be exacerbated by the re-legalization of the yellow dog device. It, of course, amplifies and cements the economic power enjoyed by employers under a "freedom of contract" regime by ensuring that employees will be able to combine their resources only upon the former's sufferance.[68] In effect, the yellow dog device allows employers to sit on both sides of the table, by permitting them largely to determine and regulate the strength of employees' bargaining power. Reduced to its basics, Professor Epstein's model ensures that the more powerful party in the market will dictate the terms of employment, and that that party will be the employer.

Unfortunately, Professor Epstein leaves unexamined and apparently unappreciated the essence of collective bargaining: its function as a method through which employees and employers jointly establish a comprehensive scheme of industrial self-government.[69] In David Feller's words, collective bargaining provides:

> a system of law to govern matters much more important to the employee than those governed by most public law: his right to a job and to a promotion, the hours at which and the conditions under which he is required to work, his right to refuse or to share in the opportunity to work overtime, the length and scheduling of his vacations, and so forth.[70]

> personal and authoritarian-hierarchical relations which actually exist in the capitalistic enterprise. While the authoritarian relationships are thus drained of all normal sentimental content, authoritarian constraint not only continues but, at least under certain circumstances, even increases. The more comprehensive the realm of structures whose existence depends in a specific way on "discipline," that of capitalist commercial establishments, the more relentlessly can authoritarian constraint be exercised within them, and the smaller will be the circle of those in whose hands the power to use this type of constraint is concentrated and who also hold the power to have such authority guaranteed to them by the legal order.

M. WEBER, *supra* note 59, at 731.

68. Professor Epstein's arguments would appear to permit employers nearly boundless ability to control the associational ties that their employees might form. For example, it appears that an employer could lawfully require, as a condition of employment, that an applicant agree to abjure certain religious practices or refrain from joining or assisting a given (or all) political parties. Like the choice between assenting to a yellow dog clause or remaining unemployed, under Professor Epstein's premises, one cannot argue that these choices are illusory because of economic inequality between the parties. Assuming that there is no use or threat of force involved, the only objection that can be interposed to the legal system's recognition of the validity of these clauses is that the applicant has a precontractual right to demand both political party membership and employment, or a precontractual right to engage in certain religious practices and employment. Assuming that the employer in question is a private person or entity, with no relation to the state, such rights would seem to exist only if, like the right to one's own person, they are recognized as being basic and inalienable. Significantly, no less a moral authority than the Pope, JOHN PAUL II, LABOREM EXERCENS (ON HUMAN WORK) § 20, at 48–49 (1981) and no less a political authority than President Reagan, N.Y. Times, Oct. 10, 1982, at 16, col. 1 (address in reaction to the banning of Solidarity by the Polish government on October 9, 1982) have proclaimed that union membership is such a right.

69. The Supreme Court recognized this key aspect of collective bargaining in its landmark opinion in Steelworkers v. Warrior & Gulf Navigation Co., 363 U.S. 574, 580 (1960) ("A collective bargaining agreement is an effort to erect a system of industrial self-government." Consequently, stated the Court, the agreement "is more than a contract; it is a generalized code . . . ." *Id.* at 578).

70. Feller, *A General Theory of the Collective Bargaining Agreement*, 61 CAL. L. REV. 663, 761

The duty to bargain affords employees the opportunity to participate in the framing and administration of the terms and rules that govern the worker-employer relationship.[71] This modification of the character of rulemaking and administration in the workplace from a unilateral and authoritarian process to one of bilateral consultation is the gist of collective bargaining as established by the National Labor Relations Act.[72] It is this—the sharing of power—that underlies much of the resistance to the idea of collective bargaining, and to the Act itself.

Contrary to the impression that one might receive from Professor Epstein's description, a central principle of the American model of collective bargaining is the exclusion of government from the parties' relationship. A noteworthy feature of the framework the Act establishes for the creation of this private system of law, and one that distinguishes the practice of collective bargaining in the United States from that in other nations, is the concept of free collective bargaining. The National Labor Relations Act neither regulates the relationship of the parties once collective bargaining begins, nor specifies any of the substantive terms that must become part of the agreement; in fact, it does not even require that an agreement be reached.[73] As the Court has said, "Congress intended that the parties should have wide latitude in their negotiations, unrestricted by any governmental power to regulate the substantive solution of their differences."[74] The making of this private law to govern the workplace thus goes forward in private, its provisions not subject to governmental oversight. Consistent with their private character, the overwhelming majority of collective bargaining agreements also provide for a private dispute-resolution system, arbitration to settle disagreements about the interpretation and application of these "codes."[75]

There are other misperceptions about the effects of unionization and bargaining that one may carry away from Professor Epstein's piece. Among these are the notions that unionized establishments are less productive[76] than non-unionized firms and that unions increase wage ine-

(1973).

71. For an elucidation of this view, see *id.* at 720–24.

72. As Professor Feller observes, "The agreement reached as a result of this bargaining becomes the rule governing the stated portion of the enterprise. It is not an agreement on the terms on which union members will work but an agreement on the rules which management will observe with respect to all employees." *Id.* at 736. For a brief explication of the incentives management has to accept unions, see *id.* at 761–71.

73. *See, e.g.*, NLRB v. Insurance Agents Int'l Union, 361 U.S. 477, 488 (1960); NLRB v. American Nat'l Ins. Co., 343 U.S. 395, 401–02 (1952).

74. *NLRB v. Insurance Agents Int'l Union*, 361 U.S. at 488.

75. Over 95% of collective bargaining agreements contain provision for arbitration. U.S. Bureau of Labor Statistics, Dep't of Labor Bull. No. 1425-6, Arbitration Procedures (1966).

76. *See* R. FREEMAN & J. MEDOFF, *supra* note 1, at 21–22, 162–80.

quality.[77] As the latest empirical research demonstrates, these (and a number of other widely held beliefs about the effects of unions) are not true.[78] This is not to suggest that the authors believe that the Wagner Act was a piece of statutory drafting without peer, or that every aspect of unionization is an unalloyed good. It is to suggest that the Norris-LaGuardia and Wagner Acts, by affording employees the associational rights enjoyed by employers, and the opportunity to participate in setting and administering the terms under which they work, do much to increase individual freedom and decrease authoritarian constraint.[79] They do so not only in the workplace, but in the political realm as well, through ensuring that employees are free to join groups that can represent their interests in an organized way, just as corporations and business lobbies represent entrepreneurs.

The fact that unions and other mediating groups do not exist or are highly controlled in totalitarian systems of both the right and left is not coincidental. As Derek Bok and John Dunlop point out, unions make an important contribution to the democratic process in a society dominated by large organizations through providing "a coordinated and coherent political voice to workers who would otherwise be largely disorganized," and by increasing "the political participation of poorer segments of society. . . ."[80] In contemplating Professor Epstein's arguments, one does well to regard the outcomes his suggested scheme encourages, and to recall Justice Holmes' acute observation that it is considerations of social advantage, not logic, that determine the configurations of one's legal arguments.[81]

As Archibald Cox has observed,[82] one of the principal things labor asked of the law was the unfettered right to form, join and assist unions. It is this right that the Norris-LaGuardia Act removed from private determination, through outlawing the yellow dog device. It is this right of free association that the National Labor Relations Act affirmatively guarantees

77. *See id.* at 20, 78-93. Professors Freeman and Medoff observe that the claim that unions increase wage inequality:

> is wrong not because the effect to which it directs attention—raising wages of some workers at the expense of other workers—does not occur. It does. The claim is wrong because the increase in inequality induced by monopoly wage effects is dwarfed by three other trade union effects on wages that reduce inequality: union wage policies lower inequality of wages *within* establishments; union wage policies favor equal pay for equal work *across* establishments; and union wage gains for blue-collar labor reduce inequality between white-collar and blue-collar workers.

Id. at 78.

78. *See id*; S. SLICHTER, J. HEALY & E. LIVERNASH, *supra* note 1.

79. *See supra* note 67.

80. D. BOK & J. DUNLOP, LABOR AND THE AMERICAN COMMUNITY 425 (1970). Concerning the strength of unions' political power, see R. FREEMAN & J. MEDOFF, *supra* note 2, at 191-206.

81. Vegelahn v. Guntner, 167 Mass. 92, 106 (1896) (Holmes, J., dissenting).

82. A. COX, LAW AND THE NATIONAL LABOR POLICY 2 (1960).

employees, and which is the Act's cornerstone. This right is one for which blood has been shed and lives placed in jeopardy here and elsewhere. To even suggest removing it on the basis of the sort of argument put forth by Professor Epstein is an affront to all those who struggled to make it a reality.

NATIONAL LABOR RELATIONS BOARD *v.* CATHOLIC BISHOP OF CHICAGO ET AL.

CERTIORARI TO THE UNITED STATES COURT OF APPEALS FOR THE SEVENTH CIRCUIT

No. 77–752. Argued October 30, 1978—Decided March 21, 1979

The National Labor Relations Board (NLRB) certified unions as bargaining agents for lay teachers in schools operated by respondents, which refused to recognize or bargain with the unions; the NLRB issued cease-and-desist orders against respondents, holding that it had properly assumed jurisdiction over the schools. Exercise of jurisdiction was asserted to be in line with its policy of declining jurisdiction only when schools are "completely religious" not just "religiously associated," as it found to be the case here, because the schools taught secular as well as religious subjects. On respondents' challenges to the NLRB orders, the Court of Appeals denied enforcement, holding that the NLRB standard failed to provide a workable guide for the exercise of its discretion and that the NLRB's assumption of jurisdiction was foreclosed by the Religion Clauses of the First Amendment. *Held:* Schools operated by a church to teach both religious and secular subjects are not within the jurisdiction granted by the National Labor Relations Act, and the NLRB was therefore without authority to issue the orders against respondents. Pp. 499–507.

(a) There would be a significant risk of infringement of the Religion Clauses of the First Amendment if the Act conferred jurisdiction over church-operated schools. Cf. *Lemon* v. *Kurtzman,* 403 U. S. 602, 617. Pp. 501–504.

(b) Neither the language of the statute nor its legislative history discloses any affirmative intention by Congress that church-operated schools be within the NLRB's jurisdiction, and, absent a clear expression of Congress' intent to bring teachers of church-operated schools within the NLRB's jurisdiction, the Court will not construe the Act in such a way as would call for the resolution of difficult and sensitive First Amendment questions. Pp. 504–507.

559 F. 2d 1112, affirmed.

BURGER, C. J., delivered the opinion of the Court, in which STEWART, POWELL, REHNQUIST, and STEVENS, JJ., joined. BRENNAN, J., filed a dissenting opinion, in which WHITE, MARSHALL, and BLACKMUN, JJ., joined, *post*, p. 508.

Solicitor General McCree argued the cause for petitioner. With him on the briefs were *Kenneth S. Geller, John S. Irving, Carl L. Taylor, Norton J. Come,* and *Carol A. De Deo.*

Don H. Reuben argued the cause for respondents. With him on the brief were *Lawrence Gunnels, James A. Serritella, James A. Klenk,* and *Jerome J. O'Dowd.**

MR. CHIEF JUSTICE BURGER delivered the opinion of the Court.

This case arises out of the National Labor Relations Board's exercise of jurisdiction over lay faculty members at two groups of Catholic high schools. We granted certiorari to consider two questions: (a) Whether teachers in schools operated by a church to teach both religious and secular subjects are within the jurisdiction granted by the National Labor Relations Act; and (b) if the Act authorizes such jurisdiction, does its exercise violate the guarantees of the Religion Clauses of the First Amendment? 434 U. S. 1061 (1978).

**J. Albert Woll* and *Laurence Gold* filed a brief for the American Federation of Labor and Congress of Industrial Organizations as *amicus curiae* urging reversal.

Briefs of *amici curiae* urging affirmance were filed by *Leo Pfeffer* and *Earl W. Trent, Jr.*, for the Baptist Joint Committee on Public Affairs; by *Thomas Stephen Neuberger* for the Center for Law and Religious Freedom of the Christian Legal Society; by *Warren L. Johns, Walter E. Carson, Lee Boothby,* and *Robert J. Hickey* for the General Conference of Seventh-Day Adventists; and by *David Goldberger* and *Barbara P. O'Toole* for the Roger Baldwin Foundation of the American Civil Liberties Union, Inc., Illinois Division.

Briefs of *amici curiae* were filed by *Lawrence A. Poltrock* and *Bruce E. Endy* for the American Federation of Teachers (AFL-CIO); by *Sharp Whitmore* for certain Catholic High Schools in the Archdiocese of Los Angeles and the Diocese of Orange; and by *George E. Reed* and *Patrick F. Geary* for the United States Catholic Conference.

I

One group of schools is operated by the Catholic Bishop of Chicago, a corporation sole; the other group is operated by the Diocese of Fort Wayne-South Bend, Inc. The group operated by the Catholic Bishop of Chicago consists of two schools, Quigley North and Quigley South.[1] Those schools are termed "minor seminaries" because of their role in educating high school students who may become priests. At one time, only students who manifested a positive and confirmed desire to be priests were admitted to the Quigley schools. In 1970, the requirement was changed so that students admitted to these schools need not show a definite inclination toward the priesthood. Now the students need only be recommended by their parish priest as having a potential for the priesthood or for Christian leadership. The schools continue to provide special religious instruction not offered in other Catholic secondary schools. The Quigley schools also offer essentially the same college-preparatory curriculum as public secondary schools. Their students participate in a variety of extracurricular activities which include secular as well as religious events. The schools are recognized by the State and accredited by a regional educational organization.[2]

The Diocese of Fort Wayne-South Bend, Inc., has five high schools.[3] Unlike the Quigley schools, the special recom-

[1] The Catholic Bishop operates other schools in the Chicago area, but they were not involved in the proceedings before the Board.

[2] As explained to the Board's Hearing Officer, in Illinois the term "approval" is distinct from "recognition." Before a school may operate, it must be approved by the State's Department of Education. Approval is given when a school meets the minimal requirements under state law, such as for compulsory attendance; approval does not require any evaluation of the school's program. Recognition, which is not required to operate, is given only after the school has passed the State's evaluation.

[3] The Diocese also has 47 elementary schools. They were not involved in the proceedings before the Board.

mendation of a priest is not a prerequisite for admission. Like the Quigley schools, however, these high schools seek to provide a traditional secular education but oriented to the tenets of the Roman Catholic faith; religious training is also mandatory. These schools are similarly certified by the State.[4]

In 1974 and 1975, separate representation petitions were filed with the Board by interested union organizations for both the Quigley and the Fort Wayne-South Bend schools; representation was sought only for lay teachers.[5] The schools challenged the assertion of jurisdiction on two grounds: (a) that they do not fall within the Board's discretionary jurisdictional criteria; and (b) that the Religion Clauses of the First Amendment preclude the Board's jurisdiction. The Board rejected the jurisdictional arguments on the basis of its decision in *Roman Catholic Archdiocese of Baltimore,* 216 N. L. R. B. 249 (1975). There the Board explained that its policy was to decline jurisdiction over religiously sponsored organizations "only when they are completely religious, not just religiously associated." *Id.,* at 250. Because neither group of schools was found to fall within the Board's "completely religious" category, the Board ordered elections. *Catholic Bishop of Chicago,* 220 N. L. R. B. 359 (1975).[6]

---

[4] As explained to the Board's Hearing Officer, "certification" by the State of Indiana is roughly equivalent to "recognition" by the State of Illinois. Both are voluntary procedures which involve some evaluation by the state educational authorities.

[5] The certification and order cover only "all full-time and regular part-time lay teachers, including physical education teachers . . . ; and excluding rectors, procurators, dean of studies, business manager, director of student activities, director of formation, director of counseling services, office clerical employees, maintenance employees, cafeteria workers, watchmen, librarians, nurses, all religious faculty, and all guards and supervisors as defined in the Act . . . ." *Catholic Bishop of Chicago,* 220 N. L. R. B. 359, 360 (1975).

[6] The decision concerning the Diocese of Fort Wayne-South Bend, Inc., is not reported.

In the Board-supervised election at the Quigley schools, the Quigley Education Alliance, a union affiliated with the Illinois Education Association, prevailed and was certified as the exclusive bargaining representative for 46 lay teachers. In the Diocese of Fort Wayne-South Bend, the Community Alliance for Teachers of Catholic High Schools, a similar union organization, prevailed and was certified as the representative for the approximately 180 lay teachers. Notwithstanding the Board's order, the schools declined to recognize the unions or to bargain. The unions filed unfair labor practice complaints with the Board under §§ 8 (a)(1) and (5) of the National Labor Relations Act, 49 Stat. 452, as amended, 29 U. S. C. §§ 158 (a) (1) and (5). The schools opposed the General Counsel's motion for summary judgment, again challenging the Board's exercise of jurisdiction over religious schools on both statutory and constitutional grounds.

The Board reviewed the record of previous proceedings and concluded that all of the arguments had been raised or could have been raised in those earlier proceedings. Since the arguments had been rejected previously, the Board granted summary judgment, holding that it had properly exercised its statutory discretion in asserting jurisdiction over these schools.[7] The Board concluded that the schools had violated the Act and ordered that they cease their unfair labor practices and that they bargain collectively with the unions. *Catholic*

[7] The Board relied on its reasoning in *Cardinal Timothy Manning, Roman Catholic Archbishop of the Archdiocese of Los Angeles,* 223 N. L. R. B. 1218 (1976): "We also do not agree that the schools are religious institutions intimately involved with the Catholic Church. It has heretofore been the Board's policy to decline jurisdiction over institutions only when they are completely religious, not just religiously associated. *Roman Catholic Archdiocese of Baltimore, Archdiocesan High Schools,* 216 NLRB 249 (1975). The schools perform in part the secular function of educating children, and in part concern themselves with religious instruction. Therefore, we will not decline to assert jurisdiction over these schools on such a basis." 223 N. L. R. B., at 1218.

Bishop of Chicago, 224 N. L. R. B. 1221 (1976); *Diocese of Fort Wayne-South Bend, Inc.,* 224 N. L. R. B. 1226 (1976).

II

The schools challenged the Board's orders in petitions to the Court of Appeals for the Seventh Circuit. That court denied enforcement of the Board's orders. 559 F. 2d 1112 (1977).[8] The court considered the Board's actions in relation to its discretion in choosing to extend its jurisdiction only to religiously affiliated schools that were not "completely religious." It concluded that the Board had not properly exercised its discretion, because the Board's distinction between "completely religious" and "merely religiously associated" failed to provide a workable guide for the exercise of discretion:

> "We find the standard itself to be a simplistic black or white, purported rule containing no borderline demarcation of where 'completely religious' takes over or, on the other hand, ceases. In our opinion the dichotomous 'completely religious—merely religiously associated' standard provides no workable guide to the exercise of discretion. The determination that an institution is so completely a religious entity as to exclude any viable secular components obviously implicates very sensitive questions of faith and tradition. *See, e. g.,* [*Wisconsin* v.] *Yoder, . . .* 406 U. S. 205 [(1972)]." *Id.,* at 1118.

The Court of Appeals recognized that the rejection of the Board's policy as to church-operated schools meant that the Board would extend its jurisdiction to all church-operated

[8] Cf. *Caulfield* v. *Hirsch,* 95 LRRM 3164 (ED Pa. 1977) (enjoining Board from asserting jurisdiction over elementary schools in Archdiocese of Philadelphia). This case is presently under review by the Court of Appeals for the Third Circuit. See App. to Pet. for Cert. in *Caulfield* v. *Hirsch,* O. T. 1977, No. 77-1411, p. A76, cert. denied, 436 U. S. 957 (1978).

schools. The court therefore turned to the question of whether the Board could exercise that jurisdiction, consistent with constitutional limitations. It concluded that both the Free Exercise Clause and the Establishment Clause of the First Amendment foreclosed the Board's jurisdiction. It reasoned that from the initial act of certifying a union as the bargaining agent for lay teachers the Board's action would impinge upon the freedom of church authorities to shape and direct teaching in accord with the requirements of their religion. It analyzed the Board's action in this way:

> "At some point, factual inquiry by courts or agencies into such matters [separating secular from religious training] would almost necessarily raise First Amendment problems. If history demonstrates, as it does, that Roman Catholics founded an alternative school system for essentially religious reasons and continued to maintain them as an 'integral part of the religious mission of the Catholic Church,' *Lemon* [v. *Kurtzman,* 403 U. S. 602], 616 [(1971)], courts and agencies would be hard pressed to take official or judicial notice that these purposes were undermined or eviscerated by the determination to offer such secular subjects as mathematics, physics, chemistry, and English literature." *Ibid.*

The court distinguished local regulations which required fire inspections or state laws mandating attendance, reasoning that they did not "have the clear inhibiting potential upon the relationship between teachers and employers with which the present Board order is directly concerned." *Id.,* at 1124. The court held that interference with management prerogatives, found acceptable in an ordinary commercial setting, was not acceptable in an area protected by the First Amendment. "The real difficulty is found in the chilling aspect that the requirement of bargaining will impose on the exercise of the bishops' control of the religious mission of the schools." *Ibid.*

III

The Board's assertion of jurisdiction over private schools is, as we noted earlier, a relatively recent development. Indeed, in 1951 the Board indicated that it would not exercise jurisdiction over nonprofit, educational institutions because to do so would not effectuate the purposes of the Act. *Trustees of Columbia University in the City of New York,* 97 N. L. R. B. 424. In 1970, however, the Board pointed to what it saw as an increased involvement in commerce by educational institutions and concluded that this required a different position on jurisdiction. In *Cornell University,* 183 N. L. R. B. 329, the Board overruled its *Columbia University* decision. *Cornell University* was followed by the assertion of jurisdiction over nonprofit, private secondary schools. *Shattuck School,* 189 N. L. R. B. 886 (1971). See also *Judson School,* 209 N. L. R. B. 677 (1974). The Board now asserts jurisdiction over all private, nonprofit, educational institutions with gross annual revenues that meet its jurisdictional requirements whether they are secular or religious. 29 CFR § 103.1 (1978). See, *e. g., Academia San Jorge,* 234 N. L. R. B. 1181 (1978) (advisory opinion stating that Board would not assert jurisdiction over Catholic educational institution which did not meet jurisdictional standards); *Windsor School, Inc.,* 199 N. L. R. B. 457, 200 N. L. R. B. 991 (1972) (declining jurisdiction where private, proprietary school did not meet jurisdictional amounts).

That broad assertion of jurisdiction has not gone unchallenged. But the Board has rejected the contention that the Religion Clauses of the First Amendment bar the extension of its jurisdiction to church-operated schools. Where the Board has declined to exercise jurisdiction, it has done so only on the grounds of the employer's minimal impact on commerce. Thus, in *Association of Hebrew Teachers of Metropolitan Detroit,* 210 N. L. R. B. 1053 (1974), the Board did not assert jurisdiction over the Association which offered courses in Jewish culture in after-school classes, a nursery school, and a college. The Board termed the Association an "isolated instance of [an] atypical employer." *Id.*, at 1058–1059. It explained: "Whether an employer falls within a given 'class' of enterprise depends upon those of its activities which are predominant and give the employing enterprise its character. . . . [T]he fact that an employer's activity . . . is dedicated to a sectarian religious purpose is not a sufficient reason for the Board to refrain from asserting jurisdiction." *Id.*, at 1058. Cf. *Board of Jewish Education of Greater Washington, D. C.*, 210 N. L. R. B. 1037 (1974). In the same year the Board asserted jurisdiction over an Association chartered by the State of New York to operate diocesan high schools. *Henry M. Hald High School Assn.*, 213 N. L. R. B. 415 (1974). It rejected the argument that its assertion of jurisdiction would produce excessive governmental entanglement with religion. In the Board's view, the Association had chosen to entangle itself with the secular world when it decided to hire lay teachers. *Id.*, at 418 n. 7.[9]

When it ordered an election for the lay professional employees at five parochial high schools in Baltimore in 1975, the Board reiterated its belief that exercise of its jurisdiction is not contrary to the First Amendment:

> "[T]he Board's policy in the past has been to decline jurisdiction over similar institutions only when they are completely religious, not just religiously associated, and the Archdiocese concedes that instruction is not limited to religious subjects. That the Archdiocese seeks to provide an education based on Christian principles does not lead to a contrary conclusion. Most religiously associated institutions seek to operate in conformity with

[9] The Board went on to explain that the rights guaranteed by § 7 of the Act, 29 U. S. C. § 157, were "a part of our national heritage established by Congress, [and] were a legitimate exercise of Congress' constitutional power." 213 N. L. R. B., at 418 n. 7.

their religious tenets." *Roman Catholic Archdiocese of Baltimore,* 216 N. L. R. B., at 250.

The Board also rejected the First Amendment claims in *Cardinal Timothy Manning, Roman Catholic Archbishop of the Archdiocese of Los Angeles,* 223 N. L. R. B. 1218, 1218 (1976): "Regulation of labor relations does not violate the First Amendment when it involves a *minimal intrusion* on religious conduct and is necessary to obtain [the Act's] objective." (Emphasis added.)

The Board thus recognizes that its assertion of jurisdiction over teachers in religious schools constitutes some degree of intrusion into the administration of the affairs of church-operated schools. Implicit in the Board's distinction between schools that are "completely religious" and those "religiously associated" is also an acknowledgment of some degree of entanglement. Because that distinction was measured by a school's involvement with commerce, however, and not by its religious association, it is clear that the Board never envisioned any sort of religious litmus test for determining when to assert jurisdiction. Nevertheless, by expressing its traditional jurisdictional standards in First Amendment terms, the Board has plainly recognized that intrusion into this area could run afoul of the Religion Clauses and hence preclude jurisdiction on constitutional grounds.

IV

That there are constitutional limitations on the Board's actions has been repeatedly recognized by this Court even while acknowledging the broad scope of the grant of jurisdiction. The First Amendment, of course, is a limitation on the power of Congress. Thus, if we were to conclude that the Act granted the challenged jurisdiction over these teachers we would be required to decide whether that was constitutionally permissible under the Religion Clauses of the First Amendment.

Although the respondents press their claims under the Religion Clauses, the question we consider first is whether Congress intended the Board to have jurisdiction over teachers in church-operated schools. In a number of cases the Court has heeded the essence of Mr. Chief Justice Marshall's admonition in *Murray* v. *The Charming Betsy,* 2 Cranch 64, 118 (1804), by holding that an Act of Congress ought not be construed to violate the Constitution if any other possible construction remains available. Moreover, the Court has followed this policy in the interpretation of the Act now before us and related statutes.

In *Machinists* v. *Street,* 367 U. S. 740 (1961), for example, the Court considered claims that serious First Amendment questions would arise if the Railway Labor Act were construed to allow compulsory union dues to be used to support political candidates or causes not approved by some members. The Court looked to the language of the Act and the legislative history and concluded that they did not permit union dues to be used for such political purposes, thus avoiding "serious doubt of [the Act's] constitutionality." *Id.,* at 749.

Similarly in *McCulloch* v. *Sociedad Nacional de Marineros de Honduras,* 372 U. S. 10 (1963), a case involving the Board's assertion of jurisdiction over foreign seamen, the Court declined to read the National Labor Relations Act so as to give rise to a serious question of separation of powers which in turn would have implicated sensitive issues of the authority of the Executive over relations with foreign nations. The international implications of the case led the Court to describe it as involving "public questions particularly high in the scale of our national interest." *Id.,* at 17. Because of those questions the Court held that before sanctioning the Board's exercise of jurisdiction " 'there must be present the affirmative intention of the Congress clearly expressed.' " *Id.,* at 21–22 (quoting *Benz* v. *Compania Naviera Hidalgo,* 353 U. S. 138, 147 (1957)).

The values enshrined in the First Amendment plainly rank high "in the scale of our national values." In keeping with the Court's prudential policy it is incumbent on us to determine whether the Board's exercise of its jurisdiction here would give rise to serious constitutional questions. If so, we must first identify "the affirmative intention of the Congress clearly expressed" before concluding that the Act grants jurisdiction.

V

In recent decisions involving aid to parochial schools we have recognized the critical and unique role of the teacher in fulfilling the mission of a church-operated school. What was said of the schools in *Lemon* v. *Kurtzman,* 403 U. S. 602, 617 (1971), is true of the schools in this case: "Religious authority necessarily pervades the school system." The key role played by teachers in such a school system has been the predicate for our conclusions that governmental aid channeled through teachers creates an impermissible risk of excessive governmental entanglement in the affairs of the church-operated schools. For example, in *Lemon, supra,* at 617, we wrote:

> "In terms of potential for involving some aspect of faith or morals *in secular subjects,* a textbook's content is ascertainable, but a teacher's handling of a subject is not. We cannot ignore the danger that a teacher under religious control and discipline poses to the separation of the religious from the purely secular aspects of pre-college education. The conflict of functions inheres in the situation." (Emphasis added.)

Only recently we again noted the importance of the teacher's function in a church school: "Whether the subject is 'remedial reading,' 'advanced reading,' or simply 'reading,' a teacher remains a teacher, and the danger that religious doctrine will become intertwined with secular instruction persists." *Meek* v. *Pittenger,* 421 U. S. 349, 370 (1975). Cf.

Wolman v. *Walter*, 433 U. S. 229, 244 (1977). Good intentions by government—or third parties—can surely no more avoid entanglement with the religious mission of the school in the setting of mandatory collective bargaining than in the well-motivated legislative efforts consented to by the church-operated schools which we found unacceptable in *Lemon, Meek,* and *Wolman.*

The Board argues that it can avoid excessive entanglement since it will resolve only factual issues such as whether an anti-union animus motivated an employer's action. But at this stage of our consideration we are not compelled to determine whether the entanglement is excessive as we would were we considering the constitutional issue. Rather, we make a narrow inquiry whether the exercise of the Board's jurisdiction presents a significant risk that the First Amendment will be infringed.

Moreover, it is already clear that the Board's actions will go beyond resolving factual issues. The Court of Appeals' opinion refers to charges of unfair labor practices filed against religious schools. 559 F. 2d, at 1125, 1126. The court observed that in those cases the schools had responded that their challenged actions were mandated by their religious creeds. The resolution of such charges by the Board, in many instances, will necessarily involve inquiry into the good faith of the position asserted by the clergy-administrators and its relationship to the school's religious mission. It is not only the conclusions that may be reached by the Board which may impinge on rights guaranteed by the Religion Clauses, but also the very process of inquiry leading to findings and conclusions.[10]

The Board's exercise of jurisdiction will have at least one other impact on church-operated schools. The Board will be called upon to decide what are "terms and conditions of

---

[10] This kind of inquiry and its sensitivity are illustrated in the examination of Monsignor O'Donnell, the Rector of Quigley North, by the Board's Hearing Officer, which is reproduced in the appendix to this opinion.

employment" and therefore mandatory subjects of bargaining. See 29 U. S. C. § 158 (d). Although the Board has not interpreted that phrase as it relates to educational institutions, similar state provisions provide insight into the effect of mandatory bargaining. The Oregon Court of Appeals noted that "nearly everything that goes on in the schools affects teachers and is therefore arguably a 'condition of employment.'" *Springfield Education Assn.* v. *Springfield School Dist. No. 19,* 24 Ore. App. 751, 759, 547 P. 2d 647, 650 (1976).

The Pennsylvania Supreme Court aptly summarized the effect of mandatory bargaining when it observed that the "introduction of a concept of mandatory collective bargaining, regardless of how narrowly the scope of negotiation is defined, necessarily represents an encroachment upon the former autonomous position of management." *Pennsylvania Labor Relations Board* v. *State College Area School Dist.,* 461 Pa. 494, 504, 337 A. 2d 262, 267 (1975). Cf. *Clark County School Dist.* v. *Local Government Employee-Management Relations Board,* 90 Nev. 442, 447, 530 P. 2d 114, 117–118 (1974). See M. Lieberman & M. Moskow, Collective Negotiations for Teachers 221–247 (1966). Inevitably the Board's inquiry will implicate sensitive issues that open the door to conflicts between clergy-administrators and the Board, or conflicts with negotiators for unions. What we said in *Lemon, supra,* at 616, applies as well here:

> "[P]arochial schools involve substantial religious activity and purpose.
>
> "The substantial religious character of these church-related schools gives rise to entangling church-state relationships of the kind the Religion Clauses sought to avoid." (Footnote omitted.)

Mr. Justice Douglas emphasized this in his concurring opinion in *Lemon,* noting "the admitted and obvious fact that the *raison d'être* of parochial schools is the propagation of a religious faith." 403 U. S., at 628.

The church-teacher relationship in a church-operated school differs from the employment relationship in a public or other nonreligious school. We see no escape from conflicts flowing from the Board's exercise of jurisdiction over teachers in church-operated schools and the consequent serious First Amendment questions that would follow. We therefore turn to an examination of the National Labor Relations Act to decide whether it must be read to confer jurisdiction that would in turn require a decision on the constitutional claims raised by respondents.

VI

There is no clear expression of an affirmative intention of Congress that teachers in church-operated schools should be covered by the Act. Admittedly, Congress defined the Board's jurisdiction in very broad terms; we must therefore examine the legislative history of the Act to determine whether Congress contemplated that the grant of jurisdiction would include teachers in such schools.

In enacting the National Labor Relations Act in 1935, Congress sought to protect the right of American workers to bargain collectively. The concern that was repeated throughout the debates was the need to assure workers the right to organize to counterbalance the collective activities of employers which had been authorized by the National Industrial Recovery Act. But congressional attention focused on employment in private industry and on industrial recovery. See, *e. g.,* 79 Cong. Rec. 7573 (1935) (remarks of Sen. Wagner), 2 National Labor Relations Board, Legislative History of the National Labor Relations Act, 1935, pp. 2341–2343 (1949).

Our examination of the statute and its legislative history indicates that Congress simply gave no consideration to church-operated schools. It is not without significance, however, that the Senate Committee on Education and Labor chose a college professor's dispute with the college as an example of employer-employee relations *not* covered by the Act. S. Rep. No. 573, 74th Cong., 1st Sess., 7 (1935), 2 Legislative History, *supra,* at 2307.

Congress' next major consideration of the jurisdiction of the Board came during the passage of the Labor Management Relations Act of 1947—the Taft-Hartley Act. In that Act Congress amended the definition of "employer" in § 2 of the original Act to exclude nonprofit hospitals. 61 Stat. 137, 29 U. S. C. § 152 (2) (1970 ed.). There was some discussion of the scope of the Board's jurisdiction but the consensus was that nonprofit institutions in general did not fall within the Board's jurisdiction because they did not affect commerce. See H. R. 3020, 80th Cong., 1st Sess. (1947), 1 National Labor Relations Board, Legislative History of the Labor Management Relations Act, 1947, p. 34 (1948) (hereinafter Leg. Hist.); H. R. Rep. No. 245, 80th Cong., 1st Sess., 12 (1947), 1 Leg. Hist. 303; H. R. Conf. Rep. No. 510, 80th Cong., 1st Sess., 3, 32 (1947), 1 Leg. Hist. 507, 536; 93 Cong. Rec. 4997 (1947), 2 Leg. Hist. 1464 (remarks of Sens. Tydings and Taft).[11]

The most recent significant amendment to the Act was passed in 1974, removing the exemption of nonprofit hospitals. Pub. L. 93–360, 88 Stat. 395. The Board relies upon that amendment as showing that Congress approved the Board's exercise of jurisdiction over church-operated schools. A close examination of that legislative history, however, reveals nothing to indicate an affirmative intention that such schools be within the Board's jurisdiction. Since the Board did not assert jurisdiction over teachers in a church-operated

[11] The National Labor Relations Act was amended again when Congress passed the Labor-Management Reporting and Disclosure Act in 1959. 73 Stat. 519. That Act made no changes in the definition of "employer" and the legislative history contains no reference to church-operated schools. See generally National Labor Relations Board, Legislative History of the Labor-Management Reporting and Disclosure Act of 1959 (1959).

school until after the 1974 amendment, nothing in the history of the amendment can be read as reflecting Congress' tacit approval of the Board's action.

During the debate there were expressions of concern about the effect of the bill on employees of religious hospitals whose religious beliefs would not permit them to join a union. 120 Cong. Rec. 12946, 16914 (1974), Legislative History of the Coverage of Nonprofit Hospitals under the National Labor Relations Act, 1974, 93d Cong., 2d Sess., 118, 331–332 (1974) (remarks of Sen. Ervin and Rep. Erlenborn). The result of those concerns was an amendment which reflects congressional sensitivity to First Amendment guarantees:

> "Any employee of a health care institution who is a member of and adheres to established and traditional tenets or teachings of a bona fide religion, body, or sect which has historically held conscientious objections to joining or financially supporting labor organizations shall not be required to join or financially support any labor organization as a condition of employment; except that such employee may be required, in lieu of periodic dues and initiation fees, to pay sums equal to such dues and initiation fees to a nonreligious charitable fund exempt from taxation under section 501 (c)(3) of title 26, chosen by such employee from a list of at least three such funds, designated in a contract between such institution and a labor organization, or if the contract fails to designate such funds, then to any such fund chosen by the employee." 29 U. S. C. § 169.

The absence of an "affirmative intention of the Congress clearly expressed" fortifies our conclusion that Congress did not contemplate that the Board would require church-operated schools to grant recognition to unions as bargaining agents for their teachers.

The Board relies heavily upon *Associated Press* v. *NLRB,*

301 U. S. 103 (1937). There the Court held that the First Amendment was no bar to the application of the Act to the Associated Press, an organization engaged in collecting information and news throughout the world and distributing it to its members. Perceiving nothing to suggest that application of the Act would infringe First Amendment guarantees of press freedoms, the Court sustained Board jurisdiction. *Id.*, at 131–132. Here, on the contrary, the record affords abundant evidence that the Board's exercise of jurisdiction over teachers in church-operated schools would implicate the guarantees of the Religion Clauses.

Accordingly, in the absence of a clear expression of Congress' intent to bring teachers in church-operated schools within the jurisdiction of the Board, we decline to construe the Act in a manner that could in turn call upon the Court to resolve difficult and sensitive questions arising out of the guarantees of the First Amendment Religion Clauses.

Affirmed.

APPENDIX TO OPINION OF THE COURT

Q. [by Hearing Officer] Now, we have had quite a bit of testimony already as to liturgies, and I don't want to beat a dead horse; but let me ask you one question: If you know, how many liturgies are required at Catholic parochial high schools; do you know?

A. I think our first problem with that would be defining liturgies. That word would have many definitions. Do you want to go into that?

Q. I believe you defined it before, is that correct, when you first testified?

A. I am not sure. Let me try briefly to do it again, okay?

Q. Yes.

A. A liturgy can range anywhere from the strictest sense of the word, which is the sacrifice of the Mass in the Roman

Catholic terminology. It can go from that all the way down to a very informal group in what we call shared prayer.

Two or three individuals praying together and reflecting their own reactions to a scriptural reading. All of these—and there is a big spectrum in between those two extremes—all of these are popularly referred to as liturgies.

Q. I see.

A. Now, possibly in repeating your question, you could give me an idea of that spectrum, I could respond more accurately.

Q. Well, let us stick with the formal Masses. If you know, how many Masses are required at Catholic parochial high schools?

A. Some have none, none required. Some would have two or three during the year where what we call Holy Days of Obligation coincide with school days. Some schools on those days prefer to have a Mass within the school day so the students attend there, rather than their parish churches. Some schools feel that is not a good idea; they should always be in their parish church; so that varies a great deal from school to school.

MR. JUSTICE BRENNAN, with whom MR. JUSTICE WHITE, MR. JUSTICE MARSHALL, and MR. JUSTICE BLACKMUN join, dissenting.

The Court today holds that coverage of the National Labor Relations Act does not extend to lay teachers employed by church-operated schools. That construction is plainly wrong in light of the Act's language, its legislative history, and this Court's precedents. It is justified solely on the basis of a canon of statutory construction seemingly invented by the Court for the purpose of deciding this case. I dissent.

I

The general principle of construing statutes to avoid unnecessary constitutional decisions is a well-settled and salutary one. The governing canon, however, is *not* that expressed by the Court today. The Court requires that there be a "clear expression of an affirmative intention of Congress" before it will bring within the coverage of a broadly worded regulatory statute certain persons whose coverage might raise constitutional questions. *Ante,* at 504. But those familiar with the legislative process know that explicit expressions of congressional intent in such broadly inclusive statutes are not commonplace. Thus, by strictly or loosely applying its requirement, the Court can virtually remake congressional enactments. This flouts Mr. Chief Justice Taft's admonition "that amendment may not be substituted for construction, and that a court may not exercise legislative functions to save [a] law from conflict with constitutional limitation." *Yu Cong Eng* v. *Trinidad,* 271 U. S. 500, 518 (1926). See *Aptheker* v. *Secretary of State,* 378 U. S. 500, 515 (1964); *Jay* v. *Boyd,* 351 U. S. 345, 357 n. 21 (1956); *Shapiro* v. *United States,* 335 U. S. 1, 31, and n. 40 (1948); *United States* v. *Sullivan,* 332 U. S. 689, 693 (1948); *Hopkins Savings Assn.* v. *Cleary,* 296 U. S. 315, 335 (1935).[1]

---

[1] The Court's new canon derives from the statement, " 'there must be present the affirmative intention of the Congress clearly expressed,' " in *McCulloch* v. *Sociedad Nacional de Marineros de Honduras,* 372 U. S. 10, 21–22 (1963). Reliance upon that case here is clearly misplaced. The question in *McCulloch* was whether the National Labor Relations Act extended to foreign seamen working aboard foreign-flag vessels. No question as to the constitutional power of Congress to cover foreign crews was presented. Indeed, all parties agreed that Congress was constitutionally empowered to reach the foreign seamen involved while they were in American waters. *Id.,* at 17. The only question was whether Congress had intended to do so.

The *McCulloch* Court held that Congress had not meant to reach disputes between foreign shipowners and their foreign crews. *McCulloch,* however, did not turn simply upon an absence of affirmative evidence that Congress wanted to reach alien seamen, but rather upon the fact, as a prior case had already held, that the legislative history " 'inescapably describe[d] the boundaries of the Act as including only the workingmen of

The settled canon for construing statutes wherein constitutional questions may lurk was stated in *Machinists* v. *Street,* 367 U. S. 740 (1961), cited by the Court, *ante,* at 500:

> " 'When the validity of an act of the Congress is drawn in question, and even if a serious doubt of constitutionality is raised, it is a cardinal principle that this Court will first ascertain whether a construction of the statute is *fairly possible* by which the question may be avoided.' *Crowell* v. *Benson,* 285 U. S. 22, 62." *Id.,* at 749–750 (emphasis added).[2]

Accord, *Pernell* v. *Southall Realty,* 416 U. S. 363, 365 (1974); *Johnson* v. *Robison,* 415 U. S. 361, 367 (1974); *Curtis* v. *Loether,* 415 U. S. 189, 192 n. 6 (1974); *Ashwander* v. *TVA,* 297 U. S. 288, 348 (1936) (Brandeis, J., concurring); *Moore Ice Cream Co.* v. *Rose,* 289 U. S. 373, 379 (1933). This limitation to constructions that are "fairly possible," and "reasonable," see *Yu Cong Eng* v. *Trinidad, supra,* at 518, acts as a

---

our own country and its possessions,' " *Id.,* at 18, quoting *Benz* v. *Compania Naviera Hidalgo,* 353 U. S. 138, 144 (1957). The Court also noted that under well-established rules of international law, "the law of the flag state ordinarily governs the internal affairs of a ship. See *Wildenhus's Case,* [120 U. S. 1,] 12." 372 U. S., at 21. In light of that contrary legislative history and domestic and international precedent, it is not at all surprising that *McCulloch* balked at holding foreign seamen covered without a strong affirmative showing of congressional intent. As the Court today admits, there is no such contrary legislative history or precedent with respect to jurisdiction over church-operated schools. *Ante,* at 504. The *McCulloch* statement, therefore, has no role to play in this case.

[2] In *Street,* the Court construed the Railway Labor Act as not permitting the use of an employee's compulsorily checked-off union dues for political causes with which he disagreed. As in *McCulloch,* see n. 1, *supra,* it so held not because of an absence of affirmative evidence that Congress *did* mean to permit such uses, but rather because the language and history of the Act indicated affirmatively that Congress *did not* mean to permit such constitutionally questionable practices. See 367 U. S., at 765–770.

brake against wholesale judicial dismemberment of congressional enactments. It confines the judiciary to its proper role in construing statutes, which is to interpret them so as to give effect to congressional intention. The Court's new "affirmative expression" rule releases that brake.

II

The interpretation of the National Labor Relations Act announced by the Court today is not "fairly possible." The Act's wording, its legislative history, and the Court's own precedents leave "the intention of the Congress . . . revealed too distinctly to permit us to ignore it because of mere misgivings as to power." *Moore Ice Cream Co.* v. *Rose, supra,* at 379. Section 2 (2) of the Act, 29 U. S. C. § 152 (2), defines "employer" as

> ". . . any person acting as an agent of an employer, directly or indirectly, *but shall not include* the United States or any wholly owned Government corporation, or any Federal Reserve Bank, or any State or political subdivision thereof, or any person subject to the Railway Labor Act, as amended from time to time, or any labor organization (other than when acting as an employer), or anyone acting in the capacity of officer or agent of such labor organization." (Emphasis added.)

Thus, the Act covers all employers not within the eight express exceptions. The Court today substitutes amendment for construction to insert one more exception—for church-operated schools. This is a particularly transparent violation of the judicial role: The legislative history reveals that Congress itself considered and rejected a very similar amendment.

The pertinent legislative history of the NLRA begins with the Wagner Act of 1935, 49 Stat. 449. Section 2 (2) of that Act, identical in all relevant respects to the current section, excluded from its coverage neither church-operated schools nor any other private nonprofit organization.[3] Accordingly, in applying that Act, the National Labor Relations Board did not recognize an exception for nonprofit employers, even when religiously associated.[4] An argument for an implied nonprofit exemption was rejected because the design of the Act was as clear then as it is now: "[N]either charitable institutions nor their employees are exempted from operation of the Act by its terms, although certain other employers and employees are exempted." *Central Dispensary & Emergency Hospital,* 44 N. L. R. B. 533, 540 (1942) (footnotes omitted), enf'd, 79 U. S. App. D. C. 274, 145 F. 2d 852 (1944). Both the lower courts and this Court concurred in the Board's construction. See *Polish National Alliance* v. *NLRB,* 322 U. S. 643 (1944), aff'g 136 F. 2d 175 (CA7 1943); *Associated Press* v. *NLRB,* 301 U. S. 103 (1937), aff'g 85 F. 2d 56 (CA2 1936); *NLRB* v. *Central Dispensary & Emergency Hospital,* 79 U. S. App. D. C. 274, 145 F. 2d 852 (1944).

The Hartley bill, which passed the House of Representa-

---

[3] Section 2 (2), 49 Stat. 450, stated:

"The term 'employer' includes any person acting in the interest of an employer, directly or indirectly, but shall not include the United States, or any State or political subdivision thereof, or any person subject to the Railway Labor Act, as amended from time to time, or any labor organization (other than when acting as an employer), or anyone acting in the capacity of officer or agent of such labor organization."

[4] See *Christian Board of Publication,* 13 N. L. R. B. 534, 537 (1939), enf'd, 113 F. 2d 678 (CA8 1940); *American Medical Assn.,* 39 N. L. R. B. 385, 386 (1942); *Central Dispensary & Emergency Hospital,* 44 N. L. R. B. 533, 539 (1942), enf'd, 79 U. S. App. D. C. 274, 145 F. 2d 852 (1944); *Henry Ford Trade School,* 58 N. L. R. B. 1535, 1536 (1944); *Polish National Alliance,* 42 N. L. R. B. 1375, 1380 (1942), enf'd, 136 F. 2d 175 (CA7 1943), aff'd, 322 U. S. 643 (1944); *Associated Press,* 1 N. L. R. B. 788, 790, enf'd, 85 F. 2d 56 (CA2 1936), aff'd, 301 U. S. 103 (1937). In unpublished decisions, the Board also exercised jurisdiction over the YWCA and the Welfare & Recreational Association. See *Central Dispensary & Emergency Hospital,* 44 N. L. R. B., at 538 n. 8.

tives in 1947, would have provided the exception the Court today writes into the statute:

> "The term 'employer' . . . shall not include . . . any corporation, community chest, fund, or foundation organized and operated exclusively for *religious,* charitable, scientific, literary, or *educational* purposes, . . . no part of the net earnings of which inures to the benefit of any private shareholder or individual . . . ." (Emphasis added.) H. R. 3020, 80th Cong., 1st Sess., § 2 (2) (Apr. 18, 1947), reprinted in National Labor Relations Board, Legislative History of the Labor Management Relations Act, 1947, pp. 160–161 (hereinafter, 1947 Leg. Hist.).

But the proposed exception was not enacted.[5] The bill reported by the Senate Committee on Labor and Public Welfare did not contain the Hartley exception. See S. 1126, 80th Cong., 1st Sess., § 2 (2) (Apr. 17, 1947), 1947 Leg. Hist. 99, 102. Instead, the Senate proposed an exception limited to nonprofit hospitals, and passed the bill in that form. See H. R. 3020, 80th Cong., 1st Sess., § 2 (2) (Senate, May 13, 1947), 1947 Leg. Hist. 226, 229. The Senate version was accepted by the House in conference, thus limiting the exception

[5] A number of reasons were offered for the rejection of the Hartley bill's exception. Some Congressmen strongly opposed the exception, see 93 Cong. Rec. 3446 (1947) (remarks of Rep. Klein); some were opposed to additional exceptions to the Board's jurisdiction, see *id.,* at 4997 (remarks of Sen. Taft); and some thought it unnecessary, see H. R. Conf. Rep. No. 510, 80th Cong., 1st Sess., 32 (1947), 1947 Leg. Hist. 536. See generally *NLRB* v. *Wentworth Institute,* 515 F. 2d 550, 555 (CA1 1975) ("[P]erhaps the most obvious, interpretation of the rejection of the House exclusion would be that Congress meant to include nonprofit organizations [within the scope of the Act]"); Sherman & Black, The Labor Board and the Private Nonprofit Employer: A Critical Examination of the Board's Worthy Cause Exemption, 83 Harv. L. Rev. 1323, 1331–1337 (1970). But whatever the reasons, it is clear that an amendment similar to that made by the Court today was proposed and rejected in 1947.

for nonprofit employers to nonprofit hospitals. Ch. 120, 61 Stat. 136.[6]

Even that limited exemption was ultimately repealed in 1974. Pub. L. 93-360, 88 Stat. 395. In doing so, Congress confirmed the view of the Act expressed here: that it was intended to cover all employers—including nonprofit employers—unless expressly excluded, and that the 1947 amendment excluded only nonprofit hospitals. See H. R. Rep. No. 93-

---

[6] The Board's contemporaneous construction of the 1947 amendment was that only nonprofit hospitals were intended to be exempt. In 1950, for example, in asserting jurisdiction over a nonprofit religious organization, the Board stated:

"The Employer asserts that, as it is a nonprofit organization which is engaged in purely religious activities, it is not engaged in commerce within the meaning of the Act. We find no merit in this contention. . . . As this Board and the courts have held, it is immaterial that the Employer may be a nonprofit organization, or that its activities may be motivated by considerations other than those applicable to enterprises which are, in the generally accepted sense, commercial." *Sunday School Board of the Southern Baptist Convention,* 92 N. L. R. B. 801, 802.

It is true that in *Trustees of Columbia University,* 97 N. L. R. B. 424 (1951), the Board indicated that it would not exercise jurisdiction over nonprofit, educational institutions; but it expressly did so as a matter of discretion, affirming that the activities of the University did come within the Act and the Board's jurisdiction. *Id.,* at 425. That 1951 discretionary decision does not undermine the validity of the Board's determination in *Cornell University,* 183 N. L. R. B. 329 (1970), that changing conditions—particularly the increasing impact of such institutions on interstate commerce—now required a change in policy leading to the renewed exercise of Board jurisdiction. As we emphasized in *NLRB* v. *Weingarten, Inc.,* 420 U. S. 251, 265-266 (1975):

"To hold that the Board's earlier decisions froze the development of this important aspect of the national labor law would misconceive the nature of administrative decisionmaking. '"Cumulative experience" begets understanding and insight by which judgments . . . are validated or qualified or invalidated. The constant process of trial and error, on a wider and fuller scale than a single adversary litigation permits, differentiates perhaps more than anything else the administrative from the judicial process.' *NLRB* v. *Seven-Up Co.,* 344 U. S. 344, 349 (1953)."

1051, p. 4 (1974), reprinted in Senate Committee on Labor and Public Welfare, Legislative History of the Coverage of Nonprofit Hospitals under the National Labor Relations Act, 1974, p. 272 (Comm. Print 1974) (hereafter 1974 Leg. Hist.); 120 Cong. Rec. 12938 (1974), 1974 Leg. Hist. 95 (Sen. Williams); 120 Cong. Rec. 16900 (1974), 1974 Leg. Hist. 291 (Rep. Ashbrook).[7] Moreover, it is significant that in considering the 1974 amendments, the Senate expressly rejected an amendment proposed by Senator Ervin that was analogous to the one the Court today creates—an amendment to exempt nonprofit hospitals operated by religious groups. 120 Cong. Rec. 12950, 12968 (1974), 1974 Leg. Hist. 119, 141. Senator Cranston, floor manager of the Senate Committee bill and primary opponent of the proposed religious exception, explained:

> "[S]uch an exception for religiously affiliated hospitals would seriously erode *the existing national policy which holds religiously affiliated institutions generally such as* proprietary nursing homes, residential communities, and *educational facilities to the same standards as their nonsectarian counterparts.*" 120 Cong. Rec. 12957 (1974), 1974 Leg. Hist. 137 (emphasis added).

---

[7] The House Report stated: "Currently, the only broad area of charitable, eleemosynary, educational institutions wherein the Board does not now exercise jurisdiction concerns the nonprofit hospitals, explicitly excluded by section 2 (2) of the Act. . . . [T]he bill removes the existing Taft-Hartley exemption in section 2 (2) of the Act. It restores to the employees of nonprofit hospitals the same rights and protections enjoyed by the employees of proprietary hospitals and most all other employees." H. R. Rep. No. 93-1051, p. 4 (1974), 1974 Leg. Hist. 272. Similarly, Senator Williams, Chairman of the Senate Committee on Labor and Public Welfare, criticized the nonprofit-hospital exemption as "not only inconsistent with the protection enjoyed by proprietary hospitals and other types of health care institutions, but it is also inconsistent with the coverage of other nonprofit activities." 120 Cong. Rec. 12938 (1974), 1974 Leg. Hist. 95. See also 120 Cong. Rec. 16900 (1974), 1974 Leg. Hist. 291 (Rep. Ashbrook).

See also *ibid.* (Sen. Javits); 120 Cong. Rec. 12957 (1974), 1974 Leg. Hist. 138 (Sen. Williams).[8]

In construing the Board's jurisdiction to exclude church-operated schools, therefore, the Court today is faithful to neither the statute's language nor its history. Moreover, it is also untrue to its own precedents. "This Court has consistently declared that in passing the National Labor Relations Act, Congress intended to and did vest in the Board the fullest *jurisdictional* breadth constitutionally permissible under the Commerce Clause. See, *e. g., Guss* v. *Utah Labor Board,* 353 U. S. 1, 3; *Polish Alliance* v. *Labor Board,* 322 U. S. 643, 647–648; *Labor Board* v. *Fainblatt,* 306 U. S. 601, 607." *NLRB* v. *Reliance Fuel Oil Corp.,* 371 U. S. 224, 226 (1963) (emphasis in original). As long as an employer is within the reach of Congress' power under the Commerce Clause—and no one doubts that respondents are—the Court has held him to be covered by the Act regardless of the nature of his activity. See, *e. g., Polish National Alliance* v. *NLRB,* 322 U. S. 643 (1944) (nonprofit fraternal organization). Indeed, *Associated Press* v. *NLRB,* 301 U. S. 103 (1937), construed the Act to

[8] The Court relies upon the fact that the 1974 amendments provided that "[a]ny *employee* of a health care institution who is a member of . . . a bona fide religion . . . which has historically held conscientious objections to joining . . . labor organizations shall not be required to join . . . any labor organization as a condition of employment . . . ." 29 U. S. C. § 169 (emphasis added). This is, of course, irrelevant to the instant case, as no employee has alleged that he was required to join a union against his religious principles and not even the respondent employers contend that collective bargaining itself is contrary to their religious beliefs. Recognizing this, the Court has limited its inference from the amendment to the proposition that it reflects "congressional sensitivity to First Amendment guarantees." *Ante,* at 506. This is quite true, but its usefulness as support for the Court's opinion is completely negated by the rejection of the Ervin amendment, see text, *supra,* which makes clear the balance struck by Congress. While Congress agreed to exclude conscientiously objecting employees, it expressly refused to sanction an exclusion for all religiously affiliated employers.

cover editorial employees of a nonprofit news-gathering organization despite a claim—precisely parallel to that made here—that their inclusion rendered the Act in violation of the First Amendment.[9] Today's opinion is simply unable to explain the grounds that distinguish that case from this one.[10]

Thus, the available authority indicates that Congress intended to include—not exclude—lay teachers of church-operated schools. The Court does not counter this with evidence that Congress *did* intend an exception it never stated. Instead, despite the legislative history to the contrary, it construes the Act as excluding lay teachers only because Congress did not state explicitly that they were covered. In Mr. Justice Cardozo's words, this presses "avoidance of a

---

[9] *Associated Press* stated the employer's argument as follows:

"The conclusion which the petitioner draws is that whatever may be the case with respect to employees in its mechanical departments it must have absolute and unrestricted freedom to employ and to discharge those who, like Watson, edit the news, that there must not be the slightest opportunity for any bias or prejudice personally entertained by an editorial employee to color or to distort what he writes, and that the Associated Press cannot be free to furnish unbiased and impartial news reports unless it is equally free to determine for itself the partiality or bias of editorial employees. So it is said that any regulation protective of union activities, or the right collectively to bargain on the part of such employees, is necessarily an invalid invasion of the freedom of the press." 301 U. S., at 131.

[10] The Court would distinguish *Associated Press* on the ground that there the Court "[p]erceiv[ed] nothing to suggest that application of the Act would infringe First Amendment guarantees . . . [while h]ere, on the contrary, the record affords abundant evidence that the Board's exercise of jurisdiction . . . would implicate the guarantees of the Religion Clauses." *Ante,* at 507. But this is mere assertion. The Court does not explain *why* the press' First Amendment problem in *Associated Press* was any less substantial than the church-supported schools' First Amendment challenge here. In point of fact, the problems raised are of precisely the same difficulty. The Court therefore cannot square its judicial "reconstruction" of the Act in this case with the refusal to rewrite the same Act in *Associated Press.*

difficulty . . . to the point of disingenuous evasion." *Moore Ice Cream Co.* v. *Rose,* 289 U. S., at 379.[11]

III

Under my view that the NLRA includes within its coverage lay teachers employed by church-operated schools, the constitutional questions presented would have to be reached. I do not now do so only because the Court does not. See *Sierra Club* v. *Morton,* 405 U. S. 727, 755 (1972) (BRENNAN, J., dissenting). I repeat for emphasis, however, that while the resolution of the constitutional question is not without difficulty, it is irresponsible to avoid it by a cavalier exercise in statutory interpretation which succeeds only in defying congressional intent. A statute is not "a nose of wax to be changed from that which the plain language imports . . . ." *Yu Cong Eng* v. *Trinidad,* 271 U. S., at 518.

---

[11] Not even the Court's redrafting of the statute causes all First Amendment problems to disappear. The Court's opinion implies limitation of its exception to church-operated schools. That limitation is doubtless necessary since this Court has already rejected a more general exception for nonprofit organizations. See *Polish National Alliance* v. *NLRB,* 322 U. S. 643 (1944). But such an exemption, available only to church-operated schools, generates a possible Establishment Clause *question* of its own. *Walz* v. *Tax Comm'n,* 397 U. S. 664 (1970), does not put that question to rest, for in upholding the property tax exemption for churches there at issue, we emphasized that New York had "not singled out . . . churches as such; rather, it has granted exemption to all houses of religious worship within a broad class of property owned by nonprofit, quasi-public corporations . . . ." *Id.,* at 673. Like the Court, "at this stage of [my] consideration [I am] not compelled to determine whether the [Establishment Clause problem] is [as significant] as [I] would were [I] considering the constitutional issue." *Ante,* at 502. It is enough to observe that no matter which way the Court turns in interpreting the Act, it cannot avoid constitutional questions.

Syllabus

TRANS WORLD AIRLINES, INC. *v.* HARDISON ET AL.

CERTIORARI TO THE UNITED STATES COURT OF APPEALS FOR THE EIGHTH CIRCUIT

No. 75–1126. Argued March 30, 1977—Decided June 16, 1977*

Respondent Hardison (hereafter respondent) was employed by Trans World Airlines (TWA), petitioner in No. 75–1126, in a department that operated 24 hours a day throughout the year in connection with an airplane maintenance and overhaul base. Respondent was subject to a seniority system in a collective-bargaining agreement between TWA and the International Association of Machinists & Aerospace Workers (union), petitioner in No. 75–1385, whereby the most senior employees have first choice for job and shift assignments as they become available, and the most junior employees are required to work when enough employees to work at a particular time or in a particular job to fill TWA's needs cannot be found. Because respondent's religious beliefs prohibit him from working on Saturdays, attempts were made to accommodate him, and these were temporarily successful mainly because on his job at the time he had sufficient seniority regularly to observe Saturday as his Sabbath. But when he sought, and was transferred to, another job where he was asked to work Saturdays and where he had low seniority, problems began to arise. TWA agreed to permit the union to seek a change of work assignments, but the union was not willing to violate the seniority system, and respondent had insufficient seniority to bid for a shift having Saturdays off. After TWA rejected a proposal that respondent work only four days a week on the ground that this would impair critical functions in the airline operations, no accommodation could be reached, and respondent was discharged for refusing to work on Saturdays. Then, having first invoked the administrative remedy provided by Title VII of the Civil Rights Act of 1964, respondent brought an action for injunctive relief against TWA and the union, claiming that his discharge constituted religious discrimination in violation of § 703 (a)(1) of the Act, which makes it an unlawful employment practice for an employer to discriminate against an employee on the basis of his religion. He also made certain other charges against the union. His claim of religious discrimination was based on

*Together with No. 75–1385, *International Assn. of Machinists & Aerospace Workers, AFL–CIO, et al.* v. *Hardison et al.*, also on certiorari to the same court.

the 1967 Equal Employment Opportunity Commission (EEOC) guidelines in effect at the time requiring an employer, short of "undue hardship," to make "reasonable accommodations" to the religious needs of its employees, and on similar language in the 1972 amendments to Title VII. The District Court ruled in favor of both TWA and the union, holding that the union's duty to accommodate respondent's religious beliefs did not require it to ignore the seniority system, and that TWA had satisfied its "reasonable accommodations" obligation. The Court of Appeals affirmed the judgment for the union but reversed the judgment for TWA, holding that TWA had not satisfied its duty to accommodate respondent's religious needs under the EEOC guidelines. The court took the view that TWA had rejected three reasonable alternatives, any one of which would have satisfied its obligation without undue hardship: (1) Within the framework of the seniority system, TWA could have permitted respondent to work a four-day week, utilizing a supervisor or another worker on duty elsewhere, even though this would have caused other shop functions to suffer; (2) TWA could have filled respondent's Saturday shift from other available personnel, even though this would have involved premium overtime pay; and (3) TWA could have arranged a "swap" between respondent and another employee either for another shift or for the Sabbath days, even though this would have involved a breach of the seniority system. *Held:* TWA, which made reasonable efforts to accommodate respondent's religious needs, did not violate Title VII, and each of the Court of Appeals' suggested alternatives would have been an undue hardship within the meaning of the statute as construed by the EEOC guidelines. Pp. 76–85.

(a) The seniority system itself represented a significant accommodation to the needs, both religious and secular, of all of TWA's employees. Pp. 77–78.

(b) TWA itself cannot be faulted for having failed to work out a shift or job swap for respondent. Both the union and TWA had agreed to the seniority system; the union was unwilling to entertain a variance over the objections of employees senior to respondent; and for TWA to have arranged unilaterally for a swap would have breached the collective-bargaining agreement. An agreed-upon seniority system is not required to give way to accommodate religious observances, and it would be anomalous to conclude that by "reasonable accommodations" Congress meant that an employer must deny the shift and job preferences of some employees, as well as deprive them of their contractual rights, in order to accommodate or prefer the religious needs of others. Title VII does not require an employer to go that far. Pp. 79–81.

(c) Under § 703 (h) of Title VII, absent a discriminatory purpose, the operation of a seniority system cannot be an unlawful employment practice even if the system is discriminatory in its effect. Pp. 81–82.

(d) To require TWA to bear more than a *de minimis* cost in order to give respondent Saturdays off would be an undue hardship, for, like abandonment of the seniority system, to require TWA to bear additional costs when no such costs are incurred to give other employees the days off that they want would involve unequal treatment of employees on the basis of their religion. Absent clear statutory language or legislative history to the contrary, the statute, the paramount concern of which is to eliminate discrimination in employment, cannot be construed to require an employer to discriminate against some employees in order to enable others to observe their Sabbath. Pp. 84–85.

527 F. 2d 33, reversed.

WHITE, J., delivered the opinion of the Court, in which BURGER, C. J., and STEWART, BLACKMUN, POWELL, REHNQUIST, and STEVENS, JJ., joined. MARSHALL, J., filed a dissenting opinion, in which BRENNAN, J., joined, *post*, p. 85.

George E. Feldmiller argued the cause for petitioner in No. 75–1126. With him on the brief was *Dick H. Woods. Mozart G. Ratner* argued the cause for petitioners in No. 75–1385. With him on the briefs were *Plato E. Papps* and *Michael D. Gordon.*

William F. Pickett argued the cause for respondent Hardison in both cases. With him on the brief was *Thomas L. Hogan.*

Nathan Lewin argued the cause for the National Jewish Commission on Law and Public Affairs as *amicus curiae* urging affirmance. With him on the brief were *Dennis Rapps* and *Howard I. Rhine.*†

---

†Briefs of *amici curiae* urging reversal were filed by *William L. Hungate, Edwin D. Akers, Jr., Charles A. Newman,* and *A. William Rolf* for the Chrysler Corp.; and by *Jay S. Siegel, Robert E. Williams,* and *Douglas S. McDowell* for the Equal Employment Advisory Council.

Briefs of *amici curiae* urging affirmance were filed by *Acting Solicitor General Friedman, Assistant Attorney General Days, Deputy Solicitor General Wallace, Allan A. Ryan, Jr., Brian K. Landsberg, Dennis J.*

MR. JUSTICE WHITE delivered the opinion of the Court.

Section 703 (a)(1) of the Civil Rights Act of 1964, Title VII, 78 Stat. 255, 42 U. S. C. § 2000e–2 (a)(1), makes it an unlawful employment practice for an employer to discriminate against an employee or a prospective employee on the basis of his or her religion. At the time of the events involved here, a guideline of the Equal Employment Opportunity Commission (EEOC), 29 CFR § 1605.1 (b) (1968), required, as the Act itself now does, 42 U. S. C. § 2000e (j) (1970 ed., Supp. V), that an employer, short of "undue hardship," make "reasonable accommodations" to the religious needs of its employees. The issue in this case is the extent of the employer's obligation under Title VII to accommodate an employee whose religious beliefs prohibit him from working on Saturdays.

I

We summarize briefly the facts found by the District Court. 375 F. Supp. 877 (WD Mo. 1974).

Petitioner Trans World Airlines (TWA) operates a large maintenance and overhaul base in Kansas City, Mo. On June 5, 1967, respondent Larry G. Hardison was hired by TWA to work as a clerk in the Stores Department at its Kansas City base. Because of its essential role in the Kansas City operation, the Stores Department must operate 24 hours per day, 365 days per year, and whenever an employee's job in that department is not filled, an employee must be

---

Dimsey, and *Abner W. Sibal* for the United States et al.; by *Frank J. Kelley*, Attorney General, *Robert A. Derengoski*, Solicitor General, and *Michael A. Lockman* and *Gary G. Kress*, Assistant Attorneys General, for the State of Michigan; by *Beverly Gross* for the New York State Division of Human Rights; by *Joel M. Gora* and *Leo Pfeffer* for the American Civil Liberties Union; by *Mr. Pfeffer* for the Central Conference of American Rabbis et al.; by *Warren L. Johns* for the General Conference of Seventh-Day Adventists; and by *Ralph K. Helge* for the Worldwide Church of God.

shifted from another department, or a supervisor must cover the job, even if the work in other areas may suffer.

Hardison, like other employees at the Kansas City base, was subject to a seniority system contained in a collective-bargaining agreement[1] that TWA maintains with petitioner International Association of Machinists and Aerospace Workers (IAM).[2] The seniority system is implemented by the union steward through a system of bidding by employees for particular shift assignments as they become available. The most senior employees have first choice for job and shift assignments, and the most junior employees are required to work when the union steward is unable to find enough people willing to work at a particular time or in a particular job to fill TWA's needs.

In the spring of 1968 Hardison began to study the religion known as the Worldwide Church of God. One of the tenets of that religion is that one must observe the Sabbath by refraining from performing any work from sunset on Friday until sunset on Saturday. The religion also proscribes work on certain specified religious holidays.

When Hardison informed Everett Kussman, the manager of the Stores Department, of his religious conviction regarding

---

[1] The TWA-IAM agreement provides in pertinent part:

"The principle of seniority shall apply in the application of this Agreement in all reductions or increases of force, preference of shift assignment, vacation period selection, in bidding for vacancies or new jobs, and in all promotions, demotions, or transfers involving classifications covered by this Agreement.

"Except as hereafter provided in this paragraph, seniority shall apply in selection of shifts and days off within a classification within a department . . . ." App. 214.

[2] TWA is the petitioner in No. 75-1126. Petitioners in No. 75-1385 are the international, local, and district levels of IAM, hereinafter collectively referred to as IAM or the union.

observance of the Sabbath, Kussman agreed that the union steward should seek a job swap for Hardison or a change of days off; that Hardison would have his religious holidays off whenever possible if Hardison agreed to work the traditional holidays when asked; and that Kussman would try to find Hardison another job that would be more compatible with his religious beliefs. The problem was temporarily solved when Hardison transferred to the 11 p. m.–7 a. m. shift. Working this shift permitted Hardison to observe his Sabbath.

The problem soon reappeared when Hardison bid for and received a transfer from Building 1, where he had been employed, to Building 2, where he would work the day shift. The two buildings had entirely separate seniority lists; and while in Building 1 Hardison had sufficient seniority to observe the Sabbath regularly, he was second from the bottom on the Building 2 seniority list.

In Building 2 Hardison was asked to work Saturdays when a fellow employee went on vacation. TWA agreed to permit the union to seek a change of work assignments for Hardison, but the union was not willing to violate the seniority provisions set out in the collective-bargaining contract,[3] and Hardison had insufficient seniority to bid for a shift having Saturdays off.

A proposal that Hardison work only four days a week was rejected by the company. Hardison's job was essential, and on weekends he was the only available person on his shift to perform it. To leave the position empty would have impaired supply shop functions, which were critical to airline operations; to fill Hardison's position with a supervisor or an

[3] The union did have a Relief Committee organized to deal with the emergency problems of its members. The record reveals that in the past this Committee had been instrumental in arranging for temporary adjustments in work schedules to meet the needs of union members; but the record also reveals that the Relief Committee had almost never arranged permanent changes in work assignments and that Hardison never sought the assistance of that Committee.

employee from another area would simply have undermanned another operation; and to employ someone not regularly assigned to work Saturdays would have required TWA to pay premium wages.

When an accommodation was not reached, Hardison refused to report for work on Saturdays. A transfer to the twilight shift proved unavailing since that schedule still required Hardison to work past sundown on Fridays. After a hearing, Hardison was discharged on grounds of insubordination for refusing to work during his designated shift.

Hardison, having first invoked the administrative remedy provided by Title VII, brought this action for injunctive relief in the United States District Court against TWA and IAM, claiming that his discharge by TWA constituted religious discrimination in violation of Title VII, 42 U. S. C. § 2000e–2 (a)(1). He also charged that the union had discriminated against him by failing to represent him adequately in his dispute with TWA and by depriving him of his right to exercise his religious beliefs. Hardison's claim of religious discrimination rested on 1967 EEOC guidelines requiring employers "to make reasonable accommodations to the religious needs of employees" whenever such accommodation would not work an "undue hardship," 29 CFR § 1605.1 (1968), and on similar language adopted by Congress in the 1972 amendments to Title VII, 42 U. S. C. § 2000e (j) (1970 ed., Supp. V).

After a bench trial, the District Court ruled in favor of the defendants. Turning first to the claim against the union, the District Court ruled that although the 1967 EEOC guidelines were applicable to unions, the union's duty to accommodate Hardison's belief did not require it to ignore its seniority system as Hardison appeared to claim.[4] As for Hardison's

[4] The District Court voiced concern that if it did not find an undue hardship in such circumstances, accommodation of religious observances might impose " 'a priority of the religious over the secular' " and thereby raise significant questions as to the constitutional validity of the statute

claim against TWA, the District Court rejected at the outset TWA's contention that requiring it in any way to accommodate the religious needs of its employees would constitute an unconstitutional establishment of religion. As the District Court construed the Act, however, TWA had satisfied its "reasonable accommodations" obligation, and any further accommodation would have worked an undue hardship on the company.

The Court of Appeals for the Eighth Circuit reversed the judgment for TWA. 527 F. 2d 33 (1975). It agreed with the District Court's constitutional ruling, but held that TWA had not satisfied its duty to accommodate. Because it did not appear that Hardison had attacked directly the judgment in favor of the union, the Court of Appeals affirmed that judgment without ruling on its substantive merits.

In separate petitions for certiorari TWA and IAM contended that adequate steps had been taken to accommodate Hardison's religious observances and that to construe the statute to require further efforts at accommodation would create an establishment of religion contrary to the First Amendment of the Constitution. TWA also contended that the Court of Appeals improperly ignored the District Court's findings of fact.

We granted both petitions for certiorari. 429 U. S. 958 (1976). Because we agree with petitioners that their conduct was not a violation of Title VII,[5] we need not reach the other questions presented.

---

under the Establishment Clause of the First Amendment. 375 F. Supp. 877, 883 (WD Mo. 1974), quoting Edwards & Kaplan, Religious Discrimination and the Role of Arbitration Under Title VII, 69 Mich. L. Rev. 599, 628 (1971).

[5] Because the judgment in its favor was affirmed by the Court of Appeals, the union was a prevailing party below; and Hardison has not filed a petition for certiorari seeking to change that judgment. It may thus appear anomalous to have granted the union's petition for certiorari as well as that of TWA. But the union's view is that the judgment below

II

The Court of Appeals found that TWA had committed an unlawful employment practice under § 703 (a)(1) of the Act, 42 U. S. C. § 2000e–2 (a)(1), which provides:

> "(a) It shall be an unlawful employment practice for an employer—
>
> "(1) to fail or refuse to hire or to discharge any individual, or otherwise to discriminate against any individual with respect to his compensation, terms, conditions, or privileges of employment, because of such individual's race, color, religion, sex, or national origin."

The emphasis of both the language and the legislative history of the statute is on eliminating discrimination in employment; similarly situated employees are not to be treated differently solely because they differ with respect to race, color, religion, sex, or national origin.[6] This is true regardless of whether

---

against TWA seriously involves union interests, because the rationale of the Court of Appeals' opinion, as the union understands it, "necessarily and explicitly assumes that petitioner Unions are legally obligated to waive or vary provisions of their collective bargaining agreement in order to accommodate respondent Hardison's beliefs, if called upon by TWA to do so." Pet. for Cert. in No. 75–1385, p. 2. This would appear to be the position of Hardison and the EEOC in this Court. Since we reverse the judgment against TWA, we need not pursue further the union's status in this Court.

[6] See *McDonald* v. *Santa Fe Trail Transportation Co.*, 427 U. S. 273, 278–279 (1976); *Franks* v. *Bowman Transportation Co.*, 424 U. S. 747, 763 (1976); *McDonnell Douglas Corp.* v. *Green*, 411 U. S. 792, 800 (1973); *Griggs* v. *Duke Power Co.*, 401 U. S. 424, 429–430 (1971).

From the outset, Congress has said that "[t]he purpose of [Title VII] is to eliminate, through the utilization of formal and informal remedial procedures, discrimination in employment based on race, color, religion, or national origin." H. R. Rep. No. 914, 88th Cong., 1st Sess., 26 (1963). See 110 Cong. Rec. 13079–13080 (1964) (remarks of Sen. Clark). When Congress amended Title VII in 1972, it did not waver from its principal goal. While Congressmen differed on the best methods to eliminate discrimination in employment, no one questioned the desirability of

the discrimination is directed against majorities or minorities. *McDonald* v. *Santa Fe Trail Transportation Co.*, 427 U. S. 273, 280 (1976). See *Griggs* v. *Duke Power Co.*, 401 U. S. 424, 431 (1971).

The prohibition against religious discrimination soon raised the question of whether it was impermissible under § 703 (a)(1) to discharge or refuse to hire a person who for religious reasons refused to work during the employer's normal workweek. In 1966 an EEOC guideline dealing with this problem declared that an employer had an obligation under the statute "to accommodate to the reasonable religious needs of employees . . . where such accommodation can be made without serious inconvenience to the conduct of the business." 29 CFR § 1605.1 (1967).

In 1967 the EEOC amended its guidelines to require employers "to make reasonable accommodations to the religious needs of employees and prospective employees where such accommodations can be made without undue hardship on the conduct of the employer's business." 29 CFR § 1605.1 (1968). The EEOC did not suggest what sort of accommodations are "reasonable" or when hardship to an employer becomes "undue." [7]

---

seeking that goal. Compare H. R. Rep. No. 92-238 (1971) (majority report of the Committee of the Whole House), with *id.*, at 58 (minority report).

[7] The EEOC expressed the view that "undue hardship, for example, may exist where the employee's needed work cannot be performed by another employee of substantially similiar qualifications during the period of absence of the Sabbath observer," 29 CFR § 1605.1 (1968). This single example was by no means intended to be exhaustive. In substance, the EEOC left further definition of its guidelines to its review of "each case on an individual basis in an effort to seek an equitable application of these guidelines to the variety of situations which arise due to the varied religious practices of the American people." *Ibid.* The EEOC at that time did not purport to change the view expressed in its 1966 guidelines that work schedules generally applicable to all employees may not be unreasonable, even if they do not "operate with uniformity . . . upon

This question—the extent of the required accommodation—remained unsettled when this Court, in *Dewey* v. *Reynolds Metals Co.*, 402 U. S. 689 (1971), affirmed by an equally divided Court the Sixth Circuit's decision in 429 F. 2d 324 (1970). The discharge of an employee who for religious reasons had refused to work on Sundays was there held by the Court of Appeals not to be an unlawful employment practice because the manner in which the employer allocated Sunday work assignments was discriminatory in neither its purpose nor effect; and consistent with the 1967 EEOC guidelines, the employer had made a reasonable accommodation of the employee's beliefs by giving him the opportunity to secure a replacement for his Sunday work.[8]

In part "to resolve by legislation" some of the issues raised in *Dewey,* 118 Cong. Rec. 706 (1972) (remarks of Sen. Randolph), Congress included the following definition of religion in its 1972 amendments to Title VII:

> "The term 'religion' includes all aspects of religious observance and practice, as well as belief, unless an employer demonstrates that he is unable to reasonably accom-

---

the religious observances of [all] employees." The EEOC's present view, expressed in an *amicus curiae* brief filed in support of Hardison and the Court of Appeals' judgment, is now otherwise, at least to some extent.

[8] Judgment entered by an equally divided Court is not "entitled to precedential weight," *Neil* v. *Biggers,* 409 U. S. 188, 192 (1972). Our ruling in *Dewey* thus does not resolve the questions there presented. Other factors, as well, make the impact of *Dewey* inconclusive. The conduct alleged to be an unlawful employment practice occurred prior to the promulgation of the 1967 guidelines, and the Court of Appeals expressed the view that those guidelines should not be given retroactive effect. Also, an earlier ruling by an arbitrator was held to have conclusively resolved the religious discrimination question in favor of the employer. But see *Alexander* v. *Gardner-Denver Co.,* 415 U. S. 36 (1974). Finally, the employer in *Dewey* was not excused from a duty to accommodate; the Court of Appeals simply held that the employer had satisfied any obligation that it might have had under the statute.

modate to an employee's or prospective employee's religious observance or practice without undue hardship on the conduct of the employer's business." § 701 (j), 42 U. S. C. § 2000e (j) (1970 ed., Supp. V).

The intent and effect of this definition was to make it an unlawful employment practice under § 703 (a)(1) for an employer not to make reasonable accommodations, short of undue hardship, for the religious practices of his employees and prospective employees. But like the EEOC guidelines, the statute provides no guidance for determining the degree of accommodation that is required of an employer. The brief legislative history of § 701 (j) is likewise of little assistance in this regard.[9] The proponent of the measure, Senator Jennings

---

[9] Section 701 (j) was added to the 1972 amendments on the floor of the Senate. The legislative history of the measure consists chiefly of a brief floor debate in the Senate, contained in less than two pages of the Congressional Record and consisting principally of the views of the proponent of the measure, Senator Jennings Randolph. 118 Cong. Rec. 705–706 (1972).

The Congressional Record, 118 Cong. Rec. 706–713 (1972), also contains reprints of *Dewey* and *Riley* v. *Bendix Corp.*, 330 F. Supp. 583 (MD Fla. 1971), rev'd, 464 F. 2d 1113 (CA5 1972), as well as a brief synopsis of the new provision, which makes reference to *Dewey*, 118 Cong. Rec. 7167 (1972). The significance of the legislative references to prior case law is unclear. In *Riley* the District Court ruled that an employer who discharged an employee for refusing to work on his Sabbath had not committed an unfair labor practice even though the employer had not made any effort whatsoever to accommodate the employee's religious needs. It is clear from the language of § 701 (j) that Congress intended to change this result by requiring some form of accommodation; but this tells us nothing about how much an employer must do to satisfy its statutory obligation.

The reference to *Dewey* is even more opaque:

"The purpose of this subsection is to provide the statutory basis for EEOC to formulate guidelines on discrimination because of religion such as those challenged in *Dewey* v. *Reynolds Metals Company*, 429 F. 2d 325 (6th Cir. 1970), *Affirmed by an equally divided court*, 402 U. S. 689

Randolph, expressed his general desire "to assure that freedom from religious discrimination in the employment of workers is for all time guaranteed by law," 118 Cong. Rec. 705 (1972), but he made no attempt to define the precise circumstances under which the "reasonable accommodation" requirement would be applied.[10]

In brief, the employer's statutory obligation to make reasonable accommodation for the religious observances of its employees, short of incurring an undue hardship, is clear, but the reach of that obligation has never been spelled out by Congress or by EEOC guidelines. With this in mind, we turn to a consideration of whether TWA has met its obliga-

(1971)." 118 Cong. Rec. 7167 (1972). Clearly, any suggestion in *Dewey* that an employer may not be required to make *reasonable* accommodation for the religious needs of its employees was disapproved by § 701 (j); but Congress did not indicate that "reasonable accommodation" requires an employer to do more than was done in *Dewey,* apparently preferring to leave that question open for future resolution by the EEOC. See also n. 8, *supra.*

[10] Cases decided by the Courts of Appeals since the enactment of the 1972 amendments to Title VII similarly provide us with little guidance as to the scope of the employer's obligation. In circumstances where an employer has declined to take steps that would burden some employees in order to permit another employee or prospective employee to observe his Sabbath, the Fifth, Sixth, and Tenth Circuits have found no violation for failure to accommodate. *Williams* v. *Southern Union Gas Co.,* 529 F. 2d 483 (CA10 1976); *Reid* v. *Memphis Publishing Co.,* 521 F. 2d 512 (CA6 1975), cert. denied, 429 U. S. 964 (1976), pet. for rehearing pending, No. 75–1105; *Johnson* v. *U. S. Postal Service,* 497 F. 2d 128 (CA5 1974). But the Fifth and Sixth Circuits have also reached the opposite conclusion on similar facts. *Draper* v. *United States Pipe & Foundry Co.,* 527 F. 2d 515 (CA6 1975); *Cummins* v. *Parker Seal Co.,* 516 F. 2d 544 (CA6 1975), aff'd by equally divided Court, 429 U. S. 65 (1976); *Riley* v. *Bendix Corp.,* 464 F. 2d 1113 (CA5 1972). These apparent intra-Circuit conflicts may be explainable on the basis of the differing facts of each case, but neither the Fifth nor the Sixth Circuit has suggested a theory of decision to justify the differing results that have been reached.

tion under Title VII to accommodate the religious observances of its employees.

III

The Court of Appeals held that TWA had not made reasonable efforts to accommodate Hardison's religious needs under the 1967 EEOC guidelines in effect at the time the relevant events occurred.[11] In its view, TWA had rejected three reasonable alternatives, any one of which would have satisfied its obligation without undue hardship. First, within the framework of the seniority system, TWA could have permitted Hardison to work a four-day week, utilizing in his place a supervisor or another worker on duty elsewhere. That this would have caused other shop functions to suffer was insufficient to amount to undue hardship in the opinion of the Court of Appeals. Second—according to the Court of Appeals, also within the bounds of the collective-bargaining contract—the company could have filled Hardison's Saturday shift from other available personnel competent to do the job, of which the court said there were at least 200. That this would have involved premium overtime pay was not deemed an undue hardship. Third, TWA could have arranged a "swap between Hardison and another employee either for another shift or for the Sabbath days." In response to the assertion that this would have involved a breach of the senior-

[11] Ordinarily, an EEOC guideline is not entitled to great weight where, as here, it varies from prior EEOC policy and no new legislative history has been introduced in support of the change. *General Electric Co.* v. *Gilbert,* 429 U. S. 125, 140–145 (1976). But where "Congress has not just kept its silence by refusing to overturn the administrative construction, but has ratified it with positive legislation," *Red Lion Broadcasting Co.* v. *FCC,* 395 U. S. 367, 381–382 (1969) (footnote omitted), the guideline is entitled to some deference, at least sufficient in this case to warrant our accepting the guideline as a defensible construction of the pre-1972 statute, *i. e.,* as imposing on TWA the duty of "reasonable accommodation" in the absence of "undue hardship." We thus need not consider whether § 701 (j) must be applied retroactively to the facts of this litigation.

ity provisions of the contract, the court noted that it had not been settled in the courts whether the required statutory accommodation to religious needs stopped short of transgressing seniority rules, but found it unnecessary to decide the issue because, as the Court of Appeals saw the record, TWA had not sought, and the union had therefore not declined to entertain, a possible variance from the seniority provisions of the collective-bargaining agreement. The company had simply left the entire matter to the union steward who the Court of Appeals said "likewise did nothing."

We disagree with the Court of Appeals in all relevant respects. It is our view that TWA made reasonable efforts to accommodate and that each of the Court of Appeals' suggested alternatives would have been an undue hardship within the meaning of the statute as construed by the EEOC guidelines.

A

It might be inferred from the Court of Appeals' opinion and from the brief of the EEOC in this Court that TWA's efforts to accommodate were no more than negligible. The findings of the District Court, supported by the record, are to the contrary. In summarizing its more detailed findings, the District Court observed:

> "TWA established as a matter of fact that it did take appropriate action to accommodate as required by Title VII. It held several meetings with plaintiff at which it attempted to find a solution to plaintiff's problems. It did accommodate plaintiff's observance of his special religious holidays. It authorized the union steward to search for someone who would swap shifts, which apparently was normal procedure." 375 F. Supp., at 890–891.

It is also true that TWA itself attempted without success to find Hardison another job. The District Court's view was that TWA had done all that could reasonably be expected within the bounds of the seniority system.

The Court of Appeals observed, however, that the possibility of a variance from the seniority system was never really posed to the union. This is contrary to the District Court's findings and to the record. The District Court found that when TWA first learned of Hardison's religious observances in April 1968, it agreed to permit the union's steward to seek a swap of shifts or days off but that "the steward reported that he was unable to work out scheduling changes and that he understood that no one was willing to swap days with plaintiff." *Id.*, at 888. Later, in March 1969, at a meeting held just two days before Hardison first failed to report for his Saturday shift, TWA again "offered to accommodate plaintiff's religious observance by agreeing to any trade of shifts or change of sections that plaintiff and the union could work out . . . . Any shift or change was impossible within the seniority framework and the union was not willing to violate the seniority provisions set out in the contract to make a shift or change." *Id.*, at 889. As the record shows, Hardison himself testified that Kussman was willing, but the union was not, to work out a shift or job trade with another employee. App. 76–77.

We shall say more about the seniority system, but at this juncture it appears to us that the system itself represented a significant accommodation to the needs, both religious and secular, of all of TWA's employees. As will become apparent, the seniority system represents a neutral way of minimizing the number of occasions when an employee must work on a day that he would prefer to have off. Additionally, recognizing that weekend work schedules are the least popular, the company made further accommodation by reducing its work force to a bare minimum on those days.

B

We are also convinced, contrary to the Court of Appeals, that TWA itself cannot be faulted for having failed to work out a shift or job swap for Hardison. Both the union and TWA had agreed to the seniority system; the union was unwilling to entertain a variance over the objections of men senior to Hardison; and for TWA to have arranged unilaterally for a swap would have amounted to a breach of the collective-bargaining agreement.

(1)

Hardison and the EEOC insist that the statutory obligation to accommodate religious needs takes precedence over both the collective-bargaining contract and the seniority rights of TWA's other employees. We agree that neither a collective-bargaining contract nor a seniority system may be employed to violate the statute,[12] but we do not believe that the duty to accommodate requires TWA to take steps inconsistent with the otherwise valid agreement. Collective bargaining, aimed at effecting workable and enforceable agreements between management and labor, lies at the core of our national labor policy, and seniority provisions are universally included in these contracts. Without a clear and express indication from Congress, we cannot agree with Hardison and the EEOC that an agreed-upon seniority system must give way when necessary to accommodate religious observances. The issue is important and warrants some discussion.

[12] "This Court has long held that employee expectations arising from a seniority system agreement may be modified by statutes furthering a strong public policy interest." *Franks* v. *Bowman Transportation Co.*, 424 U. S., at 778. Cf. *Alexander* v. *Gardner-Denver Co.*, 415 U. S. 36 (1974). In *Franks* we held that it was permissible to award retroactive seniority to victims of past discrimination in order to implement the strong congressional policy of making victims of discrimination whole. *Franks* is not dispositive of the present case since here there is no evidence of past discrimination that must be remedied. Not only is the "make-whole" policy not present in this case, but, as we shall see, the strong congressional policy against discrimination in employment argues against interpreting the statute to require the abrogation of the seniority rights of some employees in order to accommodate the religious needs of others.

Any employer who, like TWA, conducts an around-the-clock operation is presented with the choice of allocating work schedules either in accordance with the preferences of its employees or by involuntary assignment. Insofar as the varying shift preferences of its employees complement each other, TWA could meet its manpower needs through voluntary work scheduling. In the present case, for example, Hardison's supervisor foresaw little difficulty in giving Hardison his religious holidays off since they fell on days that most other employees preferred to work, while Hardison was willing to work on the traditional holidays that most other employees preferred to have off.

Whenever there are not enough employees who choose to work a particular shift, however, some employees must be assigned to that shift even though it is not their first choice. Such was evidently the case with regard to Saturday work; even though TWA cut back its weekend work force to a skeleton crew, not enough employees chose those days off to staff the Stores Department through voluntary scheduling. In these circumstances, TWA and IAM agreed to give first preference to employees who had worked in a particular department the longest.

Had TWA nevertheless circumvented the seniority system by relieving Hardison of Saturday work and ordering a senior employee to replace him, it would have denied the latter his shift preference so that Hardison could be given his. The senior employee would also have been deprived of his contractual rights under the collective-bargaining agreement.

It was essential to TWA's business to require Saturday and Sunday work from at least a few employees even though most employees preferred those days off. Allocating the burdens of weekend work was a matter for collective bargaining. In considering criteria to govern this allocation, TWA and the union had two alternatives: adopt a neutral system, such as seniority, a lottery, or rotating shifts; or allocate days off in accordance with the religious needs of its employees. TWA would have had to adopt the latter in order to assure Hardison and others like him of getting the days off necessary for strict observance of their religion, but it could have done so only at the expense of others who had strong, but perhaps nonreligious, reasons for not working on weekends. There were no volunteers to relieve Hardison on Saturdays, and to give Hardison Saturdays off, TWA would have had to deprive another employee of his shift preference at least in part because he did not adhere to a religion that observed the Saturday Sabbath.

Title VII does not contemplate such unequal treatment. The repeated, unequivocal emphasis of both the language and the legislative history of Title VII is on eliminating discrimination in employment, and such discrimination is proscribed when it is directed against majorities as well as minorities. See *supra,* at 71–72. Indeed, the foundation of Hardison's claim is that TWA and IAM engaged in religious *discrimination* in violation of 703 (a)(1) when they failed to arrange for him to have Saturdays off. It would be anomalous to conclude that by "reasonable accommodation" Congress meant that an employer must deny the shift and job preference of some employees, as well as deprive them of their contractual rights, in order to accommodate or prefer the religious needs of others, and we conclude that Title VII does not require an employer to go that far.

(2)

Our conclusion is supported by the fact that seniority systems are afforded special treatment under Title VII itself. Section 703 (h) provides in pertinent part:

> "Notwithstanding any other provision of this subchapter, it shall not be an unlawful employment practice for an employer to apply different standards of compensation, or different terms, conditions, or privileges of em-

> ployment pursuant to a bona fide seniority or merit system . . . provided that such differences are not the result of an intention to discriminate because of race, color, religion, sex, or national origin . . . ." 42 U. S. C. § 2000e–2 (h).

"[T]he unmistakable purpose of § 703 (h) was to make clear that the routine application of a bona fide seniority system would not be unlawful under Title VII." *Teamsters* v. *United States*, 431 U. S. 324, 352 (1977). See also *United Air Lines, Inc.* v. *Evans*, 431 U. S. 553 (1977). Section 703 (h) is "a definitional provision; as with the other provisions of § 703, subsection (h) delineates which employment practices are illegal and thereby prohibited and which are not." *Franks* v. *Bowman Transportation Co.*, 424 U. S. 747, 758 (1976). Thus, absent a discriminatory purpose, the operation of a seniority system cannot be an unlawful employment practice even if the system has some discriminatory consequences.

There has been no suggestion of discriminatory intent in this case. "The seniority system was not designed with the intention to discriminate against religion nor did it act to lock members of any religion into a pattern wherein their freedom to exercise their religion was limited. It was coincidental that in plaintiff's case the seniority system acted to compound his problems in exercising his religion." 375 F. Supp., at 883. The Court of Appeals' conclusion that TWA was not limited by the terms of its seniority system was in substance nothing more than a ruling that operation of the seniority system was itself an unlawful employment practice even though no discriminatory purpose had been shown. That ruling is plainly inconsistent with the dictates of § 703 (h), both on its face and as interpreted in the recent decisions of this Court.[13]

---

[13] *Franks* v. *Bowman Transportation Co.*, is not to the contrary. In *Franks* we held that "once an illegal discriminatory practice occurring after the effective date of the Act is proved," 424 U. S., at 762, § 703 (h) does not bar an award of retroactive seniority status to victims of that

As we have said, TWA was not required by Title VII to carve out a special exception to its seniority system in order to help Hardison to meet his religious obligations.[14]

discriminatory practice. Here the suggested exception to the TWA–IAM seniority system would not be remedial; the operation of the seniority system itself is said to violate Title VII. In such circumstances, § 703 (h) unequivocally mandates that there is no statutory violation in the absence of a showing of discriminatory purpose. See *United Air Lines, Inc.* v. *Evans,* 431 U. S. 553, 558–560 (1977).

[14] Despite its hyperbole and rhetoric, the dissent appears to agree with—at least it stops short of challenging—the fundamental proposition that Title VII does not require an employer and a union who have agreed on a seniority system to deprive senior employees of their seniority rights in order to accommodate a junior employee's religious practices. This is the principal issue on which TWA and the union came to this Court. The dissent is thus reduced to (1) asserting that the statute requires TWA to accommodate Hardison even though substantial expenditures are required to do so; and (2) advancing its own view of the record to show that TWA could have done more than it did to accommodate Hardison without violating the seniority system or incurring substantial additional costs. We reject the former assertion as an erroneous construction of the statute. As for the latter, we prefer the findings of the District Judge who heard the evidence. Thus, the dissent suggests that through further efforts TWA or the union might have arranged a temporary or permanent job swap within the seniority system, despite the District Court's express finding, supported by the record, that "[t]he seniority provisions . . . precluded the possibility of plaintiff's changing his shift." 375 F. Supp., at 884. Similarly, the dissent offers two alternatives—sending Hardison back to Building 1 or allowing him to work extra days without overtime pay—that it says could have been pursued by TWA or the union, even though neither of the courts below even hinted that these suggested alternatives would have been feasible under the circumstances. Furthermore, Buildings 1 and 2 had separate seniority lists, and insofar as the record shows, a return to Building 1 would not have solved Hardison's problems. Hardison himself testified that he "gave up" his Building 1 seniority when he came to Building 2, App. 104, and that the union would not accept his early return to Building 1 in part "because the problem of seniority came up again." *Id.*, at 71. We accept the District Court's findings that TWA had done all that it could do to accommodate Hardison's religious beliefs without either incurring substantial costs or violating the seniority rights of other employees. See 375 F. Supp., at 891.

C

The Court of Appeals also suggested that TWA could have permitted Hardison to work a four-day week if necessary in order to avoid working on his Sabbath. Recognizing that this might have left TWA short-handed on the one shift each week that Hardison did not work, the court still concluded that TWA would suffer no undue hardship if it were required to replace Hardison either with supervisory personnel or with qualified personnel from other departments. Alternatively, the Court of Appeals suggested that TWA could have replaced Hardison on his Saturday shift with other available employees through the payment of premium wages. Both of these alternatives would involve costs to TWA, either in the form of lost efficiency in other jobs or higher wages.

To require TWA to bear more than a *de minimis* cost in order to give Hardison Saturdays off is an undue hardship.[15] Like abandonment of the seniority system, to require TWA to bear additional costs when no such costs are incurred to give other employees the days off that they want would involve unequal treatment of employees on the basis of their religion. By suggesting that TWA should incur certain costs in order to give Hardison Saturdays off the Court of Appeals would in effect require TWA to finance an additional Saturday off and then to choose the employee who will enjoy it on the basis of his religious beliefs. While incurring extra costs to secure a replacement for Hardison might remove the necessity of compelling another employee to work involun-

[15] The dissent argues that "the costs to TWA of either paying overtime or not replacing respondent would [not] have been more than *de minimis.*" *Post,* at 92 n. 6. This ignores, however, the express finding of the District Court that "[b]oth of these solutions would have created an undue burden on the conduct of TWA's business," 375 F. Supp., at 891, and it fails to take account of the likelihood that a company as large as TWA may have many employees whose religious observances, like Hardison's, prohibit them from working on Saturdays or Sundays.

tarily in Hardison's place, it would not change the fact that the privilege of having Saturdays off would be allocated according to religious beliefs.

As we have seen, the paramount concern of Congress in enacting Title VII was the elimination of discrimination in employment. In the absence of clear statutory language or legislative history to the contrary, we will not readily construe the statute to require an employer to discriminate against some employees in order to enable others to observe their Sabbath.

Reversed.

MR. JUSTICE MARSHALL, with whom MR. JUSTICE BRENNAN joins, dissenting.

One of the most intractable problems arising under Title VII of the Civil Rights Act of 1964, 42 U. S. C. § 2000e *et seq.*, has been whether an employer is guilty of religious discrimination when he discharges an employee (or refuses to hire a job applicant) because of the employee's religious practices. Particularly troublesome has been the plight of adherents to minority faiths who do not observe the holy days on which most businesses are closed—Sundays, Christmas, and Easter—but who need time off for their own days of religious observance. The Equal Employment Opportunity Commission has grappled with this problem in two sets of regulations, and in a long line of decisions. Initially the Commission concluded that an employer was "free under Title VII to establish a normal workweek . . . generally applicable to all employees," and that an employee could not "demand any alteration in [his work schedule] to accommodate his religious needs." 29 CFR §§ 1605.1 (a)(3), (b)(3) (1967). Eventually, however, the Commission changed its view and decided that employers must reasonably accommodate such requested schedule changes except where "undue hardship" would result—for example, "where the employee's needed work cannot be performed by another employee of substantially similar qualifications during the period of absence." 29 CFR § 1605.1 (b) (1976).[1] In amending Title VII in 1972 Congress confronted the same problem, and adopted the second position of the EEOC. Pub. L. 92–261, § 2(7), 86 Stat. 103, codified at 42 U. S. C. § 2000e (j) (1970 ed., Supp. V). Both before and after the 1972 amendment the lower courts have considered at length the circumstances in which employers must accommodate the religious practices of employees, reaching what the Court correctly describes as conflicting results, *ante,* at 75 n. 10. And on two occasions this Court has attempted to provide guidance to the lower courts, only to find ourselves evenly divided. *Parker Seal Co.* v. *Cummins,* 429 U. S. 65 (1976); *Dewey* v. *Reynolds Metals Co.,* 402 U. S. 689 (1971).

Today's decision deals a fatal blow to all efforts under Title VII to accommodate work requirements to religious practices. The Court holds, in essence, that although the EEOC regulations and the Act state that an employer must make reasonable adjustments in his work demands to take account of religious observances, the regulation and Act do not

[1] The Court's statement that in promulgating the second guidelines "[t]he EEOC . . . did not purport to change the view expressed in its 1966 guidelines that work schedules generally applicable to all employees may not be unreasonable," *ante,* at 72 n. 7, is incomprehensible. The preface to the later guidelines, 32 Fed. Reg. 10298 (1967), states that the "Commission hereby amends § 1605.1, Guidelines on Discrimination Because of Religion. . . . Section 1605.1 as amended shall read as follows . . . ." Thus the later guidelines expressly repealed the earlier guidelines. Moreover, the example of "undue hardship" given in the new guidelines and quoted in text makes clear that the Commission believed, contrary to its earlier view, that in certain instances employers would be required to excuse employees from work for religious observances.

In its decisions subsequent to the formulation of the guidelines, the Commission has consistently held that employers must accommodate Sabbath observances where substitute employees are available. Compare CCH EEOC Decisions (1973) ¶¶ 6060, 6154, with, *e. g.,* ¶¶ 6120, 6310, 6367.

really mean what they say. An employer, the Court concludes, need not grant even the most minor special privilege to religious observers to enable them to follow their faith. As a question of social policy, this result is deeply troubling, for a society that truly values religious pluralism cannot compel adherents of minority religions to make the cruel choice of surrendering their religion or their job. And as a matter of law today's result is intolerable, for the Court adopts the very position that Congress expressly rejected in 1972, as if we were free to disregard congressional choices that a majority of this Court thinks unwise. I therefore dissent.

I

With respect to each of the proposed accommodations to respondent Hardison's religious observances that the Court discusses, it ultimately notes that the accommodation would have required "unequal treatment," *ante,* at 81, 84–85, in favor of the religious observer. That is quite true. But if an accommodation can be rejected simply because it involves preferential treatment, then the regulation and the statute, while brimming with "sound and fury," ultimately "signif[y] nothing."

The accommodation issue by definition arises only when a neutral rule of general applicability conflicts with the religious practices of a particular employee. In some of the reported cases, the rule in question has governed work attire; in other cases it has required attendance at some religious function; in still other instances, it has compelled membership in a union; and in the largest class of cases, it has concerned work schedules.[2] What all these cases have in common is an employee who could comply with the rule only by violating what the employee views as a religious commandment. In each

[2] Many of the cases are collected in Annot., 22 ALR Fed. 580 (1975). For a perceptive discussion of the issues posed by the cases see Note, Accommodation of an Employee's Religious Practices Under Title VII, 1976 U. Ill. L. Forum 867.

instance, the question is whether the employee is to be exempt from the rule's demands. To do so will always result in a privilege being "allocated according to religious beliefs," *ante,* at 85, unless the employer gratuitously decides to repeal the rule *in toto.* What the statute says, in plain words, is that such allocations are required unless "undue hardship" would result.

The point is perhaps best made by considering a not altogether hypothetical example. See CCH EEOC Decisions (1973) ¶ 6180. Assume that an employer requires all employees to wear a particular type of hat at work in order to make the employees readily identifiable to customers. Such a rule obviously does not, on its face, violate Title VII, and an employee who altered the uniform for reasons of taste could be discharged. But a very different question would be posed by the discharge of an employee who, for religious reasons, insisted on wearing over her hair a tightly fitted scarf which was visible through the hat. In such a case the employer could accommodate this religious practice without undue hardship—or any hardship at all. Yet as I understand the Court's analysis—and nothing in the Court's response, *ante,* at 83 n. 14, 84 n. 15, is to the contrary—the accommodation would not be required because it would afford the privilege of wearing scarfs to a select few based on their religious beliefs. The employee thus would have to give up either the religious practice or the job. This, I submit, makes a mockery of the statute.

In reaching this result, the Court seems almost oblivious of the legislative history of the 1972 amendments to Title VII which is briefly recounted in the Court's opinion, *ante,* at 73–75. That history is far more instructive than the Court allows. After the EEOC promulgated its second set of guidelines requiring reasonable accommodations unless undue hardship would result, at least two courts issued decisions questioning, whether the guidelines were consistent with Title VII. *Dewey* v. *Reynolds Metals Co.,* 429 F. 2d 324 (CA6 1970), aff'd by equally divided Court, 402 U. S. 689 (1971); *Riley* v. *Bendix Corp.,* 330 F. Supp. 583 (MD Fla. 1971), rev'd, 464 F. 2d 1113 (CA5 1972). These courts reasoned, in language strikingly similar to today's decision, that to excuse religious observers from neutral work rules would "discriminate against . . . other employees" and "constitute unequal administration of the collective-bargaining agreement." *Dewey* v. *Reynolds Metals Co., supra,* at 330. They therefore refused to equate "religious discrimination with failure to accommodate." 429 F. 2d, at 335. When Congress was reviewing Title VII in 1972, Senator Jennings Randolph informed the Congress of these decisions which, he said, had "clouded" the meaning of religious discrimination. 118 Cong. Rec. 706 (1972). He introduced an amendment, tracking the language of the EEOC regulation, to make clear that Title VII requires religious accommodation, even though unequal treatment would result. The primary purpose of the amendment, he explained, was to protect Saturday Sabbatarians like himself from employers who refuse "to hire or to continue in employment employees whose religious practices rigidly require them to abstain from work in the nature of hire on particular days." *Id.,* at 705. His amendment was unanimously approved by the Senate on a roll-call vote, *id.,* at 731, and was accepted by the Conference Committee, H. R. Rep. No. 92–899, p. 15 (1972); S. Rep. No. 92–681, p. 15 (1972), whose report was approved by both Houses, 118 Cong. Rec. 7169, 7573 (1972). Yet the Court today, in rejecting any accommodation that involves preferential treatment, follows the *Dewey* decision in direct contravention of congressional intent.

The Court's interpretation of the statute, by effectively nullifying it, has the singular advantage of making consideration of petitioners' constitutional challenge unnecessary. The Court does not even rationalize its construction on this ground, however, nor could it, since "resort to an alternative construction to avoid deciding a constitutional question is appropriate only when such a course is 'fairly possible' or when the statute provides a 'fair alternative' construction." *Swain* v. *Pressley,* 430 U. S. 372, 378 n. 11 (1977). Moreover, while important constitutional questions would be posed by interpreting the law to compel employers (or fellow employees) to incur substantial costs to aid the religious observer,[3] not all accommodations are costly, and the constitutionality of the statute is not placed in serious doubt simply because it sometimes requires an exemption from a work rule. Indeed, this Court has repeatedly found no Establishment Clause problems in exempting religious observers from state-imposed duties, *e. g., Wisconsin* v. *Yoder,* 406 U. S. 205, 234–235, n. 22 (1972); *Sherbert* v. *Verner,* 374 U. S. 398, 409 (1963); *Zorach* v. *Clauson,* 343 U. S. 306 (1952), even when the exemption was in no way compelled by the Free Exercise Clause, *e. g., Gillette* v. *United States,* 401 U. S. 437 (1971); *Welsh* v. *United States,* 398 U. S. 333, 371–372 (1970) (WHITE, J., dissenting); *Sherbert* v. *Verner, supra,* at 422 (Harlan, J., dissenting); *Braunfeld* v. *Brown,* 366 U. S. 599, 608 (1961) (dictum); *McGowan* v. *Maryland,* 366 U. S. 420, 520 (1961) (opinion of Frankfurter, J.).[4] If the State does not establish

[3] Because of the view I take of the facts, see Part II, *infra,* I find it unnecessary to decide how much cost an employer must bear before he incurs "undue hardship." I also leave for another day the merits of any constitutional objections that could be raised if the law were construed to require employers (or employees) to assume significant costs in accommodating.

[4] The exemption here, like those we have upheld, can be claimed by any religious practitioner, a term that the EEOC has sensibly defined to include atheists, *e. g*, CCH EEOC Decisions (1973) ¶ 6316, see also *Young* v. *Southwestern Savings & Loan Assn.,* 509 F. 2d 140 (CA5 1975), and persons not belonging to any organized sect but who hold "'[a] sincere and meaningful belief which occupies in the life of its possessor a place parallel to that filled by the God of those admittedly qualifying for the exemption,'" CCH Employment Practices ¶ 6500, quoting *United States* v. *Seeger,* 380 U. S. 163, 176 (1965). The purpose and primary effect of requiring such exemptions is the wholly secular one of securing

religion over nonreligion by excusing religious practitioners from obligations owed the State, I do not see how the State can be said to establish religion by requiring employers to do the same with respect to obligations owed the employer. Thus, I think it beyond dispute that the Act does—and, consistently with the First Amendment, can—require employers to grant privileges to religious observers as part of the accommodation process.

II

Once it is determined that the duty to accommodate sometimes requires that an employee be exempted from an otherwise valid work requirement, the only remaining question is whether this is such a case: Did TWA prove that it exhausted all reasonable accommodations, and that the only remaining alternatives would have caused undue hardship on TWA's business? To pose the question is to answer it, for all that the District Court found TWA had done to accommodate respondent's Sabbath observance was that it "held several meetings with [respondent] . . . [and] authorized the union steward to search for someone who would swap shifts." 375 F. Supp. 877, 890–891 (WD Mo. 1974). To conclude that TWA, one of the largest air carriers in the Nation, would have suffered undue hardship had it done anything more defies both reason and common sense.

The Court implicitly assumes that the only means of accommodation open to TWA were to compel an unwilling employee to replace Hardison; to pay premium wages to a voluntary substitute; or to employ one less person during

---

equal economic opportunity to members of minority religions. Cf., *e. g., Lemon* v. *Kurtzman,* 403 U. S. 602 (1971). And the mere fact that the law sometimes requires special treatment of religious practitioners does not present the dangers of "sponsorship, financial support, and active involvement of the sovereign in religious activity," against which the Establishment Clause is principally aimed, *Walz* v. *Tax Comm'n,* 397 U. S. 664, 668 (1970).

respondent's Sabbath shift.[5] Based on this assumption, the Court seemingly finds that each alternative would have involved undue hardship not only because Hardison would have been given a special privilege, but also because either another employee would have been deprived of rights under the collective-bargaining agreement, *ante,* at 80–81, or because "more than a *de minimis* cost," *ante,* at 84, would have been imposed on TWA. But the Court's myopic view of the available options is not supported by either the District Court's findings or the evidence adduced at trial. Thus, the Court's conclusion cannot withstand analysis, even assuming that its rejection of the alternatives it does discuss is justifiable.[6]

---

[5] It is true that these are the only options the Court of Appeals discussed. But that court found that TWA could have adopted these options without undue hardship; once that conclusion is rejected it is incumbent on this Court to decide whether any other alternatives were available that would not have involved such hardship.

[6] I entertain grave doubts on both factual and legal grounds about the validity of the Court's rejection of the options it considers. As a matter of fact, I do not believe the record supports the Court's suggestion that the costs to TWA of either paying overtime or not replacing respondent would have been more than *de minimis.* While the District Court did state, as the Court notes, *ante,* at 84 n. 15, that both alternatives "would have created an undue burden on the conduct of TWA's business," 375 F. Supp., at 891, the court did not explain its understanding of the phrase "undue burden," and may have believed that such a burden exists whenever any cost is incurred by the employer, no matter how slight. Thus the District Court's assertion falls far short of a factual "finding" that the costs of these accommodations would be more than *de minimis.* Moreover, the record is devoid of any evidence documenting the extent of the "efficiency loss" TWA would have incurred had it used a supervisor or an already scheduled employee to do respondent's work, and while the stipulations make clear what overtime would have cost, the price is far from staggering: $150 for three months, at which time respondent would have been eligible to transfer back to his previous department. The Court's suggestion that the cost of accommodation must be evaluated in light of the "likelihood that . . . TWA may have many employees whose religious observances . . . prohibit them from working on Satur-

To begin with, the record simply does not support the Court's assertion, made without accompanying citations, that "[t]here were no volunteers to relieve Hardison on Saturdays," *ante*, at 81. Everett Kussman, the manager of the department in which respondent worked, testified that he had made no effort to find volunteers, App. 136,[7] and the union stipulated that its steward had not done so either, *id.*, at 158.[8] Thus, contrary to the Court's assumption, there may have been one or more employees who, for reasons of either sympathy or personal convenience, willingly would have substi-

days or Sundays," *ante* at 84 n. 15, is not only contrary to the record, which indicates that only one other case involving a conflict between work schedules and Sabbath observance had arisen at TWA since 1945, Tr. 312–314, but also irrelevant, since the real question is not whether such employees exist but whether they could be accommodated without significant expense. Indeed, to the extent that TWA employed Sunday as well as Saturday Sabbatarians, the likelihood of accommodation being costly would diminish, since trades would be more feasible.

As a matter of law, I seriously question whether simple English usage permits "undue hardship" to be interpreted to mean "more than *de minimis* cost," especially when the examples the guidelines give of possible undue hardship is the absence of a qualified substitute, *supra*, at 85–86. I therefore believe that in the appropriate case we would be compelled to confront the constitutionality of requiring employers to bear more than *de minimis* costs. The issue need not be faced here, however, since an almost cost-free accommodation was possible.

[7] Wilbur Stone, Director of Industrial Relations, Technical Service, at TWA confirmed Kussman's testimony. App. 157–158. In its Response to Plaintiff's Suggested Findings of Fact, TWA conceded that it "did not attempt to find a replacement for plaintiff." App. in No. 74–1424 (CA6), p. 191, ¶ 3 (1).

[8] The Court relies, *ante*, at 78, on the District Court's conclusory assertion that "[a]ny shift or change was impossible within the seniority framework." 375 F. Supp., at 889. But the District Court also found that "TWA did not take part in the search for employees willing to swap shifts . . . and it was admitted at trial that the Union made no real effort." *Id.*, at 888. Thus, the District Court's statement concerning the impact of "the seniority framework" lends no support to the Court's assertion that there were no volunteers. See also n. 10, *infra*.

tuted for respondent on Saturdays until respondent could either regain the non-Saturday shift he had held for the three preceding months [9] or transfer back to his old department where he had sufficient seniority to avoid Saturday work. Alternatively, there may have been an employee who preferred respondent's Thursday-Monday daytime shift to his own; in fact, respondent testified that he had informed Kussman and the union steward that the clerk on the Sunday-Thursday night shift (the "graveyard" shift) was dissatisfied with his hours. *Id.*, at 70. Thus, respondent's religious observance might have been accommodated by a simple trade of days or shifts without necessarily depriving any employee of his or her contractual rights [10] and without

[9] Respondent lost the non-Sabbath shift when an employee junior to him went on vacation. The vacation was to last only two weeks, however, and the record does not explain why respondent did not regain his shift at the end of that time.

[10] If, as appears likely, no one senior to the substitute employee desired respondent's Sabbath assignment or his Thursday-Monday shift, then the substitute could have transferred to respondent's position without depriving anyone of his or her seniority expectations. Similarly, if, as also appears probable, no one senior to respondent desired the substitute's spot, respondent could have assumed it. Such a trade would not have deprived any employee of seniority expectations. The trade apparently still would have violated the collective-bargaining agreement, however, since the agreement authorized transfers only to vacant jobs. This is undoubtedly what the District Court meant when it found that "the seniority framework" precluded shift changes. See n. 8, *supra*. Indeed, the first time in the District Court's opinion that such a finding appears, it is preceded by the finding that "there were no jobs open for bid." 375 F. Supp., at 884.

Even if a trade could not have been arranged without disrupting seniority expectations TWA could have requested the Union Relief Committee to approve an exemption. The record reveals that the Committee's function was to ameliorate the rigidity of the system, App. 130, and that on at least one occasion it had approved a permanent transfer apparently outside the seniority system, *id.*, at 144.

imposing significant costs on TWA. Of course, it is also possible that no trade—or none consistent with the seniority system—could have been arranged. But the burden under the EEOC regulation is on TWA to establish that a reasonable accommodation was not possible. 29 CFR § 1605.1 (c) (1976). Because it failed either to explore the possibility of a voluntary trade or to assure that its delegate, the union steward, did so, TWA was unable to meet its burden.

Nor was a voluntary trade the only option open to TWA that the Court ignores; to the contrary, at least two other options are apparent from the record. First, TWA could have paid overtime to a voluntary replacement for respondent—assuming that someone would have been willing to work Saturdays for premium pay—and passed on the cost to respondent. In fact, one accommodation Hardison suggested would have done just that by requiring Hardison to work overtime when needed at regular pay. Under this plan, the total overtime cost to the employer—and the total number of overtime hours available for other employees—would not have reflected Hardison's Sabbath absences. Alternatively, TWA could have transferred respondent back to his previous department where he had accumulated substantial seniority, as respondent also suggested.[11] Admittedly, both options would have violated the collective-bargaining agreement; the former because the agreement required that employees working over 40 hours per week receive premium pay, and the latter because the agreement prohibited employees from trans-

[11] The Court states, *ante*, at 83 n. 14, that because of TWA's departmental seniority system, such a transfer "would not have solved Hardison's problems." But respondent testified without contradiction that had he returned to his previous department he would have regained his seniority in that department, and thereby could have avoided work on his Sabbath. App. 70–71. According to respondent, the only objection that was raised to this solution was that it violated the rule prohibiting transfers twice within six months. *Ibid.*

ferring departments more than once every six months. But neither accommodation would have deprived any other employee of rights under the contract or violated the seniority system in any way.[12] Plainly an employer cannot avoid his duty to accommodate by signing a contract that precludes all reasonable accommodations; even the Court appears to concede as much, *ante,* at 79. Thus I do not believe it can be even seriously argued that TWA would have suffered "undue hardship" to its business had it required respondent to pay the extra costs of his replacement, or had it transferred respondent to his former department.[13]

What makes today's decision most tragic, however, is not that respondent Hardison has been needlessly deprived of his livelihood simply because he chose to follow the dictates of his conscience. Nor is the tragedy exhausted by the impact it will have on thousands of Americans like Hardison who could be forced to live on welfare as the price they must pay for

---

[12] The accommodations would have disadvantaged respondent to some extent, but since he suggested both options I do not consider whether an employer would satisfy his duty to accommodate by offering these choices to an unwilling employee. Cf. *Draper* v. *United States Pipe & Foundry Co.*, 527 F. 2d 515 (CA6 1975) (employer does not discharge his duty to accommodate by offering to transfer an electrician to an unskilled position).

[13] Of course, the accommodations discussed in the text would have imposed some administrative inconvenience on TWA. Petitioners do not seriously argue, however, that this consequence of accommodation makes the statute violative of the Establishment Clause. Were such an argument to be made, our prior decision upholding exemptions from state-created duties, see *supra,* at 90, would provide a complete answer, since the exemptions we have sustained have placed not inconsiderable burdens on private parties. For example, the effect of excusing conscientious objectors from military conscription is to require a nonobjector to serve instead, yet we have repeatedly upheld this exemption. *E. g., Selective Draft Law Cases,* 245 U. S. 366, 389–390 (1918). See also *Gallagher* v. *Crown Kosher Market,* 366 U. S. 617, 627 (1961) (upholding law prohibiting private citizens from engaging in specified activities within a fixed distance from places of public worship).

worshiping their God.[14] The ultimate tragedy is that despite Congress' best efforts, one of this Nation's pillars of strength—our hospitality to religious diversity—has been seriously eroded. All Americans will be a little poorer until today's decision is erased.

I respectfully dissent.

[14] Ironically, the fiscal costs to society of today's decision may exceed the costs that would accrue if employers were required to make all accommodations without regard to hardship, since it is clear that persons on welfare cannot be denied benefits because they refuse to take jobs that would prevent them from observing religious holy days, see *Sherbert* v. *Verner*, 374 U. S. 398 (1963).

GOVERNMENT REGULATION OF RELIGION THROUGH LABOR AND EMPLOYMENT DISCRIMINATION LAWS*

David L. Gregory**

TABLE OF CONTENTS

I. *INTRODUCTION* 27
II. *THE FAILURE OF GOVERNMENT REGULATION TO PROTECT THE RELIGIOUS EMPLOYEE FROM DISCRIMINATION IN THE SECULAR WORKPLACE* 30
   A. Title VII: Reasonable Accommodation of the Employee, or the Employer's Undue Hardship 30
   B. The Further (Un)free Exercise of Religion: Loss of Employment and Loss of Eligibility for Unemployment Compensation Benefits 34
III. *GOVERNMENT REGULATION AND THE MANAGERIAL PREROGATIVES OF THE RELIGIOUS EMPLOYER* 35
   A. Labor Relations 37
   B. Religious Employer Exemption from Title VII 44
   C. Wage, Hour, and Workers' Disability Compensation Law 51
   D. Immigration Law 62
IV. *CONCLUSION* 65

I. INTRODUCTION

This Article will assess the policies, operations, and ramifications of government regulation of religion through labor and employment

---

* This Article is based on an address delivered at the "Seventh Annual National Conference on Labor and Employment Law: Critical Issues for 1992" held January 30-31, 1992 at Clearwater, Florida. This conference was presented by the Stetson University College of Law Center for Dispute Resolution.

** Professor of Law, St. John's University School of Law. B.A., The Catholic University of America, 1973; M.B.A., Wayne State University, 1977; J.D., University of Detroit, 1980; LL.M., Yale University, 1982; J.S.D., Yale University, 1987. Ralph Somma and Mark Varrichio, members of the Class of 1992 of St. John's University School of Law, provided excellent research assistance.

discrimination laws. Special attention will be devoted to elucidating Supreme Court and recent important federal appellate court decisions.

Recent decisions have left the individual religious employee, who is most often in need of effective protection against unlawful discrimination in secular employment on the basis of religion, largely bereft of constitutional and statutory safeguards. Meanwhile, the statist,[1] pro-management,[2] Burger/Rehnquist Supreme Court has repeatedly enhanced the managerial prerogatives of religious, institutional employers, essentially liberating these employers' labor and employment practices from government oversight.

The Burger/Rehnquist Court has consistently demonstrated inordinate judicial deference to institutional employer interests. Such deference has occurred at the expense of both the employee's constitutional right to the free exercise of religion in the workplace and the statutory right to be free from discrimination in employment on the basis of religion. The Supreme Court began this dramatic subordination of employee rights to the prerogatives of institutional employers in a series of important decisions beginning in 1977.[3] As the Burger and now Rehnquist Court matured, this activist, pro-institutional, statist jurisprudence became increasingly inimical to the severely debilitated First Amendment[4] and Title VII[5] rights of religious employ-

---

1. For commentary on the statist ideology of the Burger/Rehnquist Court, see Robert M. Cover, *The Supreme Court 1982 Term: Foreword: Nomos and Narrative*, 97 HARV. L. REV. 4 (1983); Rex E. Lee, *The Supreme Court's 1983 Term: Individual Rights, Freedom, and the Statue of Liberty*, 19 GA. L. REV. 1 (1984); Abner J. Mikva, *The Burger Court Evaluated: Some Good Marks from Unexpected Quarters*, 82 NW. U. L. REV. 808 (1988); Charles A. Reich, *The Individual Sector*, 100 YALE L.J. 1409 (1991).

2. I have previously analyzed the pro-management jurisprudence of the Burger/Rehnquist Court and of the Reagan National Labor Relations Board. *See generally* David L. Gregory, *Labor Contract Rejection in Bankruptcy: The Supreme Court's Attack on Labor in* NLRB v. Bildisco, 25 B.C.L. REV. 539 (1984); David L. Gregory & Raymond T. Mak, *Significant Decisions of the National Labor Relations Board, 1984: The Reagan Board 'Celebrates' The Fiftieth Anniversary of the National Labor Relations Act*, 18 CONN. L. REV. 7 (1985).

3. TWA v. Hardison, 432 U.S. 63 (1977).

4. "Congress shall make no law respecting an establishment of religion, or prohibiting the free exercise thereof . . . . " U.S. CONST. amend. I.

5. 42 U.S.C. § 2000e (1988). Title VII reads, in pertinent part:

(a) It shall be an unlawful employment practice for an employer

> (1) to fail or refuse to hire or to discharge any individual, or otherwise to discriminate against any individual with respect to his compensation, terms, conditions, or privileges of employment, because of such individual's race, color, religion, sex, or national origin . . . .

Id. § 2000e-2.

ees, provisions which theoretically were designed to promote free exercise of religion and to protect employees against unlawful employment discrimination on the basis of religion. The sharply polarized decisions of the Burger Court of the late 1970s are now simply accepted, largely without dissent, by virtually all of the members of the current Rehnquist Court. Several decisions by the Supreme Court and the courts of appeals between 1977 and 1992 illuminate both the most troubling jurisprudential diminutions of the free exercise and Title VII rights of individual religious employees and, correspondingly, the generally enhanced managerial discretion enjoyed when religion itself functions as the institutional employer in the secular workplace.[6]

Part II of this Article will analyze the textually demonstrable but functionally feeble protections for the religious employee in the secular workplace. The primary focus will be upon the unprotected employee and the salient case law that has dramatically debilitated Title VII of the Federal Civil Rights Act of 1964,[7] a statute designed to protect against discrimination in employment on the basis of, inter alia, the employee's religion. Concomitantly, the Supreme Court has largely vitiated the other major source of legal protections for the religious employee: the Free Exercise Clause of the First Amendment of the Constitution. The Supreme Court has consistently failed to protect the secular employment of the religious employee. Most recently, the Supreme Court has endorsed even the denial of unemployment compensation insurance eligibility of the employee terminated from secular employment for exercising purportedly protected religious observance.[8] Part II will chart this important chapter in the continuing tragedy of labor.

Part III will examine the significant prerogatives enjoyed by religion when it functions as the institutional employer. The contrast is

---

6. Although it falls beyond the scope of this Article, an interesting line of cases has begun to consider whether religious owners and senior managers of a secular employer may impose their religious norms upon subordinate employees. Thus far, Title VII has protected the subordinate employees. 42 U.S.C. § 2000e-2(a) (1988). *See* EEOC v. Townley Eng'g & Mfg. Co., 859 F.2d 610 (9th Cir. 1988), *cert. denied*, 489 U.S. 1077 (1989); Young v. Southwestern Sav. & Loan Ass'n, 509 F.2d 140 (5th Cir. 1975); State v. Sport & Health Club, Inc., 370 N.W.2d 844 (Minn. 1985), *appeal dismissed*, 478 U.S. 1015 (1986); *see generally* David L. Gregory, *The Role of Religion in the Secular Workplace*, 4 NOTRE DAME J.L. ETHICS & PUB. POL'Y 749 (1990); Laura S. Underkuffler, *"Discrimination" On the Basis of Religion: An Examination of Attempted Value Neutrality in Employment*, 30 WM. & MARY L. REV. 581 (1989).

7. 42 U.S.C. § 2000e (1988). *See supra* note 5.

8. Employment Div., Dep't of Human Resources v. Smith, 494 U.S. 872 (1990).

quite dramatic given the essentially unprotected religious employee in this employment regime. When the institutional, mainstream religion functions as the employer, its managerial prerogatives have been enhanced by government deregulation, especially through case law construction.

Is there any realistic chance of apprehending a specter of government regulation by undue intrusion into, or excessive entanglement of government with, religion through labor and employment discrimination laws? On the contrary! Deregulation, the public policy paradigm of the past decade, has been the prevailing motif as we approach the millennium. Only those employees of religious institutional employers who perform wholly secular functions and become irrevocably and systemically marginalized at the very bottom of workplace hierarchies have any realistic hope of receiving some passing judicial interest; thus these employees only occasionally obtain the bare protections of minimum wage or worker's disability compensation laws. Likewise, only marginalized and decidedly non-institutional religious employers who deliberately bear witness in opposition to the pernicious policies of the government (for example, those employers who consciously provide employment to undocumented aliens, because of the employers' principled deliberate disregard of immigration control laws) are at risk of intrusive and coercive government regulation.

This Article will conclude with a critical assessment of this current legal regime and its possible consequences for religion, the worlds of employment (and unemployment), and public policy.

II. THE FAILURE OF GOVERNMENT REGULATION TO PROTECT THE RELIGIOUS EMPLOYEE FROM DISCRIMINATION IN THE SECULAR WORKPLACE

A. Title VII: Reasonable Accommodation of the Employee, or the Employer's Undue Hardship

Trans World Airlines v. Hardison[9] marked the beginning of the contemporary Supreme Court's debilitation of employees' Title VII protections against unlawful discrimination on the basis of religion. Justice White wrote for the seven member Court majority, with Justices Brennan and Marshall in dissent.

Trans World Airlines ("TWA") hired Larry G. Hardison to work

9. 432 U.S. 63 (1977).

in TWA's Stores Department. The Stores Department was crucial to TWA's operations and therefore had to operate twenty-four hours per day, 365 days per year. Hardison was subject to a seniority system designed through a collective-bargaining agreement that TWA negotiated with the International Association of Machinists and Aerospace Workers, the union which represented Hardison's bargaining unit. Under the labor agreement, the most senior employees had first choice for job and shift assignments. In the spring of 1968, Hardison joined the Worldwide Church of God, which forbade its Sabbatarian[10] members to work on the Sabbath and proscribed work on specified religious holidays. Hardison informed his supervisor of his work schedule shift conflict with his Sabbath. The problem was temporarily resolved by transferring Hardison to a different area. Later, he voluntarily transferred back to an area where he did not have enough seniority to avoid working on his Sabbath. Hardison was asked to work, but he refused to report. After a hearing, Hardison was discharged for insubordination — refusing to work his designated shift. Hardison claimed that his discharge constituted unlawful religious discrimination in violation of Title VII of the Federal Civil Rights Act of 1964.

The Supreme Court held that TWA's discharge of Hardison did not violate Title VII. The Court explained that an employer must make reasonable accommodation of the religious needs of its employees. Based on the facts, however, the Court opined that TWA made reasonable efforts to accommodate Hardison's religious practices and Sabbath observance as required by Title VII. In addition, TWA had done all it reasonably could to accommodate the employee's religious practices within the bounds of the collective-bargaining agreement's seniority system. Therefore, stated the Court, the employer's duty to accommodate Hardison's religious observance and his refusal to work on his Saturday Sabbath did not require TWA to take steps inconsistent with the seniority system of the valid collective-bargaining agreement.

The Court placed great weight on the seniority system of the la-

---

10. *See* WEBSTER'S THIRD NEW COLLEGIATE DICTIONARY 1994 (1981). The term "Sabbatarian" refers to those who observe their Sabbath on Saturday. Anyone who observes a Sabbath, regardless of the day of the week on which it is observed, is also considered a Sabbatarian. There are well over one million non-Sunday Sabbatarians in the United States, including Jews, Muslims, Seventh-Day Adventists, and members of the World Wide Church of God. James A. Kushner, *Toward the Central Meaning of Religious Liberty: Non-Sunday Sabbatarians and the Sunday Closing Cases Revisited*, 35 Sw. L.J. 557, 558 n.5 (1981).

bor contract. While the Court recognized that religious observances are a reality, religious low-seniority employees cannot always get first choice of shifts in order to remain observant. If there are not enough employees to work Saturdays, the seniority system in this particular collective-bargaining agreement made seniority the determinative factor in shift/days-off assignments. Title VII does not stand for the proposition that the employer need deprive higher seniority employees of labor contract seniority and shift rights in order to accommodate junior employees' religious preferences. Neither the employer nor the labor union were required by Title VII to make special exception to the labor contract's seniority system in order to accommodate employees' religious obligations. The Court found that "to require TWA to bear more than de minimis cost in order to give Hardison Saturdays off is an undue hardship not required by Title VII."[11] The costs of giving junior employees days off to accommodate their religion, while abandoning or violating the labor contract's seniority system, would result in unequal treatment of employees on the basis of religion.

The dissent, written by Justice Marshall and joined by Justice Brennan, regarded the majority opinion as a fatal judicial blow to the Title VII statutory requirement to accommodate religious practices in the work place. Justice Marshall argued that accommodation should not be rejected simply because it involved unequal treatment. Title VII required employers to grant privileges as part of the accommodation process, and, according to the dissent, a huge carrier like TWA could have borne the burden of the extra costs without undue hardship.

With the *Hardison* decision, the employer's Title VII duty to reasonably accommodate the religious practices of the observant employee was utterly minimized by the Court. According to the Court's calculation, any accommodation measure of the employee by the employer that resulted in more than a "de minimis" cost to the employer was an unreasonable "undue hardship," and thus was not required of the employer by Title VII. This effective judicial relief of the employer from its statutory duty to reasonably accommodate the employee's religious observance was, if possible, made even more

11. "The term 'religion' includes all aspects of religious observance and practice, as well as belief, unless an employer demonstrates that he is unable to reasonably accommodate to an employee's or prospective employee's religious observance or practice without undue hardship on the conduct of the employer's business." 42 U.S.C. § 2000e(j) (1988).

complete by the 1986 Supreme Court decision of *Ansonia Board of Education v. Philbrook*.[12] In this decision, Chief Justice Rehnquist wrote for the seven member majority, and Justices Marshall and Stevens filed opinions concurring in part and dissenting in part.

Philbrook was employed by the Ansonia School Board since 1962 to teach business classes. In 1968, Philbrook was baptized into the Worldwide Church of God. The church required its members to refrain from working on designated holy days, which caused Philbrook to miss six school days per year. Pursuant to the collective-bargaining agreement between the school board and the teacher's union, teachers were granted three days of annual leave for observance of religious holidays. They could not, however, use any accumulated sick leave for religious observances. Philbrook used the three days contractually granted for religious holidays each year. Since Philbrook needed three more days off each year in order to observe his religion, he asked the school board either to adopt the policy of allowing use of three days of personal business for the purposes of religious observance or, in the alternative, to allow him to pay the cost of a substitute and receive full pay for additional days off for religious observances. The school board rejected Philbrook's alternative requests.

Philbrook sued, alleging that the prohibition on the use of "necessary personal business" leave for religious observance violated Title VII. He sought both damages and injunctive relief. Although it remanded the case for further factual findings, and thus did not issue a dispositive decision, the Court reiterated that the employer met its statutory obligations. Significantly, the employer is not required to acquiesce to the employee's most desired and most beneficial accommodation. As Chief Justice Rehnquist summarized:

> Thus, where the employer has already reasonably accommodated the employee's religious needs, the statutory inquiry is at an end. The employer need not further show that each of the employee's alternative accommodations would result in undue hardship. As *Hardison* illustrates, the extent of undue hardship on the employer's business is at issue only where the employer claims that it is unable to offer any reasonable accommodation without such hardship.[13]

Through these two important decisions, the Supreme Court es-

12. 479 U.S. 60 (1986).

13. *Id.* at 68-69. Case law continues to follow these precedents. *See, e.g.*, Ryan v. United States Dep't of Justice, 950 F.2d 458 (7th Cir. 1991) (FBI agent discharged for not investigating acts of civil disobedience against government policies).

sentially relieved the secular employer of its statutory duty to reasonably accommodate the religious employee; anything beyond de minimis cost caused by the employer's accommodation of the employee will be an "undue hardship" to the employer, which is beyond the employer's Title VII duty to reasonably accommodate the observations, practices, and beliefs of the religious employee.

B. The Further (Un)free Exercise of Religion: Loss of Employment and Loss of Eligibility for Unemployment Compensation Benefits

Employment Division, Department of Human Resources v. Smith,[14] decided by the Supreme Court in 1990, quickly became one of the most controversial (un)free exercise[15] of religion decisions in First Amendment religion clauses jurisprudence. *Smith* may have effectively ended the isolated line of free exercise decisions which had previously sustained eligibility for state unemployment compensation insurance benefits for those whose exercise of religion precluded continuation of employment.[16]

---

14. 494 U.S. 872 (1990). The decision immediately engendered a firestorm of very critical commentary. *See* Milner Ball, *The Unfree Exercise of Religion*, 20 CAP. U. L. REV. 39 (1991); James D. Gordon, *Free Exercise on the Mountaintop*, 79 CAL. L. REV. 91 (1991); David L. Gregory & Charles S. Russo, *Let Us Pray (But Not "Them"!): The Troubled Jurisprudence of Religious Liberty*, 65 ST. JOHN'S L. REV. 273 (1991); Michael W. McConnell, *A Response to Professor Marshall*, 58 U. CHI. L. REV. 329 (1991); Michael W. McConnell, *Free Exercise Revisionism and the Smith Decision*, 57 U. CHI. L. REV. 1109 (1990); Richard K. Sherwin, *Rhetorical Pluralism and the Discourse Ideal: Countering* Division of Employment v. Smith, *a Parable of Pagans, Politics, and Majoritarian Rule*, 85 NW. U. L. REV. 388 (1991); Steven D. Smith, *The Rise and Fall of Religious Freedom in Constitutional Discourse*, 140 U. PA. L. REV. 149 (1991); David E. Steinberg, *Religious Exemptions as Affirmative Action*, 40 EMORY L.J. 77 (1991); Danielle A. Hess, Note, *The Undoing Of Mandatory Free Exercise Accommodation*, 66 WASH. L. REV. 587 (1991); Kenneth Marin, Note, Employment Division v. Smith: *The Supreme Court Alters the State of Free Exercise Doctrine*, 40 AM. U. L. REV. 1431 (1991); Jennifer E. Bennett Overton, Note, *The Illusory Enforcement of First Amendment Freedom*: Employment Division, Department of Human Resources v. Smith *and the Abandonment of the Compelling Governmental Interest Test*, 69 N.C. L. REV. 1332 (1991); Tom C. Rawlings, Note, Employment Division, Department of Human Resources v. Smith: *The Supreme Court Deserts the Free Exercise Clause*, 25 GA. L. REV. 567 (1991). *But see* William P. Marshall, *The Case Against the Constitutionally Compelled Free Exercise Exemption*, 40 CASE. W. RES. L. REV. 357 (1990); William P. Marshall, *In Defense of* Smith *and Free Exercise Revisionism*, 58 U. CHI. L. REV. 308 (1991).

15. For the interesting concept of (un)free exercise of religion, I am indebted to Professor Milner Ball. *See* Ball, *supra* note 14.

16. *See* Frazee v. Illinois Dep't. of Employment Sec., 489 U.S. 829 (1989) (Christian refusing job requiring Sunday work could not be denied unemployment benefits under Free Exercise Clause); Hobbie v. Unemployment Appeals Comm'n, 480 U.S. 136 (1987) (Seventh-day Advent-

Alfred Smith and Galen Black were members of the Native American Church. They ingested peyote sacramentally during the religious ceremonies of their church. Consequently, they were terminated from their employment as drug and alcohol counselors at the Douglas County Council on Alcohol and Drug Abuse, a private, nonprofit rehabilitation center in Oregon. The state agency then denied them unemployment compensation benefits, based on the terminations for work-related misconduct.

Writing for the Court, Justice Scalia posited that the Court's precedents never held that an individual's religious practices relieved one from the duty to comply with a law prohibiting criminal conduct (in this case, drug use) that the state was free to regulate.[17] Further, he rejected the firmly entrenched compelling governmental interest test that heretofore had to be satisfied in order to sustain the constraint on the free exercise of religion.[18]

After *Smith*, the free exercise rights of the religious employee to retain employment or to obtain unemployment compensation benefits have been reduced to dependence upon the sufferance of the political majority. The Court has removed independent judicial protection of the free exercise rights of the religious employee in the secular workplace. The pernicious *Smith* decision encapsulates the major theme of Part II of this Article. The Supreme Court has stripped the individual religious employee of viable legal protections from employment discrimination on the basis of religion for the foreseeable future. The religious individual is at the dubious mercy of the secular employer and the pro-managerial legal regime.

III. GOVERNMENT REGULATION AND THE MANAGERIAL PREROGATIVES OF THE RELIGIOUS EMPLOYER

When a well-recognized, mainstream religious institution acts as the employer, the Supreme Court has been very deferential to the

---

ist discharged for refusing to work on Sabbath could not be denied unemployment compensation benefits under Free Exercise Clause); Thomas v. Review Bd., 450 U.S. 707 (1981) (Jehovah's Witness quitting employment because religious beliefs prevented him from producing weapons was entitled to unemployment compensation benefits under the Free Exercise Clause); Sherbert v. Verner, 374 U.S. 398 (1963) (Seventh-day Adventist need not agree to work on Sabbath to be eligible for unemployment compensation benefits). *But see* Thornton v. Caldor Inc., 472 U.S. 703 (1985) (Connecticut statute which granted religious employees absolute right not to work on their Sabbath violated Establishment Clause).

17. 494 U.S. at 878-79 (1990).

18. *Id.* at 886-87.

employer, often at the expense of the rights of employees. Those who advocate strict separation of church and state may see the Court's deference to the managerial prerogatives of the religious institutional employer as a violation of the Establishment Clause of the First Amendment.[19] That, obviously, is not a perspective recently shared by the current Court. The irony, of course, is that while this Court has increasingly "accommodated" government preferences for religion that would have been Establishment Clause violations during the Warren Court era, this Court has concomitantly vitiated the employer's Title VII duty to reasonably accommodate the religious employees' practices.

The internal labor relations of the religious employer generally will be free from the National Labor Relations Act ("NLRA") and the jurisdiction of the National Labor Relations Board ("NLRB"). The Court has made it virtually impossible for employees of religious employers to bargain collectively in a unionized context. The Court also has broadly interpreted the Title VII exemption for religious employers, thus enabling these employers to discriminate on the basis of otherwise protected classifications, in deference to the employer's religious doctrines.[20]

Fortunately, the religious employer has not had a complete carte

19. For extensive compilations of references to separationist and accommodationist theoreticians of Establishment Clause jurisprudence, see David L. Gregory, *The First Amendment Religion Clauses and Labor and Employment Law in the Supreme Court 1984 Term*, 31 N.Y.L. Sch. L. Rev. 1, 7-10 nn.14-15 (1986) [hereinafter Gregory, *First Amendment Religious Clauses*]; Gregory & Russo, *supra* note 14, at 290-91 nn.60-63.

20. Title VII provides, in pertinent part:

> Notwithstanding any other provision of this subchapter, (1) it shall not be an unlawful employment practice for an employer to hire and employ individuals, for an employment agency to classify, or refer for employment any individual, for a labor organization to classify its membership or to classify or refer for employment any individual, or for an employer, labor organization, or joint labor-management committee controlling apprenticeship or other training or retraining programs to admit or employ any individual in any such program, on the basis of his religion, sex, or national origin in those certain instances where religion, sex, or national origin is a bona fide occupational qualification reasonably necessary to the normal operation of that particular business or enterprise, and (2) it shall not be an unlawful employment practice for a school, college, university, or other educational institution or institution of learning to hire and employ employees of a particular religion if such school, college, university, or other educational institution or institution of learning is, in whole or in substantial part, owned, supported, controlled, or managed by a particular religion or by a particular religious corporation, association, or society, or if the curriculum of such school, college, university, or other educational institution or institution of learning is directed toward the propagation of a particular religion.

42 U.S.C. § 2000e-2(e) (1988).

blanche from the judiciary. When the religious employer is engaging in purely secular, commercial functions, the religious employer may, on those occasions, be subject to secular labor and employment discrimination law regulations. This has recently occurred, for example, in the context of federal courts of appeals mandating religious employers' compliance with the reporting requirements of the Immigration Reform and Control Act[21] and the minimum wage provisions of the Federal Fair Labor Standards Act.[22]

A. Labor Relations

In *NLRB v. Catholic Bishop*,[23] Chief Justice Burger, writing for a bare five-member majority of the Court, opined that the NLRB did not have jurisdiction to investigate unfair labor practice charges brought against the Catholic Bishop of Chicago. The Bishop was the employer of the complaining faculty members working in schools operated under the auspices of the Catholic Church.

The NLRA would have reduced the ability of the Catholic Church to avoid faculty unionization if this powerful institution had been subject to its mandates.[24] Although the Court majority expressed extreme sensitivity to the Free Exercise and Establishment Clauses of the First Amendment of the Constitution, it refrained from any substantive inquiry into the possible intersection of those clauses with labor law principles. Chief Justice Burger summarized:

> Accordingly, in the absence of a clear expression of Congress' intent to bring teachers in church-operated schools within the jurisdiction of the Board, we decline to construe the Act in a manner that could in turn call upon the Court to resolve difficult and sensitive questions arising out of the guarantees of the First Amendment Religion Clauses.[25]

The NLRB originally found that the Catholic Bishop, as the institutional employer of the lay faculty members at the schools oper-

---

21. 8 U.S.C. § 1324(a) (1988).
22. 29 U.S.C. §§ 201-219 (1988).
23. 440 U.S. 490 (1979). For critical commentary upon the decision, see David L. Gregory & Charles S. Russo, *Overcoming* NLRB v. Yeshiva Univ. *by the Implementation of Catholic Labor Theory*, 41 LABOR L.J. 55 (1990); David L. Gregory, *The Right to Unionize as a Fundamental Human and Civil Right*, 9 MISS. COLL. L. REV. 135 (1988) [hereinafter Gregory, *The Right to Unionize*]; David L. Gregory, *Catholic Labor Theory and the Transformation of Work*, 45 WASH. & LEE L. REV. 119 (1988) [hereinafter Gregory, *Catholic Labor Theory*].
24. 29 U.S.C. § 151 (1988).
25. 440 U.S. at 507.

ated under auspices of the Catholic Church, had violated the NLRA and had committed unfair labor practices by refusing to recognize or to bargain with the faculty union. In 1974 and 1975, separate representation petitions were filed with the NLRB by the faculty union. The Catholic Bishop challenged the assertion of jurisdiction by the NLRB. The court of appeals agreed with the Catholic Bishop. The Free Exercise and Establishment Clauses precluded the NLRB from exercising jurisdiction over the schools of the Catholic Church and over the Catholic Bishop as the institutional employer.

In a highly technical decision, which deliberately did not reach or address the underlying merits of the Bishop's unfair labor practices of refusing to recognize or to bargain with the faculty unions, the Supreme Court affirmed the decision of the Seventh Circuit. In his opinion for the majority of the Court, Chief Justice Burger pointed to the legislative history of the NLRA, which revealed nothing to indicate that church-operated schools would be within the jurisdiction of the NLRB. The Chief Justice referred specifically to the debate behind an amendment to the NLRA, which reflected certain First Amendment guarantees, and argued "the absence of an 'affirmative intention of the Congress clearly expressed' fortifies our conclusion that Congress did not contemplate that the Board would require church-operated schools to [recognize] unions as bargaining agents for their teachers."[26] The Supreme Court therefore affirmed the decision of the Seventh Circuit. While the Court recognized that the Board's jurisdiction was broad, it again pointed to the legislative history of the NLRA. Finding nothing in the legislative history which would endorse the Board jurisdiction sought by the faculty union in this case, the Court decided the Board must decline jurisdiction over labor law matters in church-operated schools. The alternative, noted the Court, would lead to mandatory bargaining, which in turn would cause too many conflicts with church administrators.[27]

In a powerful, sharp dissent by Justice Brennan, joined by Justices White, Marshall, and Blackmun, the majority opinion was characterized as a failed lesson in statutory construction. The dissent argued that the majority opinion failed to consider the NLRA's language and history. The dissent further asserted that the majority ignored its own precedents, which held that the jurisdiction of the NLRB is extremely broad. The dissent plainly would have included

26. *Id.* at 506 (quoting Benz v. Compania Navier Hidalgo, 353 U.S. 138, 147 (1957)).
27. *Id.* at 503-04.

church-operated schools within the jurisdiction of the Board.

In its 1991 decision of *NLRB v. Hanna Boys Center*,[28] the Ninth Circuit partially addressed the open question from *Catholic Bishop*: namely, whether the NLRB could constitutionally assert jurisdiction over any aspect of a church-operated school's work force.

Hanna Boys Center was a Roman Catholic owned and operated school for boys. It provided education and residential supervision for boys age ten through seventeen. Its articles of incorporation stated that its purpose included "mental, moral, physical, and spiritual training" of homeless or neglected boys, as well as providing for their "protection, care and education."[29] Control of Hanna was vested in a board of directors and an executive director. The board could include as many as forty-five members, only four of which could be clergy. The executive director was appointed by the President/Bishop of the Santa Rosa Diocese, subject to the approval of the board. The executive director formally need not be, but always had been, a priest. No employee or student of Hanna was required to be Roman Catholic or associated with any other religious organization. Hanna's students were required to attend chapel every morning for prayers and Mass on Sundays and Holy Days. The curriculum included a mandatory "moral guidance" class taught by nuns on the faculty. The court found that the Catholic faith "is woven thoroughly into the institution."[30]

The subject of the dispute involved a union's petition to the NLRB to represent lay non-faculty employees of Hanna: child-care workers, recreation assistants, cooks, cooks' helpers, and maintenance workers. This unit, as stipulated by the union and Hanna, voted in favor of representation. The NLRB upheld its regional director's assertion of jurisdiction. The Board ruled that *Catholic Bishop* did not prohibit jurisdiction over all employees of church-operated schools, but only over teachers employed by church-operated schools. The teaching function is much more closely involved with the promulgation and proselytization of the principles of Catholic doctrine than are the activities of food service and maintenance.[31] In order to ob-

28. 940 F.2d 1295 (9th Cir. 1991).

29. *Id.* at 1297.

30. *Id.* at 1304.

31. For other decisions recognizing the close relationship of the teaching function to the religion's mission, see Pime v. Loyola Univ., 803 F.2d 351 (7th Cir. 1986) (Jesuit Catholic University could reserve faculty tenure track opportunity for Jesuits, in order to preserve Jesuit Catholic character of institution); Maguire v. Marquette Univ., 627 F. Supp. 1499 (E.D. Wisc.

tain review of the NLRB's decision, Hanna refused to bargain with the Union. On appeal, Hanna argued that *Catholic Bishop* stood for the proposition that church-operated schools could not constitutionally fall, in any degree whatsoever, within the coverage of the NLRA or the jurisdiction of the NLRB. Hanna referred to the Supreme Court's finding that "Congress simply gave no consideration to church-operated schools."[32]

The Ninth Circuit explained that the ruling in *Catholic Bishop* was not as broad as Hanna had proposed: "[t]he facts of *Catholic Bishop* are confined to the Board's jurisdiction over teachers. Other employees of parochial schools, whether professional or 'blue collar,' are expressly excluded from the ruling."[33] The court of appeals explained that *Catholic Bishop* instead avoided the difficult constitutional questions that may arise if the NLRB had jurisdiction over teachers in church-operated schools, a decision "clearly founded on the 'unique role' of teachers in accomplishing the religious goals of the school."[34]

However, the appellate court proceeded to evaluate the duties of

---

1986) (First Amendment precludes inquiry by court of whether plaintiff is qualified to teach in the theology department); Dolter v. Wahlert High Sch., 483 F. Supp. 266 (N.D. Iowa 1980) (Catholic school can discharge pregnant unmarried teacher for violation of church teachings). *But see* Ohio Civil Rights Comm'n v. Dayton Christian Sch., Inc., 477 U.S. 619, 628 (1986) (state civil rights agency had jurisdiction to investigate pregnant teacher's complaint where her contract was not renewed due to church's view that mothers should stay home with preschool age children); EEOC v. Mississippi College, 626 F.2d 477 (5th Cir. 1980), *cert. denied*, 453 U.S. 912 (1981) (EEOC could investigate female professor's challenge under Title VII of college's practice of only male faculty teaching Bible courses). On August 15, 1990, Pope John Paul II promulgated an apostolic constitution on Catholic universities, entitled *Ex Corde Ecclesiae* (From the Heart of the Church). It requires the majority of faculty to be practicing Catholics and requires all other faculty to be respectful of Catholic doctrine. *See* Charles H. Wilson, *Ex Corde Ecclesiae: The New Apostolic Constitution for Catholic Universities*, 34 CATH. LAW. 17 (1991). For an examination of the intersection of Title VII and the employment status of clergy, see Daniel Abuhoff, *Title VII and the Appointment of Women Clergy: A Statutory and Constitutional Quagmire*, 13 COLUM. J.L. & SOC. PROBS. 256 (1977); Bruce N. Bagni, *Discrimination in the Name of the Lord: A Critical Evaluation of Discrimination by Religious Organizations*, 79 COLUM. L. REV. 1514 (1979). In 1991, the Executive Committee of the Association of American Law Schools adopted amendments to its Regulation 6.17 and now prohibits member law schools from discriminating in employment on the basis of sexual orientation. It remains to be seen whether any law schools with religious affiliations which continue to discriminate will be removed from AALS membership. *Discussion Forum on Issues Involving the Amendment of Executive Committee Regulation 6.17 Law Schools with a Religious Affiliation or Purpose*, ASS'N OF AM. L. SCH. ANN. MEETING PROC. (Jan. 5, 1992).

32. 940 F.2d at 1301.

33. *Id.*

34. *Id.* (quoting *Catholic Bishop*, 440 U.S. at 501).

Hanna's secular employees because "the rationale of *Catholic Bishop* would also support the exclusion from the Board's jurisdiction of other employment relationships if they involved the same constitutional problems inherent in the relationship between teachers and church-operated schools."[35]

The Ninth Circuit quickly rejected any suggestion that Hanna's recreation assistants, cooks, cooks' helpers, and maintenance workers could be characterized as "teachers" whose functions were "particularly involved with the accomplishment of the religious goals" of Hanna.[36] Regarding the child-care workers, the court found no indication that they were required to, or in fact did, "involve themselves in the religious or secular teaching" of the children. The court relied on the NLRB's findings that the role of the child-care workers was not "significantly involved with religion."[37] The NLRB described their duties as follows: " 'Child-care workers "shepherd" the boys from their cottages to chapel, supervise the boys in their cottages, and make sure the boys do their housekeeping chores and homework . . . , see that the boys say their prayers, and select a boy to say the evening prayer.' "[38] The job description listed one of the eight responsibilities of a child-care worker as " '[t]eaching values: ethical principles, religious observances.' "[39] The qualifications section contained no reference to religion. The court characterized the duties of the child-care workers as akin to those of a "dormitory monitor, an authority figure to supervise the entrants when they are not in class."[40] The court stated that the NLRB's findings were supported by the fact that Hanna had stipulated to the bargaining unit which included the child-care workers with the cooks and maintenance workers, suggesting that Hanna considered them to be similarly situated for labor relations purposes.

The court considered the constitutionality of the NLRB's exercise of jurisdiction over Hanna. The court analyzed this question under the classic three-part test announced in *Lemon v. Kurtzman*,[41] which held that to pass constitutional muster a statute must: (1) have a secular legislative purpose, (2) have a primary effect that neither

---

35. *Id.* at 1302.
36. *Id.*
37. *Id.*
38. *Id.* (quoting Hanna Boys Ctr., 284 N.L.R.B. 1080, 1083 (1987)).
39. *Id.* (quoting *Hanna*, 284 N.L.R.B. at 1083).
40. *Id.*
41. 403 U.S. 602, *reh'g denied*, 404 U.S. 876 (1971).

advances nor inhibits religion, and (3) not foster excessive government entanglement with religion. The court found Congress' purpose in enacting the NLRA to be "clearly secular — to minimize industrial strife by protecting employees' rights to organize and bargain collectively."[42] The court also found that the primary effect of the NLRA is to "require collective bargaining and reduce labor disruptions, rather than to promote or deter the acceptance or perpetuation of any religion."[43] Considering the "entanglement" prong, the court reiterated the three *Lemon* factors: "the character and purpose of the institution that is benefitted, the nature of the aid that the State provides, and the resulting relationship between government and the religious authority."[44]

First, the court determined that Hanna's primary purpose and character — to provide housing, education, and therapy to homeless or neglected boys — was secular. Second, the court decided that the nature of the activity affected by assertion of the NLRB's jurisdiction would not involve the NLRB in issues of theology. This was because the "religious mission and character" of Hanna was furthered, not by those in the disputed bargaining unit, but by priests, nuns, religious brothers, and professional workers who were excluded from any bargaining unit. Finally, the court concluded that the resulting relationship between the government and Hanna would only require government involvement with respect to specific charges filed by those in the disputed bargaining unit. It would not involve the Board in "continuing or systematic monitoring of the Church's activities and should not involve monitoring the religious aspects of Hanna's activities at all."[45] Thus, the court concluded that the minimal burden imposed on Hanna by the assertion of the NLRB's jurisdiction would not require the type of entanglement that would violate the Establishment Clause.

Hanna also argued that NLRB jurisdiction over those disputed employees would violate Hanna's right to free exercise of religion. The court noted that, after the parties had filed their briefs, the Supreme Court decided *Employment Division, Department of Human Resources v. Smith.*[46] *Smith* held that the Free Exercise Clause is not

42. 940 F.2d at 1303.
43. *Id.*
44. *Id.* (citing *Lemon*, 403 U.S. at 612-13).
45. *Id.* at 1304.
46. 494 U.S. 872 (1990).

violated if a law is generally applicable, does not have as its "object" the burdening of religion (thus having only an incidental effect on religious practices or beliefs), and does not give rise to a "hybrid claim" by violating a constitutional right in addition to free exercise of religion.[47]

The court found it unnecessary to consider *Smith* further, because it found that Hanna's free exercise claims "would not survive even the less restrictive *Sherbert* balancing test,"[48] which requires weighing three factors: (1) how much Board jurisdiction would interfere with the exercise of religious beliefs; (2) the existence of a compelling or overriding state interest justifying a burden on religious beliefs; and (3) whether accommodating those beliefs would unduly interfere with the fulfillment of the government interest.[49]

The Ninth Circuit held that the NLRB's jurisdiction would not interfere with the free exercise of religion of anyone at Hanna. "Catholic doctrine has no objection to unionization or collective bargaining."[50] Because the non-secular employees were not involved in the advancement of the church's religious mission, the court was convinced that NLRB involvement in labor disputes would be "confined to the secular aspects of Hanna's operations."[51] Weighing the compelling government interest in "promoting the peaceful settlement of industrial disputes" against the "minimal showing of any impact" on religious belief or practice, the court held that NLRB jurisdiction would not impermissibly interfere with Hanna's free exercise of religion. This 1991 decision from the Ninth Circuit is an interesting and important refinement of the unwarranted absolute principle of *Catholic Bishop*. While the core teaching function of, and the teaching employees within, the institutional religious employer when it functions as educator is not subject to the NLRA or to the jurisdiction of the NLRB, employees otherwise engaged in secular functions of the religious employer should have the protections of federal labor law. Teaching can be inextricably intertwined with doctrinal proselytization; non-teaching functions do not share such a close nexus with the doctrinal religious precepts.

---

47. 940 F.2d at 1305 (quoting *Smith*, 110 S. Ct. at 1601-02). *See supra* text accompanying notes 14-18.

48. *Id.*

49. *See* Sherbert v. Verner, 374 U.S. 398, 403 (1963).

50. *Id.* at 1306. In fact, Catholic doctrine and social teaching has powerfully supported the rights and dignity of all workers. *See* Gregory, *Catholic Labor Theory*, *supra* note 23.

51. 940 F.2d at 1306.

B. Religious Employer Exemption from Title VII

In 1987, the Supreme Court sustained without dissent the religiously-affiliated institutional employer's prerogative to summarily terminate competent, long-service employees, in *Corporation of Presiding Bishop v. Amos*.[52]

The Deseret Gymnasium was a nonprofit facility open to the public and operated by the Corporation of the Presiding Bishop of the Church of Jesus Christ of Latter-Day Saints and the Corporation of the President of the Church of Jesus Christ of Latter-Day Saints. Both of these are religious entities associated with an unincorporated religious association sometimes called the Mormon Church. Arthur Mayson worked at the Gymnasium for approximately sixteen years. He was discharged in 1981 because he failed to qualify for a temple recommend, a certificate that he was a member of the church and eligible to attend its temples. Mayson alleged that his discharge was unlawful discrimination on the basis of religion. The church maintained that section 702 of Title VII[53] shielded it from liability. Mayson argued that if this federal civil rights statute permitted religious employers to discriminate on religious grounds in their employment of persons for obviously non-religious, secular jobs, section 702 of Title VII then would unconstitutionally violate the Establishment Clause of the First Amendment.

The Supreme Court unanimously reversed the decision of the lower federal court, which had found in favor of the former employee-plaintiff. The Court examined whether section 702 of Title VII violated the Establishment Clause. Specifically, did the section 702 statutory exemption for the church from Title VII have the primary effect of unconstitutionally advancing religion, in violation of the Establishment Clause? The Court resolved the question in the negative.

---

52. 483 U.S. 327 (1987). For commentary on the decision, see Frederick M. Gedicks, *Toward a Constitutional Jurisprudence of Religious Group Rights*, 1989 Wis. L. Rev. 99; Jennifer M. Burman, Note, Corporation of Presiding Bishop v. Amos: *The Supreme Court and Religious Discrimination by Religious Educational Institutions*, 3 Notre Dame J.L. Ethics & Pub. Pol'y 629 (1988); Karen M. Crupi, Comment, *The Relationship Between Title VII and the First Amendment Religion Clauses: The Unconstitutional Schism of* Corporation of the Presiding Bishop v. Amos, 53 Alb. L. Rev. 421 (1989); Scott Klundt, Note, *Permitting Religious Employers to Discriminate on the Basis of Religion: Application to For-Profit Activities*, 1988 B.Y.U. L. Rev. 221; Scott D. McLure, Note, *Religious Preferences in Employment Decisions: How Far May Religious Organizations Go?*, 1990 Duke L.J. 587.

53. 42 U.S.C. § 2000e-2 (1988).

The Court measured the facts of the case, as well as the statute, against the Establishment Clause, using the multi-part *Lemon* test.[54] The Court concluded that, under the first prong of the *Lemon* test, it was permissible for Congress to attempt to minimize government involvement with religions' decisionmaking processes.[55] Under the second prong, the Court stated that a law is not necessarily unconstitutional simply because it allows churches to advance religion. In order to violate this prong, the Court reasoned that it would be necessary to show that the government itself had advanced religion through its own activities and influence. Finally, under the third prong of the *Lemon* test, the Court concluded that there was no unconstitutional entanglement raised by section 702 of Title VII.

Recent decisions by courts of appeals continue to follow the rationale of the Court in *Amos*. Religious employers consequently remain free from government regulation that would otherwise risk running afoul of the Establishment Clause's excessive entanglement prohibition.

In *Scharon v. St. Luke's Presbyterian Hospital*,[56] in 1991, the Eighth Circuit decided that a chaplain's age and sex discrimination claims against the church-affiliated hospital for which she worked could not be adjudicated in civil court without violating the First Amendment. The plaintiff, the Reverend Anne Scharon, an ordained Episcopal priest, was employed by the defendant St. Luke's Hospital as a chaplain in the Department of Pastoral Care. According to the

---

54. *See supra* text accompanying note 41.

55. 483 U.S. at 336 (citation omitted).

56. 929 F.2d 360 (8th Cir. 1991). For earlier cases exhibiting unwillingness to examine the institutional religious employer's treatment of clergy as ecclesiastical matters, see Serbian E. Orthodox Diocese for the United States and Can. v. Milivojevich, 426 U.S. 696 (1976); Rayburn v. General Conference of Seventh-day Adventists, 772 F.2d 1164 (4th Cir. 1985), *cert. denied*, 478 U.S. 1020 (1986); EEOC v. Southwestern Baptist Theological Seminary, 651 F.2d 277 (5th Cir.), *cert. denied*, 456 U.S. 905 (1981); McClure v. Salvation Army, 460 F.2d 553 (5th Cir.) (upholding dismissal of claim of sex discrimination brought by Salvation Army minister), *cert. denied*, 409 U.S. 896 (1972). *See also* David A. Fielder, Note, *Serving God or Caesar: Constitutional Limits on the Regulation of Religious Employers*, 51 Mo. L. Rev. 779 (1986). Of course, it remains to be seen if courts will manifest the same degree of reluctance to examine whether the religious employer has reasonably accommodated disabled clergy within the meaning of the Americans with Disabilities Act of 1990 ("ADA"). The accommodations required of employers by the ADA appear, at least in the statutory black letter, much more substantive than the de minimis standard of Title VII. Steven A. Holmes, *When The Disabled Face Rejection from Churches That Nurtured Them*, N.Y. Times, September 30, 1991, at A10 (After church refused to redesign church sanctuary to accommodate her wheel chair, Presbyterian associate minister with multiple sclerosis quit her position because she felt humiliated at having to be carried to the pulpit).

job description, some of the principal duties and responsibilities of a chaplain were to render " 'pastoral care, pastoral counseling . . . and liturgical services for persons in the hospital.' "[57] According to the job description, such work is seventy percent of a chaplain's duties. The court found that Scharon's duties were both religious and secular, and that, in addition to the counseling, she performed over 350 "religious solemn rites" in one nine-month period. In order to qualify for the position of chaplain, an applicant needed to have a Master of Divinity degree from an accredited seminary and be ordained and endorsed by a "religious faith group."[58] Scharon brought an action alleging that she was fired because of her age and her sex in violation of the Federal Age Discrimination in Employment Act[59] ("ADEA") and Title VII. St. Luke's Hospital maintained that Scharon was fired because her supervisor, also an ordained Episcopal priest, believed that she was "violating several canonical laws."[60] The supervisor terminated Scharon with the "advise and consent of the Episcopal Bishop."[61]

Using the three-part analytical approach developed by the Supreme Court in *NLRB v. Catholic Bishop*,[62] the court of appeals had to decide whether the application of the ADEA and Title VII to the case would create a serious constitutional problem, whether Congress intended the ADEA and Title VII to apply to the case, and whether the statutes could constitutionally be applied.

First, the court found that the claims asserted by Scharon would "without a doubt" give rise to serious constitutional questions. Second, the court found it clear that Title VII should apply to the employment relationship. The court, however, following the Supreme Court in *Catholic Bishop*, avoided the question of whether the ADEA was applicable; it found no language in the ADEA or in its legislative history to indicate congressional intent that the statute should be applied to a church-affiliated institution such as St. Luke's. The court's decision therefore focused on the third prong of *Catholic Bishop*: whether the ADEA and Title VII constitutionally could be applied to regulate the internal employment practices of the institutional religious employer. *Catholic Bishop* had simplisticly avoided the consti-

57. 929 F.2d at 361 (alteration in original).
58. *Id.*
59. 29 U.S.C. §§ 621-634 (1988).
60. 929 F.2d at 361.
61. *Id.*
62. 440 U.S. 490 (1979).

tutional issue, on the rationale that Congress had expressed no clear intention that the NLRB was to have jurisdiction over religious schools.

To decide the constitutional question, the court of appeals applied the three-part *Lemon* test.[63] The court summarily dismissed the first two parts of that inquiry and held that both the ADEA and Title VII have secular purposes, and that neither has the principal or primary effect of advancing or inhibiting religion. The court thus concluded that the case turned on whether applying Title VII and the ADEA to the present situation would require excessive government entanglement with religion.

The court described the "substantial religious character"[64] of St. Luke's hospital. The hospital's board of directors consisted of four church representatives. Its articles of association could only be amended with the approval of the Episcopal Diocese and the local Presbytery of the Presbyterian Church. The court accorded great weight to its findings that although the hospital could arguably be characterized as a secular institution, St. Luke's was "acting as a religious institution as Scharon's employer."[65] Furthermore, as the chaplain at the hospital, Scharon was "clergy."[66] "She was not a secular employee who happened to perform such religious duties; she was a spiritual employee who also performed some secular duties."[67] Scharon argued that the court could avoid excessive entanglement by adjudicating only the sex and age claims, and not the religious issues which she claimed were pretextual reasons for her discharge. Quoting *Catholic Bishop*, the court stated that " 'the resolution of such charges . . . will necessarily involve inquiry into the good faith of the position asserted by the clergy-administrators.' "[68] "It is not only the conclusions that may be reached which may impinge on the rights guaranteed by the Religion Clauses, but also the very process of the inquiry."[69] Therefore, the court of appeals concluded, "personnel decisions by church-affiliated institutions affecting clergy *are* per se religious matters"[70] and not reviewable by the civil courts. To do so

---

63. *See supra* text accompanying note 41.
64. 929 F.2d at 362.
65. *Id.*
66. *Id.*
67. *Id.*
68. *Id.* at 363 (alteration in original) (quoting *Catholic Bishop*, 440 U.S. at 502 (1979)).
69. *Id.*
70. *Id.*

would require the secular courts to interpret the meaning of religious doctrine and canonical law and determine whether such doctrine and law were properly applied in a particular case. The court added that "[t]his is precisely the kind of judicial second-guessing of decision-making by religious organizations the Free Exercise Clause forbids."[71]

The Third Circuit articulated a similar rationale in finding for the defendant Catholic Bishop of Pittsburgh in *Little v. Wuerl*.[72] The case considered whether Title VII applied to a Catholic school that discriminated against a non-Catholic lay teacher because her conduct did not conform to Catholic mores.

Susan Little, a Protestant, was hired by the St. Mary Magdalene Parish to teach elementary school children at its Roman Catholic school. While Little did not teach Catholic theology, she attended Catholic ceremonies with her pupils and participated in the school's seminars that were designed to "strengthen their ability to impart 'Catholic' values to students."[73] The employment contract contained a Cardinal's clause, which read: " 'Teacher recognizes the religious nature of the Catholic School and agrees that Employer has the right to dismiss a teacher for serious public immorality, public scandal, or public rejection of the official teachings, doctrine or laws of the Roman Catholic Church . . . . ' "[74] Just cause for termination was defined to include failure to comply with the terms and conditions of an employee policy handbook. The handbook states that an example of a violation of the Cardinal's Clause "would be the entry by a teacher into a marriage which is not recognized by the Catholic Church."[75]

During her employment at the Catholic school, Little was divorced and later remarried by a Justice of the Peace. After a one-year leave of absence, Little, a tenured teacher, was denied a contract renewal. The parties stipulated that Little was not rehired "because she had remarried . . . without pursuing the proper canonical process available from the Roman Catholic Church to obtain validation of her second marriage."[76] The Parish's pastor testified that he considered Susan Little's action in publicly rejecting the laws of the Church by marrying a Catholic without proper validation "[to be] a serious contradiction of the Church's teachings and laws on the indissolubil-

71. *Id.*

72. 929 F.2d 944 (3rd Cir. 1991).

73. *Id.* at 945.

74. *Id.* (quoting from the Parish's employment contract).

75. *Id.* at 946.

76. *Id.*

ity of Christian marriage and the sacramental nature of the marriage bond."[77] The Parish changed its policy two years prior to Little's application for renewal. The new policy favored hiring only Catholics and required any school hiring a non-Catholic to obtain special permission. The policy change did not apply to teachers such as Little who were already employed.

Little brought an action, claiming she had been denied employment on the basis of religion in violation of Title VII. The district court granted the Parish summary judgment. It found that the Parish's decision not to renew Little's employment contract was covered under the "religious organization" exemption to Title VII. The court of appeals considered Little's claims under the analysis of *Catholic Bishop*. The Third Circuit found that to apply the religious discrimination prohibition of Title VII to the Parish's decision would "raise substantial constitutional questions" because it would "arguably violate" the Free Exercise and Establishment Clauses of the First Amendment.[78] The circuit court combined the first and third prongs of *Catholic Bishop* in its analysis. The court noted that personnel decisions made by religious organizations affecting the ministers they employ are clearly within the religious organization exemption to Title VII. Furthermore, the court remarked that prohibition of religious discrimination "against non-minister employees where the position involved has any religious significance is uniformly recognized as constitutionally suspect, if not forbidden."[79] The court concluded that the Parish's free exercise rights would be "obviously endangered" if it were to review the decision not to renew Little's employment contract because the court would be forced to decide what constitutes the official doctrine of the Roman Catholic Church and whether the plaintiff rejected them.[80]

The court also found that application of Title VII's prohibition against religious discrimination to the Parish would be suspect because it would create excessive government entanglement with religion in violation of the Establishment Clause. Relying on *Catholic Bishop*, the court refused to conduct an inquiry into the claims asserted by the plaintiff, because to do so would require "[f]ederal court oversight" of the Parish's decision that would result in an in-

77. *Id.*

78. *Id.* at 947 (citing *Catholic Bishop*, 440 U.S. at 500-01).

79. *Id.* at 948.

80. *Id.*

vestigation into the employer's religious mission.[81] The process of review itself, the court held, might constitute excessive entanglement.

The court was faced with an interesting interpretive task. Title VII provides an exemption that permits religious educational organizations to hire and employ employees of a particular religion. The court was required to determine what it means to be "of a particular religion."[82] When the Parish hired Little, it was fully aware that she was a Protestant. Her religious affiliation never changed. Little could have plausibly argued, therefore, that the Parish's decision not to rehire her could not have been based upon whether she was "of a particular religion." The court found that Little was nonetheless refused reemployment because she was not "of a particular religion." The court looked to the Title VII, section 701(j) definition of religion, which states that the term religion "includes all aspects of religious observance and practice, as well as belief."[83] This definition is applicable to the exemption clauses as well as to the prohibition clauses. Although the court found no indication that Congress considered the effect of the definition on the exemption, it found that this broad definition was intended to be "solicitous of religious organizations' desire to create communities faithful to their religious principles."[84] Being of a "particular religion," the court held, "involves more than denominational affiliation[;] . . . it includes conduct considered by the employer or the employee to have religious significance."[85] Therefore, the court concluded that Title VII's exemption for religious organizations covered the Parish's decision not to rehire Little because of her remarriage, a marriage regarded by the Parish as "inconsistent with its religious principles."[86]

As the result of these salient Supreme Court decisions in *Catholic Bishop* and *Amos* and the courts of appeals decisions in their wake, neither the legal regimes nor religion has been enhanced. Rather, on both conceptual and practical levels, labor law doctrine, the First Amendment religion clauses, and Title VII protections

81. *Id.*

82. *Id.* at 950.

83. *Id.* (quoting 7 U.S.C. § 701(i) (1988)). For an excellent analysis of the meaning of "religion," see m. elisabeth bergeron, Note, *"New Age" or New Testament? Toward a More Faithful Interpretation of "Religion,"* 65 St. John's L. Rev. 365 (1991); *see also* Jesse H. Choper, *Defining "Religion" in the First Amendment*, 1982 U. Ill. L. Rev. 579; Kent Greenawalt, *Religion as a Concept in Constitutional Law*, 72 Cal. L. Rev. 753 (1984).

84. 929 F.2d at 950.

85. *Id.*

86. *Id.* at 951.

against discrimination in employment because of religion, have all been debilitated by the Court's jurisprudence. The only consistent "winner" in these cases has been the institutional religious employer. More significant and ominous is the Supreme Court's inexorable move to a pro-institutional, "statist" bias, thus effectuating an insidious calculus of interests that routinely subordinates individual employees who generally lack corporate institutional power and influence. It is ironic that religious employers emulate Caesar and take full advantage of this statist jurisprudence in order to insure the continued subordination of their employees and the debilitation of their employees' labor and employment discrimination law rights.[87] However, it is important to note that this has not invariably occurred when neutral regulations in federal immigration and federal minimum wage law have been at issue. In these cases, when the religious employer is engaged in overtly secular employment functions quite distinct from the religious mission, the employer has been generally held subject to the neutral regulations of the secular legal regime.

C. Wage, Hour, and Workers' Disability Compensation Law

In *Tony & Susan Alamo Foundation v. Secretary of Labor*,[88] the Supreme Court in 1985 placed a partial brake on what has otherwise been remarkable judicial deference to the managerial prerogatives of the religious employer. The Court unanimously affirmed that federal wage and hour laws protected employees engaged in the commercial, secular activities of the religious employer. The Alamo Foundation was a nonprofit religious organization incorporated under California law. Its professed primary mission was Christian evangelism and ac-

87. This allusion to Caesar refers to a story in the New Testament. During the life of Christ, the Pharisees, the elitest Jewish priests, constantly attempted to entrap him. On one occasion, they asked Jesus whether it was lawful to pay taxes to Caesar, knowing that if he answered "yes," he would speak blasphemy by acknowledging that homage was owing to a mere earthly leader. However, if he answered "no," he would be guilty of sedition against the Roman rulers.

Jesus frustrated the Pharisees' plan by asking whose image was engraved on the tribute money. When they answered that it was Caesar's, he responded, "Render to Caesar the things that are Caesar's, and to God the things that are God's." *Matthew* 22:15-22; *Mark* 12:13-17; *Luke* 20:20-26.

Religious employers emulate Caesar by demanding loyalty and conformity from employees in the name, but not the spirit, of religious doctrine. Thus, they use their status as religious institutions to consolidate their power over individuals, a goal which is repugnant to Judeo-Christian doctrine.

88. 471 U.S. 290 (1985).

tive corporal works of mercy to disadvantaged persons. The Foundation's income was generated from operating commercial businesses, ranging from service stations, hotels, farms, and construction companies to a candy producer and distributor. These businesses were staffed by 300 of the Foundation's "associates." They received minimal food, clothing, and shelter, but not cash wages or salaries. Most characterized themselves as religious volunteers and disclaimed rights to any wages. Nevertheless, the Court affirmed the lower court's finding that they were covered "employees" within the meaning of the Federal Fair Labor Standards Act ("FLSA"). The Foundation unsuccessfully argued that it should be exempt from the federal minimum wage and hour law because its commercial enterprises were "infused with a religious purpose."[89] The Court, rejecting this position, summarized:

> The Foundation's businesses serve the general public in competition with ordinary commercial enterprises . . . and the payment of substandard wages would undoubtedly give petitioners and similar organizations an advantage over their competitors. It is exactly this kind of "unfair method of competition" that the [FLSA] was intended to prevent . . . and the admixture of religious motivation does not alter a business's effect on commerce.[90]

The core rationale of the *Alamo Foundation* decision has been reiterated in subsequent decisions of courts of appeals involving wage, hour, and worker's disability compensation law applied to religious employers. As I have elsewhere noted, this decision indicates that "religious organizations do not have carte blanche to exploit persons employed in their commercial ventures."[91]

Recent decisions in the courts of appeals have closely followed *Alamo*. In *Brock v. Wendell's Woodwork*,[92] the Secretary of Labor brought suit against two commercial enterprises, seeking to enforce the FLSA's minimum wage requirements and its prohibition of child labor.

Members of a separatist religious sect, the Shiloh True Light Church, rejected institutionalized formal education. They instead opted to teach their children at home "in relative freedom from worldly influences and in accordance with their parents' understand-

89. *Id.* at 298.
90. *Id.* at 299.
91. *See* Gregory, *First Amendment Religion Clauses*, *supra* note 19, at 24.
92. 867 F.2d 196 (4th Cir. 1989).

ing of Scriptural teaching."[93] This parental instruction occupied half the usual institutional school day, thereby allowing the children's education to be supplemented by a vocational training program. Through an arrangement with the church, certain employers "having the same religious motivations as the parents" provided apprenticeship type training. This was designed to "insulate the children from idleness, to teach them marketable skills, to provide them with savings for the later launching of their own careers and to inculcate in them a scripturally mandated work ethic."[94]

The defendant Wendell's Woodwork used powersaws and forklifts in its woodwork manufacturing process. As part of their vocational training, members' children, some as young as nine and ten years of age, operated power equipment. Wendell's controlling officers were church members. Another defendant, McGee Brothers, a masonry contractor, similarly employed church members' children as part of the vocational training program. The children were engaged in laying brick and cinderblock; they transported material and mixed mortar; and, they worked on scaffolds when chimneys were being constructed. Four of the five owners of McGee Brothers were church members.

The Secretary of Labor sought to enforce the minimum wage requirements and the child labor proscriptions of the FLSA. The district court upheld the application of the FLSA. On appeal, defendants conceded application of the minimum wage requirements, but they contended that enforcement of the minimum age requirements would violate their First Amendment free exercise rights. Defendants therefore claimed an exemption from the child labor laws.

In upholding the district court's application of the FLSA to the defendants' commercial enterprises, the Fourth Circuit emphasized the perilous nature of some of the positions which had been filled by church members' children. The court indicated that FLSA regulations classified some of these jobs as "hazardous" and not to be performed by anyone under eighteen years of age. The court further noted that the FLSA prohibits employment of anyone under fourteen.

Based on the analysis in *Alamo Foundation*, the court of appeals found that the federal government had a "substantial interest in reg-

93. *Id.* at 197.
94. *Id.*

ulating child labor, even to the point of prohibition."[95] The government's interest was sufficiently compelling to override the church members' sincere convictions that they were rearing their children in the manner dictated by their religious beliefs. Although the court recognized the "spiritual worth" of the vocational training program, it concluded that those religious beliefs, served by employing children in "commercial enterprises that compete with other enterprises fully subject to labor laws," could not "immunize" the defendant employers from the proscriptions and requirements of the FLSA.[96]

In *Dole v. Shenandoah Baptist Church*,[97] in 1990, the Fourth Circuit again sustained the constitutionality of the child labor laws and minimum wage requirements of the FLSA to a church-operated school. The Shenandoah Baptist Church operated the Roanoke Valley Christian Schools to support Christian education, which the church regarded as a vital mission. The schools' full time curriculum included Bible study, and biblical materials were further integrated with traditional academic studies. The schools compensated the teachers with a $6,000 per-year base salary. Because this low salary made it difficult to attract teachers, Shenandoah instituted a "head-of-household" salary supplement. The Pastor explained that "the Bible clearly teaches that the husband is the head of the house . . . . We moved in that direction, thinking that our opportunity and responsibility of basing our practice on clear biblical teaching would not be a matter of question."[98] All married male teachers received the supplement, but married women were not eligible. However, three divorced females with dependents did receive the supplement. Ninety-one persons who worked at Roanoke Valley as support personnel also were paid less than the hourly minimum wage. These workers included bus drivers, custodians, kitchen workers, bookkeepers, and secretaries.

The Secretary of Labor and the EEOC sued, asserting that Shenandoah had violated two components of the FLSA. The government alleged that Shenandoah paid support personnel less than the minimum wage, in violation of the FLSA minimum wage requirement and had paid female teachers less than male teachers performing the same job, in violation of the equal pay requirements. The district

95. *Id.* at 199.
96. *Id.* at 198-99.
97. 899 F.2d 1389 (4th Cir.), *cert. denied*, 111 S. Ct. 131 (1990).
98. *Id.* at 1392.

court found that Shenandoah had violated both aspects of the FLSA, and it awarded backpay to Shenandoah's support personnel and teachers. On appeal, Shenandoah argued that Roanoke Valley was not subject to the strictures of the FLSA, and that applying the statute to a church-run school would violate the Free Exercise and Establishment Clauses of the First Amendment and the Equal Protection Clause of the Constitution.

The Fourth Circuit stated that two conditions are necessary for the FLSA to apply: Roanoke had to be an "enterprise" within the definition of the FLSA, and the teachers and support staff had to be "employees." The court of appeals held that the legislative history of a 1966 amendment to the FLSA, which brought public and private schools within the meaning of "enterprise," demonstrated Congress' intent to treat church-operated schools as enterprises. The amendment explicitly covered private nonprofit schools and deemed the activities performed in the operation of the school to be "performed for a business purpose."

Shenandoah nevertheless contended that the FLSA should not apply to its church-run school, because of the inseparable nature of the school and church. Relying on the *Amos* decision, Shenandoah first argued that the court was required to exempt its school from the FLSA. The court, however, pointed out that *Amos* stood for the proposition that Congress could provide for an exemption of religious institutions without running afoul of the First Amendment, but that such an exemption was not constitutionally mandated.

Shenandoah also argued that its teachers were not "employees," but instead were ministers and therefore included within the "ministerial exemption" from the FLSA. Shenandoah claimed that the teachers taught from a "pervasively religious perspective," led students in prayer, and, as a condition of employment, were required to subscribe to the "Shenandoah statement of faith."[99]

The court, however, interpreted the ministerial exemption as dependent on the teachers' function. Noting that Roanoke Valley teachers served no priestly function and belonged to no religious order, the court ruled that the teachers were "employed as lay teachers in a church-operated private school."[100] The court therefore construed the ministerial exemption narrowly and concluded that Congress intended church-operated schools such as Roanoke Valley to be

99. *Id.* at 1396.
100. *Id.* at 1396-97.

within the FLSA.

Shenandoah asserted that application of the FLSA would unconstitutionally burden the church's free exercise of its religious beliefs and unlawfully impair the church's ability to administer its relationship with employees, thereby usurping its " 'power to decide free from state interference, matters of church government as well as those of faith and doctrine.' "[101] Shenandoah further maintained that its "head-of-household" salary supplement was based on sincerely held religious beliefs — namely the biblical precept which established the husband as the absolute head of the house. Finally, the support personnel, intervenors in this action, claimed that allowing the government to set their wages, rather than the church "acting under divine guidance, would deprive them of blessings they would otherwise receive by allowing their Lord to supply their needs."[102]

In reviewing Shenandoah's free exercise claim, the court of appeals applied a three-part analysis: (1) it examined the burden on the exercise of sincerely held religious beliefs; (2) it determined whether the state has a compelling interest to justify this burden; and (3) it balanced the burden on the free exercise against the exemption's hindrance to the state's goal. Under the first prong of this inquiry, the court found that any burden on Shenandoah's free exercise rights that might arise by application of the FLSA would be limited. The Bible does not mandate a pay differential based on sex. Neither did church doctrine prevent equal pay or minimum wage. Therefore, the court concluded that "the pay requirements at issue do not cut to the heart of Shenandoah beliefs."[103] The court noted that the church was presently in compliance with the FLSA, that Shenandoah had no objection to complying with state fire, health, and safety requirements, and that it had withheld income tax from employees' wages and paid social security tax. The court also held that the increased payroll expenses that accompany FLSA compliance are not determinative in a free exercise claim. The court followed the dictates of *Alamo*: If the support staff continued to object to the government-mandated minimum wage, they had "the option of volunteering their services or returning to Shenandoah all or part of their back-pay awards."[104]

The court found that the government had compelling reasons to

101. *Id.* at 1397 (quoting Kedroff v. Saint Nicholas Cathedral, 344 U.S. 94, 116 (1952)).
102. *Id.*
103. *Id.*
104. *Id.* at 1398.

apply the minimum wage and equal pay provisions of the FLSA to Roanoke Valley: Maintaining a minimum living standard and remedying the problem of employment discrimination were " 'interests of the highest order.' "[105] Finally, weighing the limited burden on Shenandoah's free exercise rights against the government's compelling interest in applying the statute, the balance was obviously resolved in favor of the application of the FLSA to Roanoke Valley. The court found that the state's goals would be undermined if it were to exempt Roanoke Valley from compliance with the FLSA. "There is no principled way of exempting the school without exempting all other sectarian schools and thereby the thousands of lay teachers and staff members of their payrolls . . . . Congress has here created a comprehensive statute, and a less restrictive means of attaining its aims is not available."[106]

The court found that application of the FLSA to the church-run schools would not be a violation of the Establishment Clause. Shenandoah asserted that the application of the FLSA would violate the second prong of *Lemon* because the ministerial exemption of the FLSA impermissibly favors the Roman Catholic Church by granting the exemption to nuns and priests, and not to the teachers and staff at Roanoke Valley. The court disagreed, and observed that the exemption "is facially neutral, encompassing ministers, deacons, and members of religious orders in any faith, not exclusively Catholic nuns and priests."[107] This accommodation of free exercise values, the court held, is not an Establishment Clause violation.[108]

Shenandoah also argued that the government inspection, monitoring and review required by the FLSA would constitute an impermissible government entanglement with internal religious matters. The application of the FLSA to Roanoke Valley would thus fail the third prong of the *Lemon* test. Citing *Alamo*, the court instead found that while the administrative requirements of the FLSA might impose a burden "in terms of paperwork," such a burden was "not significantly more intrusive into religious affairs" than other state administrative regulations with which Shenandoah had willingly complied.[109] Shenandoah's final constitutional argument asserted

---

105. *Id.* (quoting Wisconsin v. Yoder, 406 U.S. 205, 215 (1972)).
106. 899 F.2d at 1399.
107. *Id.*
108. *Id.*
109. *Id.*

that the ministerial exemption violates equal protection guarantees in that it "creates a suspect classification which invidiously discriminates against adherents of religions that do not have formal religious orders."[110] The court, however, determined that once a statute passed the rigors of *Lemon*, all that was needed to uphold the statute was a showing that Congress had chosen a rational classification to further a legitimate end. The court upheld the exemption which it held to be a "rational means of creating a buffer between church and state."[111]

In *DeArment v. Harvey*,[112] in 1991, the Eighth Circuit also held that application of the FLSA to a church-operated school does not run afoul of the First Amendment religion clauses. D.L. Harvey was the pastor at the Rose City Pentecostal Church of God, which operated the Rose City Academy "as an integral part of the church."[113] The school, which provided education for children in kindergarten through twelfth grade, used a "self-study program" that taught all subjects from a "biblical point of view."[114] Each class was moderated by a supervisor, assisted by a classroom monitor. Neither the supervisors nor the monitors were required to be church members, but Pastor Harvey testified that each supervisor and monitor must be a "born again" Christian. All of the supervisors and monitors had either high school diplomas or had completed a GED program. None of them, however, were certified by any teachers' association. Both groups worked with the children, but they did not conduct formal classroom instruction; supervisors graded papers, answered student questions, conducted prayer, and counseled the students. The court characterized the monitors' duties as equivalent to teachers' aides in the public schools. All monitors and supervisors who testified stated that they considered their teaching to be a part of their pastoral ministry.

The Secretary of Labor instituted suit to enforce the record keeping and wage-hour requirements of the FLSA. The district court found the church was an employer and its supervisors and monitors, employees, within the meaning of the FLSA; therefore the FLSA was applicable and had been violated. The Eighth Circuit held that the *Shenandoah* court had correctly decided the applicability of the

---

110. *Id.* at 1400.
111. *Id.*
112. 932 F.2d 721 (8th Cir. 1991).
113. *Id.*
114. *Id.*

FLSA to a church-run school and would be followed.

A religious employer's secular functions are subject to state workers' compensation law. In *South Ridge Baptist Church v. Industrial Commission of Ohio,*[115] the Sixth Circuit rejected the church's challenge to the constitutionality of applying Ohio's mandatory workers' compensation program to the nonprofit religious corporation. Ohio's workers' compensation program mandated that all employers in the state must contribute semiannually to a state-administered insurance fund established for the payment of benefits to injured employees, with two relevant exceptions. First, "employee" was defined not to include ministers of churches. Second, an employer could avoid paying premiums into the state fund by electing to self-insure and thus pay benefits directly to its injured employees.[116]

South Ridge Baptist Church, an Ohio nonprofit religious corporation, characterized itself as " 'an independent, fundamental, Bible-believing, Bible-teaching and preaching Church' " which " 'strive[s] to be absolutely obedient to fundamental doctrines of the Bible and seeks to operate and live in accordance with historical Baptist doctrine.' "[117] The church declared that its religious beliefs were founded in the conviction "that the Bible is the supreme and final authority in religious faith and practice."[118] Based on Biblical teachings, the church asserted that its participation in the state's workers' compensation program would "violate God's command that Jesus is the head of the church and that its funds are God's, to be spent for Biblical purposes."[119] The church did not pursue the self-insurance option. The church alleged that the Ohio workers' compensation statute violated the Free Exercise and Establishment Clauses. The district court found that the state interest of compensating injured workers and protecting the solvency of its compensation program were sufficiently compelling to override the burden the program placed on the church's free exercise rights. Further, the court held that the scheme was the least restrictive means available since it granted an exemption to self-insured employers. Finally, the court held that the system's administrative requirements did not impermissibly entangle government with religion in violation of the Establishment Clause.

---

115. 911 F.2d 1203 (6th Cir. 1990), *cert. denied*, 111 S. Ct. 754 (1991).
116. *Id.* at 1204.
117. *Id.* (quoting from affidavits submitted by the church).
118. *Id.*
119. *Id.*

On appeal to the Sixth Circuit, the church conceded that the workers' compensation program advanced compelling state interests. The Church claimed, however, that the district court erred in granting defendants summary judgment because they had failed to prove as a matter of law that mandatory participation of all employers, including churches, was the least restrictive means available.

In resolving the free exercise claim, the Sixth Circuit applied the three-part analysis utilized by the Supreme Court in *United States v. Lee*.[120] It weighed (1) the magnitude of the burden on the exercise of religion, (2) the existence of a compelling state interest justifying the burden, and (3) the extent to which accommodation of the church would impede the state's objectives. The Sixth Circuit found that the state's interest in preserving the solvency of the workers' compensation program alone was sufficiently compelling to dispatch South Ridge's free exercise claim. The court placed heavy reliance on *Lee*, which held that the Free Exercise Clause was not violated by compelling an Amish employer to pay taxes into the federal social security system. In *Lee*, the Supreme Court found that the federal government's interest in maintaining the fiscal vitality of its old age and unemployment benefits system through mandatory participation was "very high." The Sixth Circuit indicated that Ohio's interest is "at least as great since it is based on the state's fundamental police power to safeguard the welfare of its citizens."[121] Although it failed to explain the nature of South Ridge's activities which subjected it to the workers' compensation program, the court of appeals implicitly characterized them as commercial:

> Congress and the courts have been sensitive to the needs flowing from the Free Exercise Clause, but every person cannot be shielded from all burdens incident to exercising every aspect of the right to practice religious beliefs. When followers of a particular sect enter into commercial activity as a matter of choice, the limits they accept on their own conduct as a matter of conscience and faith are not to be superimposed on the statutory schemes which are binding on others in that activity.[122]

The Sixth Circuit also found that the Supreme Court in *Lee* had "implicitly incorporated the least restrictive means test . . . in stat-

---

120. 455 U.S. 252, 255-60 (1982) (holding that the imposition of social security taxes on an Amish employer, who objected to the tax on free exercise grounds, was not unconstitutional).

121. 911 F.2d at 1208.

122. *Id.* at 1207 (citation omitted).

ing that a restriction on religious liberty must be 'essential' to the compelling government interest."[123] South Ridge argued that Ohio's mandatory workers' compensation program was not the least restrictive means available, since it did not grant the church an exemption from coverage. The church invoked *Lee*, which found that an exemption from the social security tax for "[s]elf-employed persons in a religious community having its own 'welfare' system"[124] would not unduly interfere with the fulfillment of the governmental interest. The Sixth Circuit, distinguishing the exemption in *Lee*, stated that "[c]onfining the . . . exemption to the self-employed provided for a narrow category which was readily identifiable. Self-employed persons in a religious community having its own 'welfare' system are distinguishable from the generality of wage earners employed by others."[125] Like the ministerial exemption from Ohio's workers' compensation program, the self-employed exemption from the social security tax in *Lee* did not " 'impose the employer's religious faith on the employee.' "[126] The court concluded that the "limited and regulated self-insurance option [to Ohio's workers' compensation program] fully secures the state's interest in protecting its workers; it could be expected that a blanket exemption of churches would not."[127] Finally, the court concluded that "decisions regarding the coverage of a tax program are properly for the legislative branch."[128]

The church alleged excessive entanglement of government with religion based upon inspection of church records, forced disbursement of church funds to a state program, record keeping and reporting requirements, categorizing employees according to risk, and enforcement actions for nonpayment of premiums. The court of appeals, following the guidance provided in *Corporation of Presiding Bishop v. Amos*[129] and *Dole v. Shenandoah Baptist Church*,[130] held that the administrative burdens imposed on South Ridge under the Ohio workers' compensation program would not constitute an excessive government entanglement. " '[R]outine regulatory interaction [such as application of neutral tax laws] which involves no inquiries

123. *Id.*
124. *Id.* (quoting United States v. Lee, 455 U.S. 252, 261 (1987)).
125. *Id.* (quoting *Lee*, 455 U.S. at 261).
126. *Id.* at 1209 (quoting *Lee*, 455 U.S. at 261).
127. *Id.*
128. *Id.*
129. 483 U.S. 327 (1987).
130. 899 F.2d 1389 (4th Cir.), *cert. denied*, 111 S. Ct. 131 (1990).

into religious doctrine, . . . no delegation of state power to a religious body, . . . and no "detailed monitoring and close administrative contact" between secular and religious bodies, . . . does not of itself violate the nonentanglement command.' "[131]

D. Immigration Law

Religious employers who witness their opposition to the restrictive immigration policies of the government through action have predictably been subject to intrusive and coercive government regulation. "Divine obedience" will be regarded by Caesar[132] as the most uncivil and unprotected disobedience, a further manifestation of the prevailing statist jurisprudence of the federal judiciary.

In 1990, the Second Circuit decided in *Intercommunity Center for Justice & Peace v. Immigration & Naturalization Service*[133] that a religious organization is subject to the verification requirements and sanctions of the Immigration Reform and Control Act of 1986 ("IRC").

The Intercommunity Center for Justice and Peace ("ICJP"), an organization of forty-one Roman Catholic communities, joined as plaintiffs to obtain a judgment that they were exempt from the employer verification and sanctions provisions of the Immigration Reform and Control Act ("IRC") of 1986 on the grounds that its enforcement against them would violate the Free Exercise Clause.

The IRC requires employers to verify that each of their employees is authorized to work in the United States. Civil fines may be imposed if an employer violates these verification requirements or knowingly employs an unauthorized alien. Furthermore, a pattern or practice of knowingly employing unauthorized aliens may result in criminal punishment. The ICJP asserted that application of the IRC would violate their free exercise rights. They maintained that Roman Catholic Church teachings impose upon them a duty to provide "food, clothing, shelter and means to sustain their own lives to all people without regard to residence, nationality or immigration status," and that they were compelled to offer employment to people in need, without regard to immigration status, as part of their religious

131. 911 F.2d at 1210 (alteration in original) (quoting Hernandez v. Comm'r, 490 U.S. 680, 696-97 (1989)).

132. *See supra* note 87.

133. 910 F.2d 42 (2d Cir. 1990).

ministries.[134] Relying on *NLRB v. Catholic Bishop*, the ICJP also argued that, absent an explicit statement in the IRC that it should be applied to religious organizations, they are exempt. To apply the IRC to the ICJP would cause impermissible government entanglement with religion in violation of the Establishment Clause.

The court described the religion clauses of the First Amendment as "providing full protection for religious beliefs but only limited protection for overt acts prompted by those beliefs."[135] The First Amendment contains an absolute proscription of legislative regulation of religious beliefs. Religious practice, however, is not afforded absolute protection. The court did, however, recognize that Congress may not discriminate against religion by "banning acts only when they are engaged in for religious reasons or only because of the religious belief that they display."[136] The court of appeals analogized Congress' interest in controlling the flow of aliens to that of maintaining a uniform tax system, "which has been found to be a compelling governmental interest that overrides free exercise claims."[137] The court observed that although the ICJP sought an exemption only for its members, it was not alone; over 100 amici of the Roman Catholic Church had urged support for the ICJP. This obvious indication of the potential for innumerable applications for religious exemption would seem to implicate the third part of the *Lemon* test. In dismissing ICJP's free exercise claim, the court relied in part on *Employment Division, Dep't. of Human Resources v. Smith*. "The [IRC] neither regulates religious beliefs nor burdens acts because of their religious expression or motivation. Rather, it is a valid, neutral law of general application that happens to compel action contrary to certain religious beliefs. No free exercise claim exists under such circumstances."[138]

The ICJP proposed a limited exemption for "those whose religion requires them not to discriminate on the basis of immigration as an integral part of their religious mission" to avoid the impermissible government entanglement that would otherwise result from the application of the IRC to such a religious organization.[139] The Second Circuit, however, refused to accept the notion that the application of

---

134. *Id.* at 43-44.
135. *Id.* at 44.
136. *Id.* (quoting Sherbert v. Verner, 374 U.S. 398, 402 (1963)).
137. *Id.* at 46.
138. *Id.* at 44.
139. *Id.* at 45.

the IRC here would result in "governmental inquiries into religious beliefs."[140] The court opined that the existing exemptions for household employees and employees hired prior to November 1986, unlike the exemption proposed by the ICJP, has "no relation to religion. No day-to-day inspection is required . . . . The proposed exemption would require an inquiry into whether or not a particular religious requirement is essential to an individual's religious mission."[141] Such an exemption, the court concluded, would transform a neutral statute into one which would require excessive governmental entanglement with religion. The court accordingly rejected the Establishment Clause claim.

In *American Friends Service Commission Corp. v. Thornburgh*,[142] in 1991, the Ninth Circuit also upheld the constitutionality of the verification and sanctions provisions of the IRC as applied to a Quaker charity and relief organization. The American Friends Service Committee ("AFSC") was a Quaker organization whose activities included charitable and relief work. The AFSC failed to comply with the IRC because it believed that to do so would violate the religious beliefs and practices of its members. The AFSC contended that its beliefs require that it not "refuse human beings work — thus depriving them of the means to feed and clothe themselves and their children — simply because they may be strangers to our land." The Ninth Circuit applied *Smith*[143] to find the IRC a "valid and neutral law of general applicability."[144] Therefore, AFSC's free exercise claim failed because " 'prohibiting the exercise of religion . . . is not the *object* of the [law] but merely the incidental effect of a generally applicable and otherwise valid provision.' "[145]

The court of appeals refused to accept AFSC's argument that its claims fell within the "hybrid claims" exception to *Smith*. Such claims, which contain another substantive constitutional challenge in addition to the free exercise claim, are "restricted to express constitutional protections such as freedom of speech, and firmly recognized substantive due process rights such as the privacy right in rearing children."[146] The court declared that to recognize a "hybrid claims"

140. *Id.*
141. *Id.* at 45.
142. 941 F.2d 808 (9th Cir. 1991), *superseded by* 951 F.2d 957 (1992).
143. *See supra* text accompanying notes 14-18.
144. *Id.* at 810 (quoting *Smith*, 494 U.S. at 878).
145. *Id.* (alteration in original) (quoting *Smith*, 494 U.S. at 878).
146. *Id.* at 810-11.

exception by accepting the substantive due process "right to hire" claim (a claim of "slight constitutional weight") in addition to a free exercise claim, would eviscerate the *Smith* decision.[147]

IV. CONCLUSION

Both judicial and academic commentators have long recognized the potential tensions between the Establishment and the Free Exercise Clauses. The Title VII exemption, which allows the religious employer to discriminate in employment in order to carry on its activities, exacerbates these tensions. Some courts have strongly suggested that this Title VII exemption may itself violate the Establishment Clause.[148] Yet, the total absence of any exemption whatsoever would at least arguably run afoul of the religious employer's free exercise rights. I will refrain from proposing yet another sophisticated, multipart test intended to harmonize the law but most certainly doomed to frustration.[149] As I have concluded elsewhere, "the tension in our

---

147. *Id.* at 811.

148. King's Garden, Inc. v. FCC, 498 F.2d 51, 55 (D.C. Cir. 1974) (In strong dictum, the court suggested the Title VII, section 702 exemption unconstitutionally advanced and established religion, because the exemption "invites religious groups and them alone, to impress a test of faith on job categories, and indeed whole enterprises, having nothing to do with the exercise of religion."), *cert. denied*, 419 U.S. 996 (1974); Fedlstrin v. Christian Science Monitor, 555 F. Supp. 974, 975-76 (D. Mass. 1983) (reporter not hired for paper because he was not a Christian Scientist). *But see* Larsen v. Kirkham, 499 F. Supp. 960 (D. Utah 1980), *aff'd without opinion* (10th Cir. 1982), *cert. denied*, 464 U.S. 849 (1983).

149. To sample a variety of proposals purporting to resolve Title VII matters while avoiding constitutional problems, see, *e.g.*, Carl H. Esbeck, *Establishment Clause Limits on Governmental Interference with Religious Organizations*, 41 WASH. & LEE L. REV. 347, 409, 420 (1984) ("[P]ervasively religious" organizations "should be entirely exempt from equal employment legislation . . . . Governmental involvement should be prohibited when there is a measurable risk that worship, the religious teaching and propagation of the beliefs of the religious association, or the moral discipline of its members would be inhibited."); Gedicks, *supra* note 52 (proposing absolute autonomy of religious groups in setting membership terms); Douglas Laycock, *Towards a General Theory of the Religion Clauses: The Case of Church Labor Relations and the Right to Church Autonomy*, 81 COLUM. L. REV. 1373, 1373 (1981) (Unless government can assert compelling interest, "churches have a constitutionally protected interest in managing their own institutions free of government interference.").

See also Ira C. Lupu, *Free Exercise Exemption and Religious Institutions: The Case of Employment Discrimination*, 67 B.U. L. REV. 391, 395, 439 (1987).

> [T]he right of a religious institution to discriminate in what would otherwise be unlawful ways should be viewed as driven by and coterminous with the associational rights of its members — that is, it can utilize its membership criteria as employment criteria . . . . Such associations may exclude from employment opportunities members of groups marked for protection by civil rights laws *if and only if members of those groups are also barred from membership in the church.*

Id. at 439.

religion clauses and Title VII jurisprudence can never be fully harmonized. However, with sensitivity and concern for everyone's rights, delicate balances can be achieved, if carefully and constantly recalibrated."[150]

It is highly unlikely that the current Supreme Court will sufficiently consider the interests of religious employees upon this theoretical balancing spectrum for the foreseeable future. Religious employers will probably continue to receive the Court's favoritism, not because of sensitivities to unconstitutional establishment or to the employers' free exercise claims per se, but rather due to a majority of the Justices' near-automatic deference to the hierarchical institutional status of employers *qua* employers. So long as a majority of the Justices perceive religious employers as important statist instruments who reinforce the mainstream social, political, and legal order, these employers will continue to have virtual carte blanche in their labor relations, employment policies, and operations. One of the deepest ironies in this highly skewed scenario is that the increasingly accommodationist Court actually only accommodates the religious employers, and remains hostile or oblivious to the possibility of affording anything more than utterly de minimis "reasonable accommodation" to the religious employee of the secular organization.

The best instrumental means for at least partially rectifying this gross imbalance was proposed by Elizabeth Bradley.[151] To resolve the "difficult and sensitive" issue of the extent to which the religion clauses compel or prohibit government regulation of labor and employment, courts should concentrate on the job activities of the employee, rather than on the nature of the employer organization. This would radically and appropriately reconfigure the jurisprudential perspective from the employer to the employee.

> The fact finder should determine, first, whether the employee was hired from the secular marketplace, and second, whether her em-

---

See also Shelley K. Wessels, *The Collision of Religious Exercise and Governmental Nondiscrimination Policies*, 41 STAN. L. REV. 1201 (1989).

> I conclude that a religious interest should be absolutely protected against discrimination claims when the religious group advocates the religious interest in the context of its activity as a religious community "turned inward," a religious group should be required to adhere to antidiscrimination provisions, however, when it functions as community "turned outward," toward the world.

Id. at 1204.

150. Gregory, *supra* note 6, at 763.

151. Elizabeth Bradley, Note, *A New Approach to NLRB Jurisdiction over the Employment Practices of Religious Institutions*, 54 U. CHI. L. REV. 243 (1987).

> ployment activities can be distinguished from activities ordinarily performed in a secular setting only by reference to the theology of the religious organization. If the answer to both these questions is affirmative, or if an affirmative finding on one prong sufficiently outweighs a negative finding on the other, then Title VII, the NLRA, and other fair labor statutes are applicable. Otherwise, the particular activities in question should be exempt.[152]

This focus on the employee's job activities will avoid the constitutional problem of excessive entanglement that inquiry into the nature of the employer's organization invites. Whether Bradley's test will be recognized by this Supreme Court, whatever the test's jurisprudential virtues, is highly problematic because of the Court's congenital inability to appreciate, let alone adopt, the employee's perspective in any hierarchical employment relationship.

Even if a relandscaping of the contour of statutory and constitutional law were likely, religious employers have a greater, transcendent responsibility to treat their employees with the dignity and decency internally mandated by the tenets of the religion. Unfortunately, some religious institutions may be tempted to invoke the secular doctrine of the legal regime to avoid the higher internal obligations of the religion. If so, these employers will have disingenuously assumed the role of Caesar in the workplace.[153]

Last year marked the centennial of the Catholic papal encyclical *Rerum Novarum*. In 1891, Pope Leo XIII forcefully promoted the dignity of all workers and the rights to form labor unions and to receive compensation for service to human beings. That powerful mandate has inspired the Catholic Church's eloquent social teaching on labor throughout this century. Yet some Catholic institutions, as employers, have not implemented the church's social teaching; instead, they have insidiously invoked secular labor law to deny the collective bargaining rights and aspirations of their workers, in contravention of the church's pronouncements. These machinations of secular law by religious employers, often to avoid the teachings of the very religion they putatively espouse, are more than insidious; they are profoundly wrong. This hypocritical practice can and must cease, not necessarily through the counteruse or reform of secular law, but also through the moral witness and suasion of the religious community upon its phari-

---

152. *Id.* at 244.
153. *See supra* note 87 and accompanying text.

saical institutional elites.[154]

Every religious employer must first respond to the dictates of its faith: On the job, are its workers treated with the decency and dignity internally mandated by the religion? If the religious employer instead is using the secular law to avoid its religious duties to workers, it will probably remain beyond the reach of the secular law, given the ineluctable pro-employer jurisprudence of this Supreme Court. But, in this hellish scenario, the manipulative "religious" employer who deliberately emulates Caesar ultimately will have to answer to a court higher than any earthly high court.

Government deregulation of religion through the judicial vitiation of the labor and employment discrimination laws ultimately may produce less significant ramifications than religious employers' compliance with their own higher law. Affording workers dignified and decent working conditions will help to render "society better, more just, and more humane in the daily lives of all working people."[155] Changes will occur through the force of internal moral suasion upon religious institutional employers, not through secular law reform. These changes will effect a new judicial focus upon the role and function of the employee to replace the Court's skewed deference to the institutional employer. Such a focus would hopefully result in more appropriate application of secular labor and employment discrimination laws to protect both employees who are not essential to an employer's core religious function and to religious individuals employed by secular institutions. Unfortunately, the prospects of such change are highly unlikely at the Supreme Court level for the foreseeable future, absent Congressional action to clarify intent and strengthen existing statutes. Therefore, the legal system will probably continue to deregulate religion through the judicial vitiation of labor and employment discrimination laws.

---

154. *See* David L. Gregory & Charles S. Russo, *Overcoming* NLRB v. Yeshiva University *by the Implementation of Catholic Labor Theory*, 41 Lab. L.J. 55, 63 (1990).

> [D]ecisions such as *NLRB v. Catholic Bishop of Chicago* should likewise become quickly irrelevant in Catholic employment environments. In light of the Church's unequivocal and powerful labor theory, it is simply morally preposterous that any Catholic employer continue to raise First Amendment or constitutional preemption claims in order to avoid collective bargaining with its workers, if and when the majority of the workers wish to unionize.

Id.

155. *See* Gregory, *The Right to Unionize*, *supra* note 23, at 157.

COMMUNICATIONS WORKERS OF AMERICA ET AL. *v.* BECK ET AL.

CERTIORARI TO THE UNITED STATES COURT OF APPEALS FOR THE FOURTH CIRCUIT

No. 86–637. Argued January 11, 1988—Decided June 29, 1988

Section 8(a)(3) of the National Labor Relations Act (NLRA) permits an employer and a union to enter into an agreement requiring all employees in the bargaining unit to pay union dues as a condition of continued employment, whether or not the employees become union members. Petitioner Communications Workers of America (CWA) entered into a collective-bargaining agreement that contains a union-security clause under which all represented employees who do not become union members must pay the union "agency fees" in amounts equal to the dues paid by union members. Respondents, bargaining-unit employees who chose not to become union members, filed this suit in Federal District Court, challenging CWA's use of their agency fees for purposes other than collective bargaining, contract administration, or grievance adjustment (hereinafter "collective-bargaining" activities). They alleged that expenditure of their fees on activities such as organizing the employees of other employers, lobbying for labor legislation, and participating in social, charitable, and political events violated CWA's duty of fair representation, § 8(a)(3), and the First Amendment. The court concluded that CWA's collection and disbursement of agency fees for purposes other than collective-bargaining activities violated the associational and free speech rights of objecting nonmembers, and granted injunctive relief and an order for reimbursement of excess fees. The Court of Appeals, preferring to rest its judgment on a ground other than the Constitution, ultimately concluded, *inter alia*, that the collection of nonmembers' fees for purposes unrelated to collective bargaining violated CWA's duty of fair representation.

Held:

1. The courts below properly exercised jurisdiction over respondents' claims that exactions of agency fees beyond those necessary to finance collective-bargaining activities violated the judicially created duty of fair representation and respondents' First Amendment rights. Although the National Labor Relations Board (Board) had primary jurisdiction over respondents' § 8(a)(3) claim, cf. *San Diego Building Trades Council* v. *Garmon*, 359 U. S. 236, the courts below were not precluded from deciding the merits of that claim insofar as such a decision was necessary

to the disposition of respondents' duty-of-fair-representation challenge. Federal courts may resolve unfair labor practice questions that emerge as collateral issues in suits brought under independent federal remedies. Respondents did not attempt to circumvent the Board's primary jurisdiction by casting their statutory claim as a violation of CWA's duty of fair representation. Instead, the necessity of deciding the scope of § 8(a)(3) arose because CWA and its copetitioner local unions sought to defend themselves on the ground that the statute authorizes the type of union-security agreement in issue. Pp. 742–744.

2. Section 8(a)(3) does not permit a union, over the objections of dues-paying nonmember employees, to expend funds collected from them on activities unrelated to collective-bargaining activities. Pp. 744–762.

(a) The decision in *Machinists* v. *Street*, 367 U. S. 740—holding that § 2, Eleventh of the Railway Labor Act (RLA) does not permit a union, over the objections of nonmembers, to expend agency fees on political causes—is controlling, for § 8(a)(3) and § 2, Eleventh are in all material respects identical. Their nearly identical language reflects the fact that in both Congress authorized compulsory unionism only to the extent necessary to ensure that those who enjoy union-negotiated benefits contribute to their cost. Indeed, Congress, in 1951, expressly modeled § 2, Eleventh on § 8(a)(3), which it had added to the NLRA by the Taft-Hartley Act only four years earlier, and emphasized that it was extending to railroad labor the same rights and privileges of the union shop that were contained in the Taft-Hartley Act. Pp. 744–747.

(b) Section 8(a)(3) was intended to correct abuses of compulsory unionism that had developed under "closed shop" agreements and, at the same time, to require, through union-security clauses, that nonmember employees pay their share of the cost of benefits secured by the union through collective bargaining. These same concerns prompted Congress' later amendment of the RLA. Given the parallel purpose, structure, and language of § 8(a)(3) and § 2, Eleventh, both provisions must be interpreted in the same manner. Only the most compelling evidence would support a contrary conclusion, and petitioners have not proffered such evidence here. Pp. 747–754.

(c) Petitioners claim that the union-security provisions of the RLA and NLRA should be read differently in light of the different history of unionism in the regulated industries—that is, the tradition of voluntary unionism in the railway industry prior to the 1951 amendment of the RLA and the history of compulsory unionism in NLRA-regulated industries prior to 1947. Petitioners contend that because agreements requiring the payment of uniform dues were not among the specific abuses Congress sought to remedy in the Taft-Hartley Act, § 8(a)(3) cannot plausibly be read to prohibit the collection of fees in excess of those necessary to cover the costs of collective bargaining. This argument is unpersuasive because the legislative history of § 8(a)(3) shows that Congress was concerned with numerous and systemic abuses of the closed shop and therefore resolved to ban the closed shop altogether; to the extent it permitted union-security agreements at all, Congress was guided—as it was in its later amendment of the RLA—by the principle that those enjoying the benefits of union representation should contribute their fair share to the expense of securing those benefits. Moreover, it is clear that Congress understood its actions in 1947 and 1951 to have placed the respective regulated industries on an equal footing insofar as compulsory unionism was concerned. Pp. 754–756.

(d) The fact that in the Taft-Hartley Act Congress expressly considered proposals regulating union finances but ultimately placed only a few limitations on the collection and use of dues and fees, and otherwise left unions free to arrange their financial affairs as they saw fit, is not sufficient to compel a broader construction of § 8(a)(3) than that accorded § 2, Eleventh in *Street*. The legislative history of § 8(a)(3) shows that Congress was concerned with the dues and rights of union members, not the agency fees and rights of nonmembers. The absence, in such legislative history, of congressional concern for the rights of nonmembers is consistent with the view that Congress understood § 8(a)(3) to afford nonmembers adequate protection by authorizing the collection of only those fees necessary to finance collective-bargaining activities. Nor is there any merit to the contention that, because unions had previously used members' dues for a variety of purposes in addition to collective-bargaining agreements, Congress' silence in 1947 as to the uses to which unions could put nonmembers' fees should be understood as an acquiescence in such union practices. Pp. 756–761.

(e) *Street* cannot be distinguished on the theory that the construction of § 2, Eleventh was merely expedient to avoid the constitutional question—as to the use of fees for political causes that nonmembers find objectionable—that otherwise would have been raised because the RLA (unlike the NLRA) pre-empts state laws banning union-security agreements and thus nonmember fees were compelled by "governmental action." Even assuming that the exercise of rights permitted, though not compelled, by § 8(a)(3) does not involve state action, and that the NLRA and RLA therefore differ in such respect, nevertheless the absence of any constitutional concerns in this case would not warrant reading the nearly identical language of § 8(a)(3) and § 2, Eleventh differently. Pp. 761–762.

800 F. 2d 1280, affirmed.

BRENNAN, J., delivered the opinion of the Court, in which REHNQUIST, C. J., and WHITE, MARSHALL, and STEVENS, JJ., joined, and in Parts I and II of which BLACKMUN, O'CONNOR, and SCALIA, JJ., joined. BLACKMUN, J., filed an opinion concurring in part and dissenting in part, in which O'CONNOR and SCALIA, JJ., joined, *post*, p. 763. KENNEDY, J., took no part in the consideration or decision of the case.

Laurence Gold argued the cause for petitioners. With him on the briefs were *Thomas S. Adair*, *James Coppess*, and *George Kaufmann*.

Edwin Vieira, Jr., argued the cause for respondents. With him on the brief was *Hugh L. Reilly*.*

JUSTICE BRENNAN delivered the opinion of the Court.

Section 8(a)(3) of the National Labor Relations Act of 1935 (NLRA), 49 Stat. 452, as amended, 29 U. S. C. § 158(a)(3), permits an employer and an exclusive bargaining representative to enter into an agreement requiring all employees in the bargaining unit to pay periodic union dues and initiation fees as a condition of continued employment, whether or not the employees otherwise wish to become union members. Today we must decide whether this provision also permits a union, over the objections of dues-paying nonmember employees, to expend funds so collected on activities unrelated to collective bargaining, contract administration, or grievance adjustment, and, if so, whether such expenditures violate the union's duty of fair representation or the objecting employees' First Amendment rights.

**David M. Silberman* filed a brief for the American Federation of Labor and Congress of Industrial Organizations as *amicus curiae* urging reversal.

Briefs of *amici curiae* urging affirmance were filed for the Landmark Legal Foundation by *Jerald L. Hill* and *Mark J. Bredemeier;* for the Pacific Legal Foundation et al. by *Ronald A. Zumbrun* and *Anthony T. Caso;* and for Senator Jesse Helms et al. by *Thomas A. Farr*, *W. W. Taylor, Jr.*, and *Robert A. Valois*.

Solicitor General Fried, *Deputy Solicitor General Cohen*, *Norton J. Come*, and *Linda Sher* filed a brief for the United States as *amicus curiae*.

I

In accordance with § 9 of the NLRA, 49 Stat. 453, as amended, 29 U. S. C. § 159, a majority of the employees of American Telephone and Telegraph Company and several of its subsidiaries selected petitioner Communications Workers of America (CWA) as their exclusive bargaining representative. As such, the union is empowered to bargain collectively with the employer on behalf of all employees in the bargaining unit over wages, hours, and other terms and conditions of employment, § 9(a), 29 U. S. C. § 159(a), and it accordingly enjoys "broad authority . . . in the negotiation and administration of [the] collective bargaining contract." *Humphrey* v. *Moore*, 375 U. S. 335, 342 (1964). This broad authority, however, is tempered by the union's "statutory obligation to serve the interests of all members without hostility or discrimination toward any," *Vaca* v. *Sipes*, 386 U. S. 171, 177 (1967), a duty that extends not only to the negotiation of the collective-bargaining agreement itself but also to the subsequent enforcement of that agreement, including the administration of any grievance procedure the agreement may establish. *Ibid.* CWA chartered several local unions, copetitioners in this case, to assist it in discharging these statutory duties. In addition, at least in part to help defray the considerable costs it incurs in performing these tasks, CWA negotiated a union-security clause in the collective-bargaining agreement under which all represented employees, including those who do not wish to become union members, must pay the union "agency fees" in "amounts equal to the periodic dues" paid by union members. Plaintiffs' Complaint ¶ 11 and Plaintiffs' Exhibit A–1, 1 Record. Under the clause, failure to tender the required fee may be grounds for discharge.

In June 1976, respondents, 20 employees who chose not to become union members, initiated this suit challenging CWA's use of their agency fees for purposes other than collective bargaining, contract administration, or grievance adjustment (hereinafter "collective-bargaining" or "representational" activities). Specifically, respondents alleged that the union's expenditure of their fees on activities such as organizing the employees of other employers, lobbying for labor legislation, and participating in social, charitable, and political events violated petitioners' duty of fair representation, § 8(a)(3) of the NLRA, the First Amendment, and various common-law fiduciary duties. In addition to declaratory relief, respondents sought an injunction barring petitioners from exacting fees above those necessary to finance collective-bargaining activities, as well as damages for the past collection of such excess fees.

The District Court concluded that the union's collection and disbursement of agency fees for purposes other than bargaining unit representation violated the associational and free speech rights of objecting nonmembers, and therefore enjoined their future collection. 468 F. Supp. 93 (Md. 1979). Applying a "clear and convincing" evidentiary standard, the District Court concluded that the union had failed to show that more than 21% of its funds were expended on collective-bargaining matters. App. to Pet. for Cert. 119a. The court ordered reimbursement of all excess fees respondents had paid since January 1976, and directed the union to institute a recordkeeping system to segregate accounts for representational and noncollective-bargaining activities. *Id.*, at 125a, 108a–109a.

A divided panel of the United States Court of Appeals for the Fourth Circuit agreed that respondents stated a valid claim for relief under the First Amendment, but, preferring to rest its judgment on a ground other than the Constitution, concluded that the collection of nonmembers' fees for purposes unrelated to collective bargaining violated § 8(a)(3). 776 F. 2d 1187 (1985). Turning to the specific activities challenged, the majority noted that the District Court's adoption of a "clear and convincing" standard of proof was improper, but found that for certain categories of expenditures, such as lobbying, organizing employees in other companies, and funding various community services, the error was harmless inasmuch as the activities were indisputably unrelated to bargaining unit representation. The majority remanded the case for reconsideration of the remaining expenditures, which the union claimed were made in connection with valid collective-bargaining activities. Chief Judge Winter dissented. *Id.*, at 1214. He concluded that § 8(a)(3) authorized exaction of fees in amounts equivalent to full union dues, including fees expended on nonrepresentational activities, and that the negotiation and enforcement of agreements permitting such exactions was private conduct incapable of violating the constitutional rights of objecting nonmembers.

On rehearing, the en banc court vacated the panel opinion and by a 6-to-4 vote again affirmed in part, reversed in part, and remanded for further proceedings. 800 F. 2d 1280 (1986). The court explained in a brief *per curiam* opinion that five of the six majority judges believed there was federal jurisdiction over both the § 8(a)(3) and the duty-of-fair-representation claims, and that respondents were entitled to judgment on both. Judge Murnaghan, casting the deciding vote, concluded that the court had jurisdiction over only the duty-of-fair-representation claim; although he believed that § 8(a)(3) permits union-security clauses requiring payment of full union dues, he concluded that the collection of such fees from nonmembers to finance activities unrelated to collective bargaining violates the union's duty of fair representation. All six of these judges agreed with the panel's resolution of the specific allocations issue and accordingly remanded the action. Chief Judge Winter, joined by three others, again dissented for the reasons set out in his earlier panel dissent.

The decision below directly conflicts with that of the United States Court of Appeals for the Second Circuit. See *Price* v. *Auto Workers*, 795 F. 2d 1128 (1986). We granted certiorari to resolve the important question concerning the validity of such agreements, 482 U. S. 904 (1987), and now affirm.

II

At the outset, we address briefly the jurisdictional question that divided the Court of Appeals. Respondents sought relief on three separate federal claims: that the exaction of fees beyond those necessary to finance collective-bargaining activities violates § 8(a)(3); that such exactions violate the judicially created duty of fair representation; and that such exactions violate respondents' First Amendment rights. We think it clear that the courts below properly exercised jurisdiction over the latter two claims, but that the National Labor Relations Board (NLRB or Board) had primary jurisdiction over respondents' § 8(a)(3) claim.

In *San Diego Building Trades Council* v. *Garmon*, 359 U. S. 236 (1959), we held that "[w]hen an activity is arguably subject to § 7 or § 8 of the [NLRA], the States *as well as the federal courts* must defer to the exclusive competence of the [Board] if the danger of state interference with national policy is to be averted." *Id.*, at 245 (emphasis added). A simple recitation of respondents' § 8(a)(3) claim reveals that it falls squarely within the primary jurisdiction of the Board: respondents contend that, by collecting and using agency fees for nonrepresentational purposes, the union has contravened the express terms of § 8(a)(3), which, respondents argue, provides a limited authorization for the collection of only those fees necessary to finance collective-bargaining activities. There can be no doubt, therefore, that the challenged fee-collecting activity is "subject to" § 8.

While the five-judge plurality of the en banc court did not explain the basis of its jurisdictional holding, the panel majority concluded that because courts have jurisdiction over challenges to union-security clauses negotiated under § 2, Eleventh of the Railway Labor Act (RLA), 64 Stat. 1238, 45 U. S. C. § 152, Eleventh, which is in all material respects identical to § 8(a)(3), there must be a parity of federal jurisdiction over § 8(a)(3) claims. Unlike the NLRA, however, the RLA establishes no agency charged with administering its provisions, and instead leaves it to the courts to determine the validity of activities challenged under the Act. The primary jurisdiction of the NLRB, therefore, cannot be diminished by analogies to the RLA, for in this regard the two labor statutes do not parallel one another. The Court of Appeals erred, then, to the extent that it concluded it possessed jurisdiction to pass directly on respondents' § 8(a)(3) claim.

The court was not precluded, however, from deciding the merits of this claim insofar as such a decision was necessary to the disposition of respondents' duty-of-fair-representation challenge. Federal courts may resolve unfair labor practice questions that "emerge as collateral issues in suits brought under independent federal remedies," *Connell Construction Co.* v. *Plumbers*, 421 U. S. 616, 626 (1975), and one such remedy over which federal jurisdiction is well settled is the judicially implied duty of fair representation. *Vaca* v. *Sipes*, 386 U. S. 171 (1967). This jurisdiction to adjudicate fair-representation claims encompasses challenges leveled not only at a union's contract administration and enforcement efforts, *id.*, at 176–188, but at its negotiation activities as well. *Ford Motor Co.* v. *Huffman*, 345 U. S. 330 (1953). Employees, of course, may not circumvent the primary jurisdiction of the NLRB simply by casting statutory claims as violations of the union's duty of fair representation. Respondents, however, have done no such thing here; rather, they claim that the union failed to represent their interests fairly and without hostility by negotiating and enforcing an agreement that allows the exaction of funds for purposes that do not serve their interests and in some cases are contrary to their personal beliefs. The necessity of deciding the scope of § 8(a)(3) arises because *petitioners* seek to defend themselves on the ground that the statute authorizes precisely this type of agreement. Under these circumstances, the Court of Appeals had jurisdiction to decide the § 8(a)(3) question raised by respondents' duty-of-fair-representation claim.[1]

III

Added as part of the Labor Management Relations Act, 1947, or Taft-Hartley Act, § 8(a)(3) makes it an unfair labor practice for an employer "by discrimination in regard to hire or tenure of employment . . . to encourage or discourage membership in any labor organization." 29 U. S. C. § 158 (a)(3). The section contains two provisos without which all union-security clauses would fall within this otherwise broad condemnation: the first states that nothing in the Act "preclude[s] an employer from making an agreement with a labor organization . . . to require as a condition of employment membership therein" 30 days after the employee attains employment, *ibid.;* the second, limiting the first, provides:

> "[N]o employer shall justify any discrimination against an employee for nonmembership in a labor organization (A) if he has reasonable grounds for believing that such membership was not available to the employee on the same terms and conditions generally applicable to other members, or (B) if he has reasonable grounds for believing that membership was denied or terminated for reasons other than the failure . . . to tender the periodic

[1] The courts below, of course, possessed jurisdiction over respondents' constitutional challenges. Whether or not the NLRB entertains constitutional claims, see *Florida Gulf Coast Building & Construction Trades Council (Edward J. DeBartolo Corp.)*, 273 N. L. R. B. 1431, 1432 (1985) (Board "will presume the constitutionality of the Act [it] administer[s]"); *Handy Andy, Inc.*, 228 N. L. R. B. 447, 452 (1977) (Board lacks the authority "to determine the constitutionality of mandatory language in the Act"); see also *Johnson* v. *Robison*, 415 U. S. 361, 368 (1974) ("Adjudication of the constitutionality of congressional enactments has generally been thought beyond the jurisdiction of administrative agencies"); cf. *NLRB* v. *Catholic Bishop of Chicago*, 440 U. S. 490, 495–499 (1979) (reviewing Board's history of determining its jurisdiction over religious schools in light of Free Exercise Clause concerns), such claims would not fall within the Board's primary jurisdiction.

dues and the initiation fees uniformly required as a condition of acquiring or retaining membership." *Ibid.*

Taken as a whole, § 8(a)(3) permits an employer and a union[2] to enter into an agreement requiring all employees to become union members as a condition of continued employment, but the "membership" that may be so required has been "whittled down to its financial core." *NLRB* v. *General Motors Corp.*, 373 U. S. 734, 742 (1963). The statutory question presented in this case, then, is whether this "financial core" includes the obligation to support union activities beyond those germane to collective bargaining, contract administration, and grievance adjustment. We think it does not.

Although we have never before delineated the precise limits § 8(a)(3) places on the negotiation and enforcement of union-security agreements, the question the parties proffer is not an entirely new one. Over a quarter century ago we held that § 2, Eleventh of the RLA does not permit a union, over the objections of nonmembers, to expend compelled agency fees on political causes. *Machinists* v. *Street*, 367 U. S. 740 (1961). Because the NLRA and RLA differ in certain crucial respects, we have frequently warned that decisions construing the latter often provide only the roughest of guidance when interpreting the former. See, *e. g.*, *Street*, *supra*, at 743; *First National Maintenance Corp.* v. *NLRB*, 452 U. S. 666, 686, n. 23 (1984). Our decision in *Street*, however, is far more than merely instructive here: we believe it is controlling, for § 8(a)(3) and § 2, Eleventh are in all material respects identical.[3] Indeed, we have previously described

---

[2] Section 8(b)(2) makes it unlawful for unions "to cause or attempt to cause an employer to discriminate against an employee in violation of subsection (a)(3)," 29 U. S. C. § 158(b)(2); accordingly, the provisos to § 8(a)(3) also allow unions to seek and enter into union-security agreements.

[3] Section 2, Eleventh provides, in pertinent part:

"Notwithstanding any other provisions of this chapter, or of any other statute or law of the United States, or Territory thereof, or of any State, any carrier or carriers as defined in this chapter and a labor organization or

the two provisions as "statutory equivalent[s]," *Ellis* v. *Railway Clerks*, 466 U. S. 435, 452, n. 13 (1984), and with good reason, because their nearly identical language reflects the fact that in both Congress authorized compulsory unionism only to the extent necessary to ensure that those who enjoy union-negotiated benefits contribute to their cost. Thus, in amending the RLA in 1951, Congress expressly modeled § 2, Eleventh on § 8(a)(3), which it had added to the NLRA only four years earlier, and repeatedly emphasized that it was extending "to railroad labor the same rights and privileges of the union shop that are contained in the Taft-Hartley Act." 96 Cong. Rec. 17055 (1951) (remarks of Rep. Brown).[4] In

labor organizations duly designated and authorized to represent employees in accordance with the requirements of this chapter shall be permitted—

"(a) to make agreements, requiring, as a condition of continued employment, that within sixty days following the beginning of such employment, or the effective date of such agreements, whichever is later, all employees shall become members of the labor organization representing their craft or class: *Provided*, That no such agreement shall require such condition of employment with respect to employees to whom membership is not available upon the same terms and conditions as are generally applicable to any other member or with respect to employees to whom membership was denied or terminated for any reason other than the failure of the employee to tender the periodic dues, initiation fees, and assessments (not including fines and penalties) uniformly required as a condition of acquiring or retaining membership." 45 U. S. C. § 152, Eleventh.

Although § 2, Eleventh allows termination of an employee for failure to pay "periodic dues, initiation fees, *and assessments (not including fines and penalties)*," the italicized language was added to the RLA only because some railway unions required only nominal dues, and financed their bargaining activities through monthly assessments; having added "assessments" as a proper element of agency fees, Congress simply clarified that the term did not refer, as it often did in the parlance of other industries, to fines or penalties. See *Machinists* v. *Street*, 367 U. S., at 766. In addition, § 2, Eleventh pre-empts state laws that would otherwise ban union shops. This difference, however, has no bearing on the types of union-security agreements that the statute permits, and thus does not distinguish the union shop authorization of § 2, Eleventh from that of § 8(a)(3).

[4] See also S. Rep. No. 2262, 81st Cong., 2d Sess., 3 (1950) ("[T]he terms of [the bill] are substantially the same as those of the Labor-Management

these circumstances, we think it clear that Congress intended the same language to have the same meaning in both statutes.

A

Both the structure and purpose of § 8(a)(3) are best understood in light of the statute's historical origins. Prior to the enactment of the Taft-Hartley Act of 1947, 61 Stat. 140, § 8(3) of the Wagner Act of 1935 (NLRA) permitted majority unions to negotiate "closed shop" agreements requiring employers to hire only persons who were already union members.

Relations Act"); H. R. Rep. No. 2811, 81st Cong., 2d Sess., 4 (1950) (the bill allows unions "to negotiate agreements with railroads and airlines of a character permitted in the case of labor organizations in the other large industries of the country"); 96 Cong. Rec. 15737 (1950) (remarks of Sen. Hill) ("The bill . . . is designed merely to extend to employees and employers subject to the [RLA] rights now possessed by employees and employers under the Taft-Hartley Act"); *id.*, at 15740 (remarks of Sen. Lehman) ("The railroad brotherhoods should have the same right that any other union has to negotiate for the union shop"); *id.*, at 16267 (remarks of Sen. Taft) ("[T]he bill inserts in the railway mediation law almost the exact provisions . . . of the Taft-Hartley law"); *id.*, at 17049 (remarks of Rep. Beckworth) (the bill permits railway unions "to bring about agreements with carriers providing for union shops, a principle enacted into law in the Taft-Hartley bill"); *id.*, at 17055 (remarks of Rep. Biemiller) ("[The] provision . . . gives to railway labor the right to bargain for the union shop just as any other labor group in the country may do"); *id.*, at 17056 (remarks of Rep. Bennett) ("The purpose of the bill is to amend the [RLA] to give railroad workers . . . the same right to enjoy the benefits and privileges of a union-shop arrangement that is now accorded to all workmen in most other types of employment"); *ibid.* (remarks of Rep. Heselton) ("[T]his bill primarily provides for the same kind of treatment of railroad and airline employees as is now accorded employees in all other industries under existing law"); *id.*, at 17059 (remarks of Rep. Harris) ("The fundamental proposition involved in the bill [is to extend] the national policy expressed in the Taft-Hartley Act regarding the lawfulness of . . . the union shop . . . to . . . railroad and airline labor organizations"); *id.*, at 17061 (remarks of Rep. Vursell) ("This bill simply extends to the railroad workers and employers the benefit of this provision now enjoyed by all other laboring men under the Taft-Hartley Act").

See *Algoma Plywood Co.* v. *Wisconsin Employment Relations Board*, 336 U. S. 301, 307–311 (1949). By 1947, such agreements had come under increasing attack, and after extensive hearings Congress determined that the closed shop and the abuses associated with it "create[d] too great a barrier to free employment to be longer tolerated." S. Rep. No. 105, 80th Cong., 1st Sess., 6 (1947) (S. Rep.), Legislative History of Labor Management Relations Act, 1947 (Committee Print compiled for the Subcommittee on Labor of the Senate Committee on Labor and Public Welfare), p. 412 (1974) (Leg. Hist.). The 1947 Congress was equally concerned, however, that without such agreements, many employees would reap the benefits that unions negotiated on their behalf without in any way contributing financial support to those efforts. As Senator Taft, one of the authors of the 1947 legislation, explained, "the argument . . . against abolishing the closed shop . . . is that if there is not a closed shop those not in the union will get a free ride, that the union does the work, gets the wages raised, then the man who does not pay dues rides along freely without any expense to himself." 93 Cong. Rec. 4887 (1947), Leg. Hist. 1422.[5] Thus, the Taft-Hartley Act was

[5] This sentiment was repeated throughout the hearings and lengthy debate that preceded passage of the bill. See, *e. g.*, 93 Cong. Rec. 3557 (1947), Leg. Hist. 740 (remarks of Rep. Jennings) (because members of the minority "would get the benefit of that contract made between the majority of their fellow workmen and the management . . . it is not unreasonable that they should go along and contribute dues like the others"); 93 Cong Rec. 3558, Leg. Hist. 741 (remarks of Rep. Robison) ("If [union-negotiated] benefits come to the workers all alike, is it not only fair that the beneficiaries, whether the majority or the minority, contribute their equal share in securing these benefits?"); 93 Cong. Rec. 3837, Leg. Hist. 1010 (remarks of Sen. Taft) ([T]he legislation, "in effect, . . . say[s], that no one can get a free ride in such a shop. That meets one of the arguments for a union shop. The employee has to pay the union dues"); S. Rep., at 6, Leg. Hist. 412 ("In testifying before this Committee, . . . leaders of organized labor have stressed the fact that in the absence of [union-security] provisions many employees sharing the benefits of what unions are able to ac-

> "intended to accomplish twin purposes. On the one hand, the most serious abuses of compulsory unionism were eliminated by abolishing the closed shop. On the other hand, Congress recognized that in the absence of a union-security provision 'many employees sharing the benefits of what unions are able to accomplish by collective bargaining will refuse to pay their share of the cost.'" *NLRB* v. *General Motors Corp.*, 373 U. S., at 740–741 (quoting S. Rep., at 6, Leg. Hist. 412).

The legislative solution embodied in § 8(a)(3) allows employers to enter into agreements requiring all the employees in a given bargaining unit to become members 30 days after being hired as long as such membership is available to all workers on a nondiscriminatory basis, but it prohibits the mandatory discharge of an employee who is expelled from the union for any reason other than his or her failure to pay initiation fees or dues. As we have previously observed, Congress carefully tailored this solution to the evils at which it was aimed:

> "Th[e] legislative history clearly indicates that Congress intended to prevent utilization of union security agreements for any purpose other than to compel payment of union dues and fees. Thus Congress recognized the validity of unions' concerns about 'free riders,' *i. e.*, employees who receive the benefits of union representation but are unwilling to contribute their *fair share* of financial support to such union, and gave unions the power to contract to meet *that problem* while withholding from unions the power to cause the discharge of employees for any other reason." *Radio Officers* v. *NLRB*, 347 U. S. 17, 41 (1954) (emphasis added).

---

complish by collective bargaining will refuse to pay their share of the cost"). See also H. R. Rep. No. 245, 80th Cong., 1st Sess., 80 (1947) (H. R. Rep.), Leg. Hist. 371 ("[Closed shop] agreements prevent nonunion workers from sharing in the benefits resulting from union activities without also sharing in the obligations").

Indeed, "Congress' decision to allow union-security agreements *at all* reflects its concern that . . . the parties to a collective bargaining agreement be allowed to provide that there be no employees who are getting the benefits of union representation without paying for them." *Oil Workers* v. *Mobil Oil Corp.*, 426 U. S. 407, 416 (1976) (emphasis added).

This same concern over the resentment spawned by "free riders" in the railroad industry prompted Congress, four years after the passage of the Taft-Hartley Act, to amend the RLA. As the House Report explained, 75 to 80% of the 1.2 million railroad industry workers belonged to one or another of the railway unions. H. R. Rep. No. 2811, 81st Cong., 2d Sess., 4 (1950). These unions, of course, were legally obligated to represent the interests of all workers, including those who did not become members; thus nonunion workers were able, at no expense to themselves, to share in all the benefits the unions obtained through collective bargaining. *Ibid.* Noting that the "principle of authorizing agreements for the union shop and the deduction of union dues has now become firmly established as a national policy for all industry subject to the Labor Management Relations Act of 1947," the House Report concluded that "[n]o sound reason exists for continuing to deny to labor organizations subject to the Railway Labor Act the right to negotiate agreements with railroads and airlines of a character permitted in the case of labor organizations in the other large industries of the country." *Ibid.*

In drafting what was to become §2, Eleventh, Congress did not look to §8(a)(3) merely for guidance. Rather, as Senator Taft argued in support of the legislation, the amendment "inserts in the railway mediation law almost the exact provisions, so far as they fit, of the Taft-Hartley law, so that the conditions regarding the union shop and the check-off are carried into the relations between railroad unions and the railroads." 96 Cong. Rec. 16267 (1950).[6] This was the universal understanding, among both supporters and opponents, of the purpose and effect of the amendment. See n. 4, *supra.* Indeed, railroad union representatives themselves proposed the amendment that incorporated in § 2, Eleventh, § 8(a)(3)'s prohibition against the discharge of employees who fail to obtain or maintain union membership for any reason other than nonpayment of periodic dues; in offering this proposal the unions argued, in terms echoing the language of the Senate Report accompanying the Taft-Hartley Act, that such a prohibition "remedies the alleged abuses of compulsory union membership . . . , yet makes possible the elimination of the 'free rider' and the sharing of the burden of maintenance by all of the beneficiaries of union activity." Hearings on H. R. 7789 before the House Committee on Interstate and Foreign Commerce, 81st Cong., 2d Sess., 253 (1950).

In *Street* we concluded "that § 2, Eleventh contemplated compulsory unionism to force employees to share the costs of negotiating and administering collective agreements, and the costs of the adjustment and settlement of disputes," but that Congress did not intend "to provide the unions with a means for forcing employees, over their objection, to support political causes which they oppose." 367 U. S., at 764. Constru-

---

[6] Although Senator Taft qualified his comparison by explaining that the provisions of the Taft-Hartley law were incorporated into the RLA "so far as they fit," this qualification merely reflected the fact that the laws were not identical in all respects, their chief difference inhering in their preemptive effect, or lack thereof, on all state regulation of union-security agreements. See n. 3, *supra.* This difference, of course, does not detract from the near identity of the provisions insofar as they confer on unions and employers authority to enter into union-security agreements, nor does it in any way undermine the force of Senator Taft's comparison with respect to this authority. Indeed, Taft himself explained that he initially "objected to some of the original terms of the bill, but when the [bill's] proponents agreed to accept amendments which made the provisions *identical* with the Taft-Hartley law," he decided to support the law. 96 Cong. Rec. 16267 (1950) (emphasis added).

ing the statute in light of this legislative history and purpose, we held that although § 2, Eleventh on its face authorizes the collection from nonmembers of "periodic dues, initiation fees, and assessments . . . *uniformly required* as a condition of acquiring or retaining membership" in a union, 45 U. S. C. § 152, Eleventh (b) (emphasis added), this authorization did not "ves[t] the unions with unlimited power to spend exacted money." 367 U. S., at 768. We have since reaffirmed that "Congress' essential justification for authorizing the union shop" limits the expenditures that may properly be charged to nonmembers under § 2, Eleventh to those "necessarily or reasonably incurred for the purpose of performing the duties of an exclusive [bargaining] representative." *Ellis* v. *Railway Clerks*, 466 U. S., at 447–448. Given the parallel purpose, structure, and language of § 8(a)(3), we must interpret that provision in the same manner.[7] Like § 2, Eleventh,

---

[7] We note that the NLRB, at least for a time, also took the position that the uniform "periodic dues and initiation fees" required by § 8(a)(3) were limited by the congressional concern with free riders to those fees necessary to finance collective-bargaining activities. In *Teamsters Local No. 959*, 167 N. L. R. B. 1042, 1045 (1967), the Board explained:

"[T]he right to charge 'periodic dues' granted unions by the proviso to Section 8(a)(3) is concerned exclusively with the concept that those enjoying the benefits of collective bargaining should bear their fair share of the costs incurred by the collective-bargaining agent in representing them. But it is manifest that dues that do not contribute, and are not intended to contribute, to the cost of operation of a union in its capacity as collective-bargaining agent cannot be justified as necessary for the elimination of 'free riders.'"

The Board, however, subsequently repudiated that view. See *Detroit Mailers Union No. 40*, 192 N. L. R. B. 951, 952 (1971).

Notwithstanding this unequivocal language, the dissent advises us, *post*, at 767, n. 5, that we have misread *Teamsters Local*. Choosing to ignore the above-quoted passage, the dissent asserts that the Board never "embraced . . . the view," *post*, at 767, n. 5, that "periodic dues and initiation fees" are limited to those that finance the union in its capacity as collective-bargaining agent, because in *Teamsters Local* itself the Board concluded that the dues in question "were actually 'special purpose funds,'" and were thus "'assessments' not contemplated by the proviso to § 8(a)(3)." *Post*, at 767, n. 5

§ 8(a)(3) permits the collection of "periodic dues and initiation fees uniformly required as a condition of acquiring or retaining membership" in the union,[8] and like its counterpart in the RLA, § 8(a)(3) was designed to remedy the inequities posed by "free riders" who would otherwise unfairly profit from the

(quoting *Teamsters Local, supra,* at 1044). This observation, however, avails the dissent nothing; obviously, once the Board determined that the dues were not used for collective-bargaining purposes, the conclusion that they were not dues within the meaning of § 8(a)(3) followed automatically. Under the dissent's reading, had the union simply built the increase into its dues base, rather than initially denominating it as a "special assessment," it would have been entitled to exact the fees as "periodic dues" and spend them for precisely the same purposes without running afoul of § 8(a)(3). The Board made entirely clear, however, that it was the *purpose* of the fee, not the manner in which it was collected, that controlled, and thus explained that "[m]onies collected for a credit union or building fund even if regularly recurring, as here, are obviously not 'for the maintenance of the' [union] as an organization, but are for a 'special purpose' and could be terminated without affecting *the continued existence of [the union] as the bargaining representative.*" *Teamsters Local, supra,* at 1045 (emphasis added). Finally, the dissent's portrayal of *Teamsters Local* as part of an unbroken string of consistent Board decisions on the issue is belied by the dissenting statement in *Detroit Mailers,* in which member Jenkins, who joined the decision in *Teamsters Local,* charged that the Board had ignored the clear holding of that earlier case. 192 N. L. R. B., at 952–953.

[8] Construing both § 8(a)(3) and § 2, Eleventh as permitting the collection and use of only those fees germane to collective bargaining does not, as petitioners seem to believe, read the term "uniform" out of the statutes. The uniformity requirement makes clear that the costs of representational activities must be borne equally by all those who benefit; without this language, unions could conceivably establish different dues rates both among members and between members and nonmembers, and thereby apportion the costs of collective bargaining unevenly. Indeed, the uniformity requirement inures to the benefit of dissident union members as well, by ensuring that if the union discriminates against them by charging higher dues, their failure to pay such dues cannot be grounds for discharge. See § 8(b)(2), 29 U. S. C. § 158(b)(2) (making it an unfair labor practice for a union "to cause or attempt to cause an *employer* to discriminate against an employee . . . with respect to whom membership in [the union] has been denied or terminated on some ground other than [the] failure to tender the periodic dues and initiation fees uniformly required") (emphasis added).

Taft-Hartley Act's abolition of the closed shop. In the face of such statutory congruity, only the most compelling evidence could persuade us that Congress intended the nearly identical language of these two provisions to have different meanings. Petitioners have not proffered such evidence here.

B

(1)

Petitioners claim that the union-security provisions of the RLA and NLRA can and should be read differently in light of the vastly different history of unionism in the industries the two statutes regulate. Thus they note that in *Street* we emphasized the "long-standing tradition of voluntary unionism" in the railway industry prior to the 1951 amendment, and the fact that in 1934 Congress had expressly endorsed an "open shop" policy in the RLA. 367 U. S., at 750. It was this historical background, petitioners contend, that led us to conclude that in amending the RLA in 1951, Congress "did not completely abandon the policy of full freedom of choice embodied in the 1934 Act, but rather made inroads on it for the limited purpose of eliminating the problems created by the 'free rider.'" *Id.*, at 767. The history of union security in industries governed by the NLRA was precisely the opposite: under the Wagner Act of 1935, all forms of compulsory unionism, including the closed shop, were permitted. Petitioners accordingly argue that the inroads Congress made in 1947 on the policy of compulsory unionism were likewise limited, and were designed to remedy only those "carefully-defined" abuses of the union shop system that Congress had expressly identified. Brief for Petitioners 42. Because agreements requiring the payment of uniform dues were not among these specified abuses, petitioners contend that § 8(a)(3) cannot plausibly be read to prohibit the collection of fees in excess of those necessary to cover the costs of collective bargaining.

We find this argument unpersuasive for several reasons. To begin with, the fact that Congress sought to remedy "the most serious abuses of compulsory union membership," S. Rep., at 7, Leg. Hist. 413, hardly suggests that the Taft-Hartley Act effected only limited changes in union-security practices. Quite to the contrary, in *Street* we concluded that Congress' purpose in amending the RLA was "limited" precisely because Congress did not perceive voluntary unionism as the source of widespread and flagrant abuses, and thus modified the railroad industry's open shop system only to the extent necessary to eliminate the problems associated with "free riders." That Congress viewed the Wagner Act's regime of compulsory unionism as seriously flawed, on the other hand, indicates that its purposes in overhauling that system were, if anything, far less limited, and not, as petitioners and the dissent contend, equally circumspect. Not surprisingly, therefore—and in stark contrast to petitioners' "limited inroads" theory—congressional opponents of the Taft-Hartley Act's union-security provisions understood the Act to provide only the most grudging authorization of such agreements, permitting "union-shop agreement[s] only under limited and administratively burdensome conditions." S. Rep., pt. 2, p. 8, Leg. Hist. 470 (Minority Report). That understanding comports with our own recognition that "Congress' decision to allow union-security agreements *at all* reflects its concern that . . . the parties to a collective bargaining agreement be allowed to provide that there be no employees who are getting the benefits of union representation without paying for them." *Oil Workers* v. *Mobil Oil Corp.*, 426 U. S., at 416 (emphasis added). Congress thus did not set out in 1947 simply to tinker in some limited fashion with the NLRA's authorization of union-security agreements. Rather, to the extent Congress preserved the status quo, it did so because of the considerable evidence adduced at congressional hearings indicating that "such agreements promoted stability by eliminating 'free riders,'" S. Rep., at 7,

Leg. Hist. 413, and Congress accordingly "gave unions the power to contract to meet *that problem* while withholding from unions the power to cause the discharge of employees for any other reason." *Radio Officers* v. *NLRB*, 347 U. S., at 41 (emphasis added). We therefore think it not only permissible but altogether proper to read § 8(a)(3), as we read § 2, Eleventh, in light of this animating principle.

Finally, however much union-security practices may have differed between the railway and NLRA-governed industries prior to 1951, it is abundantly clear that Congress itself understood its actions in 1947 and 1951 to have placed these respective industries on an equal footing insofar as compulsory unionism was concerned. Not only did the 1951 proponents of the union shop propose adding to the RLA language nearly identical to that of § 8(a)(3), they repeatedly insisted that the purpose of the amendment was to confer on railway unions precisely the same right to negotiate and enter into union-security agreements that all unions subject to the NLRA enjoyed. See n. 4, *supra*. Indeed, a subtheme running throughout the comments of these supporters was that the inequity of permitting "free riders" in the railroad industry was especially egregious in view of the fact that the Taft-Hartley Act gave exclusive bargaining representatives in all other industries adequate means to redress such problems. It would surely come as a surprise to these legislators to learn that their efforts to provide these same means of redress to railway unions were frustrated by the very historical disparity they sought to eliminate.

(2)

Petitioners also rely on certain aspects of the Taft-Hartley Act's legislative history as evidence that Congress intended to permit the collection and use of full union dues, including those allocable to activities other than collective bargaining. Again, however, we find this history insufficient to compel a broader construction of § 8(a)(3) than that accorded § 2, Eleventh in *Street*.

First and foremost, petitioners point to the fact that Congress expressly considered proposals regulating union finances but ultimately placed only a few limitations on the collection and use of dues and fees, and otherwise left unions free to arrange their financial affairs as they saw fit. In light of this history and the specific prohibitions Congress did enact, petitioners argue that there is no warrant for implying any further limitations on the amount of dues equivalents that unions may collect or the manner in which they may use them. As originally passed, § 7(b) of the House bill guaranteed union members the "right to be free from unreasonable or discriminatory financial demands of" unions. Leg. Hist. 176. Similarly, § 8(c) of the bill, the so-called "bill of rights for union members," H. R. Rep., at 31, Leg. Hist. 322, set out 10 protections against arbitrary action by union officers, one of which made it an unfair labor practice for a union to impose initiation fees in excess of $25 without NLRB approval, or to fix dues in amounts that were unreasonable, nonuniform, or not approved by majority vote of the members. *Id.*, at 53. In addition, § 304 of the bill prohibited unions from making contributions to or expenditures on behalf of candidates for federal office. *Id.*, at 97–98. The conferees adopted the latter provision, see *Pipefitters* v. *United States*, 407 U. S. 385, 405 (1972), and agreed to a prohibition on "excessive" initiation fees, see § 8(b)(5), 29 U. S. C. § 158(b)(5), but the Senate steadfastly resisted any further attempts to regulate internal union affairs. Referring to the House provisions, Senator Taft explained:

> "[T]he Senate conferees refused to agree to the inclusion of this subsection in the conference agreement since they felt that it was unwise to authorize an agency of the Government to undertake such elaborate policing of the internal affairs of unions as this section contemplated . . . . In the opinion of the Senate conferees the language

> which protected an employee from losing his job if a union expelled him for some reason other than nonpayment of dues and initiation fees, uniformly required of all members, was considered sufficient protection." 93 Cong. Rec. 6443 (1947), Leg. Hist. 1540.

Petitioners would have us infer from the demise of this "bill of rights" that Congress "'rejected . . . general federal restrictions on either the dues equivalents that employees may be required to pay or the uses to which unions may put such dues-equivalents,'" and that aside from the prohibition on political expenditures Congress placed no limitations on union exactions other than the requirement that they be equal to uniform dues. Brief for Petitioners 39–40 (quoting Brief for United States as *Amicus Curiae* 19). We believe petitioners' reliance on this legislative compromise is misplaced. The House bill did not purport to set out the rights of *nonmembers* who are compelled to pay union dues, but rather sought to establish a "bill of rights for union *members*" vis-à-vis their union leaders. H. R. Rep., at 31, Leg. Hist. 322 (emphasis added). Thus, § 8(c) of the House bill sought to regulate, among other things, the ability of unions to fine, discipline, suspend, or expel members; the manner in which unions conduct certain elections or maintain financial records; and the extent to which they can compel contributions to insurance or other benefit plans, or encumber the rights of members to resign. Leg. Hist. 52–56. The debate over these provisions focused on the desirability of Government oversight of internal union affairs, and a myriad of reasons having nothing whatever to do with the rights of nonmembers accounted for Congress' decision to forgo such detailed regulation. In rejecting any limitation on dues, therefore, Congress was not concerned with restrictions on "dues-equivalents," but rather with the administrative burdens and potential threat to individual liberties posed by Government regulation of purely internal union matters.[9]

It simply does not follow from this that Congress left unions free to exact dues equivalents from nonmembers in any amount they please, no matter how unrelated those fees may be to collective-bargaining activities. On the contrary, the complete lack of congressional concern for the rights of nonmembers in the debate surrounding the House "bill of rights" is perfectly consistent with the view that Congress understood § 8(a)(3) to afford nonmembers adequate protection by authorizing the collection of only those fees necessary to finance collective-bargaining activities: because the amount of such fees would be fixed by their underlying purpose—defraying the costs of collective bargaining—Congress would have every reason to believe that the lack of any limitations on union dues was entirely irrelevant so far as the rights of nonmembers were concerned. In short, we think it far safer and far more appropriate to construe § 8(a)(3) in light of its legislative justification, *i. e.*, ensuring that nonmembers who obtain the benefits of union representation can be made to pay for them, than by drawing inferences from Congress' rejection of a proposal that did not address the rights of nonmembers at all.

Petitioners also deem it highly significant that prior to 1947 unions "'rather typically'" used their members' dues for a "'variety of purposes . . . in addition to meeting the . . . costs of collective bargaining,'" *Retail Clerks* v. *Schermerhorn*, 373 U. S. 746, 754 (1963), and yet Congress, which was presumably well aware of the practice, in no way limited the

---

[9] See, *e. g.*, H. R. Rep., at 76–77, Leg. Hist. 367–368 (Minority Views) (charging that Government regulation was essentially impossible; that the encroachment on the rights of voluntary organizations such as unions was "without parallel"; and that such regulation invited harassment by rival unions and employers, and ultimately complete governmental control over union affairs).

uses to which unions could put fees collected from nonmembers. This silence, petitioners suggest, should be understood as congressional acquiescence in these practices. The short answer to this argument is that Congress was equally well aware of the same practices by railway unions, see *Street*, 367 U. S., at 767 ("We may assume that Congress was . . . fully conversant with the long history of intensive involvement of the railroad unions in political activities"); *Ellis*, 466 U. S., at 446 ("Congress was adequately informed about the broad scope of union activities"), yet neither in *Street* nor in any of the cases that followed it have we deemed Congress' failure in § 2, Eleventh to prohibit or otherwise regulate such expenditures as an endorsement of fee collections unrelated to collective-bargaining expenses. We see no reason to give greater weight to Congress' silence in the NLRA than we did in the RLA, particularly where such silence is again perfectly consistent with the rationale underlying § 8(a)(3): prohibiting the collection of fees that are not germane to representational activities would have been redundant if Congress understood § 8(a)(3) simply to enable unions to charge nonmembers only for those activities that actually benefit them.

Finally, petitioners rely on a statement Senator Taft made during floor debate in which he explained how the provisos of § 8(a)(3) remedied the abuses of the closed shop. "The great difference [between the closed shop and the union shop]," the Senator stated, "is that [under the union shop] a man can get a job without joining the union or asking favors of the union. . . . The fact that the employee has to pay dues to the union seems to me to be much less important." 93 Cong. Rec. 4886 (1947), Leg. Hist. 1422. On its face, the statement—made during a lengthy legislative debate—is somewhat ambiguous, for the reference to "union dues" could connote "full union dues" or could as easily be a shorthand method of referring to "collective-bargaining-related dues." In any event, as noted above, Senator Taft later described § 2, Eleventh as "almost the exact provisions . . . of the Taft-Hartley law," 96 Cong.

Rec. 16267 (1950), and we have construed the latter statute as permitting the exaction of only those dues related to representational activities. In view of Senator Taft's own comparison of the two statutory provisions, his comment in 1947 fails to persuade us that Congress intended virtually identical language in two statutes to have different meanings.

(3)

We come then to petitioners' final reason for distinguishing *Street.* Five years prior to our decision in that case, we ruled in *Railway Employees* v. *Hanson*, 351 U. S. 225 (1956), that because the RLA pre-empts all state laws banning union-security agreements, the negotiation and enforcement of such provisions in railroad industry contracts involves "governmental action" and is therefore subject to constitutional limitations. Accordingly, in *Street* we interpreted § 2, Eleventh to avoid the serious constitutional question that would otherwise be raised by a construction permitting unions to expend governmentally compelled fees on political causes that nonmembers find objectionable. See 367 U. S., at 749. No such constitutional questions lurk here, petitioners contend, for § 14(b) of the NLRA expressly preserves the authority of States to outlaw union-security agreements. Thus, petitioners' argument runs, the federal pre-emption essential to *Hanson*'s finding of governmental action is missing in the NLRA context, and we therefore need not strain to avoid the plain meaning of § 8(a)(3) as we did with § 2, Eleventh.

We need not decide whether the exercise of rights permitted, though not compelled, by § 8(a)(3) involves state action. Cf. *Steelworkers* v. *Sadlowski*, 457 U. S. 102, 121, n. 16 (1982) (union's decision to adopt an internal rule governing its elections does not involve state action); *Steelworkers* v. *Weber*, 443 U. S. 193, 200 (1979) (negotiation of collective-bargaining agreement's affirmative-action plan does not involve state action). Even assuming that it does not, and that the NLRA and RLA therefore differ in this respect, we do not believe that the absence of any constitutional concerns in this case would warrant reading the nearly identical language of § 8(a)(3) and § 2, Eleventh differently. It is, of course, true that federal statutes are to be construed so as to avoid serious doubts as to their constitutionality, and that when faced with such doubts the Court will first determine whether it is fairly possible to interpret the statute in a manner that renders it constitutionally valid. *Edward J. DeBartolo Corp.* v. *Florida Gulf Coast Building & Construction Trades Council*, 485 U. S. 568 (1988); *Crowell* v. *Benson*, 285 U. S. 22, 62 (1932). But statutory construction may not be pressed "'to the point of disingenuous evasion,'" *United States* v. *Locke*, 471 U. S. 84, 96 (1985) (quoting *George Moore Ice Cream Co.* v. *Rose*, 289 U. S. 373, 379 (1933)), and in avoiding constitutional questions the Court may not embrace a construction that "is plainly contrary to the intent of Congress." *DeBartolo*, *supra*, at 575. In *Street*, we concluded that our interpretation of § 2, Eleventh was "not only 'fairly possible' but entirely reasonable," 367 U. S., at 750, and we have adhered to that interpretation since. We therefore decline to construe the language of § 8(a)(3) differently from that of § 2, Eleventh on the theory that our construction of the latter provision was merely constitutionally expedient. Congress enacted the two provisions for the same purpose, eliminating "free riders," and that purpose dictates our construction of § 8(a)(3) no less than it did that of § 2, Eleventh, regardless of whether the negotiation of union-security agreements under the NLRA partakes of governmental action.

IV

We conclude that § 8(a)(3), like its statutory equivalent, § 2, Eleventh of the RLA, authorizes the exaction of only those fees and dues necessary to "performing the duties of an exclusive representative of the employees in dealing with the employer on labor-management issues." *Ellis*, 466 U. S., at 448. Accordingly, the judgment of the Court of Appeals is

Affirmed.

JUSTICE KENNEDY took no part in the consideration or decision of this case.

JUSTICE BLACKMUN, with whom JUSTICE O'CONNOR and JUSTICE SCALIA join, concurring in part and dissenting in part.

I agree that the District Court and the Court of Appeals properly exercised jurisdiction over respondents' duty-of-fair-representation and First Amendment claims, and that the National Labor Relations Board had primary jurisdiction over respondents' claim brought under § 8(a)(3) of the National Labor Relations Act of 1935, 49 Stat. 452, as amended, 29 U. S. C. § 158(a)(3). I also agree that the Court of Appeals had jurisdiction to decide the § 8(a)(3) question raised by respondents' duty-of-fair-representation claim.[1] I therefore join Parts I and II of the Court's opinion.

My agreement with the majority ends there, however, for I cannot agree with its resolution of the § 8(a)(3) issue. Without the decision in *Machinists* v. *Street*, 367 U. S. 740 (1961), involving the Railway Labor Act (RLA), the Court could not reach the result it does today. Our accepted mode of resolving statutory questions would not lead to a construction of § 8(a)(3) so foreign to that section's express language and legislative history, which show that Congress did not intend to limit either the amount of "agency fees" (or what the majority labels "dues-equivalents") a union may collect under a union-security agreement, or the union's expenditure of such funds. The Court's excessive reliance on *Street* to reach a

---

[1] Like the majority, I do not reach the First Amendment issue raised below by respondents, and therefore similarly do not address whether a union's exercise of rights pursuant to § 8(a)(3) involves state action. See *ante*, at 761.

contrary conclusion is manifested by its unique line of reasoning. No sooner is the language of § 8(a)(3) intoned, than the Court abandons all attempt at construction of *this* statute and leaps to its interpretation over a quarter century ago of another statute enacted by a different Congress, a statute with a distinct history and purpose. See *ante*, at 744–745. I am unwilling to offend our established doctrines of statutory construction and strain the meaning of the language used by Congress in § 8(a)(3), simply to conform § 8(a)(3)'s construction to the Court's interpretation of similar language in a different later-enacted statute, an interpretation which is itself "not without its difficulties." *Abood* v. *Detroit Board of Education*, 431 U. S. 209, 232 (1977) (characterizing the Court's decision in *Street*). I therefore dissent from Parts III and IV of the Court's opinion.

I

As the Court observes, "we have never before delineated the precise limits § 8(a)(3) places on the negotiation and enforcement of union-security agreements." *Ante*, at 745. Unlike the majority, however, I think the issue is an entirely new one. I shall endeavor, therefore, to resolve it in accordance with our well-settled principles of statutory construction.

A

As with any question of statutory interpretation, the starting point is the language of the statute itself. Section 8(a)(3) makes it unlawful for an employer to "discriminat[e] in regard to hire or tenure of employment or any term or condition of employment to encourage or discourage membership in any labor organization." 29 U. S. C. § 158(a)(3). Standing alone, this proscription, and thus § 8(b)(2)'s corollary proscription,[2] effectively would outlaw union-security agreements. The proscription, however, is qualified by two provisos. The first, which appeared initially in § 8(a)(3) of the

[2] Section 8(b)(2) makes it unlawful for a union "to cause or attempt to cause an employer" to violate § 8(a)(3). 29 U. S. C. § 158(b)(2).

NLRA as originally enacted in 1935, 49 Stat. 452, generally excludes union-security agreements from statutory condemnation by explaining that

> "nothing in [the NLRA] or in any other statute of the United States, shall preclude an employer from making an agreement with a labor organization . . . to require as a condition of employment membership therein . . . if such labor organization is the representative of the employees as provided in section 159(a) of this title . . . ." § 8(a)(3), 29 U. S. C. § 158(a)(3).

The second proviso, incorporated in § 8(a)(3) by the Taft-Hartley Amendments of 1947, 61 Stat. 141,[3] circumscribes the first proviso's general exemption by the following limitations:

> "[N]o employer shall justify any discrimination against an employee for nonmembership in a labor organization . . . if he has reasonable grounds for believing that membership was denied or terminated for reasons other than the failure of the employee to tender the periodic dues and the initiation fees uniformly required as a condition of acquiring or retaining membership."

The plain language of these statutory provisions, read together, permits an employer and union to enter into an agreement requiring *all* employees, as a condition of continued employment, to pay uniform periodic dues and initiation fees.[4] The second proviso expressly allows an employer to terminate any "employee," pursuant to a union-security agreement permitted by the first proviso, if the employee

---

[3] The Taft-Hartley Act also amended the first proviso to prohibit the application of a union-security agreement to an individual until he has been employed for 30 days. See 29 U. S. C. § 158(a)(3).

[4] This reading, of course, flows from the fact that "membership" as used in the first proviso, means not *actual* membership in the union, but rather "the payment of initiation fees and monthly dues." *NLRB* v. *General Motors Corp.*, 373 U. S. 734, 742 (1963).

fails "to tender the periodic dues and the initiation fees uniformly required as a condition of acquiring or retaining membership" in the union. 29 U. S. C. § 158(a)(3). The term "employee," as statutorily defined, includes any employee, without regard to union membership. See 29 U. S. C. § 152 (3). Union-member employees and nonunion-member employees are treated alike under § 8(a)(3).

"[W]e assume 'that the legislative purpose is expressed by the ordinary meaning of the words used.'" *American Tobacco Co.* v. *Patterson*, 456 U. S. 63, 68 (1982), quoting *Richards* v. *United States*, 369 U. S. 1, 9 (1962). The terms "dues" and "fees," as used in the proviso, can refer to nothing other than the regular, periodic dues and initiation fees paid by "voluntary" union members. This was the apparent understanding of the Court in those decisions in which it held that § 8(a)(3) permits union-security agreements. See *NLRB* v. *General Motors Corp.*, 373 U. S. 734, 736 (1963) (approving a union-security proposal that would have conditioned employment "upon the payment of sums equal to the initiation fee and regular monthly dues paid by the union members"); *Retail Clerks* v. *Schermerhorn*, 373 U. S. 746, 753 (1963) (upholding agreement requiring nonmembers to pay a "service fee [which] is admittedly the exact equal of membership initiation fees and monthly dues"). It also has been the consistent view of the NLRB,[5] "the agency en-

[5] See, *e. g.*, *In re Union Starch & Refining Co.*, 87 N. L. R. B. 779, (1949), enf'd, 186 F. 2d 1008 (CA7), cert. denied, 342 U. S. 815 (1951); *Detroit Mailers Union No. 40*, 192 N. L. R. B. 951, 951–952 (1971). In *Detroit Mailers*, the Board explained:

"Neither on its face nor in the congressional purpose behind [§ 8(a)(3)] can any warrant be found for making any distinction here between dues which may be allocated for collective-bargaining purposes and those earmarked for institutional expenses of the union. . . . '[D]ues collected from members may be used for a variety of purposes, in addition to meeting the union's costs of collective bargaining.' Unions 'rather typically' use their membership dues 'to do those things which the members authorized the union to do in their interest and on their behalf.' By virtue of Sec-

trusted by Congress with the authority to administer the NLRA." *Edward J. DeBartolo Corp.* v. *Florida Gulf Coast Building & Construction Trades Council*, 485 U. S. 568, 574 (1988). The provisos do not give any employee, union member or not, the right to pay less than the full amount of regular dues and initiation fees charged to all other bargaining-unit employees.

---

tion 8(a)(3), such dues may be required from an employee under a union-security contract so long as they are periodic and uniformly required and are not devoted to a purpose which would make their mandatory extraction otherwise inimical to public policy." *Id.*, at 952, quoting *Retail Clerks* v. *Schermerhorn*, 373 U. S., at 753–754 (internal quotations omitted).

The United States, appearing here as *amicus curiae*, maintains that position in this case.

Contrary to the Court's suggestion, the NLRB has not embraced and then "repudiated" the view that, for purposes of § 8(a)(3), "periodic dues and initiation fees" mean only "those fees necessary to finance collective-bargaining activities." *Ante*, at 752, n. 7. *Teamsters Local No. 959*, 167 N. L. R. B. 1042 (1967), does not demonstrate otherwise. In *Teamsters Local*, the NLRB held that "working dues" designated to fund a union building program and a credit union were actually "assessments" not contemplated by the proviso to § 8(a)(3). *Id.*, at 1044. The Board found that the union itself regarded the levy as a "temporary assessment," clearly distinct from its "regular dues." *Ibid.* Moreover, because the financing for the programs was constructed in such a way that the union treasury might never have received 90% of the moneys, the Board concluded that the "working dues" were actually "special purposes funds," and that "the support of such funds cannot come from 'periodic dues' as that term is used in § 8(a)(3)." *Ibid.* In *Detroit Mailers*, the NLRB distinguished such assessments from "periodic and uniformly required" dues, which, in its view, a union is not precluded from demanding of nonmembers pursuant to § 8(a)(3). 192 N. L. R. B., at 952.

While the majority credits an interpretation of *Teamsters Local* propounded by a dissenting member of the Board in *Detroit Mailers*, *ante*, at 752–753, n. 7, I prefer to take the Board's word at face value: *Teamsters Local* did not create "controlling precedent" endorsing the view of § 8(a)(3) enunciated by the Court today. 192 N. L. R. B., at 952. Significantly, the majority cannot cite one case in which the Board has held that uniformly required, periodic dues used for purposes other than "collective bargaining" are not dues within the meaning of § 8(a)(3).

The Court's conclusion that § 8(a)(3) prohibits petitioners from requiring respondents to pay fees for purposes other than those "germane" to collective bargaining, contract administration, and grievance adjustment simply cannot be derived from the plain language of the statute. In effect, the Court accepts respondents' contention that the words "dues" and "fees," as used in § 8(a)(3), refer not to the periodic amount a union charges its members but to the portion of that amount that the union expends on statutory collective bargaining.[6] See Brief for Respondents 17–20. Not only is this reading implausible as a matter of simple English usage, but it is also contradicted by the decisions of this Court and of the NLRB interpreting the section. Section 8(a)(3) does not speak of "dues" and "fees" that employees covered by a

---

[6] The Court's insistence that it has not changed the meaning of the term "uniform," see *ante*, at 753, n. 8, misses the point. The uniformity requirement obviously requires that the union can collect from nonmembers under a union-security agreement only those "periodic dues and initiation fees" collected equally from its members. But this begs the question: what "periodic dues and initiation fees"? It is the meaning of those terms which the Court misconceives.

Under our settled doctrines of statutory construction, were there any ambiguity in the meaning of § 8(a)(3)—which there is not—the Court would be constrained to defer to the interpretation of the NLRB, unless the agency's construction were contrary to the clear intent of Congress. *Chevron U. S. A. Inc.* v. *National Resources Defense Council, Inc.*, 467 U. S. 837, 842–843, and n. 9 (1984). Although the Court apparently finds such ambiguity, it fails to apply this doctrine. By reference to a narrow view of congressional "purpose" gleaned from isolated statements in the legislative history, and in reliance upon this Court's interpretation of another statute, the Court constructs an interpretation that not only finds no support in the statutory language or legislative history of § 8(a)(3), but also contradicts the Board's settled interpretation of the statutory provision. The Court previously has directed: "Where the Board's construction of the Act is reasonable, it should not be rejected 'merely because the courts might prefer another view of the statute.'" *Pattern Makers* v. *NLRB*, 473 U. S. 95, 114 (1985), quoting *Ford Motor Co.* v. *NLRB*, 441 U. S. 488, 497 (1979). Here, the only apparent motivation for holding that the Board's interpretation of § 8(a)(3) is impermissible, is the Court's view of *another* statute.

union-security agreement may be required to tender to their union representative; rather, the section speaks only of "the periodic dues and the initiation fees *uniformly required as a condition of acquiring or retaining membership*" (emphasis added). Thus, the section, by its terms, defines "periodic dues" and "initiation fees" as those dues and fees "uniformly required" of all members, not as a portion of full dues. As recognized by this Court, "dues collected from members may be used for a variety of purposes, in addition to meeting the union's costs of collective bargaining. Unions rather typically use their membership dues to do those things which the members authorize the union to do in their interest and on their behalf." *Retail Clerks* v. *Schermerhorn*, 373 U. S., at 753–754 (internal quotations omitted). By virtue of § 8(a)(3), such dues may be required from *any* employee under a union-security agreement. Nothing in § 8(a)(3) limits, or even addresses, the purposes to which a union may devote the moneys collected pursuant to such an agreement.[7]

B

The Court's attempt to squeeze support from the legislative history for its reading of congressional intent contrary to the plain language of § 8(a)(3) is unavailing. As its own discussion of the relevant legislative materials reveals, *ante*, at 747–750, there is no indication that the 1947 Congress intended to limit the union's authority to collect from nonmembers the same periodic dues and initiation fees it collects from members. Indeed, on balance, the legislative history rein-

[7] The Court's answer to the absolute lack of evidence that Congress intended to regulate such expenditures is no answer at all: the Court simply reiterates that in *Machinists* v. *Street*, 367 U. S. 740 (1961), it did not give weight to congressional silence in the RLA on this issue. See *ante*, at 760. The point, however, is *not* that the Court should give weight to Congress' silence in the NLRA; the point is that the Court must find *some* support in the NLRA for its proposition. Congress' silence simply highlights that there is no support for the Court's interpretation of the 1947 Congress' intent.

forces what the statutory language suggests: the provisos neither limit the uses to which agency fees may be put nor require nonmembers to be charged less than the "uniform" dues and initiation fees.

In *Machinists* v. *NLRB*, 362 U. S. 411 (1960), the Court stated:

> "It is well known, and the legislative history of the 1947 Taft-Hartley amendments plainly shows, that § 8(a)(3)—including its proviso—represented the Congressional response to the competing demands of employee freedom of choice and union security. Had Congress thought one or the other overriding, it would doubtless have found words adequate to express that judgment. It did not do so; it accommodated both interests, doubtless in a manner unsatisfactory to the extreme partisans of each, by drawing a line it thought reasonable. It is not for the administrators of the Congressional mandate to approach either side of that line grudgingly." *Id.*, at 418, n. 7.

The legislative debates surrounding the adoption of § 8 (a)(3) in 1947, show that in crafting the proviso to § 8(a)(3), Congress was attempting "only to 'remedy the most serious abuses of compulsory union membership . . . .'" *NLRB* v. *General Motors Corp.*, 373 U. S., at 741, quoting from the legislative history. The particular "abuses" Congress identified and attempted to correct were two: the closed shop, which "deprives management of any real choice of the men it hires" and gives union leaders "a method of depriving employees of their jobs, and in some cases [of] a means of securing a livelihood in their trade or calling, for purely capricious reasons," S. Rep. No. 105, 80th Cong., 1st Sess., 6 (1947) (S. Rep.), Legislative History of the Labor Management Relations Act, 1947 (Committee Print compiled for the Subcommittee on Labor of the Senate Committee on Labor and Public Welfare), p. 412 (1974) (Leg. Hist.); and those union shops in which the union sought to obtain indirectly the same result as that obtained through a closed shop by negotiating a union-shop agreement and maintaining a "closed" union where it was free to deny membership to an individual arbitrarily or discriminatorily and then compel the discharge of that person because of his nonmembership, 93 Cong. Rec. 3836–3837, 4193, 4885–4886 (1947), Leg. Hist. 1010, 1096-1097, 1420–1421 (remarks of Sen. Taft); 93 Cong. Rec. 4135, Leg. Hist. 1061–1062 (remarks of Sen. Ellender). Senator Taft, the chief sponsor of the Senate bill, in arguing against an amendment to proscribe all forms of union-security agreements, stated that it was unwise to outlaw union-security agreements altogether "since there had been for such a long time so many union shops in the United States, [and] since in many trades it was entirely customary and had worked satisfactorily," and that therefore the appropriate approach was to "meet the problem of dealing with the abuses which had appeared." 93 Cong. Rec. 4885, Leg. Hist. 1420.[8] "Con-

---

[8] See also, *e. g.*, 93 Cong. Rec. 3837 (1947), Leg. Hist. 1010 (remarks of Sen. Taft) ("[B]ecause the union shop has been in force in many industries for so many years . . . to upset it today probably would destroy relationships of long standing and probably would bring on more strikes than it would cure").

Despite a legislative history rife with unequivocal statements to the contrary, the Court concludes that the 1947 Congress did not set out to restrict union-security agreements in a "limited fashion." *Ante*, at 755. Quite apart from the Court's unorthodox reliance on representations of those *opposed* to the Taft-Hartley amendments, the majority's observation that "Congress viewed the Wagner Act's regime of compulsory unionism as seriously flawed," *ibid.*, begs the question. The perceived flaws were embedded in the *closed*-shop system, not the *union*-shop system. Thus, as is characteristic of the majority's opinion, its comparison to the RLA, under which there was no closed-shop system, is beside the point. See *ibid.* Congress was aware that under the NLRA, "the one system [the closed shop] ha[d] led to very serious abuses and the other system [the union shop] ha[d] not led to such serious abuses." 93 Cong. Rec. 4886 (1947), Leg. Hist. 1421 (remarks of Sen. Taft). Accordingly, Congress banned closed shops altogether, but it made only limited inroads on the union-shop system that had been in effect prior to 1947, carefully describing its limitations on such agreements. H. R. Rep. No. 245, 80th Cong.,

gress [also] recognized that in the absence of a union-security provision 'many employees sharing the benefits of what unions are able to accomplish by collective bargaining will refuse to pay their share of the cost.'" *NLRB* v. *General Motors Corp.*, 373 U. S., at 740–741, quoting S. Rep., at 6, Leg. Hist. 412.

Congress' solution was to ban the closed shop and to permit the enforcement of union-shop agreements as long as union membership is available "on the same terms and conditions" to all employees, and mandatory discharge is required only for "nonpayment of regular dues and initiation fees." S. Rep., at 7, 20, Leg. Hist. 413, 426. Congress was of the view, that, as Senator Taft stated, "[t]he fact that the employee will have to pay dues to the union seems . . . to be much less important. The important thing is that the man will have the job." 93 Cong. Rec. 4886 (1947), Leg. Hist. 1422. "[A] man can get a job with an employer and can continue in that job if, in effect, he joins the union and pays the union dues.

. . . . .

"If he pays the dues without joining the union, he has the right to be employed." 93 Cong. Rec. 4886 (1947), Leg. Hist.

1st Sess., 9 (1947), Leg. Hist. 300; S. Rep., at 6–7, Leg. Hist. 412–413. It could not be clearer from the legislative history that in enacting the provisos to § 8(a)(3), Congress attempted to deal only with specific abuses in the union-shop system, only the "actual problems that ha[d] arisen." 93 Cong. Rec. 4886 (1947), Leg. Hist. 1421 (remarks of Sen. Taft); accord, 93 Cong. Rec. 3836–3837 (1947), Leg. Hist. 1010–1011 (remarks of Sen. Taft). Congress' philosophy was that it had "to decree either an open shop or an open union. [It] decreed an open union . . . [which would] permit the continuation of existing relationships, and [would] not violently tear apart a great many long-existing relationships and make trouble in the labor movement; and yet at the same time it [would] meet the abuses which exist." 93 Cong. Rec. 4886 (1947), Leg. Hist. 1420 (remarks of Sen. Taft). Union-security agreements requiring the payment of uniform periodic dues and standard initiation fees were not among the specified abuses. There was no testimony regarding problems arising from such arrangements. Indeed, the subtext of the entire debate was that such arrangements were acceptable. The Court's suggestion to the contrary is simply untenable.

1421–1422. There is no serious doubt that what Congress had in mind was a situation in which the nonmember employee would "pay the same dues as other members of the union." 93 Cong. Rec. 4272 (1947), Leg. Hist. 1142 (remarks of Sen. Taft); accord, 93 Cong. Rec. 3557 (1947), Leg. Hist. 740 (remarks of Sen. Jennings) (members of the minority "should go along and contribute dues like the others"). In their financial obligations, therefore, these employees were "in effect," union members, and could not be discharged pursuant to a union-security agreement as long as they maintained this aspect of union "membership."[9] This solution was viewed as "tak[ing] care" of the free-rider issue. 93 Cong. Rec. 4887 (1947), Leg. Hist. 1422 (remarks of Sen. Taft).

Throughout the hearings and lengthy debate on one of the most hotly contested issues that confronted the 1947 Congress, not once did any Member of Congress suggest that § 8(a)(3) did not leave employers and unions free to adopt and enforce union-security agreements requiring all employees in the bargaining unit to pay an amount equal to full union dues and standard initiation fees. Nor did anyone suggest that § 8(a)(3) affected a union's expenditure of such funds.

Indeed, the legislative history indicates that Congress affirmatively declined to place limitations on either the amount of dues a union could charge or the uses to which it could put these dues. The Court dismisses as irrelevant the fact that Congress expressly rejected the House proposal that would have empowered the NLRB to regulate the "reasonableness" of union dues and expenditures. The Court finds meaningful the fact that "[t]he House bill did not purport to set out the

[9] The Senate Report explained: Congress "did not desire to limit the labor organization with respect to either its selection of membership or expulsion therefrom. But [it] did wish to protect the employee in his job if unreasonably expelled or denied membership. The tests provided by the amendment are based upon facts readily ascertainable and do not require the employer to inquire into the internal affairs of the union." S. Rep., at 20, Leg. Hist. 426.

rights of *nonmembers* who are compelled to pay union dues, but rather sought to establish a 'bill of rights for union *members*' vis-à-vis their union leaders. H. R. Rep., at 31, Leg. Hist. 322 (emphasis added)." *Ante*, at 758. But this is a distinction without a difference. Contrary to the Court's view, Congress viewed this proposal as directly related to § 8(a)(3); Congress clearly saw the nonmembers' interests in this context as being represented by union members.[10] Thus, Senator Taft explained the Senate conferees' reasons for refusing to accept the provisions in the House bill:

> "In the opinion of the Senate conferees[,] the language which protected an employee from losing his job if a union expelled him for some reason other than nonpayment of dues and initiation fees, uniformly required of all members, was considered sufficient protection." 93 Cong. Rec. 6443 (1947), Leg. Hist. 1540.

Congress' decision, in the course of the well-documented Senate-House compromise, not to place any general federal restrictions on the levels or uses of union dues,[11] indicates

[10] The Court appears to believe that Congress intended § 8(a)(3) to protect the interests of individual nonmembers in the uses to which the union puts their moneys. See *ante*, at 759. It could not be clearer, however, that Congress did not have this in mind at all. As Senator Taft explained to his colleague who complained that requiring a man to join a union he does not wish to join (pursuant to § 8(a)(3)) was no less restrictive than a closed shop: in enacting § 8(a)(3), Congress was not trying "to go into the broader fields of the rights of particular persons." 93 Cong. Rec. 4886 (1947), Leg. Hist. 1421.

The only "rights" protected by the § 8(a)(3) provisos are workers' employment rights. As the legislative debates reflect, Congress was principally concerned with insulating workers' jobs from capricious actions by union leaders. "The purpose of the union unfair labor practice provisions added to § 8(a)(3) was to 'preven[t] the union from inducing the employer to use the emoluments of the job to enforce the union's rules.'" *Pattern Makers* v. *NLRB*, 473 U. S., at 126 (dissenting opinion), quoting *Scofield* v. *NLRB*, 394 U. S. 423, 429 (1969).

[11] Congress placed only one limitation on the uses which can be made of union dues. "[W]ith little apparent discussion or opposition," the Senate

that it did not intend the provisos to limit the uses to which agency fees may be put.

The Court invokes what it apparently sees as a single-minded legislative purpose, namely, the eradication of a "free-rider" problem, and then views the legislative history through this narrow prism. The legislative materials demonstrate, however, that, contrary to the impression left by the Court, Congress was not guided solely by a desire to eliminate "free riders." The 1947 Congress that carefully crafted § 8(a)(3) was focusing on a quite different problem—the most serious abuses of compulsory unionism. As the majority observes, "Congress carefully tailored [its] solution to the evils at which it was aimed." *Ante*, at 749. In serving its purpose, Congress went only so far in foreclosing compulsory unionism. It outlawed closed shops altogether, but banned unions from using union-security provisions only where those provisions exact more than the initiation fees and "periodic dues" uniformly required as conditions of union

conferees adopted the House bill's prohibition limiting what unions may spend from dues money on federal elections. *Pipefitters* v. *United States*, 407 U. S. 385, 405 (1972). In § 304 of the Labor Management Relations (Taft-Hartley) Act, 61 Stat. 159–160, which is now incorporated in the Federal Election Campaign Act of 1976, 90 Stat. 490, 2 U. S. C. § 441b(a), Congress made it unlawful for a union "to make a contribution or expenditure in connection with" certain political elections, primaries, or political conventions.

The Senate conferees also agreed with the House that some safeguard was needed to prevent unions from charging new members exorbitant initiation fees that effectively "close" the union, thereby "frustrat[ing] the intent of [§ 8(a)(3)]." 93 Cong. Rec. 6443 (1947), Leg. Hist. 1540 (remarks of Sen. Taft). Hence, § 8(b)(5) was added to the final bill, which makes it an unfair labor practice for a union which has negotiated a union-security agreement to require initiation fees that the NLRB "finds excessive or discriminatory under all the circumstances." 29 U. S. C. § 158(b)(5). The Senate passed § 8(b)(5) only after receiving assurances from Senator Taft that it would not allow the NLRB to regulate union expenditures. See 93 Cong. Rec. 6859 (1947), Leg. Hist. 1623 (stressing that the provision "is limited to initiation fees and does not cover dues").

membership. Otherwise, it determined that the regulation of union-security agreements should be left to specific federal legislation and to the legislatures and courts of the several States.[12] Congress explicitly declined to mandate the kind of particularized regulation of union dues and fees which the Court attributes to it today.

II

By suggesting that the 1947 Congress was driven principally by a desire to eradicate a "free-rider" problem, the Court finds the means not only to distort the legislative justification for § 8(a)(3) and to ignore the provision's plain language, but also to draw a controlling parallelism to § 2, Eleventh of the RLA, 64 Stat. 1238, 45 U. S. C. § 152. As mistaken as the Court is in its view of Congress' purpose in enacting § 8(a)(3), the Court is even more mistaken in its reliance on this Court's interpretation of § 2, Eleventh in *Machinists* v. *Street*, 367 U. S. 740 (1961).

The text of § 8(a)(3) of the NLRA is, of course, very much like the text of the later enacted § 2, Eleventh of the RLA. This similarity, however, does not dictate the conclusion that the 1947 Congress intended § 8(a)(3) to have a meaning identical to that which the 1951 Congress intended § 2, Eleventh to have. The Court previously has held that the scope of the RLA is not identical to that of the NLRA and that courts should be wary of drawing parallels between the two stat-

[12] "It was never the intention of the [NLRA] . . . to preempt the field in this regard so as to deprive the States of their powers to prevent compulsory unionism." H. R. Conf. Rep. 510, 80th Cong., 1st Sess., 60 (1947), Leg. Hist. 564. Accordingly, Congress added § 14(b) to the final bill, which, as enacted, expressly preserves the authority of the States to regulate union-security agreements, including the use of funds collected from employees pursuant to such an agreement. See *Retail Clerks* v. *Schermerhorn*, 373 U. S., at 751–752. Many States in fact have imposed limitations on the union-security agreements that are permitted in their jurisdictions. See 2 C. Morris, The Developing Labor Law 1391–1392 (2d ed. 1983).

utes. See, *e. g.*, *First National Maintenance Corp.* v. *NLRB*, 452 U. S. 666, 686, n. 23 (1981); *Railroad Trainmen* v. *Jacksonville Terminal Co.*, 394 U. S. 369, 383 (1969). Thus, parallels between § 8(a)(3) and § 2, Eleventh, "like all parallels between the NLRA and the Railway Labor Act, should be drawn with the utmost care and with full awareness of the differences between the statutory schemes." *Chicago & N. W. R. Co.* v. *Transportation Union*, 402 U. S. 570, 579, n. 11 (1971). Contrary to the majority's conclusion, *ante*, at 750, the two provisions were not born of the "same concern[s]"; indeed, they were born of competing concerns. This Court's interpretation of § 2, Eleventh, therefore, provides no support for construing § 8(a)(3) in a fashion inconsistent with its plain language and legislative history.[13]

The considerations that enabled the Court to conclude in *Street*, 367 U. S., at 750, that it is "'fairly possible'" and "entirely reasonable" to read § 2, Eleventh to proscribe union-security agreements requiring uniform payments from all bargaining-unit employees are wholly absent with respect to § 8(a)(3). In *Street*, the Court stressed the fact that from 1926, when the RLA was first enacted, until 1951 when § 2, Eleventh assumed its present form, that Act prohibited all forms of union security and declared a "policy of complete freedom of choice of employees to join or not to join a union." *Ibid.* By 1951, however, Congress recognized "the expenses and burdens incurred by the unions in the administration of the complex scheme of the [RLA]." 367 U. S., at 751. The purpose advanced for amending the RLA in 1951 to authorize union-security agreements for the first time was "the elimi-

[13] The dissent in the original panel decision in this case appropriately observed: "If the legislative purposes behind § 8(a)(3) and § 2, Eleventh were identical, one would expect that [this] Court in *Street* would have looked to the NLRA for guidance in interpreting § 2, Eleventh. The *Street* opinion, however, does not significantly rely on or discuss either the NLRA or § 8(a)(3). Instead, it focuses on the distinctive features of the railroad industry and the Railway Labor Act in construing § 2, Eleventh." 776 F. 2d 1187, 1220 (CA4 1985).

nation of the 'free riders.'" 367 U. S., at 761. Given that background, the Court was persuaded that it was possible to conclude that "Congress did not completely abandon the policy of full freedom of choice embodied in the . . . Act, but rather made inroads on it for the limited purpose of eliminating the problems created by the 'free rider.'" *Id.*, at 767.

The NLRA does not share the RLA's underlying policy, which propelled the Court's interpretation of § 2, Eleventh in *Street*. Indeed, the history of the NLRA points in the opposite direction: the original policy of the Wagner Act was to permit all forms of union-security agreements, and such agreements were commonplace in 1947. Thus, in enacting § 8(a)(3), the 1947 Congress, unlike the 1951 Congress, was not making inroads on a policy of full freedom of choice in order to provide "a specific response," *id.*, at 751, to a particular problem facing unions. Rather, the 1947 amendments to § 8(a)(3) were designed to make an inroad into a preexisting policy of the absolute freedom of private parties under federal law to negotiate union-security agreements. It was a "limited" inroad, responding to carefully defined abuses that Congress concluded had arisen in the union-security agreements permitted by the Wagner Act. The 1947 Congress did not enact § 8(a)(3) for the "same purpose" as did the 1951 Congress in enacting § 2, Eleventh. Therefore, contrary to the Court's conclusion, *ante*, at 762, the latter purpose, "eliminating 'free riders,'" does *not* dictate our construction of § 8(a)(3), regardless of its impact on our construction of § 2, Eleventh.

In order to overcome this inevitable conclusion, the Court relies on remarks made by a few Members of the Congress in enacting the 1951 amendments to § 2, Eleventh of the RLA, which the Court contends show that the 1951 Congress viewed those amendments as identical to the amendments that had been made to § 8(a)(3) of the NLRA in 1947. See *ante*, at 756; see also *ante*, at 746, and n. 4. But even assuming the Court's view of the legislative history of § 2, Eleventh is correct (and the legislative materials do not obviously impart the message the Court receives[14]), it does not provide support for the Court's strained reading of § 8(a)(3). Its only possible relevance in this case is to evidence the 1951 Congress' understanding of a statute that particular Congress did not enact. The relevant question here, however, is what the 1947 Congress intended by the statute that *it* enacted. "[I]t is well settled that '"the views of a subsequent Congress form a hazardous basis for inferring the intent of an earlier one."'" *Russello* v. *United States*, 464 U. S. 16, 26 (1983), quoting *Jefferson County Pharmaceutical Assn.* v. *Abbott Laboratories*, 460 U. S. 150, 165, n. 27 (1983), in turn quoting *United States* v. *Price*, 361 U. S. 304, 313 (1960). See also *United States* v. *Clark*, 445 U. S. 23, 33, n. 9 (1980). It

[14] The Court overstates the clarity of what was said about § 8(a)(3) when § 2, Eleventh was amended in 1951. As the Court's recitation of various statements reflects, the extent to which the 1951 Congress saw itself engrafting onto the RLA terms *identical*, in all respects, to the terms of § 8(a)(3) is uncertain. See *ante*, at 746–747, n. 4. The remarks are only general comments about the similarity of the NLRA union-security provisions, rather than explicit comparisions of § 8(a)(3) with the provisions of the RLA. For example, Senator Taft explained: "In effect, the bill inserts in the railway mediation law *almost the exact provisions, so far as they fit*, of the Taft-Hartley law, so that the conditions regarding the union shop and the check-off are carried into the relations between railroad unions and the railroads." 96 Cong. Rec. 16267 (1950) (emphasis added). See also, *e. g.*, H. R. Rep. No. 2811, 81st Cong., 2d Sess., 4 (1950) (§ 2, Eleventh allows agreements "of a character" permitted in § 8(a)(3)); 96 Cong. Rec. 17049 (1951) (remarks of Rep. Beckworth) (§ 2, Eleventh extends to railroads "a principle" embodied in § 8(a)(3)). Especially when it is remembered that Congress was *extending* to unions in the railroad industry the authority to enter into agreements for which they previously had *no* authority, whereas the 1947 Congress had rescinded authorization for certain kinds of union-security agreements, the import of these statements is ambiguous. To borrow a phrase from the majority, I "think it far safer and far more appropriate to construe § 8(a)(3) in light of its" language and legislative history, "than by drawing inferences from" ambiguous statements made by Members of a later Congress in enacting a different statute. *Ante*, at 759.

would "surely come as a surprise" to the legislators who enacted § 8(a)(3) to learn that, in discerning their intent, the Court listens not to their voices, but to those of a later Congress. *Ante*, at 756. Unlike the majority, I am unwilling to put the 1951 legislators' words into the 1947 legislators' mouths.

The relevant sources for gleaning the 1947 Congress' intent are the plain language of § 8(a)(3), and, at least to the extent that it might reflect a clear intention contrary to the plain meaning of the statute, the legislative history of § 8(a)(3). Those sources show that the 1947 Congress did not intend § 8(a)(3) to have the same meaning the Court has attributed to § 2, Eleventh of the RLA. I therefore must disagree with the majority's assertion that the Court's decision in *Street* is "controlling" here. See *ante*, at 745.

III

In sum, I conclude that, in enacting § 8(a)(3) of the NLRA, Congress did not intend to prohibit union-security agreements that require the tender of full union dues and standard union initiation fees from nonmember employees, without regard to how the union expends the funds so collected. In finding controlling weight in this Court's interpretation of § 2, Eleventh of the RLA to reach a contrary conclusion, the Court has not only eschewed our well-established methods of statutory construction, but also interpreted the terms of § 8(a)(3) in a manner inconsistent with the congressional purpose clearly expressed in the statutory language and amply documented in the legislative history. I dissent.

Syllabus

WATERS ET AL. v. CHURCHILL ET AL.

CERTIORARI TO THE UNITED STATES COURT OF APPEALS FOR THE SEVENTH CIRCUIT

No. 92–1450. Argued December 1, 1993—Decided May 31, 1994

Petitioners fired respondent Churchill from her nursing job at a public hospital, allegedly because of statements she made to co-worker Perkins-Graham during a work break. What Churchill actually said during the conversation is in dispute. Petitioners' version was based on interviews with Perkins-Graham and one Ballew, who had overheard part of the conversation, and indicated that Churchill made disruptive statements critical of her department and of petitioners. However, in Churchill's version, which was corroborated by others who had overheard part of the conversation, her speech was largely limited to nondisruptive statements critical of the hospital's "cross-training" policy, which she believed threatened patient care. Churchill sued under 42 U. S. C. § 1983, claiming that her speech was protected under *Connick* v. *Myers*, 461 U. S. 138, 142, in which the Court held that the First Amendment protects a government employee's speech if it is on a matter of public concern and the employee's interest in expressing herself on this matter is not outweighed by any injury the speech could cause to the government's interest, as an employer, in promoting the efficiency of the public services it performs through its employees. The District Court granted petitioners summary judgment, holding that management could fire Churchill with impunity because neither version of the conversation was protected under *Connick*. The Court of Appeals reversed, concluding that Churchill's speech, viewed in the light most favorable to her, was on a matter of public concern and was not disruptive, and that the inquiry must turn on what her speech actually was, as determined by a jury, not on what the employer thought it was.

Held: The judgment is vacated, and the case is remanded.

977 F. 2d 1114, vacated and remanded.

JUSTICE O'CONNOR, joined by THE CHIEF JUSTICE, JUSTICE SOUTER, AND JUSTICE GINSBURG, concluded:

1. The *Connick* test should be applied to what the government employer reasonably thought was said, not to what the trier of fact ultimately determines to have been said. Pp. 668–679.

(a) Absent a general test for deciding when the First Amendment requires a procedural safeguard, the question must be answered on a case-by-case basis, by considering the procedure's cost and the relative

Syllabus

magnitude and constitutional significance of the risks of erroneous punishment of protected speech and of erroneous exculpation of unprotected speech that the procedure involves. In evaluating these factors here, the key is the government employer's interest in achieving its goals as effectively and efficiently as possible. Pp. 668–675.

(b) The Court of Appeals' approach gives insufficient weight to this interest, since it would force the government employer to come to its factual conclusions through procedures that substantially mirror the evidentiary rules used in court, whereas employment decisions are frequently and properly based on hearsay, past similar conduct, personal knowledge of people's credibility, and other factors that the judicial process ignores. Pp. 675–677.

(c) On the other hand, courts must not apply the *Connick* test only to the facts as the employer thought them to be, without considering the reasonableness of the employer's conclusions. It is necessary that the decisionmaker reach its conclusion about what was said in good faith, rather than as a pretext; but it does not follow that good faith alone is sufficient under the First Amendment. *Mt. Healthy City Bd. of Ed.* v. *Doyle,* 429 U. S. 274, and *Pickering* v. *Board of Ed. of Township High School Dist. 205, Will Cty.*, 391 U. S. 563, distinguished. P. 677.

(d) Thus, if an employment action is based on what an employee supposedly said, and a reasonable supervisor would recognize that there is a substantial likelihood that what was actually said was protected, the First Amendment requires that the manager proceed with the care that a reasonable manager would use before making an employment decision of the sort involved in the particular case. In situations in which reasonable employers would disagree about who is to be believed, or how much investigation needs to be done, or how much evidence is needed to come to a particular conclusion, many different courses of action will necessarily be reasonable, and only procedures outside the range of what a reasonable manager would use may be condemned as unreasonable. Pp. 677–678.

2. Applying the foregoing to this case demonstrates that petitioners must win if they really did believe Perkins-Graham's and Ballew's story, and fired Churchill because of it. That belief, based on the investigation petitioners conducted, would have been entirely reasonable. Moreover, as a matter of law, the potential disruptiveness of Churchill's speech would have rendered it unprotected under the *Connick* test. Nonetheless, the District Court erred in granting petitioners summary judgment, since Churchill has produced enough evidence to create a material issue of disputed fact about whether she was actually fired because of disruptive statements, or because of nondisruptive state-

ments about cross-training, or because of other statements she may have made earlier. If either of the latter is so, the court will have to determine whether the statements in question were protected speech. Pp. 679–682.

JUSTICE SCALIA, joined by JUSTICE KENNEDY and JUSTICE THOMAS, concluded that the Court should adhere to its previously stated rule that a public employer's disciplining of an employee violates the First Amendment only if it is in retaliation for the employee's speech on a matter of public concern, see, *e. g., Pickering* v. *Board of Ed. of Township High School Dist. 205, Will Cty.*, 391 U. S. 563, 572, and should not add to this prohibition a requirement that the employer conduct an investigation before taking disciplinary action. The plurality's recognition of a broad new First Amendment right to an investigation before dismissal for speech is unprecedented and unpredictable in its application and consequences. In light of the requirement of a pretext inquiry, it is also superfluous to the disposition of this case and unnecessary for the protection of public-employee speech on matters of public concern. Judicial inquiry into the genuineness of a public employer's asserted permissible justification for an employment decision—be it unprotected speech, general insubordination, or laziness—is all that is necessary to avoid the targeting of "public interest" speech condemned in *Pickering.* See, *e. g., Mt. Healthy City Bd. of Ed.* v. *Doyle*, 429 U. S. 274, 287. Churchill's right not to be dismissed in retaliation for her expression of views on a matter of public concern was not violated, since she was dismissed for another reason, erroneous though it may have been. Pp. 686–694.

O'CONNOR, J., announced the judgment of the Court and delivered an opinion, in which REHNQUIST, C. J., and SOUTER and GINSBURG, JJ., joined. SOUTER, J., filed a concurring opinion, *post*, p. 682. SCALIA, J., filed an opinion concurring in the judgment, in which KENNEDY and THOMAS, JJ., joined, *post*, p. 686. STEVENS, J., filed a dissenting opinion, in which BLACKMUN, J., joined, *post*, p. 694.

Lawrence A. Manson argued the cause for petitioners. With him on the briefs was *Donald J. McNeil.*

Richard H. Seamon argued the cause for the United States as *amicus curiae* urging reversal. With him on the brief were *Solicitor General Days, Assistant Attorney General Hunger, Acting Deputy Solicitor General Kneedler, Barbara L. Herwig,* and *Robert D. Kamenshine.*

John H. Bisbee argued the cause for respondents. With him on the brief was *Barry Nakell*.*

JUSTICE O'CONNOR announced the judgment of the Court and delivered an opinion, in which THE CHIEF JUSTICE, JUSTICE SOUTER, and JUSTICE GINSBURG join.

In *Connick* v. *Myers*, 461 U. S. 138 (1983), we set forth a test for determining whether speech by a government employee may, consistently with the First Amendment, serve as a basis for disciplining or discharging that employee. In this case, we decide whether the *Connick* test should be applied to what the government employer thought was said, or to what the trier of fact ultimately determines to have been said.

I

This case arises out of a conversation that respondent Cheryl Churchill had on January 16, 1987, with Melanie Perkins-Graham. Both Churchill and Perkins-Graham were nurses working at McDonough District Hospital; Churchill was in the obstetrics department, and Perkins-Graham was considering transferring to that department. The conversation took place at work during a dinner break. Petitioners heard about it and fired Churchill, allegedly because of it. There is, however, a dispute about what Churchill actually said, and therefore about whether petitioners were constitutionally permitted to fire Churchill for her statements.

**Richard Ruda* and *Glen D. Nager* filed a brief for the International City/County Management Association et al. as *amici curiae* urging reversal.

Briefs of *amici curiae* urging affirmance were filed for the American Nurses Association by *Ronald C. Jessamy;* for the National Education Association et al. by *Robert H. Chanin, Jeremiah A. Collins,* and *Larry P. Weinberg;* and for the Southern States Police Benevolent Association et al. by *J. Michael McGuinness.*

Charles E. Tucker, Jr., Patricia C. Benassi, and *Mary Lee Leahy* filed a brief for the National Employment Lawyers Association as *amicus curiae.*

The conversation was overheard in part by two other nurses, Mary Lou Ballew and Jean Welty, and by Dr. Thomas Koch, the clinical head of obstetrics. A few days later, Ballew told Cynthia Waters, Churchill's supervisor, about the incident. According to Ballew, Churchill took "'the cross trainee into the kitchen for . . . at least 20 minutes to talk about [Waters] and how bad things are in [obstetrics] in general.'" 977 F. 2d 1114, 1118 (CA7 1992). Ballew said that Churchill's statements led Perkins-Graham to no longer be interested in switching to the department. Supplemental App. of Defendants-Appellees in No. 91–2288 (CA7), p. 60.

Shortly after this, Waters met with Ballew a second time for confirmation of Ballew's initial report. Ballew said that Churchill "was knocking the department" and that "in general [Churchill] was saying what a bad place [obstetrics] is to work." Ballew said she heard Churchill say Waters "was trying to find reasons to fire her." Ballew also said Churchill described a patient complaint for which Waters had supposedly wrongly blamed Churchill. *Id.*, at 67–68.

Waters, together with petitioner Kathleen Davis, the hospital's vice president of nursing, also met with Perkins-Graham, who told them that Churchill "had indeed said unkind and inappropriate negative things about [Waters]." *Id.*, at 228. Also, according to Perkins-Graham, Churchill mentioned a negative evaluation that Waters had given Churchill, which arose out of an incident in which Waters had cited Churchill for an insubordinate remark. *Ibid.* The evaluation stated that Churchill "'promotes an unpleasant atmosphere and hinders constructive communication and cooperation,'" 977 F. 2d, at 1118, and "'exhibits negative behavior towards [Waters] and [Waters'] leadership through her actions and body language'"; the evaluation said Churchill's work was otherwise satisfactory, *id.*, at 1116. Churchill allegedly told Perkins-Graham that she and Waters had discussed the evaluation, and that Waters "wanted to wipe the slate clean . . . but [Churchill thought] this wasn't possible."

Supplemental App. of Defendants-Appellees in No. 91–2288, at 228. Churchill also allegedly told Perkins-Graham "that just in general things were not good in OB and hospital administration was responsible." *Id.*, at 229. Churchill specifically mentioned Davis, saying Davis "was ruining MDH." *Ibid.* Perkins-Graham told Waters that she knew Davis and Waters "could not tolerate that kind of negativism." *Ibid.*

Churchill's version of the conversation is different. For several months, Churchill had been concerned about the hospital's "cross-training" policy, under which nurses from one department could work in another when their usual location was overstaffed. Churchill believed this policy threatened patient care because it was designed not to train nurses but to cover staff shortages, and she had complained about this to Davis and Waters. According to Churchill, the conversation with Perkins-Graham primarily concerned the cross-training policy. 977 F. 2d, at 1118. Churchill denies that she said some of what Ballew and Perkins-Graham allege she said. She does admit she criticized Davis, saying her staffing policies threatened to "ruin" the hospital because they "'seemed to be impeding nursing care.'" *Ibid.* She claims she actually defended Waters and encouraged Perkins-Graham to transfer to obstetrics. *Ibid.*

Koch's and Welty's recollections of the conversation match Churchill's. *Id.*, at 1122. Davis and Waters, however, never talked to Koch or Welty about this, and they did not talk to Churchill until the time they told her she was fired. Moreover, Churchill claims, Ballew was biased against Churchill because of an incident in which Ballew apparently made an error and Churchill had to cover for her. Brief for Respondents 9, n. 12.

After she was discharged, Churchill filed an internal grievance. The president of the hospital, petitioner Stephen Hopper, met with Churchill in regard to this and heard her side of the story. App. to Pet. for Cert. 75–77. He then reviewed Waters' and Davis' written reports of their conversations with Ballew and Perkins-Graham, and had Bernice Magin, the hospital's vice president of human resources, interview Ballew one more time. Supplemental App. of Defendants-Appellees in No. 91–2288, at 108, 139–142. After considering all this, Hopper rejected Churchill's grievance.

Churchill then sued under Rev. Stat. § 1979, 42 U. S. C. § 1983, claiming that the firing violated her First Amendment rights because her speech was protected under *Connick* v. *Myers*, 461 U. S. 138 (1983). In May 1991, the United States District Court for the Central District of Illinois granted summary judgment to petitioners. The court held that neither version of the conversation was protected under *Connick:* Regardless of whose story was accepted, the speech was not on a matter of public concern, and even if it was on a matter of public concern, its potential for disruption nonetheless stripped it of First Amendment protection. Therefore, the court held, management could fire Churchill for the conversation with impunity. App. to Pet. for Cert. 45–49.

The United States Court of Appeals for the Seventh Circuit reversed. 977 F. 2d 1114 (1992). The court held that Churchill's speech, viewed in the light most favorable to her, was protected speech under the *Connick* test: It was on a matter of public concern—"the hospital's [alleged] violation of state nursing regulations as well as the quality and level of nursing care it provides its patients," *id.*, at 1122—and it was not disruptive, *id.*, at 1124.

The court also concluded that the inquiry must turn on what the speech actually was, not on what the employer thought it was. "If the employer chooses to discharge the employee without sufficient knowledge of her protected speech as a result of an inadequate investigation into the employee's conduct," the court held, "the employer runs the risk of eventually being required to remedy any wrongdoing whether it was deliberate or accidental." *Id.*, at 1127 (footnote omitted).

We granted certiorari, 509 U. S. 903 (1993), to resolve a conflict among the Circuits on this issue. Compare the decision below with *Atcherson* v. *Siebenmann*, 605 F. 2d 1058 (CA8 1979); *Wulf* v. *Wichita*, 883 F. 2d 842 (CA10 1989); *Sims* v. *Metropolitan Dade County*, 972 F. 2d 1230 (CA11 1992).

II

A

There is no dispute in this case about when speech by a government employee is protected by the First Amendment: To be protected, the speech must be on a matter of public concern, and the employee's interest in expressing herself on this matter must not be outweighed by any injury the speech could cause to "'the interest of the State, as an employer, in promoting the efficiency of the public services it performs through its employees.'" *Connick, supra*, at 142 (quoting *Pickering* v. *Board of Ed. of Township High School Dist. 205, Will Cty.*, 391 U. S. 563, 568 (1968)). It is also agreed that it is the court's task to apply the *Connick* test to the facts. 461 U. S., at 148, n. 7, and 150, n. 10.

The dispute is over how the factual basis for applying the test—what the speech was, in what tone it was delivered, what the listener's reactions were, see *id.*, at 151–153—is to be determined. Should the court apply the *Connick* test to the speech as the government employer found it to be, or should it ask the jury to determine the facts for itself? The Court of Appeals held that the employer's factual conclusions were irrelevant, and that the jury should engage in its own factfinding. Petitioners argue that the employer's factual conclusions should be dispositive. Respondents take a middle course: They suggest that the court should accept the employer's factual conclusions, but only if those conclusions were arrived at reasonably, see Brief for Respondents 39, something they say did not happen here.

We agree that it is important to ensure not only that the substantive First Amendment standards are sound, but also that they are applied through reliable procedures. This is why we have often held some procedures—a particular allocation of the burden of proof, a particular quantum of proof, a particular type of appellate review, and so on—to be constitutionally required in proceedings that may penalize protected speech. See *Freedman* v. *Maryland*, 380 U. S. 51, 58–60 (1965) (government must bear burden of proving that speech is unprotected); *Speiser* v. *Randall*, 357 U. S. 513, 526 (1958) (same); *Philadelphia Newspapers, Inc.* v. *Hepps*, 475 U. S. 767, 775–778 (1986) (libel plaintiff must bear burden of proving that speech is false); *Masson* v. *New Yorker Magazine, Inc.*, 501 U. S. 496, 510 (1991) (actual malice must be proved by clear and convincing evidence); *Bose Corp.* v. *Consumers Union of United States, Inc.*, 466 U. S. 485, 503–511 (1984) (appellate court must make independent judgment about presence of actual malice).

These cases establish a basic First Amendment principle: Government action based on protected speech may under some circumstances violate the First Amendment even if the government actor honestly believes the speech is unprotected. And though JUSTICE SCALIA suggests that this principle be limited to licensing schemes and to "deprivation[s] of the freedom of speech specifically *through the judicial process*," *post*, at 687 (emphasis in original), we do not think the logic of the cases supports such a limitation. Speech can be chilled and punished by administrative action as much as by judicial processes; in no case have we asserted or even implied the contrary. In fact, in *Speiser* v. *Randall*, we struck down procedures, on the grounds that they were insufficiently protective of free speech, which involved both administrative and judicial components. *Speiser*, like this case, dealt with a government decision to deny a speaker certain benefits—in *Speiser* a tax exemption, in this case a government job—based on what the speaker said. Our holding there did not depend on the deprivation taking place "specifically through the judicial process," and we cannot see how the result could have been any different had the process been entirely administrative, with no judicial review. We cannot sweep aside *Speiser* and the other cases cited above as easily as JUSTICE SCALIA proposes.

Nonetheless, not every procedure that may safeguard protected speech is constitutionally mandated. True, the procedure adopted by the Court of Appeals may lower the chance of protected speech being erroneously punished. A speaker is more protected if she has two opportunities to be vindicated—first by the employer's investigation and then by the jury—than just one. But each procedure involves a different mix of administrative burden, risk of erroneous punishment of protected speech, and risk of erroneous exculpation of unprotected speech. Though the First Amendment creates a strong presumption against punishing protected speech even inadvertently, the balance need not always be struck in that direction. We have never, for instance, required proof beyond a reasonable doubt in civil cases where First Amendment interests are at stake, though such a requirement would protect speech more than the alternative standards would. Compare, *e. g., California ex rel. Cooper* v. *Mitchell Brothers' Santa Ana Theater*, 454 U. S. 90, 93 (1981) *(per curiam)*, with *McKinney* v. *Alabama*, 424 U. S. 669, 686 (1976) (Brennan, J., concurring in judgment in part). Likewise, the possibility that defamation liability would chill even true speech has not led us to require an actual malice standard in all libel cases. *Dun & Bradstreet, Inc.* v. *Greenmoss Builders, Inc.*, 472 U. S. 749, 761 (1985) (plurality opinion); *Gertz* v. *Robert Welch, Inc.*, 418 U. S. 323 (1974). Nor has the possibility that overbroad regulations may chill commercial speech convinced us to extend the overbreadth doctrine into the commercial speech area. *Bates* v. *State Bar of Ariz.*, 433 U. S. 350, 380–381 (1977).

We have never set forth a general test to determine when a procedural safeguard is required by the First Amendment—just as we have never set forth a general test to determine what constitutes a compelling state interest, see *Boos* v. *Barry,* 485 U. S. 312, 324 (1988), or what categories of speech are so lacking in value that they fall outside the protection of the First Amendment, *New York* v. *Ferber,* 458 U. S. 747, 763–764 (1982), or many other matters—and we do not purport to do so now. But though we agree with JUSTICE SCALIA that the lack of such a test is inconvenient, see *post,* at 687–688, this does not relieve us of our responsibility to decide the case that is before us today. Both JUSTICE SCALIA and we agree that some procedural requirements are mandated by the First Amendment and some are not. See *post,* at 686. None of us have discovered a general principle to determine where the line is to be drawn. See *post,* at 686–688. We must therefore reconcile ourselves to answering the question on a case-by-case basis, at least until some workable general rule emerges.

Accordingly, all we say today is that the propriety of a proposed procedure must turn on the particular context in which the question arises—on the cost of the procedure and the relative magnitude and constitutional significance of the risks it would decrease and increase. And to evaluate these factors here we have to return to the issue we dealt with in *Connick* and in the cases that came before it: What is it about the government's role as employer that gives it a freer hand in regulating the speech of its employees than it has in regulating the speech of the public at large?

B

We have never explicitly answered this question, though we have always assumed that its premise is correct—that the government as employer indeed has far broader powers than does the government as sovereign. See, *e. g., Pickering,* 391 U. S., at 568; *Civil Service Comm'n* v. *Letter Carri-*

ers, 413 U. S. 548, 564 (1973); *Connick,* 461 U. S., at 147. This assumption is amply borne out by considering the practical realities of government employment, and the many situations in which, we believe, most observers would agree that the government must be able to restrict its employees' speech.

To begin with, even many of the most fundamental maxims of our First Amendment jurisprudence cannot reasonably be applied to speech by government employees. The First Amendment demands a tolerance of "verbal tumult, discord, and even offensive utterance," as "necessary side effects of . . . the process of open debate," *Cohen* v. *California,* 403 U. S. 15, 24–25 (1971). But we have never expressed doubt that a government employer may bar its employees from using Mr. Cohen's offensive utterance to members of the public or to the people with whom they work. "Under the First Amendment there is no such thing as a false idea," *Gertz, supra,* at 339; the "fitting remedy for evil counsels is good ones," *Whitney* v. *California,* 274 U. S. 357, 375 (1927) (Brandeis, J., concurring). But when an employee counsels her co-workers to do their job in a way with which the public employer disagrees, her managers may tell her to stop, rather than relying on counterspeech. The First Amendment reflects the "profound national commitment to the principle that debate on public issues should be uninhibited, robust, and wide-open." *New York Times Co.* v. *Sullivan,* 376 U. S. 254, 270 (1964). But though a private person is perfectly free to uninhibitedly and robustly criticize a state governor's legislative program, we have never suggested that the Constitution bars the governor from firing a high-ranking deputy for doing the same thing. Cf. *Branti* v. *Finkel,* 445 U. S. 507, 518 (1980). Even something as close to the core of the First Amendment as participation in political campaigns may be prohibited to government employees. *Broadrick* v. *Oklahoma,* 413 U. S. 601 (1973); *Letter Carriers, supra; Public Workers* v. *Mitchell,* 330 U. S. 75 (1947).

Government employee speech must be treated differently with regard to procedural requirements as well. For example, speech restrictions must generally precisely define the speech they target. *Baggett* v. *Bullitt*, 377 U. S. 360, 367–368 (1964); *Hustler Magazine, Inc.* v. *Falwell*, 485 U. S. 46, 55 (1988). Yet surely a public employer may, consistently with the First Amendment, prohibit its employees from being "rude to customers," a standard almost certainly too vague when applied to the public at large. Cf. *Arnett* v. *Kennedy*, 416 U. S. 134, 158–162 (1974) (plurality opinion) (upholding a regulation that allowed discharges for speech that hindered the "efficiency of the service"); *id.*, at 164 (Powell, J., concurring in part and concurring in result in part) (agreeing on this point).

Likewise, we have consistently given greater deference to government predictions of harm used to justify restriction of employee speech than to predictions of harm used to justify restrictions on the speech of the public at large. Few of the examples we have discussed involve tangible, present interference with the agency's operation. The danger in them is mostly speculative. One could make a respectable argument that political activity by government employees is generally not harmful, see *Public Workers* v. *Mitchell, supra,* at 99; or that high officials should allow more public dissent by their subordinates, see *Connick, supra,* at 168–169 (Brennan, J., dissenting); Whistleblower Protection Act of 1989, 103 Stat. 16, or that even in a government workplace the free market of ideas is superior to a command economy. But we have given substantial weight to government employers' reasonable predictions of disruption, even when the speech involved is on a matter of public concern, and even though when the government is acting as sovereign our review of legislative predictions of harm is considerably less deferential. Compare, *e. g., Connick, supra,* at 151–152; *Letter Carriers, supra,* at 566–567, with *Sable Communications of Cal., Inc.* v. *FCC*, 492 U. S. 115, 129 (1989); *Texas* v. *Johnson*,

491 U. S. 397, 409 (1989). Similarly, we have refrained from intervening in government employer decisions that are based on speech that is of entirely private concern. Doubtless some such speech is sometimes nondisruptive; doubtless it is sometimes of value to the speakers and the listeners. But we have declined to question government employers' decisions on such matters. *Connick, supra,* at 146–149.

This does not, of course, show that the First Amendment should play no role in government employment decisions. Government employees are often in the best position to know what ails the agencies for which they work; public debate may gain much from their informed opinions. *Pickering, supra,* at 572. And a government employee, like any citizen, may have a strong, legitimate interest in speaking out on public matters. In many such situations the government may have to make a substantial showing that the speech is, in fact, likely to be disruptive before it may be punished. See, *e. g., Rankin* v. *McPherson,* 483 U. S. 378, 388 (1987); *Connick, supra,* at 152; *Pickering, supra,* at 569–571. Moreover, the government may certainly choose to give additional protections to its employees beyond what is mandated by the First Amendment, out of respect for the values underlying the First Amendment, values central to our social order as well as our legal system. See, *e. g.,* Whistleblower Protection Act of 1989, *supra.*

But the above examples do show that constitutional review of government employment decisions must rest on different principles than review of speech restraints imposed by the government as sovereign. The restrictions discussed above are allowed not just because the speech interferes with the government's operation. Speech by private people can do the same, but this does not allow the government to suppress it.

Rather, the extra power the government has in this area comes from the nature of the government's mission as employer. Government agencies are charged by law with doing particular tasks. Agencies hire employees to help do those tasks as effectively and efficiently as possible. When someone who is paid a salary so that she will contribute to an agency's effective operation begins to do or say things that detract from the agency's effective operation, the government employer must have some power to restrain her. The reason the governor may, in the example given above, fire the deputy is not that this dismissal would somehow be narrowly tailored to a compelling government interest. It is that the governor and the governor's staff have a job to do, and the governor justifiably feels that a quieter subordinate would allow them to do this job more effectively.

The key to First Amendment analysis of government employment decisions, then, is this: The government's interest in achieving its goals as effectively and efficiently as possible is elevated from a relatively subordinate interest when it acts as sovereign to a significant one when it acts as employer. The government cannot restrict the speech of the public at large just in the name of efficiency. But where the government is employing someone for the very purpose of effectively achieving its goals, such restrictions may well be appropriate.

C

1

The Court of Appeals' decision, we believe, gives insufficient weight to the government's interest in efficient employment decisionmaking. In other First Amendment contexts the need to safeguard possibly protected speech may indeed outweigh the government's efficiency interests. See, *e. g., Freedman* v. *Maryland,* 380 U. S. 51 (1965); *Speiser* v. *Randall,* 357 U. S., at 526. But where the government is acting as employer, its efficiency concerns should, as we discussed above, be assigned a greater value.

The problem with the Court of Appeals' approach—under which the facts to which the *Connick* test is applied are determined by the judicial factfinder—is that it would force the government employer to come to its factual conclusions through procedures that substantially mirror the evidentiary rules used in court. The government manager would have to ask not what conclusions she, as an experienced professional, can draw from the circumstances, but rather what conclusions a jury would later draw. If she relies on hearsay, or on what she knows about the accused employee's character, she must be aware that this evidence might not be usable in court. If she knows one party is, in her personal experience, more credible than another, she must realize that the jury will not share that personal experience. If she thinks the alleged offense is so egregious that it is proper to discipline the accused employee even though the evidence is ambiguous, she must consider that a jury might decide the other way.

But employers, public and private, often do rely on hearsay, on past similar conduct, on their personal knowledge of people's credibility, and on other factors that the judicial process ignores. Such reliance may sometimes be the most effective way for the employer to avoid future recurrences of improper and disruptive conduct. What works best in a judicial proceeding may not be appropriate in the employment context. If one employee accuses another of misconduct, it is reasonable for a government manager to credit the allegation more if it is consistent with what the manager knows of the character of the accused. Likewise, a manager may legitimately want to discipline an employee based on complaints by patrons that the employee has been rude, even though these complaints are hearsay.

It is true that these practices involve some risk of erroneously punishing protected speech. The government may certainly choose to adopt other practices, by law or by contract. But we do not believe that the First Amendment requires it to do so. Government employers should be allowed to use personnel procedures that differ from the evidentiary rules used by courts, without fear that these differences will lead to liability.

2

On the other hand, we do not believe that the court must apply the *Connick* test only to the facts as the employer thought them to be, without considering the reasonableness of the employer's conclusions. Even in situations where courts have recognized the special expertise and special needs of certain decisionmakers, the deference to their conclusions has never been complete. Cf. *New Jersey* v. *T. L. O.*, 469 U. S. 325, 342–343 (1985); *United States* v. *Leon*, 468 U. S. 897, 914 (1984); *Universal Camera Corp.* v. *NLRB*, 340 U. S. 474, 490–491 (1951). It is necessary that the decisionmaker reach its conclusion about what was said in good faith, rather than as a pretext; but it does not follow that good faith is sufficient. JUSTICE SCALIA is right in saying that we have often held various laws to require only an inquiry into the decisionmaker's intent, see *post*, at 690–691, but, as discussed *supra* in Part II–A, this has not been our view of the First Amendment.

We think employer decisionmaking will not be unduly burdened by having courts look to the facts as the employer *reasonably* found them to be. It may be unreasonable, for example, for the employer to come to a conclusion based on no evidence at all. Likewise, it may be unreasonable for an employer to act based on extremely weak evidence when strong evidence is clearly available—if, for instance, an employee is accused of writing an improper letter to the editor, and instead of just reading the letter, the employer decides what it said based on unreliable hearsay.

If an employment action is based on what an employee supposedly said, and a reasonable supervisor would recognize that there is a substantial likelihood that what was actually said was protected, the manager must tread with a certain amount of care. This need not be the care with which trials, with their rules of evidence and procedure, are conducted. It should, however, be the care that a reasonable manager would use before making an employment decision—discharge, suspension, reprimand, or whatever else—of the sort involved in the particular case. JUSTICE SCALIA correctly points out that such care is normally not constitutionally required unless the employee has a protected property interest in her job, *post*, at 688; see also *Board of Regents of State Colleges* v. *Roth*, 408 U. S. 564, 576–578 (1972); but we believe that the possibility of inadvertently punishing someone for exercising her First Amendment rights makes such care necessary.

Of course, there will often be situations in which reasonable employers would disagree about who is to be believed, or how much investigation needs to be done, or how much evidence is needed to come to a particular conclusion. In those situations, many different courses of action will necessarily be reasonable. Only procedures outside the range of what a reasonable manager would use may be condemned as unreasonable.

Petitioners argue that *Mt. Healthy City Bd. of Ed.* v. *Doyle*, 429 U. S. 274 (1977), forecloses a reasonableness test, and holds instead that the First Amendment was not violated unless "'the defendant[s'] *intent* [was] to violate the plaintiff['s] constitutional rights.'" Brief for Petitioners 25; see also *post*, at 690 (SCALIA, J., dissenting). JUSTICE SCALIA makes a similar argument based on *Pickering*, *Connick*, and *Perry*, which alluded to the impropriety of management "retaliation" for protected speech. *Post*, at 689. But in all those cases the employer assertedly knew the true content of the employee's protected speech, and fired the employee in part because of it. In none of them did we have occasion to decide what should happen if the defendants hold an erroneous and unreasonable belief about what plaintiff said. These cases cannot be read as foreclosing an argument that they never dealt with. *United States* v. *L. A. Tucker Truck Lines, Inc.*, 344 U. S. 33, 38 (1952).

3

We disagree with JUSTICE STEVENS' contention that the test we adopt "provides less protection for a fundamental constitutional right than the law ordinarily provides for less exalted rights." *Post*, at 695. We have never held that it is a violation of the Constitution for a government employer to discharge an employee based on substantively incorrect information. Where an employee has a property interest in her job, the only protection we have found the Constitution gives her is a right to adequate procedure. And an at-will government employee—such as Churchill apparently was, App. to Pet. for Cert. 70—generally has no claim based on the Constitution at all.

Of course, an employee may be able to challenge the substantive accuracy of the employer's factual conclusions under state contract law, or under some state statute or common-law cause of action. In some situations, the employee may even have a federal statutory claim. See *NLRB* v. *Burnup & Sims, Inc.*, 379 U. S. 21 (1964). Likewise, the State or Federal Governments may, if they choose, provide similar protection to people fired because of their speech. But this protection is not mandated by the Constitution.

The one pattern from which our approach does diverge is the broader protection normally given to people in their relationship with the government as sovereign. See, *e. g.*, *New York Times Co.* v. *Sullivan*, 376 U. S., at 279–280, cited *post*, at 696, 699 (STEVENS, J., dissenting). But the reasons for this are those discussed *supra* in Part II–B: "[O]ur 'profound national commitment' to the freedom of speech," *post*, at 699 (STEVENS, J., dissenting), must of necessity operate differently when the government acts as employer rather than sovereign.

III

Applying the foregoing to this case, it is clear that if petitioners really did believe Perkins-Graham's and Ballew's story, and fired Churchill because of it, they must win. Their belief, based on the investigation they conducted, would have been entirely reasonable. After getting the initial report from Ballew, who overheard the conversation, Waters and Davis approached and interviewed Perkins-Graham, and then interviewed Ballew again for confirmation. In response to Churchill's grievance, Hopper met directly with Churchill to hear her side of the story, and instructed Magin to interview Ballew one more time. Management can spend only so much of their time on any one employment decision. By the end of the termination process, Hopper, who made the final decision, had the word of two trusted employees, the endorsement of those employees' reliability by three hospital managers, and the benefit of a face-to-face meeting with the employee he fired. With that in hand, a reasonable manager could have concluded that no further time needed to be taken. As respondents themselves point out, "if the belief an employer forms supporting its adverse personnel action is 'reasonable,' an employer has no need to investigate further." Brief for Respondents 39.

And under the *Connick* test, Churchill's speech as reported by Perkins-Graham and Ballew was unprotected. Even if Churchill's criticism of cross-training reported by Perkins-Graham and Ballew was speech on a matter of public concern—something we need not decide—the potential disruptiveness of the speech as reported was enough to outweigh whatever First Amendment value it might have had. According to Ballew, Churchill's speech may have substantially dampened Perkins-Graham's interest in working in obstetrics. Discouraging people from coming to work for a department certainly qualifies as disruption. Moreover, Perkins-Graham perceived Churchill's statements about Waters to be "unkind and inappropriate," and told management that she knew they could not continue to "tolerate that kind of negativism" from Churchill. This is strong evidence that Churchill's complaining, if not dealt with, threatened to undermine management's authority in Perkins-Graham's eyes. And finally, Churchill's statement, as reported by Perkins-Graham, that it "wasn't possible" to "wipe the slate clean" between her and Waters could certainly make management doubt Churchill's future effectiveness. As a matter of law, this potential disruptiveness was enough to outweigh whatever First Amendment value the speech might have had.

This is so even if, as Churchill suggests, Davis and Waters were "[d]eliberately [i]ndifferent," Brief for Respondents 31, to the possibility that much of the rest of the conversation was solely about cross-training. So long as Davis and Waters discharged Churchill only for the part of the speech that was either not on a matter of public concern, or on a matter of public concern but disruptive, it is irrelevant whether the rest of the speech was, unbeknownst to them, both on a matter of public concern and nondisruptive. The *Connick* test is to be applied to the speech for which Churchill was fired. Cf. *Connick*, 461 U. S., at 149 (evaluating the disruptiveness of part of plaintiff's speech because that part was "upon a matter of public concern *and contributed to [plaintiff's] discharge*" (emphasis added)); *Mt. Healthy*, 429 U. S., at 286–287. An employee who makes an unprotected statement is not immunized from discipline by the fact that this statement is surrounded by protected statements.

Nonetheless, we agree with the Court of Appeals that the District Court erred in granting summary judgment in petitioners' favor. Though Davis and Waters would have been justified in firing Churchill for the statements outlined above, there remains the question whether Churchill was actually fired because of those statements, or because of something else. See *Mt. Healthy*, *supra*, at 286–287.

Churchill has produced enough evidence to create a material issue of disputed fact about petitioners' actual motivation. Churchill had criticized the cross-training policy in the past; management had exhibited some sensitivity about the criticisms; Churchill pointed to some other conduct by hospital management that, if viewed in the light most favorable to her, would show that they were hostile to her because of her criticisms. 977 F. 2d, at 1125–1126. A reasonable factfinder might therefore, on this record, conclude that petitioners actually fired Churchill not because of the disruptive things she said to Perkins-Graham, but because of nondisruptive statements about cross-training that they thought she may have made in the same conversation, or because of other statements she may have made earlier. If this is so, then the court will have to determine whether those statements were protected speech, a different matter than the one before us now.

Because of our conclusion, we need not determine whether the defendants were entitled to qualified immunity. We also need not decide whether the defendants were acting pursuant to hospital policy or custom, because that question, though argued by petitioners in their merits brief, was not presented in the petition for certiorari. See *Izumi Seimitsu Kogyo Kabushiki Kaisha* v. *U. S. Philips Corp.*, 510 U. S. 27 (1993) *(per curiam)*. Rather, we vacate the judgment of the Court of Appeals and remand the case for further proceedings consistent with this opinion.

So ordered.

JUSTICE SOUTER, concurring.

I

I join JUSTICE O'CONNOR's plurality opinion stating that, under the Free Speech Clause, a public employer who reasonably believes a third-party report that an employee engaged in constitutionally unprotected speech may punish the employee in reliance on that report, even if it turns out that the employee's actual remarks were constitutionally protected. I add these words to emphasize that, in order to avoid liability, the public employer must not only reasonably investigate the third-party report, but must also actually believe it. Under the plurality's opinion, an objectively reasonable investigation that fails to convince the employer that the employee actually engaged in disruptive or otherwise unprotected speech does not inoculate the employer against constitutional liability. A public employer violates the Free Speech Clause, that is, by invoking a third-party report to penalize an employee when the employer, despite the report and the reasonable investigation into it, believes or genuinely suspects that the employee's speech was protected in its entirety or in that part on which the employer purports to rely in taking disciplinary action; or if the employer invokes the third-party report merely as a pretext to shield disciplinary action taken because of protected speech the employer believes or genuinely suspects that the employee uttered at another time.

First Amendment limitations on public employers, as the plurality explains, must reflect a balance of the public employer's interest in accomplishing its mission and the public employee's interest in speaking on matters of public concern. See *ante*, at 668–675. Where an employer penalizes an employee on the basis of a third-party report of speech that the employer should have suspected, based on the content of the report and the employer's familiarity with the employee and the workplace, to have been constitutionally protected, this balance must reflect the facts that employees' speech on matters of public concern will often (as we said of employees' union activities) "engende[r] strong emotions and giv[e] rise to active rumors," and, critically, that "the example of employees who are discharged on false charges would or might have a deterrent effect on other employees." *NLRB* v. *Burnup & Sims, Inc.*, 379 U. S. 21, 23 (1964); see also *Rankin* v. *McPherson*, 483 U. S. 378, 384 (1987) ("'[T]he threat of dismissal from public employment is . . . a potent means of inhibiting speech'") (quoting *Pickering* v. *Board of Ed. of Township High School Dist. 205, Will Cty.*, 391 U. S. 563, 574 (1968)). As the plurality's opinion frankly recognizes, permitting public employers to punish employees in reliance on third-party reports "involve[s] some risk of erroneously punishing protected speech." *Ante,* at 676.

This is a risk that the public employer's interests justify tolerating, as the plurality's opinion explains, but only when the public employer's conduct was reasonable, see *ante,* at 677–678, and only when the employer "really did believe" the third-party report, *ante,* at 679; see also *ante,* at 680 (an employer need not investigate further " 'if the belief an employer forms supporting its adverse personnel action is "reasonable" ' ") (citation omitted); *ante,* at 677 (courts must "look to the facts as the employer reasonably found them to be") (emphasis deleted).* A public employer who did not really believe that the employee engaged in disruptive or otherwise punishable speech can assert no legitimate interest strong enough to justify chilling protected expression, whether the employer affirmatively disbelieved the third-party report or merely doubted its accuracy. Imposing liability on such an employer respects the "longstanding recognition that the First Amendment's primary aim is the full protection of speech upon issues of public concern, as well as the practical realities involved in the administration of a government office." *Connick* v. *Myers,* 461 U. S. 138, 154 (1983).

Accordingly, even though petitioners conducted an objectively reasonable investigation into Ballew's report about respondent Churchill's conversation with Perkins-Graham, I believe that petitioners' dismissal of Churchill would have violated the Free Speech Clause if after the investigation they doubted the accuracy of the report and fired Churchill for speech, or for a portion of her speech, that they genuinely suspected was nondisruptive (assuming that the speech was

*In addition, and also because of the risk of chilling protected expression, the public employer must believe that the discipline chosen is an appropriate, and not excessive, response to the employee's speech as reported. I do not understand respondents in this case to raise any claim that the discharge was pretextual in this respect.

actually on a matter of public concern). Though under the plurality's opinion the presentation of such an argument is open to Churchill on remand, Churchill would not, of course, have to rely on it if she can establish that, despite the reasonable investigation, petitioners believed that Churchill said nothing disruptive in her conversation with Perkins-Graham; that they believed that Churchill made some nondisruptive remarks to Perkins-Graham and fired her because of those remarks; or that they fired her because of nondisruptive comments about cross-training they knew she made earlier (again, assuming in each case that the speech at issue was on a matter of public concern).

II

Though JUSTICE O'CONNOR's opinion speaks for just four Members of the Court, the reasonableness test it sets out is clearly the one that lower courts should apply. A majority of the Court agrees that employers whose conduct survives the plurality's reasonableness test cannot be held constitutionally liable (assuming the absence of pretext), see *ante*, at 679–681 (plurality opinion); *post*, at 686–692 (SCALIA, J., concurring in judgment); and a majority (though a different one) is of the view that employers whose conduct fails the plurality's reasonableness test have violated the Free Speech Clause, see *ante*, at 677–678 (plurality opinion); *post*, at 694–699 (STEVENS, J., dissenting); see also *post*, at 697–698, n. 4 (STEVENS, J., dissenting) ("JUSTICE O'CONNOR appropriately rejects [JUSTICE SCALIA's] position, at least for those instances in which the employer unreasonably believes an incorrect report concerning speech that was in fact protected and disciplines an employee based upon that misunderstanding. I, of course, agree with JUSTICE O'CONNOR that discipline in such circumstances violates the First Amendment"). Accordingly, the plurality opinion may be taken to state the holding of the Court. See *Marks* v. *United States*, 430 U. S. 188, 193–194 (1977) (discussing *Book Named "John Cleland's*

Memoirs of a Woman of Pleasure" v. *Attorney General of Mass.*, 383 U. S. 413 (1966)).

JUSTICE SCALIA, with whom JUSTICE KENNEDY and JUSTICE THOMAS join, concurring in the judgment.

The central issue in this case is whether we shall adhere to our previously stated rule that a public employer's disciplining of an employee violates the Speech and Press Clause of the First Amendment only if it is in retaliation for the employee's speech on a matter of public concern. JUSTICE O'CONNOR would add to this prohibition a requirement that the employer conduct an investigation before taking disciplinary action in certain circumstances. This recognition of a broad new First Amendment procedural right is in my view unprecedented, superfluous to the decision in the present case, unnecessary for protection of public-employee speech on matters of public concern, and unpredictable in its application and consequences.

I

I do not doubt that the First Amendment contains within it some procedural prescriptions—that in some circumstances, "the freedom of speech" recognized by the Constitution consisted of a right to speak unless and until certain procedures to prevent the speech had first been complied with. Thus, for example, I have no quarrel in principle with (though I have not inquired into the historical justification for) decisions such as *Freedman* v. *Maryland*, 380 U. S. 51 (1965), which established the administrative and judicial review provisions that a film licensing process must contain in order to avoid constituting an unconstitutional prior restraint, see *Patterson* v. *Colorado ex rel. Attorney General of Colo.*, 205 U. S. 454, 462 (1907) (Holmes, J.).

We have, however, been most circumspect about acknowledging procedural components of the First Amendment. Almost all of the cases JUSTICE O'CONNOR cites as exemplars are elaborations upon the limitation on defamation suits first announced in *New York Times Co.* v. *Sullivan*, 376 U. S. 254 (1964). See, *e. g.*, *Bose Corp.* v. *Consumers Union of United States, Inc.*, 466 U. S. 485 (1984); *Philadelphia Newspapers, Inc.* v. *Hepps*, 475 U. S. 767 (1986); *Masson* v. *New Yorker Magazine, Inc.*, 501 U. S. 496 (1991). These cases deal with alleged governmental deprivation of the freedom of speech specifically *through the judicial process*, in which context procedures are necessarily central to the discussion.* *Speiser* v. *Randall*, 357 U. S. 513 (1958), also involved judicial (and pre-judicial adjudicative) process, holding that a state tax deduction could not be denied for a speech-related reason (advocacy of overthrow of the Government of the United States or of the State by unlawful means) by placing the burden of *dis*proving that speech-related reason upon the taxpayer. Moreover, although the existence of a First Amendment right was central to the Court's reasoning, the decision was squarely rested on the Due Process Clause, see *id.*, at 529, and not on the First Amendment, see *id.*, at 517, n. 3. The last case cited by JUSTICE O'CONNOR, *Freedman*, *supra*, was, as I described earlier, a prior restraint case; review and requirement of procedures were to be expected.

In today's opinion by JUSTICE O'CONNOR, our previous parsimony is abandoned, in favor of a general principle that "it is important to ensure not only that the substantive First Amendment standards are sound, but also that they are applied through reliable procedures," *ante*, at 669. Although we are assured that "not every procedure that may safeguard protected speech is constitutionally mandated," *ante*, at 670, the implication of that assurance is that many are. We never are informed how to tell mandated speech-safeguarding procedures from nonmandated ones, except for the clue that "each procedure involves a different mix of administrative burden, risk of erroneous punishment of

*Moreover, the remedy in that context is self-evident: remand for re-adjudication pursuant to the proper procedures. In the present context, by contrast, the remedy is not all clear, see *infra*, at 693–694.

protected speech, and risk of erroneous exculpation of unprotected speech," *ibid.*

The proposed right to an investigation before dismissal for speech not only expands the concept of "First Amendment procedure" into brand new areas, but brings it into disharmony with our cases involving government employment decided under the Due Process Clause. As JUSTICE O'CONNOR acknowledges, see *ante*, at 678, those cases hold that public employees who, like Churchill, lack a protected property interest in their jobs, are not entitled to any sort of a hearing before dismissal. See, *e. g.*, *Board of Regents of State Colleges* v. *Roth*, 408 U. S. 564, 577–578 (1972). Such employees can be dismissed with impunity (insofar as federal constitutional protections are concerned) for the reason, *accurate or not*, that they are incompetent, that they have been guilty of unexcused absences, that they have stolen money from the faculty honor bar—or indeed *for no reason at all.* But under JUSTICE O'CONNOR's opinion, if a reason happens to be given, and if the reason relates to speech and "there is a substantial likelihood that what was actually said was protected," (whatever that means), *ante*, at 677, an investigation to assure that the speech was not the sort protected by the First Amendment must be conducted—after which, presumably, the dismissal can still proceed even if the speech was not what the employer had thought it was, so long as it was not speech on an issue of public importance. In the present case, for example, if the requisite "First Amendment investigation" disclosed that Nurse Churchill had not been demeaning her superiors, but had been complaining about the perennial end-of-season slump of the Chicago Cubs, her dismissal, erroneous as it was, would have been perfectly OK.

This is a strange jurisprudence indeed. And the reason it is strange is that JUSTICE O'CONNOR has in effect converted the government employer's First Amendment liability with respect to "public concern" speech from liability for intentional wrong to liability for mere negligence. What she proposes is, at bottom, not new procedural protections for established First Amendment rights, but rather new First Amendment rights. *Pickering* v. *Board of Ed. of Township High School Dist. 205, Will Cty.*, 391 U. S. 563 (1968), did not require government-employer "protection" of "public concern" speech, but merely forbade government-employer hostility to such speech. "[I]t is essential," *Pickering* said, "that [public employees] be able to speak out freely on such questions without fear of *retaliatory* dismissal." *Id.*, at 572 (emphasis added). See also *Connick* v. *Myers*, 461 U. S. 138, 149 (1983) (same). The critical inquiry for the factfinder in these cases is whether the employment decision was, "in fact, made in retaliation for [the] exercise of the constitutional right of free speech." *Perry* v. *Sindermann*, 408 U. S. 593, 598 (1972). A category of employee speech is certainly not being "retaliated against" if it is no more and no less subject to being mistaken for a disciplinable infraction than is any other category of speech or conduct.

II

The creation of procedural First Amendment rights in this case is all the more remarkable because it is unnecessary to the disposition of the matter. After imposing the new duty upon government employers, JUSTICE O'CONNOR's opinion concludes that it was satisfied anyway—*i. e.*, that the investigation conducted by the hospital was "entirely reasonable." *Ante*, at 680. And then, to make the creation of the new duty doubly irrelevant, it finds that the case must be remanded anyway for a pretext inquiry: whether "petitioners actually fired Churchill not because of the disruptive things she said to Perkins-Graham, but because of nondisruptive statements about cross-training that they thought she may have made in the same conversation, or because of other statements she may have made earlier." *Ante*, at 682; see also *ante*, at 682–685 (SOUTER, J., concurring). Surely this offends the doctrine that constitutional questions that need not be addressed should be avoided.

The requirement of a pretext inquiry, I think, renders creation of the new First Amendment right of investigation not only superfluous to the disposition of the present case, but superfluous to the protection of previously established speech rights. JUSTICE O'CONNOR makes no attempt to justify the right of investigation on historical grounds (it is quite unheard of). The entire asserted basis for it is pragmatic and functional: without it the government employee's right not to be fired for his speech cannot be protected. The availability of a pretext inquiry disproves that argument. Judicial inquiry into the genuineness of a public employer's asserted permissible justification for an employment decision—be it unprotected speech, general insubordination, or laziness—is all that is necessary to avoid the targeting of "public interest" speech condemned in *Pickering*.

Our cases have hitherto considered this sort of inquiry all the protection needed. *Mt. Healthy City Bd. of Ed.* v. *Doyle*, 429 U. S. 274 (1977), involved an arguably weaker case for the public employer than the present one, in that there was a "mixed motive" for the disciplinary action—that is, the employer admitted that the "public concern" speech was part of the reason for the discharge, but asserted that other valid reasons were in any event sufficient. In deciding that case, we found no need to invent procedural requirements, but simply directed the District Court "to determine whether the Board had shown by a preponderance of the evidence that it would have reached the same decision as to respondent's [e]mployment even in the absence of the protected conduct." *Id.*, at 287. The objective, we said, was to "protec[t] against the invasion of constitutional rights without commanding undesirable consequences not necessary to the assurance of those rights." *Ibid.*

The Court considers "pretext" analysis sufficient in many other areas. See, *e. g., Eastman Kodak Co.* v. *Image Techni-*

cal Services, Inc., 504 U. S. 451, 484 (1992) (antitrust laws); *Hernandez* v. *New York*, 500 U. S. 352, 363–364 (1991) (plurality opinion) (constitutionality of peremptory challenges); *Patterson* v. *McLean Credit Union*, 491 U. S. 164, 187–188 (1989) (employment discrimination suit under 42 U. S. C. § 1981); *New York* v. *Burger*, 482 U. S. 691, 716–717, n. 27 (1987) (Fourth Amendment challenge to administrative searches); *Sure-Tan, Inc.* v. *NLRB*, 467 U. S. 883, 895–896, n. 6 (1984) (unfair labor practice suit under the National Labor Relations Act); *Geduldig* v. *Aiello*, 417 U. S. 484, 496–497, n. 20 (1974) (Equal Protection Clause sex-discrimination claim against legislation); *McDonnell Douglas Corp.* v. *Green*, 411 U. S. 792, 804–805 (1973) (discrimination claim under Title VII). And it considers "pretext" analysis sufficient in other First Amendment contexts. For example, in *Renton* v. *Playtime Theatres, Inc.*, 475 U. S. 41, 54 (1986), after holding that zoning laws restricting the location of movie theaters do not violate the First Amendment unless they are a pretext for preventing free speech, we did not think it necessary to prescribe "reasonable" procedures for zoning commissions across the Nation; we left it to factfinders to determine whether zoning regulations are prompted by legitimate or improper factors. See also *Arcara* v. *Cloud Books, Inc.*, 478 U. S. 697, 708 (1986) (O'CONNOR, J., concurring) (same). There is no reason why the same approach should not suffice here.

JUSTICE STEVENS believes that "pretext" review is inadequate, since "it provides less protection for a fundamental constitutional right than the law ordinarily provides for less exalted rights"; and "[o]rdinarily," he contends, "when someone acts to another person's detriment based upon a factual judgment, the actor assumes the risk that an impartial adjudicator may come to a different conclusion." *Post*, at 696. But that is true in contractual realms only to the extent that the contract provides a "right" whose elimination constitutes a legal "detriment." An employee dismissable at will *can* be fired on the basis of an erroneous factual judgment, with no legal recourse—which is what happened here. Churchill also had a *non*contractual right: the right not to be dismissed (even from an at-will government job) in retaliation for her expression of views on a matter of public concern. That right was not violated, since she was dismissed for another reason, erroneous though it may have been. The issue before us has nothing to do with according the deprivation of a right the ordinary degree of protection; it has to do with expanding the protection accorded a government employee's public interest speech from (1) protection against retaliation, to (2) protection against retaliation and mistake.

III

The approach to this case adopted by JUSTICE O'CONNOR's opinion provides more questions than answers, subjecting public employers to intolerable legal uncertainty. Despite the difficulties courts already encounter in distinguishing between protected and unprotected speech, see, *e. g., Miller* v. *California,* 413 U. S. 15, 22 (1973), and in determining whether speech pertains to a matter of public concern, compare *O'Connor* v. *Steeves,* 994 F. 2d 905, 915 (CA1), cert. denied, 510 U. S. 1024 (1993), with *Gillum* v. *City of Kerrville,* 3 F. 3d 117, 120–121 (CA5 1993), cert. denied, 510 U. S. 1072 (1994), JUSTICE O'CONNOR creates yet another speech-related puzzlement that government employers, judges, and juries must struggle to solve. The new constitutional duty to provide certain minimum procedural protections is triggered when "an employment action is based on what an employee supposedly said, and a reasonable supervisor would recognize that there is a substantial likelihood that what was actually said was protected," *ante,* at 677. But on what does the "reasonable supervisor" base his judgment as to whether "there is a substantial likelihood that what was actually said was protected?" Can he base it upon the *report* of what was said? Seemingly not, since otherwise JUSTICE O'CONNOR would not have found the minimum procedural protection of investigation to have been required in the present case (the report of Churchill's conversation gave no hint of protected speech). It remains entirely unclear what the employer's judgment *must* be based on. To avoid liability, he had better assume that it must be based on *what was actually said*—which means that he had better investigate the incident in order to determine whether he has an obligation to investigate the incident. Hopefully I am wrong, however, and (despite today's holding) the basis for judging whether investigation is required will be solely the *report*. Then the public employer will only have to figure out what a hypothetical reasonable supervisor would infer about actual speech from that report, and then determine whether that constructed "actual speech" has a substantial likelihood of being on a matter of public concern. May the employer at least assume that no investigation is required if the report does not *mention* speech? Or can he be liable if the recommended basis for the discipline (for example, "disrupting the workplace") had a substantial likelihood of involving speech which would have had a substantial likelihood of being on a subject of public concern? I suppose ultimately it will be up to the jury to answer all these nice, once-removed questions. Or come to think of it, perhaps it will be up to the judge. JUSTICE O'CONNOR does not specify whether all this is a question of law or fact.

JUSTICE O'CONNOR states that "employer decisionmaking will not be unduly burdened by having courts look to the facts as the employer *reasonably* found them to be." *Ante*, at 677 (emphasis in original). This explains the subsequent course of events when the employer's investigation has been found reasonable: The court (or the jury) decides whether, on the facts as found by the employer, the speech was on a matter of public concern, and if not, whether the employer's reliance on the report was pretextual. But what happens when the employer's investigation has been found unreasonable? I presume that there has then been established a violation of the procedural component of the First Amendment—the failure to treat possibly protected speech with the requisite "amount of care"—without regard to whether the employee's speech was in fact on a matter of public concern. JUSTICE O'CONNOR does not reveal what the remedy for this violation is to be. There are various possibilities: One could say that the discharge without observance of the constitutionally requisite procedures is invalid, and must be set aside unless and until those procedures are complied with. Alternatively, one could charge the employer who failed to conduct a reasonable investigation with knowledge of the protected speech that a jury later finds—producing a sort of constructive retaliatory discharge, and entitling the employee to full reinstatement and damages. Or alternatively again, the jury could be required to determine what information a reasonable investigation would have turned up, and then to decide whether it would have been permissible for the employer to fire the employee based on that information.

These are only a few of the numerous questions left unanswered by JUSTICE O'CONNOR's opinion. Loose ends are the inevitable consequence of judicial invention. We will spend decades trying to improvise the limits of this new First Amendment procedure that is unmentioned in text and unformed by tradition. It seems to me clear that game is not worth the candle, given the adequacy of "pretext" analysis to protect the constitutional interest at stake.

JUSTICE STEVENS, with whom JUSTICE BLACKMUN joins, dissenting.

This is a free country. Every American has the *right* to express an opinion on issues of public significance. In the private sector, of course, the exercise of that right may entail unpleasant consequences. Absent some contractual or statutory provision limiting its prerogatives, a private-sector employer may discipline or fire employees for speaking their minds. The First Amendment, however, demands that the government respect its employees' freedom to express their opinions on issues of public importance. As long as that expression is not unduly disruptive, it simply may not provide the basis for discipline or termination. The critical issues in a case of this kind are (1) whether the speech is protected, and (2) whether it was the basis for the sanction imposed on the employee.

Applying these standards to the case before us is quite straightforward. Everyone agrees that respondent Cheryl Churchill was fired because of what she said in a conversation with co-workers during a dinner break. Given the posture in which this case comes to us, we must assume that Churchill's statements were fully protected by the First Amendment.[1] Nevertheless, the plurality concludes that a dismissal for speech is valid as a matter of law as long as the public employer reasonably believed that the employee's speech was unprotected. See *ante*, at 677–678. This conclusion is erroneous because it provides less protection for a fundamental constitutional right than the law ordinarily provides for less exalted rights, including contractual and statutory rights applicable in the private sector.

If, for example, a hospital employee had a contract providing that she could retain her job for a year if she followed the employer's rules and did competent work, that employee

[1] On review of the Court of Appeals' reversal of a summary judgment for petitioners, we naturally accept as true the version of Churchill's statements described in her testimony and that of two supporting witnesses. See 977 F. 2d 1114, 1118–1126 (CA7 1992). According to Churchill, Thomas Koch, and Jean Welty, the dinner-break conversation concerned the merits of hospital policy, and Churchill did not direct any "personal criticism" against her supervisors. See *id.*, at 1118–1119, 1122. According to two other witnesses, Melanie Perkins-Graham and Mary Lou Ballew, Churchill's speech was filled with "unkind and inappropriate . . . things," "negativism," and personal comment about petitioner Cynthia Waters and the hospital administration. *Id.*, at 1118–1119.

could not be fired because her supervisor reasonably but mistakenly believed she had been late to work or given a patient the wrong medicine. Ordinarily, when someone acts to another person's detriment based upon a factual judgment, the actor assumes the risk that an impartial adjudicator may come to a different conclusion.[2] Our legal system generally delegates the determination of facts upon which important rights depend to neutral factfinders, notwithstanding the attendant risks of error and overdeterrence.

Federal constitutional rights merit at least the normal degree of protection. Doubts concerning the ability of juries to find the truth, an ability for which we usually have high regard, should be resolved in favor of, not against, the protection of First Amendment rights. See, *e. g., New York Times Co.* v. *Sullivan,* 376 U. S. 254, 279–280 (1964). Unfortunately, the plurality underestimates the importance of freedom of speech for the more than 18 million civilian employees of this country's Federal, State, and local Governments,[3] and subordinates that freedom to an abstract interest in bureaucratic efficiency. The need for governmental efficiency that so concerns the plurality is amply protected by the substan-

[2] In *NLRB* v. *Burnup & Sims, Inc.,* 379 U. S. 21 (1964), two employee labor organizers were fired based upon a report that they had threatened to dynamite the employer's plant if a coming representation election was unsuccessful. The National Labor Relations Board found that the employees had never made the threatening statements. Although we recognized that the employer had acted in good faith, this Court held that the discharge "plainly violated" the organizers' right under § 8 of the National Labor Relations Act. *Id.,* at 22. "Union activity," we observed, "often engenders strong emotions and gives rise to active rumors. A protected activity acquires a precarious status if innocent employees can be discharged while engaging in it, even though the employer acts in good faith." *Id.,* at 23. The plurality does not explain why First Amendment rights should receive any lesser protection than the statutory right at issue in *Burnup & Sims.*

[3] See U. S. Dept. of Commerce, Statistical Abstract of the United States 318 (113 ed. 1993) (Table No. 500) (figure from 1991).

tive limits on public employees' rights of expression. See generally *Connick* v. *Myers*, 461 U. S. 138 (1983); *Pickering* v. *Board of Ed. of Township High School Dist. 205, Will Cty.*, 391 U. S. 563 (1968). Efficiency does not demand an *additional* layer of deference to employers' "reasonable" factual errors. Today's ruling will surely deter speech that would be fully protected under *Pickering* and *Connick*.

The plurality correctly points out that we have never decided whether the governing version of the facts in public employment free speech cases is "what the government employer thought was said, or . . . what the trier of fact ultimately determines to have been said." *Ante*, at 664.[4] To

---

[4] JUSTICE SCALIA would recharacterize employees' right to free speech as a more modest protection against "retaliatory" discharges, a protection that would not extend to those terminated for speech that was fully protected but incorrectly reported. The only support he cites for this restrictive theory is that three of our prior public employment speech opinions have used the word "retaliation." See *ante*, at 688–689 (opinion concurring in judgment) (citing *Connick* v. *Myers*, 461 U. S. 138, 149 (1983); *Perry* v. *Sindermann*, 408 U. S. 593, 598 (1972); *Pickering* v. *Board of Ed. of Township High School Dist. 205, Will Cty.*, 391 U. S. 563, 572 (1968)). Our use of that word in the cases JUSTICE SCALIA cites, however, does not resolve the present question, since none of those decisions involved any factual dispute over the content of employee speech. More importantly, other passages from two of those opinions support the view that the *causal* connection between the employee's speech and her discharge is all the "retaliation" that must be shown. See *Perry*, 408 U. S., at 598 (nonrenewal of a teacher's contract "may not be predicated on his exercise of First and Fourteenth Amendment rights"); *ibid.* ("[A] teacher's public criticism of his superiors on matters of public concern may be constitutionally protected and may, therefore, be an impermissible basis for termination of his employment"); *Pickering*, 391 U. S., at 574 ("In sum, . . . a teacher's exercise of his right to speak on issues of public importance may not furnish the basis for his dismissal from public employment"). Precedent certainly does not command JUSTICE SCALIA's approach, and nothing in the First Amendment recommends a rule that makes ignorance or mistake a complete defense for a discharge based on fully protected speech. JUSTICE O'CONNOR appropriately rejects that position, at least for those instances in which the employer unreasonably believes an incorrect report

me it is clear that the latter must be controlling. The First Amendment assures public employees that they may express their views on issues of public concern without fear of discipline or termination as long as they do so in an appropriate manner and at an appropriate time and place. A violation occurs when a public employee is fired for uttering speech on a matter of public concern that is not unduly disruptive of the operations of the relevant agency. The violation does not vanish merely because the firing was based upon a reasonable mistake about what the employee said.[5] A First Amendment claimant need not allege bad faith; the controlling question is not the regularity of the agency's investigative procedures, or the purity of its motives, but whether the employee's freedom of speech has been "abridged."

The risk that a jury may ultimately view the facts differently from even a conscientious employer is not, as the plurality would have it, a needless fetter on public employers' ability to discharge their duties. It is the normal means by which our legal system protects legal rights and encourages those in authority to act with care. Here, for example, attention to "conclusions a jury would later draw," *ante*, at 676, about the content of Churchill's speech might have caused petitioners to talk to Churchill about what she said before deciding to fire her. There is nothing unfair or onerous

---

concerning speech that was in fact protected and disciplines an employee based upon that misunderstanding. I, of course, agree with JUSTICE O'CONNOR that discipline in such circumstances violates the First Amendment.

[5] The reasonableness of the public employer's mistake would, of course, bear on whether that employer should be liable for damages. See *Butz* v. *Economou*, 438 U. S. 478, 507 (1978) ("Federal officials will not be liable for mere mistakes in judgment, whether the mistake is one of fact or one of law"). It is wrong, however, to constrict the substantive reach of a public employee's right of free speech in response to such remedial considerations. See *ante*, at 677 (government employers who use reasonable procedures should be free to act "without fear [of] *liability*") (emphasis added).

about putting the risk of error on an employer in these circumstances.[6]

Government agencies are often the site of sharp differences over a wide range of important public issues. In offices where the First Amendment commands respect for candid deliberation and individual opinion, such disagreements are both inevitable and desirable. When those who work together disagree, reports of speech are often skewed, and supervisors are apt to misconstrue even accurate reports. The plurality, observing that managers "can spend only so much of their time on any one employment decision," *ante*, at 680, adopts a rule that invites discipline, rather than further discussion, when such disputes arise. That rule is unwise, for deliberation within the government, like deliberation about it, is an essential part of our "profound national commitment" to the freedom of speech. Cf. *New York Times*, 376 U. S., at 270. A proper regard for that principle requires that, before firing a public employee for her speech, management get its facts straight.

I would affirm the judgment of the Court of Appeals.

---

[6] Because there is no dispute that Churchill was fired for the content of her speech, this case does not involve the problem of determining whether the public employee would have been terminated anyway for reasons unrelated to speech. See *Mt. Healthy City Bd. of Ed.* v. *Doyle*, 429 U. S. 274 (1977).

Free Speech and Due Process in the Workplace

CYNTHIA L. ESTLUND*

INTRODUCTION 102
I. THE VALUE OF EMPLOYEE FREEDOM OF SPEECH: THREE VIEWS OF THE WORKPLACE 106
A. Speech and the Workplace as a Self-Governed Community 106
B. Speech and the Workplace as a Regulated Institution 110
C. Speech and the Workplace as Intermediate Institution 112
II. THE PROMISE OF FREE SPEECH IN THE WORKPLACE: WHAT EMPLOYEE SPEECH DOES THE LAW PROTECT? 114
A. The Scope of Protected Speech in Public Sector Employment 115
B. The Scope of Protected Speech in Private Sector Employment 116
III. WRONGS UNREMEDIED AND SPEECH UNSPOKEN: SOME EMPIRICAL EVIDENCE ON THE STATE OF FREEDOM OF EXPRESSION IN THE WORKPLACE 119
IV. THE SYSTEM OF FREEDOM OF EXPRESSION IN THE PUBLIC SECTOR WORKPLACE AND THE ROLE OF DUE PROCESS 124
A. The Wrongful Discharge Model of Free Speech Protections in the Public Sector Workplace 124
B. Due Process Protections as a Foundation for Freedom of Speech 128
V. THE SYSTEM OF FREEDOM OF EXPRESSION IN THE PRIVATE SECTOR WORKPLACE 129
A. The Wrongful Discharge Model of Free Speech Protection in the Private Sector At-Will Workplace 130
B. The Rationality of Employer Retaliation and Employee Silence in an At-Will Environment 132
C. Two Models of Due Process in the Private Sector Workplace 135
1. "Industrial Due Process" and Protection of Employee Speech 136
2. The Growth and Limitations of "Corporate Due Process" 139
D. A Brief Look Back at the Data 142
VI. SECURING FREE SPEECH THROUGH DUE PROCESS IN THE WORKPLACE: SOME PRELIMINARY OBSERVATIONS ON IMPLEMENTATION 143
A. Universalizing Due Process in the Public Sector 144
B. Universal Just Cause and Free Speech in the Private Sector: Lessons from Industrial and Corporate Due Process 146
CONCLUSION 150

---

* Leroy G. Denman, Jr., Regents Professor of Real Property Law, University of Texas School of Law. I would like to thank my colleagues Jack Getman, Sam Issacharoff, Doug Laycock, Dick Markovits, Bill Powers, and the participants in a faculty workshop at the University of Texas, as well as Michael Gottesman, J. Hoult (Rip) Verkerke, and the participants in a faculty workshop at the Northwestern University School of Law, for their helpful comments on earlier drafts. Finally, I wish to thank Ruth Silvers and Brent Caldwell for their helpful contributions as research assistants.

INTRODUCTION

Imagine a society whose citizens had free speech rights but no due process rights. The government could imprison citizens or banish them for any reason, or no reason at all, without notice or a hearing or proof of the charges; but it could not punish citizens based on their criticism of the government or other protected speech. The citizen who believed she had in fact been punished for speaking against the government could go to court and, if she could prove it, secure relief. How free would speech be in such a system? Would the citizens feel free to challenge the regime without fear of retaliation?

The questions are not idle ones, for the system that I have described is essentially that which prevails in the American workplace for the at-will employee, both public and private. Employees in both the public and the private sectors have free speech rights: the Constitution, state and federal statutes, and the common law purport to protect employees' rights to speak on various matters free from employer retaliation. But this "system of freedom of expression"[1] in the workplace lacks a crucial element of the system of freedom of expression in the society under the federal Constitution: many employees in both the public sector and the private sector enjoy no general legal protection against arbitrary discipline or discharge. They can be fired at will, for any reason or for no reason at all, subject to their ability to mount a legal challenge and to prove that the employer's true reason was the desire to punish the employee for protected speech (or was some other forbidden motive). Under this system, as in my hypothetical regime, the formal principle of freedom of expression may be largely illusory, for retaliation is readily cloaked in the guise of arbitrariness, and uncloaking it is likely to be too difficult, too time-consuming, and too costly to offer much reassurance to the typical employee.

The difficulties of proving an employer's motivation and the costs and delays of litigation undermine the effectiveness of many wrongful discharge remedies, including those against discrimination based on race, religion, ethnicity, sex, age, and handicap. But there is an additional element that should concern us when we seek to protect voluntary conduct by an individual, such as reporting of employer wrongdoing, rather than classes of individuals. The hurdles faced by the employee who is fired because of protected speech are not invisible to the employee who is deciding whether to speak up. An employee who considers whether to blow the whistle on her employer for unlawful conduct or to advocate unionization among her coworkers, but who fears she may lose her job with no readily available means of redress, is likely to be deterred from speaking. Notwithstanding the formal prohibition of retaliation against certain kinds of speech, we should expect reasonable employees to be "chilled" from speaking freely when it may put their jobs at risk. This is an important but largely unrecognized cost of the "at-will" presumption that underlies employment law for most American employees.

In this description of the workplace, it may seem that I am ignoring a crucial distinction. It is commonly thought that public employees enjoy freedom of expression; private sector employees do not. But I want to challenge that dichotomy and suggest another more important one. I will argue that real freedom of expression in the workplace depends less on the applicability of First Amendment protections than on the existence of independent protections against discharge without just cause and associated procedural

1. *See generally* THOMAS I. EMERSON, THE SYSTEM OF FREEDOM OF EXPRESSION (1972).

rights. These substantive and procedural due process rights, whether grounded in the Constitution or elsewhere, are the key to realizing the free speech rights that we already afford in principle to both public and private employees. I do not aim in this Article to question the doctrine of state action that keeps the First Amendment out of virtually all employment disputes in the private sector.[2] Rather, putting the state action question to one side is part of my strategy for uncovering and comparing the functional elements of the two systems of freedom of expression.[3]

I will thus contend that at-will public employees—though they enjoy free speech rights against their employer under the First Amendment—are extremely vulnerable without the underpinnings of basic due process protections against unjustified discharge. The Supreme Court's recent decision in *Waters v. Churchill*[4] takes a small, but still too small, step toward recognizing this link between free speech and due process. Turning to the private sector, I will argue that there is a "system of freedom of expression" consisting of a patchwork of discrete protections against employer retaliation for socially valued speech. But I will argue that the virtual absence, except in the dwindling union sector, of any functioning system of fair treatment and due process renders those speech protections nearly meaningless for the vast majority of employees. By contrast, in workplaces where the employer must show an impartial decisionmaker that there is good cause for discharge, as in the typical unionized workplace, employees enjoy much greater freedom of expression—perhaps more than many public employees protected by the First Amendment.

In short, I am making claims about the freedom of speech that employees experience at work in light of their legal environment. These contentions should be stated in the form of hypotheses. No analysis of the doctrine or case law can demonstrate that the legal environment which I describe "chills" employee freedom of speech. Evidence for my contentions would be found not in the cases adjudicating claims of retaliation, but in the silence that surrounds them—the silence of the typical employee who is neither uncommonly brave nor litigious, whose job is crucially important to her and her family, and who is guided in her actions by expectations about the consequences of those actions.

---

2. Others have done so, however. Some commentators have argued that, under a broad reading of Shelley v. Kraemer, 334 U.S. 1 (1948), a court's dismissal of a private employee's challenge to his speech-based discharge is sufficient state action to trigger the First Amendment. *See, e.g.*, Lisa B. Bingham, *Employee Free Speech in the Workplace: Using the First Amendment as Public Policy for Wrongful Discharge Actions*, 55 OHIO ST. L.J. 341, (1994); Thomas R. McCoy, *Current State Action Theories, the Jackson Nexus Requirements, and Employee Discharges by Semi-Public and State-Aided Institutions*, 31 VAND. L. REV. 785, 792-96 (1978); Cornelius J. Peck, *Unjust Discharges from Employment: A Necessary Change in the Law*, 40 OHIO ST. L.J. 1 (1979). Others have challenged the state action requirement more directly. *See, e.g.*, Terry A. Halbert, *The First Amendment in the Workplace: An Analysis and Call for Reform*, 17 SETON HALL L. REV. 42, 66-70 (1987) (questioning state action requirement); Stanley Ingber, *Rediscovering the Communal Worth of Individual Rights: The First Amendment in Institutional Contexts*, 69 TEX. L. REV. 1, 65-70 (1990). *See generally* Erwin Chemerinsky, *Rethinking State Action*, 80 NW. U. L. REV. 503 (1986) (arguing for elimination of state action requirement generally).

3. Several commentators have looked at some of the common free speech issues in the public and private sector workplace. *See* Bingham, *supra* note 2; Cynthia L. Estlund, *What Do Workers Want? Employee Interests, Public Interests, and Freedom of Expression Under the National Labor Relations Act*, 140 U. PA. L. REV. 921 (1992); Richard M. Fischl, *Labor, Management, and the First Amendment: Whose Rights Are These, Anyway?*, 10 CARDOZO L. REV. 729 (1989); Joseph R. Grodin, *Constitutional Values in the Private Sector Workplace*, 13 INDUS. REL. L.J. 1 (1991); Halbert, *supra* note 2; Ingber, *supra* note 2; Karl Klare, *The Public/Private Distinction in Labor Law*, 130 U. PA. L. REV. 1358 (1982); Robert F. Ladenson, *Free Speech in the Workplace and the Public-Private Distinction*, 7 LAW & PHIL. 247 (1988-89); Staughton Lynd, *Employee Speech in the Private and Public Workplace: Two Doctrines or One?*, 1 INDUS. REL. L. J. 711 (1977).

4. 114 S. Ct. 1878 (1994).

There is some empirical evidence to support these claims, but the data are incomplete.[5] In the meantime, it seems fair to assume that employees respond sensibly to the expected costs and benefits of speaking out. As things stand, much speech that is ostensibly protected remains very costly and produces little or no private benefit to the employee.

However we define the speech that we value and seek to protect in the workplace, that speech will not be free if the speaker must prove her right to speak and must bear the burdens of delay, uncertainty, or error in decisionmaking. Freedom of expression in the workplace, as in the society at large, requires "breathing room." I submit that the best way to give breathing room to valued workplace speech is to support existing protections of expression with a regime of substantive and procedural due process. Due process, in the form of a "just cause" requirement for discharge and a fair hearing, would both bolster the existing protections of highly valued employee speech and, incidentally, generate some protection for less exalted forms of speech that simply do not justify the extreme sanction of discharge. Due process would thus help to provide the necessary breathing room for the freedom of expression that we already purport to recognize.

I anticipate three fairly sweeping objections to a universal just cause requirement: It won't work; it isn't necessary; and it costs too much. The objection that a legally mandated just cause regime will not protect employees against retaliation and will not support freedom of expression strikes at the heart of my thesis. My belief in the value of due process is based partly on standard economic reasoning: employees should normally be expected to act on the basis of reasonable expectations about the consequences of speaking out and particularly about the possibility of discharge. The greater ease, availability, and timeliness of a remedy against retaliatory discharge offered under a due process system rather than under a wrongful discharge system reduces the cost of speaking out. Empirical evidence bolsters this analysis, including experience in the union setting. But that experience may indicate the need for some form of institutional support for employees seeking to challenge their discharge, such as some type of employee representation within or outside the workplace, in addition to individual due process.

The second objection is that a legal mandate of due process is not necessary to support legally protected speech because the threat of wrongful discharge liability will deter employers from wrongful conduct or will lead them to take precautions in the form of procedural safeguards. But the speech that is protected by law can be quite costly to employers for the same reasons that it is valuable to the public; that is why legal protection is necessary. Given the real benefits that employers might gain from the discharge of a disruptive speaker, the deterrence of other potential speakers, and the hurdles that employees face in remedying a retaliatory discharge, the prospect of liability may often be inadequate to deter punishment of valuable and legally protected speech.

The third and related objection, that universal due process is too costly, is for some the most telling objection. Given the very small percentage of discharges that are probably based on valuable or protected speech, universal just cause protection appears to be a very big and intrusive solution to a relatively small problem. Of course, the current wrongful discharge regime, only a part of which concerns the protection of speech, is itself extremely costly to employers, employees, and the economy as a whole. If it is as

5. I am undertaking a preliminary study of these questions, with the support of the Fund for Labor Relations Studies. The study will begin, and may end, with a number of open-ended interviews of nonsupervisory employees of medium and large private firms. I hope to learn more about how free employees feel to speak on issues as to which the law provides protection against employer retaliation.

ineffective as I claim it is, then the question of costs begins to look quite different. But the question of whether due process is too costly goes beyond the present project, for there are both costs and benefits to due process that lie far beyond the issue of workplace speech. My argument is therefore *not* that the benefits of due process for employee freedom of expression are sufficient to justify instituting a universal just cause regime, but that securing employee freedom of expression is an important and largely unrecognized benefit of moving toward such a regime.

There is one final response to my claim of drastic underenforcement of speech protections: "You get what you pay for." More protection would entail greater interference with managerial prerogatives and greater administrative or litigation costs as well as more of the ostensibly desirable speech. Perhaps the existing weak enforcement mechanisms afford all the protection of employee speech for which we as a society are willing to pay. For those who take this view, the greater part of my argument, which exposes the enormous gap between what the law apparently promises in terms of freedom of speech and what the law delivers, will fall on deaf ears: "So what? You simply failed to read the fine print." Stated differently: Why should we protect the employee speech that we claim to protect?

It is partly in anticipation of this question that I begin in Part I by discussing what is at stake in the protection of employee speech. Against this background I proceed in Part II to describe what employee speech the law currently protects. I conclude that existing law represents a promise of employee freedom of expression that is limited in scope—in some cases too limited—but that it is a promise well worth fulfilling, for the speech that is protected is of great value in the workplace and the society. In Part III, I examine the limited empirical evidence of the effectiveness of existing legal protections. I look at both the prevalence of discharges based on protected speech, and more importantly, the extent of freedom of speech that employees experience. The limited empirical evidence available suggests a large gap between what the law promises and what it delivers: many employees do not experience even the limited freedom of expression that the law purports to grant them.

In Parts IV and V, I return to existing law, first in the public sector and then in the private sector, to seek an explanation for that gap. But I seek that explanation not in the content of what is protected, but in the procedures and structures through which these protections are administered. In particular, I examine how those structures and procedures operate against the backgrounds both of at-will employment—which underlies the system of freedom of expression in many public sector and most private sector employment relations—and of a system of due process and just cause. In both the public and private sectors, I conclude that the current regime of wrongful discharge remedies, against the heavy backdrop of the at-will presumption, provides plainly inadequate remedies for employees fired on the basis of protected speech, but that a functioning due process system acts as an indirect but effective bulwark for the protection of employee speech. Finally, in Part VI, I will discuss very briefly some aspects of how due process safeguards might be implemented as part of the system of freedom of expression in the public and private sector workplace.

I. THE VALUE OF EMPLOYEE FREEDOM OF SPEECH: THREE VIEWS OF THE WORKPLACE

Why should we care about freedom of expression in the workplace?[6] To begin with, most adults spend a great part of their waking hours at work. The intrinsic value of free speech for individual autonomy, and its value in fostering individual self-realization and fulfillment, transcends the boundaries established by the state action doctrine. Freedom of expression at work enhances human development and well-being no less than freedom of expression in civic life.[7]

But speech is not a solitary exercise; it presupposes a listener, a conversation, and a community. Speech in the workplace, like speech in the society, can benefit the audience and the society as a whole as well as the speaker. The values served depend on how we view the workplace as an institution. First, we can see the workplace from the inside as a microcosmic society governed by management. We can also see the workplace from the outside as an object of societal control. Finally, we can see the workplace as an intermediate institution, an institution that mediates between individuals and the society as a whole, in which individuals cultivate some of the values, habits, and traits that carry over to their roles as citizens. Each of these perspectives on the workplace sheds light on the value of employee speech.[8]

A. *Speech and the Workplace as a Self-Governed Community*

The workplace is an internally governed community.[9] The employee-citizens of the workplace community are governed by management.[10] The form of government may vary. Some workplace governments are highly autocratic, relying heavily on hierarchy and close supervision. Few are governed "democratically" by the citizen-employees themselves, though many workplace governments include mechanisms for participation and representation of employees.

---

6. The values served by free speech in the workplace loosely parallel the values served by free speech in society generally. For a very few of the prominent contributions to the rich literature discussing the values served by free speech in society generally, see ALEXANDER MEIKLEJOHN, POLITICAL FREEDOM 24-28 (1960); JOHN STUART MILL, ON LIBERTY, ch. 2 (1859); FREDERICK SCHAUER, FREE SPEECH: A PHILOSOPHICAL ENQUIRY (1982); C. Edwin Baker, *Scope of the First Amendment Freedom of Speech*, 25 UCLA L. REV. 964 (1978); Thomas I. Emerson, *Toward a General Theory of the First Amendment*, 72 YALE L.J. 877 (1963); Martin H. Redish, *The Value of Free Speech*, 130 U. PA. L. REV. 591 (1982). The values underlying the First Amendment become relevant directly—not merely by analogy—in the public sector workplace. *See generally* Toni M. Massaro, *Significant Silences: Freedom of Speech in the Public Sector Workplace*, 61 S. CAL. L. REV. 1, 38-51 (1987) (arguing that important First Amendment values are at stake in public employee speech).

7. *See* DAVID W. EWING, FREEDOM INSIDE THE ORGANIZATION 11-20 (1977); Ingber, *supra* note 2, at 54, 65-68; Ladenson, *supra* note 3, at 259-60.

8. I want to offer one caveat before proceeding: I will not argue that the scope of substantive free speech protections of employees should directly correspond to the speech that I argue is valuable in the workplace. On the contrary, for most of this Article, I take as given the existing categories of protected speech, and I discuss how effectively the law really protects that speech. This discussion of the value of workplace speech is meant to serve as one kind of measuring stick for the subsequent evaluation of the system of freedom of expression that we have in the workplace and for the evaluation of my proposed just cause regime.

9. David Ewing also described the workplace as a society governed by management as he examined the state of civil liberties within the workplace. EWING, *supra* note 7, at 11-20.

10. Indeed, one could analogize the full-time, "permanent" workforce as the citizenry and the various "contingent" workers—part-time, temporary, or contract employees—as the "resident aliens," whose status is more tenuous and whose rights are more limited.

There is something like "law" within the workplace community as well. Most of the "law" that governs the conduct of the citizen-employees is the law enacted by management more or less unilaterally: rules of conduct, standards of performance, and the hierarchies and systems established by management for enforcing these rules and standards. In the unionized workplace, the employees, through their union, play a role in establishing some of the "law of the shop." The law established by management, written or unwritten, with or without the participation of a union, is what regulates the day-to-day conduct of the government and its citizens.

The law of the shop includes regulation of speech. Employers might seek to prohibit or suppress speech that helps to enforce external regulatory norms and that threatens the firm with outside scrutiny or sanctions. Employers might also regulate or punish speech that threatens the internal structures, relationships, and hierarchies through which it governs, such as harassment, rudeness, or insubordination. And just as governments may punish sedition, employers may seek to punish speech that, from their vantage point, foments rebellion against the existing workplace regime.[11] In many nonunion workplaces it appears to be widely understood that employees shall not discuss the possibility of unionization and that violation of this "rule" is punishable by discharge.[12] From the employee's perspective, this is the law of the shop.[13]

The workplace government is constrained, however, by something analogous to a constitution: the whole body of public law that governs the workplace from the outside, including the laws protecting some kinds of employee speech against employer sanctions. These laws, the content of which is discussed below, establish the framework and the minimum standards within which workplace law operates. They are no more subject to change by the internal governing structure of the workplace than is the federal constitution by a local government. The amalgam of public laws protecting speech in the private sector workplace thus functions as a kind of quasi-First Amendment for the workplace just as the First Amendment itself, in modified form, functions like a constitutional limit on the internal law of the public sector workplace. I will discuss the content and structure of this quasi-First Amendment below. For the moment, I want to focus on the protections of workplace speech.

Thinking about the workplace as a management-governed community puts a new spin on the relation between free speech and intelligent self-government. It is an article of faith that the free speech of the citizenry is essential to democratic self-governance in the society at large. Might employee free speech play an analogous role in fostering informed self-governance within the workplace?

To pose that question may seem to finesse an enormous difference between the political community and the workplace. In our society the ideal of democratic self-government is a given. It constitutes the society and the manner in which we pursue other societal objectives, and that is what makes free speech on public issues so self-evidently

11. I have argued that this is precisely how many employers, not without reason, see employee speech advocating unionization. *See* Cynthia L. Estlund, *Economic Rationality and Union Avoidance: Misunderstanding the National Labor Relations Act*, 71 TEX. L. REV. 921 (1993).

12. *See infra* notes 83-85 and accompanying text.

13. I do not, of course, mean to enter into a jurisprudential debate about whether "law" of this sort—employer dictates that violate governing positive law—can be called "law." It is as much a law from the perspective of the employee as is an unconstitutional statute or governmental practice from the perspective of the citizen who is subject to that statute or practice. In either case, the fact of unconstitutionality is somewhat academic if the means of establishing unconstitutionality are too remote or expensive or unwieldy to be an effective defense against the illegal practice.

necessary. By contrast, the ideal of workplace democracy is at best contested. The private firm, in particular, is organized to compete effectively in the relevant product market and to generate profits for its owners, not to foster the domestic well-being of its citizen-employees. Even in the public sector workplace, the instrumental goals of carrying out governmental objectives and delivering public services take precedence over the democratic nature of the workplace as an institution.[14] So whatever role free speech may have in improving democratic self-government, the question may seem misplaced in the workplace and particularly in the private profitmaking firm.

But recent developments in industrial relations scholarship and practice, as well as in corporate law and scholarship, have laid a foundation for asking this question. While employee self-governance is hardly a given, as it is in the polity as a whole, employee participation in workplace governance is increasingly viewed as both an intrinsic and an instrumental good. The intrinsic value of employee participation can be seen in the simple fact that employees are more satisfied with their work when they have an opportunity to express themselves and potentially influence workplace decisions.[15] But more than job satisfaction is at stake, for the workplace is the location where people come together for purposive, cooperative activity and where they gain or lose much of their sense of community and of self-worth.

Moral claims such as these have long been overshadowed by issues of economic efficiency in discussions of private firm governance,[16] but they have a new generation of champions in the field of corporate law. For many observers, the wave of mergers and acquisitions of the 1980's exposed the extent to which shareholder primacy subordinated the pressing concerns of other "stakeholders" in the private corporation, including workers and their communities.[17] In the wake of these developments has come a broad current of dissatisfaction with the long-prevailing paradigms of corporate law, which give shareholders the dominant claim on legal protection while leaving other parties in the

---

14. According to a plurality of the Supreme Court, this is the fundamental reason for the greater deference granted the government in its regulation of employee speech than in its regulation of the speech of citizens at large. *See* Waters v. Churchill, 114 S. Ct. 1878, 1887-88 (1994) (plurality opinion).

15. *See, e.g.*, COMMISSION ON THE FUTURE OF WORKER-MANAGEMENT RELATIONS, FACT FINDING REPORTS 30-31, 52 (1994) [hereinafter FACT FINDING REPORTS]; Karen L. Newman, *The Just Organization: Creating and Maintaining Justice in Work Environments*, 50 WASH. & LEE L. REV. 1489, 1489-95, 1498 (1993) (reviewing studies); David Sheinfeld & Sheldon S. Zalkind, *Does Civil-Liberties Climate in Organizations Correlate with Job Satisfaction and Work Alienation?*, 60 PSYCHOL. REP. 467 (1987).

16. For a discussion of the competing normative frameworks of efficiency and ethics in corporate law by a proponent of the latter, see generally Lawrence E. Mitchell, *Groundwork of the Metaphysics of Corporate Law*, 50 WASH. & LEE L. REV. 1477 (1993); *see also* Lawrence E. Mitchell, *Cooperation and Constraint in the Modern Corporation: An Inquiry into the Causes of Corporate Immorality*, 73 TEX. L. REV. 477 (1995).

17. *See* David Millon, *Communitarians, Contractarians, and the Crisis in Corporate Law*, 50 WASH. & LEE L. REV. 1373, 1373-77 (1993) [hereinafter Millon, *Communitarians*]. One much-analyzed result has been state "stakeholder" statutes that give corporate managers and directors the right, and sometimes even the duty, to consider the interests of corporate constituencies other than shareholders. Some corporate law scholars have argued for an expansive reading of these statutes. *See, e.g.*, David Millon, *Redefining Corporate Law*, 24 IND. L. REV. 223 (1991); Lawrence E. Mitchell, *A Theoretical and Practical Framework for Enforcing Corporate Constituency Statutes*, 70 TEX. L. REV. 579, 630-40 (1992); Marleen A. O'Connor, *Restructuring the Corporation's Nexus of Contracts: Recognizing a Fiduciary Duty to Protect Displaced Workers*, 69 N.C. L. REV. 1189, 1232-34 (1991); Katherine Van Wezel Stone, *Employees as Stakeholders Under State Nonshareholders Constituency Statutes*, 21 STETSON L. REV. 45 (1991). Others are critical of the statutes' theoretical underpinnings and argue for limiting constructions. *See, e.g.*, Charles Hansen, *Other Constituency Statutes: A Search for Perspective*, 46 BUS. LAW. 1355, 1375 (1991); Jonathan R. Macey, *Externalities, Firm-Specific Capital Investments, and the Legal Treatment of Fundamental Corporate Changes*, 1989 DUKE L.J. 173.

"nexus of contracts" to bargain with whatever chips their circumstances endow them.[18] For some of these new communitarians of corporate law and theory, employee voice—the opportunity to speak and to have an influence on decisions in the firm—is valued because it fulfills human needs and helps to foster a humane working environment.

Employee voice has also won champions among labor economists. In much modern thinking about workplace relations and the economy, the ideal workplace of the future is the "high-performance," high-wage, high-skill workplace. It is widely held, and was recently affirmed by the Presidential Commission on the Future of Worker-Management Relations (or the Dunlop Commission), that thoroughgoing cooperation and partnership between workers and management is a crucial prerequisite to a high-performance economy.[19] Although economists remain divided over these claims, a good deal of research shows that employee-management cooperation, particularly through the medium of collective bargaining, tends to improve productivity at the firm level by supporting employees' investment in firm-specific skills, enhancing the exchange of knowledge, and improving employee morale, loyalty, and longevity.[20]

Cooperation, in turn, requires mechanisms for fostering employee "voice" in the workplace. The Dunlop Commission, among others, has focused on the organizational structures for employee voice.[21] There has been a profusion of scholarship chronicling the decline of traditional union representation and the gradual rise, at the margins of existing law, of nonunion, management-initiated forms of employee participation.[22] Legal scholars have asked how the law can foster effective forms of employee representation including, but not limited to, traditional union representation and collective bargaining.

There is good reason to focus on participatory institutions. Employee voice, to be effective in workplace governance and in monitoring regulatory compliance, must be channeled into workable and representative structures with power within the workplace; it is important to explore alternative forms of employee representation as well as means of reinforcing the traditional right to choose union representation. But I believe that in touting the virtues and evaluating the organizational structures of employee voice without directly examining the system of employee freedom of expression, we have neglected the obvious. To be free to participate in workplace governance, to initiate new or better

18. For the classic statement of the "nexus of contracts" view, see generally FRANK EASTERBROOK & DANIEL R. FISCHEL, THE ECONOMIC STRUCTURE OF CORPORATE LAW (1991). For a concise summary, see Henry N. Butler, *The Contractual Theory of the Corporation*, 11 GEO. MASON U. L. REV. 100 (1989). For some of the recent critiques of this view, see generally William W. Bratton, Jr., *The New Economic Theory of the Firm: Critical Perspectives from History*, 41 STAN. L. REV. 1471 (1989); William W. Bratton, Jr., *The "Nexus of Contracts" Corporation: A Critical Appraisal*, 74 CORNELL L. REV. 407 (1989); Lyman Johnson, *Individual and Collective Sovereignty in the Corporate Enterprise*, 92 COLUM. L. REV. 2215 (1992). A "Partial Bibliography of Communitarian Corporate Law Scholarship" appears in Millon, *Communitarians*, *supra* note 17, at 1391-93.

19. FACT FINDING REPORTS, *supra* note 15, at 55-56.

20. Relatively high wages are, by definition, an important element of the "high-wage" economy, and higher wages lead firms to substitute capital for labor in a way that increases labor's productivity but that most economists would regard as inefficient. But the efficient type of productivity gains appear, at least in some studies, to predominate. The Dunlop Commission evaluated much of the available evidence on productivity gains from labor-management cooperation and unionization. *See id.* at 45-47. A more detailed assessment of the evidence appears in Dale Belman, *Unions, the Quality of Labor Relations, and Firm Performance*, *in* UNIONS AND ECONOMIC COMPETITIVENESS 41 (Lawrence Mishel & Paula B. Voos eds., 1992). As one economist framed the choice, "[b]etter firm performance can be the outcome of skilled workers operating with superior capital in a wholesome environment. Better performance can also be founded on sweated labor driven to higher output by necessity and insecurity." *Id.* at 72.

21. FACT FINDING REPORTS, *supra* note 15, at 55-57, 79-80 (disclosing findings on worker participation schemes and freedom to choose union representation).

22. *See* WILLIAM B. GOULD IV, AGENDA FOR REFORM (1993); PAUL C. WEILER, GOVERNING THE WORKPLACE (1990). A recent collection of articles from many leading labor scholars on these issues is found in *Symposium on the Legal Future of Employee Representation*, 69 CHI.-KENT L. REV. 1 (1993).

alternative forms of employee representation, and to choose traditional union representation, employees must be free to speak out, among themselves and with supervisors and management, about workplace issues.[23] Employees cannot be expected to act as full partners and to take the initiative in forming and reforming effective representative structures in an environment where they do not feel free to criticize and question management without risking their jobs.[24]

Many firms have recognized the benefits of employee voice and participation in firm governance, at least to some degree, and many educated observers have urged a much wider dissemination of participatory mechanisms.[25] It is evident that a wholesale shift toward codetermination and away from unfettered management prerogatives would require a dramatic cultural transformation in American business. Cultural transformation is not easily legislated. But freedom of expression, and the legal structures necessary to protect it, is something with which the American legal system has a wealth of experience. We know that self-governance in the political sphere depends on free public debate, and that free public debate requires dissident viewpoints and strong legal guarantees against government censorship and repression of information. Now that the economists have rediscovered the instrumental virtues of participation in workplace governance, it is time to take another look at the system of freedom of expression that, in the workplace as in the society, lies at the foundation of a participatory system of governance.

B. Speech and the Workplace as a Regulated Institution

The workplace is not only a self-governing community but is also an object of regulation by the government and the citizens at large. Protection of some employee speech facilitates the informed and intelligent exercise of societal control of the workplace. This is true in different ways in both the public sector and the private sector. Citizens govern the public sector workplace—government agencies and institutions—both through legislation and through political processes, including elections. Public employees are an important source of information about government operations and conduct. Protecting public employee speech from employer reprisals

---

23. Those who have focused their attention on structures for collective employee representation might argue quite persuasively that true employee free speech is at least as *dependent* on effective collective representation—or, more baldly, on employee power—as it is *necessary* for effective representation, and that the latter must come first. Fortunately, there is no pressing need to solve this conundrum unless the measures one proposes for the protection of employee free speech undermine the effort to develop effective representative structures. It seems far more likely that the two efforts would reinforce one another.

24. The Dunlop Commission notes evidence that the vast majority of unrepresented workers wants a greater voice in workplace decisionmaking and decries the lack of employee initiative in originating or reforming participatory schemes. The Commission cites employee concerns that they will alienate their employers or be fired, and that such efforts will be "risky or futile." FACT FINDING REPORTS, *supra* note 15, at 52. The statistics of unfair labor practices by employers, *see id.* at 83, and the experiences of some workers who sought union representation amply support the employees' fears of retaliation. *See id.* at 89-92. What these findings reflect, but do not address as such, is the fact that employees lack freedom of expression even on matters that are supposedly protected by law.

25. The strong economic claims on behalf of employee participation provoke an obvious question: If employee voice tends to promote productivity, why would employers suppress it? That is a deeply challenging question, and to attempt to answer it here would take me too far afield. Let me offer a few brief observations, however. First, the claim is that employee voice can contribute to productivity, but higher productivity does not necessarily translate into profits. *See* Estlund, *supra* note 11, at 948-49. Second, the powerful prevailing ideology of managerial prerogatives may well get in the way of recognizing the value to the firm of giving employees greater voice and influence. *See id.* at 932. Third, the short-term benefits of suppressing employee speech that the firm regards as harmful may overshadow the less tangible long-term benefits to the firm of freer employee discourse. *See infra* notes 141-46 and accompanying text.

potentially enhances the quality of citizens' political judgments and decisions about how public agencies should run and who should run them.[26]

Much of what the government does, however, is to regulate the private sector. Just as public employees may provide information to the public about how government works, private employees may provide information to the public about how private firms operate with regard to working conditions, product safety, environmental practices, and other matters in which the society has a well-established regulatory interest. Assuming (as I will here) that there is a legitimate public interest behind the underlying regulations—workplace safety and antidiscrimination laws, environmental and product safety regulations, etc.—then there is a public interest as well in information of the sort that employees often have about compliance with the regulations.[27] Employee speech about corporate conduct may also inform public debate about whether more or less or different forms of regulation are wise.[28]

Whistleblowing directed to public or government officials is the most dramatic example of employee speech that enhances the regulatory process. But less visible, less dramatic forms of employee speech—the day-to-day speech of ordinary employees within the workplace—may be the necessary first step toward improving safety and other working conditions as well as compliance with environmental, safety, financial, and other regulatory requirements.

Employee speech on these matters can be understood not simply as good for the public but as a "public good" in the economic sense.[29] Most dramatically, reporting of employer misconduct and threats to public safety produce goods, in the form of information, for the public at large. Moreover, the society relies heavily on employee monitoring and reporting as key elements of the enforcement scheme for most workplace regulations, many of which necessarily protect workers as a group as well as interests of the public at large in adequate working conditions.[30] Both types of employee reporting produce public goods. The employee cannot keep to herself the benefits of the information, nor can she generally share with others the significant costs she incurs in producing the information—the cost of learning about legal requirements and about the employer's conduct, as well as the risk of retaliation from the employer.[31] Protecting employee speech that informs the government or the public or even the employer about illegal or

---

26. This has been the preeminent justification for protecting public employee speech under the First Amendment. *See, e.g.*, Connick v. Myers, 461 U.S. 138, 142-44 (1983); Pickering v. Board of Educ., 391 U.S. 563, 568 (1968); *see also* Massaro, *supra* note 6, at 38-41 (discussing the value of public employee speech to the political process).

27. *See infra* notes 60-65.

28. *See* CHRISTOPHER D. STONE, WHERE THE LAW ENDS: THE SOCIAL CONTROL OF CORPORATE BEHAVIOR (1975); Estlund, *supra* note 3, at 960-67. The public interest in information about the conduct of private firms figures prominently in the literature on whistleblowing. *See infra* notes 64-65 and accompanying text.

29. The "public goods" aspect of many workplace goods is explored in RICHARD B. FREEMAN & JAMES L. MEDOFF, WHAT DO UNIONS DO? (1984); Michael H. Gottesman, *Wither Goest Labor Law: Law and Economics in the Workplace*, 100 YALE L.J. 2767, 2789-90 (1991) (reviewing PAUL C. WEILER, *supra* note 22); Steven L. Willborn, *Individual Employment Rights and the Standard Economic Objection Theory and Empiricism*, 67 NEB. L. REV. 101, 127-34 (1988). These commentators focus on public goods within the workplace. I mean to consider as well—even primarily—the external benefits to the public at large.

30. *See* WEILER, *supra* note 22, at 157-58.

31. This is the case primarily in the nonunion workplace. Several commentators have emphasized the ability of unions to overcome the public goods problem in the workplace as one of the chief advantages of unions to employees and to social efficiency. *See* sources cited *supra* note 29.

otherwise harmful conduct or conditions within the workplace may mitigate the public goods problem, and encourage employees to produce this valued information.[32]

C. Speech and the Workplace as Intermediate Institution

The workplace functions not only as a self-governing institution and as a regulated institution; it also functions as a crucial intermediate institution that stands between the individual and the state.[33] The workplace is one institution in which most adults can and must interact with others—initially strangers, often from diverse cultural, ethnic, political, and religious backgrounds—in a constructive way toward common aims. Indeed, as other intermediate communities and institutions such as neighborhoods, families, and religious congregations are battered and destabilized by the pressures of economic change and geographic mobility, the workplace is increasingly one of the few organic communities of a human scale in which many members of the society participate on a regular basis.[34] To that degree, the workplace has become an increasingly important site for the forging of those crosscutting ties that help bind together a diverse society and for the formation of "civic virtues": the habits and traits and beliefs that make good citizens.[35]

This picture of the workplace community is surely idealized, but to the extent that it is an ideal worth aspiring to, it requires that people feel reasonably free to speak their minds on what matters to them at work.[36] The ideal of the workplace as a "school for democracy" requires respect for some of the basic values and freedoms of political democracy. I do not think such respect in the workplace requires the full range of freedom of expression that the First Amendment demands in the society at large, however.

---

32. It may be possible to over-encourage employee production of information about their employers, *see* Martin H. Malin, *Protecting the Whistleblower from Retaliatory Discharge*, 10 U. MICH. J. L. REF. 277, 302-03 (1983), and even to over-enforce societal regulations of employers, *see* James W. Hubbell, *Retaliatory Discharge and the Economics of Deterrence*, 60 U. COLO. L. REV. 91 (1989). The potential for over-enforcement would not follow from the freedom of employees to speak, or from the prohibition of retaliation itself, but from allegedly excessive remedies (such as large punitive damage awards) and/or errors in adjudication that predominantly favor employees. The possible problem of over-enforcement thus does not militate against employee freedom to speak out against the employer; however, it does merit consideration in thinking about how to enforce that freedom.

33. On the importance of intermediate institutions as "schools of democracy," see ALEXIS DE TOCQUEVILLE, DEMOCRACY IN AMERICA 63 (J.D. Meyer ed. & George Lawrence trans., 1965).

34. For an early renowned statement of the crucial role of "occupational groups" in bridging the increasing chasm between the solitary individual and the polity, see EMILE DURKHEIM, SUICIDE: A STUDY IN SOCIOLOGY 378-82 (George Simpson ed. & trans. & John A. Spaulding trans., 1951). Of course the workplace itself is not immune from these same destabilizing pressures. Witness the growth of the contingent workforce—the legions of part-time, temporary, and contract employees who are taking the place of many full-time, permanent employees. *See* FACT FINDING REPORTS, *supra* note 15, at 21-22. Thomas Kohler explores the decline of unions as a crucial aspect of the "declining middle"—the deterioration of mediating institutions. *See* Thomas C. Kohler, *The Overlooked Middle*, 69 CHI.-KENT L. REV. 229, 234-39 (1993).

35. *See* Stanley Ingber, *Judging Without Judgment: Constitutional Irrelevancies and the Demise of Dialogue*, 46 RUTGERS L. REV. 1473, 562-72 (1994); Ingber, *supra* note 2, at 53-54; Thomas C. Kohler, *Individualism and Communitarianism at Work*, 1993 B.Y.U. L. REV. 727, 731-39; Massaro, *supra* note 6, at 59-61; *see also* Frank Michelman, *Law's Republic*, 97 YALE L.J. 1493, 1531 (1988) (noting the importance of the workplace as a "mediating" institution); *accord* Cass R. Sunstein, *Beyond the Republican Revival*, 97 YALE L.J. 1539, 1577-78 (1988).

36. The most important expression of these ideas in American law was perhaps in the enactment of the National Labor Relations Act in 1935. The focus then was on the creation of instruments for collective employee self-expression and self-determination. Unionization was viewed not only as a means toward pressing economic ends but also as a move toward democratization of the workplace and of society. Section 7 of the Act was held up as a vindication of the "constitutional" and "natural" rights of workers to make their voices heard. *See* Estlund, *supra* note 3, at 964-66.

Not all employee speech advances these values. The ideal of the workplace as an effective mediating institution requires a degree of civility, mutual respect, and tolerance that some speech may undermine.[37] These concerns should not overshadow the value of freedom of expression in the workplace in cultivating habits of active and responsible citizenship in the society at large. But they do complicate the picture by raising the prickly problem of harmful workplace speech.

By "harmful workplace speech" I do not mean speech that the employer deems disruptive and harmful for the same reasons that it benefits workers or the public, such as speech that exposes the employer to deserved criticism or legal liability[38] or discussion among coworkers of unionization.[39] That is not what I mean by "harmful speech."[40]

But other speech, such as personal insults, divisive gossip, racial slurs, sexual taunts, propositions, innuendo, and the like may harm coworkers and undermine employee morale, cooperative relations, and ultimately productivity within the workplace. Some speech undermines the norms of equality that are, like the speech protections discussed here, part of the "constitution" of the workplace community. Virtually all employers rely to some degree (and I have argued that they should rely increasingly) on cooperation and harmony among employees at different levels of management. How do we treat employee speech that erodes the relationships on which a more democratic and less hierarchical workplace depends?

These same dilemmas have generated passionate debate within constitutional law and theory over the extent to which the government may or even must restrict some kinds of harmful speech in order to effectuate equality, to enable the often silent to speak, or to preserve the civility and tolerance that holds together a community within which free speech is possible and meaningful.[41] These dilemmas are largely absent from the positive law of freedom of expression within the workplace, for in the private sector workplace there is no First Amendment at all, nor indeed any general principle of freedom of expression; the legal protections of socially valuable speech are like islands of protection in a sea of employer discretion.[42] The landscape of the public sector, in which the First Amendment does apply, is not so very different, for speech is protected only if it is on

37. The workplace thus replicates what Professor Post has called the paradox of public discourse: the tension between freedom of speech about community self-definition and the constraints of civility and tolerance that constitute the community within which such speech is meaningful. The resolution of that paradox in the workplace, however, can and should give greater weight to the value of constraints on speech than is appropriate in the society at large. *See* Cynthia L. Estlund, Workplace Harassment, Free Speech, and Fairness (1995) (unpublished manuscript on file with author).

38. Employees' "duty of loyalty" to their employer has increasingly given way to recognition of overriding employee rights and duties to speak and to report wrongdoing, particularly on issues affecting the public. *See* Estlund, *supra* note 3, at 988-94.

39. Employers frequently treat union advocacy as a form of "treason" or "disloyalty" and punish it accordingly, in violation of §§ 7, 8(a)(1), and (8)(a)(2) of the NLRA. 29 U.S.C. §§ 157-158(a)(1), (3) (1988); *see* Estlund, *supra* note 11, at 928-29.

40. To take account of harms such as these would require us to second guess each of the legislative or judicial decisions protecting such speech against employer retaliation. I mean to take those existing protections largely as given.

41. *See, e.g.*, Richard Delgado, *Campus Antiracism Rules: Constitutional Narratives in Collision*, 85 NW. U. L. REV. 343 (1991); Charles R. Lawrence III, *If He Hollers Let Him Go: Regulating Racist Speech on Campus*, 1990 DUKE L.J. 431; Catharine A. MacKinnon, *Pornography, Civil Rights and Speech*, 20 HARV. C.R.-C.L. L. REV. 1 (1985); Mari J. Matsuda, *Public Response to Racist Speech: Considering the Victim's Story*, 87 MICH. L. REV. 2320 (1989); Robert C. Post, *The Constitutional Concept of Public Discourse: Outrageous Opinion, Democratic Deliberation, and* Hustler Magazine v. Falwell, 103 HARV. L. REV. 603 (1990); Nadine Strossen, *Regulating Racist Speech on Campus: A Modest Proposal?*, 1990 DUKE L.J. 484.

42. Actually, that image suggests greater stability and security than it should, given the barriers to effective enforcement that I will discuss below. A better image is of a fleet of ships—large and small, more or less seaworthy—sailing over a sea of employer discretion.

matters of public concern, and even then only if it is not too "disruptive."[43] So speech that is harmful, and that is not protected by positive law, is freely punishable by the at-will employer, public or private.

Of course, to the extent that the government itself punishes workplace speech in the private sector, the First Amendment is implicated. The emerging debate over the constitutionality of Title VII's prohibition of sexual and racial harassment parallels in many respects the broader controversy over the regulation of hate speech and raises important questions about workplace speech within the constitutional scheme.[44] Those questions are not unrelated to the questions explored here, but they would take me well into the realm of First Amendment jurisprudence and far afield from the focus of this Article. I leave them for another day.[45] For the moment I am concerned with why we might choose to extend *legal protection* to some employee speech. While some employee speech may erode the network of relations that make the workplace a crucial mediating institution, and may to some extent be appropriately proscribed by law, there can be no doubt that some level of employee freedom of expression is also essential to that mediating function, and calls for the protection of some speech from employer reprisals.

These three perspectives on the workplace as an institution—the workplace as a self-governed community, the workplace as an object of regulation, and the workplace as intermediate institution—provide a normative background against which to examine the positive law. To what extent does the law reflect a societal appreciation for the value of employee speech and the importance of freedom from employer reprisals? What employee speech does the law protect? I take up these questions in Part II.

II. THE PROMISE OF FREE SPEECH IN THE WORKPLACE: WHAT EMPLOYEE SPEECH DOES THE LAW PROTECT?

Most basically, legal protection of free speech takes the form of a prohibition against punishment or suppression of speech. The First Amendment thus bars most government punishment or censorship of its citizens' speech. When we consider freedom of speech within the workplace, the employer takes the place of the government, and the prohibition and punishment of speech is accomplished primarily through discipline and discharge. Freedom of speech in the workplace, in this Article, is the freedom to speak out at or about the workplace free from the threat of discharge or serious discipline.[46] Thus, the First Amendment bars the government employer in most cases from discharging a public employee because of protected speech. Similarly, the many speech protections governing

---

43. *See infra* notes 102-11 and accompanying text.

44. For thoughtful assessments of the free speech issues raised by Title VII harassment doctrine, see Marci Strauss, *Sexist Speech in the Workplace*, 25 HARV. C.R.-C.L. L. REV. 1 (1990); Nadine Strossen, *Regulating Workplace Sexual Harassment and Upholding the First Amendment—Avoiding a Collision*, 37 VILL. L. REV. 757 (1992); Eugene Volokh, Comment, *Freedom of Speech and Workplace Harassment*, 39 UCLA L. REV. 1791 (1992); *see also* Kingsley R. Browne, *Title VII as Censorship: Hostile-Environment Harassment and the First Amendment*, 52 OHIO ST. L. J. 481 (1991). For contrary views, see Suzanne Sangree, *Title VII Prohibitions Against Hostile Environment Sexual Harassment and the First Amendment: No Collision in Sight*, 47 RUTGERS L. REV. 461, 546-51 (1995).

45. I explore those issues in another paper. *See* Estlund, *supra* note 37.

46. The denial of promotional opportunities or other more subtle discrimination based on speech may be a powerful threat as well. I will focus, however, on the more serious and tangible threats that are the subject of most speech protections in the workplace.

the private workplace prohibit or make actionable the discharge of an employee based on a particular sort of message or speech.

Beginning with the enactment of the National Labor Relations Act in 1935, and increasingly since 1960, legislatures and courts have extended the principle of freedom of expression into public and private workplaces by prohibiting employer reprisals based on various forms of communication.[47] I will begin with the more familiar developments in the public sector, where the First Amendment applies directly. Then I will turn to the more interesting and motley picture in the private sector, where a patchwork of legal protections form a kind of quasi-First Amendment for private sector employees.

A. The Scope of Protected Speech in Public Sector Employment

In *Pickering v. Board of Education*,[48] the Supreme Court announced that the First Amendment constrains government not only in its capacity as sovereign, but also, albeit to a lesser degree, in its capacity as employer. In *Connick v. Myers*,[49] the Court gave sharper form to the doctrine, establishing a threshold requirement that the employee's speech be on a matter of public concern and, for speech that meets that threshold, a balancing test in which the disruption (or fear of disruption) of the agency's operations is generally decisive.

The public concern test concisely, if not neatly, circumscribes the content of the speech of public employees that is protected by the First Amendment against employer punishment.[50] Quintessentially, employees speak on matters of public concern when they report dereliction of public duties, corruption, or threats to public health or safety.[51] On the other hand, the public concern test is often used to deny protection to employees' expression of grievances or criticism concerning workplace conditions.[52] Indeed, in the not uncommon cases in which speech is both a workplace grievance and of potential concern to the public, the employee's personal interest in the matter often disqualifies her speech from protection.[53] First Amendment doctrine thus embraces the view of the public sector workplace as an object of governance and gives no support to the value of speech in promoting self-governance and participation within the workplace,[54] nor in fostering the mediating function of the workplace.

---

47. *See generally* Clyde W. Summers, *The Privatization of Personal Freedoms and Enrichment of Democracy: Some Lessons from Labor Law*, 1986 U. ILL. L. REV. 689, 697 (noting that, with the Wagner Act, "Congress brought the First Amendment to private employment").

48. 391 U.S. 563 (1968).

49. 461 U.S. 138 (1983).

50. Several commentators have criticized the "public concern" test. *See, e.g.*, Cynthia L. Estlund, *Speech on Matters of Public Concern: The Perils of an Emerging First Amendment Category*, 59 GEO. WASH. L. REV. 1 (1990); Risa L. Lieberwitz, *Freedom of Speech in Public Sector Employment: The Deconstitutionalization of the Public Sector Workplace*, 19 U.C. DAVIS L. REV. 597 (1986); Massaro, supra note 6, at 25-33.

51. Rankin v. McPherson, 483 U.S. 378 (1987), shows that the public concern category is not strictly limited to whistleblowing about government misconduct. In *Rankin*, the Court ordered the reinstatement of an employee who was fired for a private workplace conversation, on the occasion of the shooting of President Ronald Reagan, in which she said, "[I]f they go for him again, I hope they get him." *Id.* at 381. Because the conversation involved a discussion of President Reagan's policies, and was not a workplace grievance, the Court held the statement protected.

52. *See* Estlund, *supra* note 50, at 52.

53. *See id.* In *Connick* itself, the Supreme Court held that an employee's circulation of a questionnaire concerning employee morale, trust for supervisors, and other issues relating to the fair and efficient operation of a district attorney's office, was not on matters of public concern because it was motivated by and closely tied to the employee's own dissatisfaction over a recent transfer decision. 461 U.S. at 154.

54. *See* Lieberwitz, *supra* note 50.

The First Amendment is not the only source of protection for public employee speech.[55] Federal civil service employees are legally shielded by the Whistleblower Protection Act[56] against reprisals for reporting fraud, waste, and abuse.[57] Many states have also enacted "whistleblower protection" laws that generally prohibit reprisals against public employees who report serious fraud, waste, or illegality to some proper authority or law enforcement official.[58] In addition, most federal employees and some state and municipal employees enjoy statutory protections of speech relating to unionization and collective bargaining.[59]

But only the First Amendment protects all public employees, and for present purposes it will serve as a useful paradigm for protected public employee speech. I will return below to the question of how and how effectively these protections work. For now, however, let us turn to the private sector, in which the content of the employee speech that is legally protected is much less susceptible to concise description than it is in the public sector.

B. The Scope of Protected Speech in Private Sector Employment

Employees in the private sector have, of course, no constitutional free speech rights to raise against their employer's decision to fire them. Indeed, normally employers have the right to fire their employees at will, for good reason, bad reason, or no reason at all. But the right to fire for "bad reasons" has come under sustained legal assault. In particular, a variety of federal and state statutes and common law doctrines protect particular kinds of employee speech from employer retaliation. This amalgam of legal constraints forms, in effect, a quasi-First Amendment doctrine that constrains the governance of the workplace by management. It stands outside of and above the government of the workplace much as the Constitution stands outside of and above the governments of the society.

---

55. Indeed, the free speech clause may not even be the only provision of the First Amendment that protects public employee speech. Under a recent Third Circuit decision, employees who "petition" their government employer regarding workplace concerns may be protected by the little-used "petitioning" clause of the First Amendment. San Filippo v. Bongiovanni, 30 F.3d 424 (3d Cir. 1994). In *San Filippo*, an employee brought grievances and filed lawsuits on a number of issues, some of which were not "matters of public concern." The court held that the public concern requirement did not circumscribe the independent protections of the "petition clause." *Id.* at 443. Other circuits considering the question have decided, to the contrary, that the petition clause is limited, like the speech clause, to issues of public concern. *See, e.g.*, White Plains Towing Corp. v. Patterson, 991 F.2d 1049, 1059 (2d Cir. 1993); Rice v. Ohio Dep't of Transp., 887 F.2d 716, 720-21 (6th Cir. 1989), *vacated on other grounds*, 497 U.S. 1001 (1990); Day v. South Park Indep. Sch. Dist., 768 F.2d 696, 703 (5th Cir. 1985), *cert. denied*, 474 U.S. 1101 (1986); Gearhart v. Thorne, 768 F.2d 1072, 1073 (9th Cir. 1985) (per curiam); Altman v. Hurst, 734 F.2d 1240, 1244 (7th Cir. 1984) (per curiam); Renfroe v. Kirkpatrick, 722 F.2d 714, 715 (11th Cir.) (per curiam), *cert. denied*, 469 U.S. 823 (1984).

56. 5 U.S.C. § 2302 (1994).

57. Federal employees entitled to these protections are generally precluded from pursuing their claim for damages under the First Amendment under Bush v. Lucas, 462 U.S. 367 (1983), though there are exceptions. *See generally* Barry J. Shotts, *The Scope of* Bush v. Lucas: *An Examination of Congressional Remedies for Whistleblowers*, 88 COLUM. L. REV. 587 (1988).

58. For a survey of such state laws, see MARCIA P. MICELI & JANET P. NEAR, BLOWING THE WHISTLE 260-73 (1992). Some of these laws protect private sector whistleblowers as well. *See id.*; *see also infra* notes 60-65 and accompanying text.

59. Public employee bargaining statutes in the federal government and many states reach some speech on shared employee grievances and collective bargaining. In the federal government, the Federal Service Labor Management Relations Act, 5 U.S.C. §§ 7102, 7116(a) (1988 & Supp. 1994), prohibits retaliation or discrimination based on protected union activity.

One of the most dramatic developments in employment law has been the rise of "whistleblower protection" laws and doctrines. The common law protections, which take the form of "public policy exceptions" to the employer's power to fire employees at will, are perhaps best-known.[60] Very recently, for example, a California court recognized the claim of an employee who was fired for complaining to his employer that many employees were working overtime without being paid overtime wages.[61]

Less well-known are a large and growing number of statutory whistleblower protections that prohibit reprisals against employees who make complaints, bring charges, or participate in proceedings under various regulatory statutes. Some of these statutes protect employees seeking to vindicate their own interests, individually or as part of the workforce. Antiretaliation provisions are thus routinely included in federal statutes regulating terms and conditions of employment, such as antidiscrimination laws, health and safety laws, minimum wage and maximum hours laws, and pension laws.[62] Other whistleblower provisions protect information of concern outside the workplace to the public at large. Thus, many federal laws that regulate the conduct of private firms outside the employment context, such as pollution control laws, prohibit retaliation against employees who report violations or participate in proceedings against their employer.[63]

---

60. *See, e.g.*, Adler v. American Standard Corp., 538 F. Supp. 572 (D. Md. 1982) (holding actionable discharge of employee for threatening to expose antitrust and other violations); Sheets v. Teddy's Frosted Foods, Inc., 427 A.2d 385 (Conn. 1980) (holding actionable discharge of employee for insisting that employer comply with state drug labeling requirements); Palmateer v. International Harvester Co., 421 N.E.2d 876 (Ill. 1978) (holding actionable discharge of employee who provided information to police investigating alleged criminal violations of coworker); Palmer v. Brown, 752 P.2d 685 (Kan. 1988) (holding actionable discharge of employee for refusing to promise not to report a superior's fraudulent Medicaid billing practices); Harless v. First Nat'l Bank, 246 S.E.2d 270 (W. Va. 1978) (holding actionable discharge of employee for attempting to report illegal bank overcharges to banking authorities); *cf.* Peterman v. Teamsters Local 396, 344 P.2d 25 (Cal. Ct. App. 1959) (prohibiting discharge of employee who declined to commit perjury before a legislative committee); Trombetta v. Detroit, T. & I. R.R., 265 N.W.2d 385 (Mich. Ct. App. 1978) (protecting employee who refused to alter state-mandated pollution control reports); Sabine Pilot Serv. v. Hauck, 687 S.W.2d 733 (Tex. 1985) (holding that public policy prohibits employers from firing employees who refuse to commit illegal acts). Many states have some form of public policy exception to the employment at-will doctrine, which often includes some whistleblower protections, but the doctrines are often quite narrow, and the employee's burden is heavy. *See* STUART H. BOMPEY ET AL., WRONGFUL TERMINATION OF CLAIMS: A PREVENTIVE APPROACH 51-52 (1991). For a review of the case law, see *id.* at 46-53.

61. Gould v. Maryland Sound Indus., 37 Cal. Rptr. 2d 718 (1995).

62. Among the many federal antiretaliation provisions are the following: National Labor Relations Act of 1935, 29 U.S.C. § 158(a)(4) (1988) (prohibiting employer discrimination against employees who file charges or testify under the NLRA); Fair Labor Standards Act, *id.* § 201 (1988 & Supp. 1994), and *id.* § 215(a)(3) (1988) (prohibiting retaliation against employees who file complaints or participate in proceedings); Age Discrimination in Employment Act of 1967, *id.* § 623(d) (1988 & Supp. 1994) (forbidding employer discrimination against employees who oppose or report age discrimination); Occupational Safety and Health Act of 1970, *id.* § 660(c) (1988) (prohibiting employer retaliation against employees who report employer violations of safety standards); Employee Retirement Income Security Act of 1974, *id.* §§ 1140, 1141 (1988) (prohibiting discrimination against employees who claim benefits under the Act or participate in an investigation against their employer); Migrant and Seasonal Agricultural Worker Protection Act of 1983, *id.* § 1855 (1988) (prohibiting discrimination by employer against migrant workers who file complaints or participate in an investigation under this statute); Employee Polygraph Protection Act of 1988, *id.* § 2002 (1988 & Supp. 1994) (prohibiting employers from retaliating against employees who bring or participate in actions under this Act); Federal Mine Safety and Health Act of 1977, 30 U.S.C. § 815(c) (1988) (prohibiting discharge of employees who participate in proceedings against employer for health and safety violations); Title VII of the Civil Rights Act of 1964, 42 U.S.C. § 2000e-3 (1988 & Supp. 1994) (prohibiting discrimination or discharge of employee for reporting employer violations of Act). For a partial listing of comparable state antiretaliation provisions, see BOMPEY ET AL., *supra* note 60, at 8-11.

63. Among federal statutes, see Department of Defense Authorization Act of 1987, 10 U.S.C. § 2409 (1995) (prohibiting retaliation against employees of contractors of the Department of Defense, the Coast Guard, and N.A.S.A. for reporting violations of contract law); Toxic Substances Control Act of 1976, 15 U.S.C. § 2622 (1988) (prohibiting retaliation against employees for initiating or testifying in proceedings against employer); Asbestos Hazard Emergency Response Act of 1986, *id.* § 2651 (1988) (prohibiting retaliation against employees for reporting a potential violation of this statute by a state or local educational agency); Major Fraud Act of 1988, 18 U.S.C. § 1031(g) (1988 & Supp. 1994) (prohibiting retaliation against employees for participating in prosecution against an employer accused of defrauding the United States); Surface Mining and Reclamation Act of 1977, 30 U.S.C. § 1293 (1988) (prohibiting retaliation against

Several states have enacted broader "whistleblower protection" statutes providing limited remedies for employees who suffer employer retaliation for reporting specified kinds of wrongdoing to public authorities.[64] The protection that these statutes afford varies widely and is severely limited in many instances; most significantly, employees may not be protected when they report wrongdoing to officials within their own organization.[65] Still, these laws and doctrines together protect a good deal of employee speech that employers might be inclined to suppress. These provisions suggest an emerging principle of protection for employees who report employer wrongdoing.

If whistleblowing is our paradigm of protected employee speech, as it is in the public sector under the "public concern" requirement, then we would expect very limited protection of more mundane speech relating to internal workplace governance: employee grievances, criticism of supervisors, suggestions for improved work practices, and even discussions of unionization. But ironically, as a formal matter, most private sector employees enjoy greater freedom of expression than do most public employees on the issues that matter to them most at work.[66] Indeed, the single most sweeping legal protection of employee speech in the private sector is the National Labor Relations Act, which gives employees the right to engage in "concerted activity for . . . mutual aid or protection." Section 7 applies not only to employees who are, or who seek to be, represented by a union but to almost all private sector employees, provided that they act "in concert" with one or more coworkers.[67] The NLRA is rarely used by and is largely unfamiliar to nonunion employees outside the organizing context.[68] But section 7 is a potentially significant source of free speech rights in the workplace on issues of concern to workers; it protects speech about unionization or other forms of employee

---

employees for reporting employer violations of surface mining guidelines); Water Pollution Control Act of 1948, 33 U.S.C. § 1367 (1988) (prohibiting retaliation against employees for reporting employer water pollution); Title III of the Federal Property and Administrative Services Act of 1949, 41 U.S.C. § 251 (1988), *amended by* 108 Stat. 3243, 3365 (1994) (prohibiting retaliation against employees of civilian contractors who report contract violations); Safe Drinking Water Act of 1974, 42 U.S.C. § 300j-9 (h)-(I) (1988 & Supp. 1994) (prohibiting employers from firing employees who report violations under this Act); Atomic Energy Act of 1954, *id.* § 5851 (1988 & Supp. 1994) (prohibiting employer from discharging employee who reports nuclear safety violations); Solid Waste Disposal Act of 1965, *id.* § 6971 (1988) (prohibiting retaliation against employees for reporting employer violation of solid waste disposal); Clean Air Act of 1955, *id.* § 7622 (1988) (prohibiting retaliation against employees for reporting employer violations of clean air standards); Comprehensive Environmental Response, Compensation, and Liability Act of 1980, *id.* § 9610 (1988) (prohibiting employer from firing employee for reporting or participating in investigations of CERCLA violations). For a partial listing of comparable state provisions, see BOMPEY ET AL., *supra* note 60, at 10 n.32.

64. *See, e.g.*, CONN. GEN. STAT. ANN. § 31-51(m) (West 1987); ME. REV. STAT. ANN. tit. 26, § 833 (West 1988); MICH. COMP. LAWS ANN. § 15.362 (West 1994). For a description of these laws and an analysis of their impact, see Terry M. Dworkin & Janet P. Near, *Whistleblowing Statutes: Are They Working?*, 25 AM. BUS. L.J. 241 (1987).

65. For a description and critique of the "hodgepodge" of federal whistleblower protections in the health and safety area, see *Employee Health and Safety Whistleblower Protection Act: Hearings on S. 436 Before the Subcomm. on Labor of the Senate Comm. on Labor and Human Resources*, 101st Cong., 1st Sess. 116 (1989) (report by Eugene R. Fidell) [hereinafter *Hearings*].

66. This irony is one of my points of departure in Estlund, *supra* note 3. Like a mirror image of the First Amendment, § 7 of the National Labor Relations Act excludes much speech that is directed at issues of concern primarily to the public, such as public health and safety. *See also* Grodin, *supra* note 3, at 13.

67. *See* NLRB v. Washington Aluminum Co., 370 U.S. 9 (1962). The Supreme Court held that § 7 protected four nonunion workers who walked off the job in protest of extremely cold temperatures in the workplace and that their discharge thus violated § 8(a)(1) of the NLRA.

68. Indeed, my own casual inquiries suggest that the protections that § 7 affords nonunion employees are unfamiliar to almost all law students—including those beginning a course in labor law—most lawyers, and even to many lawyers who practice "employment law." The NLRA is widely regarded as a world unto itself, one that deals strictly with unions and collective bargaining.

representation, discussion of work-related grievances, and petitioning for their redress.[69] The NLRA protects a great deal of employee communication that promotes participation and self-governance within the workplace.

What unites these various legal protections of employee speech in the private sector is more axiomatic than insightful: Each protects speech that some employers have shown a proclivity to punish. In each case some legal authority has concluded that the interest of the employee in speaking freely, and in many cases the interest of the public or of coworkers in hearing the message, outweighs the employer's interest in suppressing that message. But how effective are these protections? How free is speech that the law purports to protect?

III. Wrongs Unremedied and Speech Unspoken: Some Empirical Evidence on the State of Freedom of Expression in the Workplace

What is most important to know about the actual state of freedom of expression in the workplace cannot be gleaned from ordinary legal materials. First, how prevalent is employer retaliation against protected speech? And second, to what extent do employees feel free—free from the threat of employer retaliation—to engage in protected speech? Even the first question seems virtually unanswerable, for proof of the actual prevalence of retaliation would require a mini-trial of unknown cases that never occurred.[70] But the available evidence strongly suggests that employees continue to experience retaliation and the threat of retaliation for speech that the law purports to protect and that employee silence resounds where speech should be free.

The most detailed information on these questions comes from the federal government, whose employees are protected by the First Amendment and by the 1989 Whistleblower Protection Act.[71] The Whistleblower Protection Act prohibits reprisals against employees for reporting illegal or wasteful activity within the agency; the study, for the Merit Systems Protection Board ("MSPB"), defined whistleblowing as reporting such activity

---

69. Thus, in Republic Aviation v. NLRB, 324 U.S. 793 (1945), the Supreme Court held that employees have a right to discuss and solicit support for unionization during off-duty time in nonwork areas and that employers normally violate the NLRA if they maintain or enforce even a neutral no-solicitation rule against communication protected by § 7. That includes, for example, political literature on workplace issues—issues of concern to "employees as employees." *See* Eastex, Inc. v. NLRB, 437 U.S. 556 (1978).

70. Something comparable was done in a Harvard study of medical malpractice: medical experts examined 40,000 patient files from New York over a several-year period to determine the actual incidence of medical malpractice. The Report of the Harvard Medical Practice Study of the State of New York: Patients, Doctors & Lawyers: Medical Injury, Malpractice Litigation, and Patient Compensation in New York 2-8 (1990). Interestingly, the researchers identified many more actual incidents of malpractice than there were malpractice lawsuits filed by these patients, and there was rather little correspondence between the two sets of cases. Even if the resources were available for such a study of discharge cases, it is very unlikely that the recordkeeping practices of employers would permit an accurate assessment of the cause of unlitigated discharges. *Id.*

71. Pub. L. No. 101-12, 103 Stat. 16 (1989) (codified as amended in scattered sections of 5 U.S.C.). The Civil Service Reform Act of 1978, Pub. L. No. 95-454, 92 Stat. 1111 (1978) (codified as amended in scattered sections of 5 U.S.C.) prohibited reprisals against employees who legitimately disclosed illegal or wasteful activities. Still, studies in 1980 and 1983 revealed that "[a] large percentage of Federal employees were reluctant to report instances of illegal or wasteful activities they had observed. Further, among those who did report such activities, a significant percentage felt they experienced some form of reprisal as a result." U.S. Merit Systems Protection Board, Whistleblowing in the Federal Government: An Update i (1993) [hereinafter Update]. In response, Congress in 1989 passed the Whistleblower Protection Act, which expanded the protection of federal employee whistleblowers. *Id.*

to someone other than a friend, coworker, or family member.[72] The 1992 study of over 13,000 federal employees found the following: 18% had personally observed or seen evidence of illegal or wasteful activities in their agencies.[73] Approximately 50% of those observers had reported the wrongdoing to someone who might be in a position to address the problem.[74] Of those who did not report the wrongdoing, 59% explained that they did not think anything would be done; 33% said they feared retaliation.[75]

Of those who did report wrongdoing, 37% believed they had been subject to some form of retaliation.[76] But almost all of the reported retaliation was more subtle than discharge, demotion, or suspension. For example, employees cited poor performance appraisals (47%), shunning by coworkers or managers (49%), verbal harassment or intimidation (47%), or assignment to less desirable duties (37%).[77] Of those employees who took action against perceived reprisals, only 3% reported positive outcomes; most said that reporting the reprisals either caused them more trouble or made no difference.[78] As compared to earlier studies, the 1992 study found significantly greater willingness to speak out. The study also found more reported reprisals, albeit fewer of the more official and more serious kind.[79]

There is one glaring problem with this study and with much of the existing data on whistleblowers and retaliation: because the study surveyed current employees, it systematically excluded any employees who had been fired or who had quit in response to perceived reprisals. Still, the study is instructive. It indicates that many employees who observe wrongdoing do not report it, that many of those who do so perceive employer retaliation, albeit of a comparatively mild variety, and that many of those who do not report wrongdoing attribute their unwillingness to speak out to the fear of retaliation. That these findings were made in the federal civil service, whose employees enjoy greater job security than just about any other group of employees, raises serious concerns about the state of freedom of expression in the private sector workplace.

Other studies of whistleblowing reached similar findings. These studies tend to focus on managerial or professional employees; some fail to distinguish between public and private sector employees, and most fail to distinguish between disclosures that are protected by law and other disclosures of wrongful conduct within the organization. But these studies, together with the MSPB's study of federal employees, make up the largest body of empirical data on employee free speech. The studies generally have found that, as in the federal government, many employees who observe misconduct do not report it to anyone.[80] A significant number of those who do speak out report that they suffered

---

72. UPDATE, *supra* note 71, at 9.

73. *Id.* at i, 3. All these figures are based on the employee's own judgment that wrongdoing had taken place; they do not demonstrate the actual incidence of wrongdoing. Most of these reports involved waste and poor management rather than fraud or other unlawful activity.

74. *Id.* at 9.

75. *Id.* at 13.

76. *Id.* at 19.

77. *Id.* at 22. Others reported reassignment or transfer to a less desirable job (23%), denial of an award (30%), or denial of a promotion or training opportunity (19%). Only a tiny fraction reported being fired (1%), demoted (3%), or suspended (3%) because of their reporting.

78. *Id.* at 25.

79. *Id.* at 35.

80. *See* MICELI & NEAR, *supra* note 58, at 96-97. Among those who said that they had observed wrongdoing of some sort, between 10% and 91% said they had reported the wrongdoing to someone in authority. Excluding those such as "internal auditors," whose jobs involved the detection and reporting of wrongdoing, rates of reporting ranged from 10% to 74%. The highest rate in that group was among science professors. *See also* Janet P. Near & Marcia P. Miceli, *Whistle-Blowers in Organizations: Dissidents or Reformers?*, *in* 9 RESEARCH IN ORGANIZATIONAL BEHAVIOR 321 (Barry M.

retaliation, though most reported retaliation is of a comparatively mild type, and the reported incidence of retaliation varies dramatically from one study to another.[81] Still, it has proven harder to demonstrate decisively that the silence of many is due to a fear of retaliation.[82]

The data are less detailed and less rigorous as to other employee groups and other kinds of speech. The single most prolific source of employee free speech claims in the private sector is the NLRA's prohibition of employer retaliation based on union activity and other "concerted activity" on workplace issues. In recent times, approximately 10,000 employees per year have been ordered reinstated as a result of findings that they were discharged on the basis of protected activity. Many of these were fired on the basis of union organizing activity such as solicitation of union support, discussions with coworkers about unionization, and other forms of expressive activity.[83] These reinstatements represent only a small fraction of the discrimination charges filed. Even if many of the charges are frivolous, it seems probable that many meritorious charges do not result in a remedy or even an adjudication.[84] It thus appears that nonunion employers are demonstrably and increasingly willing to suppress union talk in violation of a sixty-year-old federal statute.

In light of prevalence of discriminatory discharges, it is not surprising that most employees—more than in the past—*believe* that pro-union talk meets with serious employer reprisals. The Dunlop Commission recently reported the results of a 1991 poll in which 79% of the employees surveyed agreed that it was either "very" or "somewhat" likely "that nonunion workers will get fired if they try to organize a union." Of employed nonunion respondents, 59% said it was likely they would lose favor with their employer if they supported an organizing drive; 41% agreed with the statement "it is likely that I will lose my job if I tried to form a union."[85] It is worth noting as well that union organizing activity is at nearly unprecedented low levels.[86] Scholars have disagreed, however, over whether these phenomena are related.[87]

Staw & L. L. Cummings eds., 1987).

81. *See* MICELI & NEAR, *supra* note 58, at 203; Near & Miceli, *supra* note 80; Janet P. Near & Marcia P. Miceli, *Retaliation Against Whistle Blowers: Predictors and Effects*, 71 J. APPLIED PSYCHOL. 137 (1986). *See generally* Tim Barnett et al., *The Internal Disclosure Policies of Private-Sector Employers: An Initial Look at Their Relationship to Employee Whistleblowing*, 12 J. BUS. ETHICS 127, 127-28 (1993). Many of these studies share the shortcoming of the federal study: they study current employees and thus exclude any who experienced reprisals that resulted in their leaving the organization.

82. According to several leading researchers in the area, "*not one* previous [empirical] study of whistle blowing supports" the seemingly logical proposition that a fear of retaliation deters whistleblowing. Marcia P. Miceli et al., *Blowing the Whistle on Data Fudging: A Controlled Field Experiment*, 21 J. APPLIED SOC. PSYCHOL. 271, 273 (1991) (emphasis in original); *see also* Near & Miceli, *supra* note 80 (noting lack of demonstrated relationship between fear of retaliation and whistleblowing); Janelle B. Dozier & Marcia P. Miceli, *Potential Predictors of Whistle-Blowing: A Prosocial Behavior Perspective*, 10 ACAD. MGMT. REV. 823, 832 (1985); Near & Miceli, *supra* note 81, at 143-44. Since then at least one study has found that employees *believe* that a fear of retaliatory discharge deters whistleblowing. *See* Elletta S. Callahan & John W. Collins, *Employee Attitudes Toward Whistleblowing: Management and Public Policy Implications*, 11 J. BUS. ETHICS 939, 944-45 (1992).

83. *See* FACT FINDING REPORTS, *supra* note 15, at 83.

84. *See infra* notes 88-92 and accompanying text.

85. FACT FINDING REPORTS, *supra* note 15, at 75 (citing Richard B. Freeman & Joel Rogers, *Who Speaks for Us? Employee Representation in a Nonunion Labor Market*, *in* EMPLOYEE REPRESENTATION: ALTERNATIVES AND FUTURE DIRECTIONS 13, 28-34 (Bruce E. Kaufman & Morris M. Kleiner, eds., 1993)).

86. *See* FACT FINDING REPORTS, *supra* note 15, at 67, 79, 81; WEILER, *supra* note 22, at 105-06.

87. Many commentators argue that employer opposition to unions, particularly in the form of discrimination against union activists, and the law's feeble response to it, are responsible for much of labor's declining membership. *See, e.g.*, FREEMAN & MEDOFF, *supra* note 29; MICHAEL GOLDFIELD, THE DECLINE OF ORGANIZED LABOR IN THE UNITED STATES 180-217 (1987); THOMAS A. KOCHAN ET AL., THE TRANSFORMATION OF AMERICAN INDUSTRIAL RELATIONS 53-80 (1986); WEILER, *supra* note 22, at 108-18; Richard B. Freeman, *Why Are Unions Faring Poorly in NLRB Representation*

Union organizing seems to be the most harshly suppressed and frequently adjudicated of all forms of protected workplace speech. The effectiveness of union talk depends on the speaker's ability to gain a following; thus retaliation may appear to be a particularly attractive option for the employer who deeply opposes the formation of a union. And because, by definition, there is a well-informed employee advocate on the scene, claims of anti-union retaliation are particularly likely to become formal charges. But these data strongly suggest that many employers do violate the law and fire employees who speak out contrary to the perceived interests of the firm.

The picture is a bit different, and the data still more incomplete, with respect to other kinds of speech. For example, in spite of the dramatic expansion of wrongful discharge doctrines, civil litigation under all those doctrines remains "rare" in relation to both total employment and the number of discharges,[88] and it is concentrated among more highly paid employees who can afford attorneys.[89] In states with private sector whistleblower protection statutes, there is very little litigation under those statutes.[90] With the glaring exception of union speech under the NLRA, there are surprisingly few proceedings under the federal statutes protecting private sector employee speech; for example, most of the whistleblower protection provisions of federal health, safety, and environmental statutes are virtually dormant.[91] Perhaps the most widely used of these provisions is the Occupational Safety and Health Act, 29 U.S.C. §§ 651-678. Several thousand complaints are filed each year, but only a tiny fraction of them result in any relief.[92]

The paucity of remedies and even adjudications under these antiretaliation statutes may be due to the infrequency of serious retaliation. It may also be due to the ignorance of

---

Elections?, *in* CHALLENGES AND CHOICES FACING AMERICAN LABOR UNIONS 45-65 (Thomas A. Kochan ed., 1985); Paul Weiler, *Striking a New Balance: Freedom of Contract and the Prospects for Union Representation*, 98 HARV. L. REV. 351 (1984); Paul Weiler, *Promises to Keep: Securing Workers' Rights to Self-Organization Under the NLRA*, 96 HARV. L. REV. 1769 (1983).

But other observers argue that employer opposition is a relatively minor factor in declining union strength, and that "structural economic changes" in the market are chiefly responsible for the decline of unions. A leading proponent of this view is Professor Leo Troy. *See* Leo Troy, *The Right to Organize Meets the Market*, *in* LIBERTY, PROPERTY, AND THE FUTURE OF CONSTITUTIONAL DEVELOPMENT 305-28 (Ellen F. Paul & Howard Dickman eds., 1990); Leo Troy, *Will a More Interventionist NLRA Revive Organized Labor*, 13 HARV. J.L. & PUB. POL'Y 583 (1990).

For a review of empirical research on the significance of public policy and employer opposition in the decline of unionization, see Gary M. Chaison & Joseph B. Rose, *The Macrodeterminants of Union Growth and Decline*, *in* THE STATE OF THE UNIONS 3, 20-30 (George Strauss et al. eds., 1991). Chaison and Rose conclude from their review of the literature that "public policy and employer opposition to unionism play important roles in union growth and serve as leading explanations of the divergence in union growth rates among industrialized countries." *Id.* at 36.

88. *See* JAMES N. DERTOUZOS & LYNN A. KAROLY, RAND INST. FOR CIVIL JUSTICE, LABOR-MARKET RESPONSES TO EMPLOYER LIABILITY xiii (1992) [hereinafter RAND Study].

89. *See* WEILER, *supra* note 22, at 82. The possibility of contingent fee arrangements does little to mitigate this disparity. Damages in wrongful discharge cases are closely tied to salary levels and are usually modest, particularly considering the 95% of cases that settle without a trial. RAND Study, *supra* note 88, at 36.

90. *See* Dworkin & Near, *supra* note 64, at 253-64. Enactment of a whistleblower protection statute was found to bring no increase in whistleblower claims (as compared with claims under the prior common law) and no more claims than otherwise comparable states with or without common law protections of whistleblowers.

91. Of sixteen federal health and safety statutes with antiretaliation provisions for private sector employees, only three generated more than forty-five claims in 1985; twelve of them generated fewer than five complaints. *See Hearings*, *supra* note 65, at A7-A8.

92. *See generally* THOMAS O. MCGARITY & SIDNEY A. SHAPIRO, WORKERS AT RISK: THE FAILED PROMISE OF THE OCCUPATIONAL SAFETY AND HEALTH ADMINISTRATION 336-40 (1993). OSHA has sole power to enforce the whistleblower protection provision, 29 U.S.C. § 660(c)(2), and "in the past OSHA has not been a diligent protector of employee whistle-blowers." Thomas O. McGarity, *Reforming OSHA: Some Thoughts for the Current Legislative Agenda*, 31 HOUS. L. REV. 99, 115 (1994). For example, of 3600 complaints filed in fiscal year 1989, 31% were dismissed by OSHA out of hand, 38% were dismissed after initial screening, 15% were withdrawn by the complainant, and 16% were deemed meritorious. Only some smaller number of these are referred to the Solicitor of Labor for civil prosecution, which is the only means of enforcement. *See* MCGARITY & SHAPIRO, *supra*, at 338.

individual employees as to what their rights are and how to protect them. Most disturbing, and most difficult to ascertain, is the possibility that many employees remain silent because they are simply unwilling to take the chance that they will suffer reprisals. There is evidence, for example, that employees routinely ignore workplace safety violations, although safety violations are more regularly reported and redressed in union shops than in nonunion shops.[93]

The same pattern is repeated in other areas in which workers have the "right" to complain about unlawful working conditions free from employer reprisals. Employees have the right under Title VII, for example, to report incidents of discrimination and harassment, and employers are prohibited from retaliation against them.[94] Yet many of those who do complain of sexual harassment end up being fired or quitting in response to what they regard as employer retaliation.[95] Many incidents of perceived sexual harassment go unreported, and many would-be complainants cite a fear of reprisals as a reason for remaining silent.[96]

The data, though they are incomplete and uneven, portray a sizable gap between the freedom of expression that the law purports to secure to employees and the freedom of expression that many employees experience. Clearly there are forces other than fear of employer reprisals that silence employees: concern about peer disapproval, pessimism about the utility of speech, and sheer inertia are powerful censors.[97] But fear of discharge or other serious economic reprisals is an especially strong deterrent, and it is one that the law purports to redress. Yet many employees appear unwilling to test the protection that the law affords them, and many of those who do so experience retaliation notwithstanding the law's protections. This incongruence between what the law promises and what employees experience raises a further question: Why does the law fail to effectively secure freedom of expression even in the limited areas singled out for protection?

Thus far I have described the content of the employee speech that is protected against employer retaliation. But the "system of freedom of expression"[98] in the workplace, like

---

93. *See* WEILER, *supra* note 22, at 157-58 & n.49; *see also* Tim Barnett, *A Preliminary Investigation of the Relationship Between Selected Organizational Characteristics and External Whistleblowing by Employees*, 11 J. BUS. ETHICS 949 (1992) (finding that incidence of external whistleblowing in general is perceived as higher in unionized organizations). There is indirect evidence of the silence of nonunion employees in many workplace accidents, for serious accidents often bring to light a history of dangerous practices that must have been evident to hundreds of employees but went unreported and unremedied notwithstanding OSHA's prohibition of retaliation based on health and safety complaints.

94. 42 U.S.C. § 2000e-3.

95. A study of 88 complaints filed in California between 1979 and 1983 found that nearly 50% of the complainants had been fired and another 23% had quit. Frances S. Coles, *Forced to Quit: Sexual Harassment Complaints and Agency Response*, 14 SEX ROLES 81, 89 (1986); *see also* BARBARA A. GUTEK, SEX AND THE WORKPLACE 58 (1985) (finding that 20% of women have quit, been transferred, been fired, or stopped applying for a job because of harassment); Peggy Crull, *The Impact of Sexual Harassment on the Job: A Profile of the Experience of 92 Women*, 3 WORKING WOMEN'S INST. REP. 1 (1979) (finding that 24% of victims were fired after complaining; another 42% quit because of employer retaliation or continued harassment). These and other sources are discussed in B. Glenn George, *The Back Door: Legitimizing Sexual Harassment Claims*, 73 B.U. L. REV. 1, 25-26 (1993).

96. Various studies have shown high levels of sexual harassment at work. *See, e.g.*, GUTEK, *supra* note 95, at 46 (53% of women surveyed reported sexual harassment); U.S. MERIT SYSTEMS PROTECTION BOARD SEXUAL HARASSMENT IN THE FEDERAL GOVERNMENT: AN UPDATE 11 (1988) (reporting that 42% of the female federal employees surveyed reported being sexually harassed); Edward Lafontaine & Leslie Tredeau, *The Frequency, Sources, and Correlates of Sexual Harassment Among Women in Traditional Male Occupations*, 15 SEX ROLES 433, 436 (1986) (finding that 75% of women respondents in engineering, science, and management reported sexual harassment). But most incidents of sexual harassment go unreported, and many who do not report harassment cite fear of "being blamed" or of more severe harassment or other reprisals. GUTEK, *supra* note 95, at 70-73; U.S. MERIT SYSTEMS PROTECTION BOARD, *supra*, at 28.

97. The whistleblowing studies all confirm the importance of these factors in accounting for employee inaction in the face of wrongdoing. *See* MICELI & NEAR, *supra* note 58, at 132-35, 175-78.

98. *See* EMERSON, *supra* note 1.

the system of freedom of expression under the First Amendment generally, is not only the content of the law's protections but also the mechanisms by which the law operates: the procedures, burdens of proof, and presumptions through which the law's protections are administered. A closer look at these aspects of the system of freedom of expression in the workplace offers some strong clues to the very partial success of that system. Part IV discusses these issues in the public sector workplace; Part V concerns the more complex—but, as it turns out, largely parallel—system of freedom of expression in the private sector.

IV. THE SYSTEM OF FREEDOM OF EXPRESSION IN THE PUBLIC SECTOR WORKPLACE AND THE ROLE OF DUE PROCESS

All public employees are protected by the First Amendment. If a public employee is fired on the basis of protected speech, she may bring a constitutional "wrongful discharge" action against her employers. But not all public employees enjoy freedom of speech. I will argue that those employees whose sole recourse against a retaliatory discharge is the slow, costly, and unreliable wrongful discharge remedy—that is, the many public employees who are terminable at will, without a reason and without a hearing—enjoy correspondingly limited freedom of expression. But those employees who enjoy independent due process rights—who cannot be fired without a good reason or without notice and a hearing—should be expected to enjoy much greater freedom of expression as well. I will begin by examining the workings of a public employee's First Amendment lawsuit challenging her discharge.

A. The Wrongful Discharge Model of Free Speech Protections in the Public Sector Workplace

The First Amendment operates in public employment quite differently than it does in society at large. The First Amendment generally establishes a broad principle of protection with a number of discrete exceptions for "unprotected speech." It is for the government to bear the burden of proving that a particular message or communication falls outside the realm of protected speech. Under *Connick v. Myers*, by contrast, the First Amendment in the governmental workplace creates an exception—speech on matters of public concern—to a general background principle of no protection, or employer discretion; the burden of proving protection rests on the employee.[99] The principle of freedom of expression in public employment is, in short, a "defining-in" sort of system, in Professor Schauer's terminology, as opposed to the "defining-out" structure that prevails under the First Amendment generally.[100]

Once the public employee-speaker has overcome the threshold "public concern" requirement and has shown that what she said constitutes protected speech, she must undertake the formidable burden of proving that her discharge was motivated by her speech. This is no mean feat in the case of a reasonably knowledgeable employer and an imperfect employee. Even if the employee can prove the existence of an unconstitutional

99. *Connick*, 461 U.S. at 146.

100. Frederick Schauer, *Categories and the First Amendment: A Play in Three Acts*, 34 VAND. L. REV. 265, 279-81 (1981). For my own application of these constructs to the doctrine of public employee speech, see Estlund, *supra* note 50.

motive, the employer has the chance to prove that it would have fired the employee anyway for reasons unrelated to her speech.[101]

Even if the employee proves that her discharge was based on constitutionally protected speech, she must still contend with far greater deference to the government's claimed justification for the discharge than would the citizen-at-large under the First Amendment: the government is required to show neither a compelling government interest nor the necessity of its means, but rather only "disruption" or a threat of disruption that outweighs the employee's interest in speaking out.[102]

The Supreme Court's decision last term in *Waters v. Churchill*[103] offers a window on how these elements interact with the "public concern" test, and adds an important twist. In *Waters*, a public hospital fired nurse Cheryl Churchill—apparently an at-will employee—based on what her superiors believed were disparaging comments about her supervisors and the department.[104] Churchill sued the hospital under § 1983[105] for firing her on the basis of constitutionally protected speech. According to Churchill, she did not disparage the department, but rather criticized a hospital policy of dealing with staff shortages by using "cross-trainees" from other departments, a policy she believed threatened patient care.[106] Churchill argued that her comments were clearly on a matter of public concern and were not sufficiently disruptive to justify discharge.[107]

The question before the Supreme Court was which of three possible versions of the employee's speech should be subjected to the *Connick* test: Is it what the employer *honestly* believed the employee said? Is it what the employer *reasonably and honestly* believed the employee said, based on its investigation of the facts? Or is it what the employee *actually* said, according to the ultimate judicial factfinder? Given these three possible standards of liability—intentional wrongdoing, negligence, or strict liability—the Court split three ways.

Justice Scalia, joined by Justices Kennedy and Thomas, took the narrowest view of the First Amendment: The government employer violates the First Amendment rights of public employees only if it acts on the basis of an unconstitutional retaliatory motive. The employee should thus have no claim if her statements, as the employer *honestly* (but

---

101. Under Mt. Healthy City Board of Education v. Doyle, 429 U.S. 274 (1976), once the employee proves that protected speech was a motivating factor in her discharge, the burden shifts to the employer to show that it would have fired the employee anyway for reasons unrelated to her speech. *Id.* at 287.

102. *Connick*, 461 U.S. at 152.

103. 114 S. Ct. 1878 (1994).

104. Nurse Mary Lou Ballew reported to Churchill's supervisor Cynthia Waters that she had overheard Churchill "knocking the department" and discouraging another nurse, Melanie Perkins-Graham, from transferring to the department. Waters and the vice president of nursing, Kathleen Davis, then spoke with Perkins-Graham, who reported that Churchill "had indeed said unkind and inappropriate negative things about [Waters]" and about Davis' administration. Waters and Davis proceeded to fire Churchill. In response to Churchill's internal grievance, the hospital president reviewed the written record, had a subordinate speak again with Ballew, and, for the first time, spoke briefly with Churchill. The hospital denied Churchill's grievance. *Id.* at 1882-83 (quoting Supplemental App. of Defendants-Appellees at 60, Churchill v. Waters, 977 F.2d 1114 (7th Cir. 1992) (No. 91-2288), *cert. granted*, 114 S. Ct. 1878 (1994)) (alteration in original).

105. 42 U.S.C. § 1983 (1988).

106. Two other witnesses to the conversation, Nurse Jean Welty and Dr. Thomas Koch, clinical head of obstetrics, later supported Churchill's report of her conversation, but nobody spoke with Welty or Koch on behalf of the hospital. *Waters*, 114 S. Ct. at 1883.

107. The district court granted summary judgment to the hospital, holding that neither version of Churchill's comments dealt with a matter of public concern, and that, even if they were of public concern, they were disruptive enough to justify discharge. Churchill v. Waters, 731 F. Supp. 311, 320-21 (C.D. Ill. 1990). The Court of Appeals reversed, holding that if the factfinder believed Churchill's testimony about what she said, her speech was on a matter of public concern and not disruptive, and was protected. What mattered for the employee's First Amendment claim, said the court, was what she actually said, not what the employer believed she had said, even if that belief was based on a reasonable investigation. Churchill v. Waters, 977 F.2d 1114, 1121-23 (7th Cir. 1992), *rev'd*, 114 S. Ct. 1878.

perhaps unreasonably) believed them to be, were unprotected. Churchill should therefore lose unless she proves on remand that the unprotected statements at issue were a mere pretext for firing her, and that she was actually fired because of past protected statements about hospital policy.[108]

Justices Stevens and Blackmun, on the other hand, took the broadest view of First Amendment liability: all that should matter is what the employee actually said, regardless of how reasonably the employer believes that she said something different and unprotected. The government may be wise to investigate what was said before firing an employee based on her speech, but under the dissenters' view the government would be liable nonetheless if the ultimate judicial factfinder later found that the employee actually said something else that was protected.[109]

But the plurality—Justices O'Connor, Rehnquist, Souter, and Ginsburg—took a middle view: The government does not incur First Amendment liability if the employee's statements, as the employer honestly *and reasonably* believed them to be, were unprotected. On this view the hospital in *Waters*, having conducted a reasonable investigation of what Churchill said,[110] could thus prevail even if Churchill might ultimately persuade the judicial factfinder that she said something different that was protected. The case was remanded, however, to give Churchill a chance to prove that her unprotected statements—or the version of those statements that the employer reasonably believed—were a pretext for firing her, and that she was in fact fired for other protected speech.[111]

The *Waters* plurality built on a line of decisions imposing procedural safeguards as necessary adjuncts to the First Amendment.[112] But "First Amendment due process," as it has evolved in these cases, is only a minor manifestation of a much more vital connection between free speech rights and due process of law. Basic procedural constraints on adverse government action provide an indispensable foundation for freedom of speech: Without independent due process rights against government deprivations of life, liberty, and property, the First Amendment would offer dissenters a very fragile shield against state retaliation. How free would speech be if the government could punish the speaker, ostensibly for speeding or theft or murder or even some unwritten crime, without notice of the prohibition and of the charges, and without probable cause or a hearing or the burden of proving its case to an impartial tribunal? How free would speech be if the speaker's only remedy in such a case were to sue the government and prove that it acted on the basis of her dissent? Yet this is roughly where existing doctrine, and every member of the Court in *Waters*, would leave the at-will public employee—an employee who, like Churchill, has no civil service protection or tenure, and who can be fired for any reason at any time.

---

108. *Waters*, 114 S. Ct. at 1893-97 (Scalia, J., concurring).

109. *Id.* at 1898-1900 (Stevens, J., concurring).

110. The investigation consisted of speaking with two witnesses, but not Churchill herself, before the discharge. *Id.* at 1882-83.

111. *Id.* at 1888-91.

112. *See, e.g.*, Freedman v. Maryland, 380 U.S. 51, 58 (1965) (holding that government must bear burden of proving that speech is unprotected); Speiser v. Randall, 357 U.S. 513, 526 (1958) (same); *cf.* Masson v. New Yorker Magazine, Inc., 501 U.S. 496 (1991) (stating that actual malice in libel action must be proved by clear and convincing evidence); Philadelphia Newspapers, Inc. v. Hepps, 475 U.S. 767, 776-77 (1986) (holding that libel plaintiff must bear burden of proving falsity); Bose Corp. v. Consumers Union of United States, Inc., 466 U.S. 485, 510-11 (1984) (affirming that appellate court must make independent judgment about presence of actual malice). *See generally* Henry P. Monaghan, *First Amendment "Due Process"*, 83 HARV. L. REV. 518 (1970).

The analogy may seem hyperbolic: discharge from a job is not equivalent to imprisonment or execution. But in fact termination of employment may be more serious than many smaller criminal penalties that trigger the full panoply of constitutional due process rights. Termination of employment is likely to have a harsher impact on one's life and well-being, and carry a greater social stigma, than would a modest criminal fine. It is no accident that, in the law and language of labor arbitration, discharge is regarded as "industrial capital punishment."[113]

Notwithstanding the existence of free speech rights under the First Amendment, the dissenting employee who can generally be fired for no good reason and without a hearing is extremely vulnerable to retaliatory discharge. Justice Douglas made this connection in his dissent in *Board of Regents of State College v. Roth*: "Without a statement of the reasons for the discharge and an opportunity to rebut those reasons . . . there is no means short of a lawsuit to safeguard the right not to be discharged for the exercise of First Amendment guarantees."[114] He thus argued for the extension of due process rights to *all* public employees faced with dismissal, in part to realize and support these employees' substantive constitutional rights. But the majority of the Court rejected this view in *Roth*,[115] and none of the opinions in *Waters* resurrects it.[116]

Consider the hurdles that face an at-will public employee who has publicly criticized her superiors' performance of their public duties, and who is subsequently fired. She may be given no reason, or she may be told that her performance has been unsatisfactory. She has no right to notice or documentation of the alleged inadequacies, or an opportunity to refute the charges. If the employee believes that she was fired because of protected speech, and if she can find a lawyer to represent her, she can file a lawsuit in which she may attempt to prove—largely through the employer's documents and witnesses still employed by the employer—that her speech was on a matter of public concern, that her discharge was actually motivated by her speech, and that the speech was not unduly disruptive.[117] In the meantime the employee may be unemployed under circumstances that may handicap her in getting another job.

In making the link between procedural safeguards and substantive protection of speech for public employees, the *Waters* plurality took an important step. But in squeezing this insight into a realm in which due process is generally absent ("at-will" public employees who have no "property interest" in continued employment) the plurality created a minefield of uncertainty and absurdity that Justice Scalia gleefully exposed. Most strikingly, Justice Scalia pointed out that "[i]n the present case, for example, if the requisite 'First Amendment investigation' disclosed that Nurse Churchill had not been demeaning her superiors, but had been complaining about the perennial end-of-season slump of the Chicago Cubs, her dismissal, erroneous as it was, would have been perfectly OK."[118]

113. *See* FRANK ELKOURI & EDNA A. ELKOURI, HOW ARBITRATION WORKS 661 n.60 (4th ed. 1985).

114. 408 U.S. 564, 585 (1972) (Douglas, J., dissenting).

115. *Id.* at 598.

116. *Waters*, 114 S. Ct. 1878.

117. The employee need not show that her speech was a "but-for" cause of her discharge, only a contributing cause. But even if the employee can prove that her protected speech was a motivating factor in her discharge, the employer can still prevail if it can show that it would have fired the employee, even absent the protected speech, for other reasons. *See* Mt. Healthy City Bd. of Educ. v. Doyle, 429 U.S. 274, 285-86 (1977).

118. *Waters*, 114 S. Ct. at 1894-95 (Scalia, J., concurring).

The problem is exaggerated in a bureaucratic context in which the ultimate decision to discharge is typically made not by the immediate supervisor or by anyone with direct knowledge of the employee's conduct and performance, but by a higher management official based on information from others. Thus, if a dissenting employee is reported, perhaps by a hostile supervisor, to have made some disruptive, unprotected comments, the decisionmaker presumably has some duty under the plurality opinion to investigate the report's accuracy before discharging the employee on that basis. But if the same employee is reported by the same hostile supervisor to have been late to work six times, or to have done her job badly, or to have worn a disagreeably brightly colored dress, the decisionmaker may fire her summarily with no need to show that its grounds were reasonable or based in fact (subject to the employee's possible effort in litigation to prove an unconstitutional motive). The *Waters* plurality effectively imposed a duty to investigate only where "an employment action is based on what an employee supposedly said, and a reasonable supervisor would recognize that there is a substantial likelihood that what was actually said was protected."[119]

Justice Scalia ascribed these absurdities to the plurality's requirement that the government act reasonably in cases involving potentially protected speech. But I would put it differently: Absurdities arise when the government is required to act reasonably *only* in cases involving speech—that is, when the government is not generally required to act reasonably in its treatment of those employees, like Churchill, whom it has chosen to employ on an at-will basis. The general power of the government to act arbitrarily and without reasons in its treatment of some of its employees—to fire them if it wishes for "complaining about the perennial end-of-season slump of the Chicago Cubs,"[120] or for wearing a brightly colored dress—renders somewhat incongruous and ill-fitting the plurality's minimal requirements of reasonableness in a particular kind of case.

The *Waters* decision adds nothing—and even Justice Stevens' dissent adds nothing—to the protection of the at-will public employee against retaliatory discharges that are unexplained or explained by something other than speech. The members of the Court divide over what happens in the case in which the employer relies explicitly on speech as the basis for a discharge. But where the employer gives no reason, or gives a reason that has nothing to do with speech, all of the opinions in *Waters* would leave the employee where she was: Her only remedy comes by way of a federal lawsuit in which she must prove that the discharge was based on protected speech. For the employee contemplating public criticism of her employer, the prospect of prevailing, perhaps after many years, in such a lawsuit, must look like a long shot. It is a gamble that many employees may reasonably decline to take.

B. Due Process Protections as a Foundation for Freedom of Speech

Waters v. Churchill adds little or nothing to the First Amendment protection of at-will public employees. It also adds nothing to the protection of those public employees who, unlike Churchill, have some form of civil service or "just cause" protection. As to those employees, the government already has the burden to reasonably investigate and evaluate

119. *Id.* at 1889 (plurality).
120. *Id.* at 1895 (Scalia, J., concurring).

whatever facts it is relying upon before imposing serious discipline, and if challenged to prove its case in a post-termination hearing. Even before termination, "[t]he tenured public employee is entitled to oral or written notice of the charges against him, an explanation of the employer's evidence, and an opportunity to present his side of the story."[121] This alone is more process than the *Waters* plurality found adequate for the at-will employee who is fired explicitly on the basis of speech.

I will call this right—the right to notice of the charges and to a hearing before an impartial decisionmaker at which the employer must show just cause for discipline or discharge and the employee may respond—"due process." Under prevailing constitutional doctrine, the substantive requirement of just cause or the like arises from statute or contract, not from the due process clause itself; the entitlement to retain one's job absent specified conditions is the "property interest" that triggers the constitutional requirement of due process.[122] But due process rights assume the existence of substantive protections, and when I refer to "due process," I include both the procedures and their substantive predicate—the right not to be fired without a good reason.

The tenured civil servant who is fired after having publicly criticized her superiors' performance of their public duties is in an altogether different position than the at-will employee discussed above. She cannot be fired but for reasons prescribed by regulation, or for just cause. She must be given notice of the charges and of the evidence, and an opportunity to present her side of the story before termination; if she is fired she may challenge the employer's claims in an administrative hearing before an impartial decisionmaker. The administrative process for adjudicating just cause discharges is much cheaper and more prompt, and consequently more accessible to most employees, than civil litigation. The employee who believes that she was actually fired because of her public criticism need not prove that the employer was so motivated, although she may seek to do so to rebut the employer's claim of just cause.

Due process rights undergird the free speech rights of public employees much as due process rights in criminal matters undergird the free speech rights of citizens generally. Indeed, I suspect that whatever greater margin of freedom of expression public employees have over private employees is enjoyed only by those protected by some form of civil service regulations or tenure, and rests as much on due process protections as it does on the ability to bring a First Amendment claim.

Waters thus suggests, but does not give much substance to, the idea of a "First Amendment due process" for public employees. That is unfortunate. Given the great difficulty and burden of litigating these cases, due process—requiring the government to give notice and a hearing and to prove a rational basis for discharge—would do more to protect the freedom of speech of many public employees than would a more generous standard of liability in a First Amendment lawsuit.

V. The System of Freedom of Expression in the Private Sector Workplace

Employees in the private sector do not enjoy even the limited constitutional right of freedom of expression at the workplace that public employees have, for their employers'

---

121. Cleveland Bd. of Educ. v. Loudermill, 470 U.S. 532, 546 (1985).
122. *See id.* at 541.

actions are not state action. Yet there is a system of freedom of expression in the workplace. Its content, described above, differs from that in the public sector, but I will argue that its structure and the probable consequences are surprisingly similar: as in the public sector, those employees who can be fired at will cannot be expected to enjoy the freedom of speech the law purports to provide them, while those employees who enjoy "due process rights" can be expected to enjoy much greater free speech rights as well.

A. The Wrongful Discharge Model of Free Speech Protections in the Private Sector At-Will Workplace

I have suggested that we think of the workplace as a community in which management governs the citizens-employees, subject to an amalgam of speech-protective laws that serves as the functional equivalent of a First Amendment doctrine (just as the various employment discrimination laws can be seen as the equivalent of the Equal Protection Clause). This quasi-First Amendment creates no general principle of freedom of speech, subject to certain defined exceptions; this is not a "defining-out" system.[123] Unlike the First Amendment generally, but like the First Amendment in public employment, the system of freedom of expression in private employment is a "defining-in" system,[124] in which the employee bears the burden of showing that her speech is within limited protected categories. But speech that is "defined-in" in the private sector consists of a number of particular, discrete exceptions stemming from different sources, rather than a single broad exception, to a general principle of no protection.

But no protection in the private sector is harsher than it is in most of the public sector, for in the great majority of private sector workplaces there is no independent principle of due process. I do not refer simply to the absence of "state action" and the inapplicability of constitutional due process; I refer rather to the absence of any general principle under which the "government"—here, firm management—must prove, by fair procedures, a rational basis for adverse action against an individual. In the private sector, of course, the background rule is quite the opposite: the law generally gives employers plenary power to discharge employees at will, for good reason, no reason, or even bad reason, including expressive activity. The at-will presumption has been dramatically eroded by a growing array of discrete "wrongful discharge" doctrines against discrimination and retaliation of various kinds, including the speech protections at issue here. But each of these protections is superimposed upon and, I will argue, undermined by the background rule of employer discretion.

The typical private sector employee is thus in much the same situation as the sizable minority of public employees who are at will and cannot rely on any general procedural or substantive guarantee of fairness to support their supposed protection against discharge based on protected speech. Without a just cause requirement for discharge, employees have no right to notice of the grounds for discharge, to a hearing before an impartial tribunal, or to proof by the employer of a fair and rational basis for the decision. That void makes employees very vulnerable to employer retaliation or discrimination. A discharge—even one that the employee claims was based on "protected" speech—stands

---

123. Schauer, *supra* note 100, at 279-81.
124. *Id.*

unless and until the employee can prove a hidden unlawful motive by way of drawn-out and often costly procedures.

The at-will rule, which lies at the foundation of employment law, casts the heavy burdens of proof and of delay on the discharged employee. The at-will rule thus continues to exercise a tremendous gravitational pull on the status and security of the employee even in the context of the many exceptions to the at-will rule. In particular, the at-will background to the system of freedom of expression undermines legal protections of speech in the private sector, whether they are enforceable through litigation or administratively.[125]

Let me take as an example of the latter the NLRA's protection of union organizing. An employee who believes he was fired for union activity may file a charge with the National Labor Relations Board ("Board"), but only the Board may prosecute a complaint.[126] Given the burden of proof and limited prosecutorial resources, it is often difficult to persuade the agency to pursue these cases without a "smoking gun," and "smoking gun" testimony on behalf of a recently discharged union activist is very hard to come by.[127] Even when the Board does prosecute, a recalcitrant employer's decision reigns until and unless a court finally orders reinstatement or some other remedy.[128] A fully litigated discrimination case lasts an average of three years under the NLRA.[129] Nor is there a pot of gold at the end of this long process. The Board's remedial powers are limited to ordering reinstatement and backpay; the NLRA provides for neither full compensation nor penalties.[130]

These features of the NLRA—the lack of a private cause of action, the heavy burden of proving employer motive, the economic burden of delay, and the lack of fully compensatory (or deterrent) remedies—are typical of the administrative schemes by which most statutory antiretaliation provisions are enforced. An agency may reject many meritorious but hard-to-prove cases, particularly when enforcement resources are tight.[131] Because these statutory schemes provide no private cause of action, an agency's refusal to act means the end of the employee's case. Remedies in administrative cases are typically limited to reinstatement and backpay, and are not fully compensatory. Fines, when they are allowed, are generally minimal.[132]

But there is good reason to believe that many potentially meritorious retaliation claims are never filed. Perhaps because of the lack of a private cause of action, most of these

---

125. Given the great number of discrete legal protections for private sector employee speech, I will describe the enforcement mechanisms at a high level of generality. The mechanisms vary in many particulars, but it is not too great a simplification to identify two kinds of enforcement schemes: private litigation and agency enforcement through a complaint and hearing procedure.

126. The agency's refusal to prosecute an unfair labor practice complaint of this kind ends the employee's case, for that decision is not reviewable, and there is no private right of action under the antidiscrimination provisions of the NLRA. *See* NLRB v. United Food & Commercial Workers Union, Local 23, 484 U.S. 112, 118-19 (1987).

127. I base these assertions partly on my own experiences with and observations of these cases; I represented a number of discharged activists and unions as a labor lawyer from 1985 to 1989.

128. Preliminary reinstatement on a showing of "probable cause" is available under some statutes, including the NLRA. *See* 29 U.S.C. § 160(j) (1988). It is rarely used.

129. FACT FINDING REPORTS, *supra* note 15, at 71; WEILER, *supra* note 22, at 235.

130. For a critique of remedies under the NLRA, see WEILER, *supra* note 22, at 234-40.

131. The difficulty of proving reprisals—particularly the causal link between the protected disclosure and the adverse action—has greatly limited the impact of the Whistleblower Protection Act for federal employees. *See* U.S. GENERAL ACCOUNTING OFFICE, WHISTLEBLOWER PROTECTION: DETERMINING WHETHER REPRISAL OCCURRED REMAINS DIFFICULT 13-14 (1992). Of 805 complaints received by the Office of Special Counsel under the Act from July 1989 through September 1991, 72.3% were dismissed for insufficient evidence; 13.5% were "disproved." Only 3.4% resulted in "corrective action." *Id.* at 13.

132. *See* MICELI & NEAR, *supra* note 58, at 243.

antiretaliation provisions are virtually unknown to employees and even to lawyers. And for most protected employee speech that is unrelated to union activity, there is typically no informed agent, such as a union, on the scene. That difference alone may account for much of the otherwise surprising contrast between the voluminous activity under the NLRA and the virtual dormancy of most other statutory antiretaliation provisions.[133] Widespread ignorance of the law combines with what is typically a very short statute of limitations to cut off many potential claims before they are recognized.[134] All this suggests that it is not the rarity of employer reprisals but rather weaknesses in the system of enforcement—some combination of employee ignorance about these provisions, inadequate agency resources, lack of political will, and vagaries of proof—that have rendered many statutory antiretaliation provisions virtually dormant.[135]

The situation is different but not markedly better with respect to those retaliation claims that are in the hands of private litigants. The employee still bears the difficult burden of proving a retaliatory motive where the employer has created the relevant documents and employs most of the potential witnesses. Further uncertainty results from the limited and indeterminate scope of the common law protections. Moreover, litigation is notoriously slow. In the face of these difficulties, lawyers play a screening role similar to the role of administrative agencies.

The decisions of private attorneys, however, cannot help but be greatly influenced by the prospective plaintiff's wealth: few low- and middle-income employees who are fired from their jobs have the savings or income to pay a lawyer's fee, and, given that backpay is a chief determinant of damages, few have the realistic prospect of a recovery sufficient to attract a lawyer to any case that would require a significant investment of time.[136] Notwithstanding the popular perception created by some highly publicized large verdicts, recovery in most wrongful discharge lawsuits amounts to the equivalent of half a year's salary.[137] Punitive damages are sometimes available, and may be necessary in some contexts.[138] But the few resulting mega-verdicts create a misleading public perception of wrongful discharge remedies, lending what the Dunlop Commission calls a "lottery-like" character to wrongful discharge litigation:[139] a few plaintiffs hit the jackpot, but the great majority of wrongfully discharged employees get little or no relief.

B. The Rationality of Employer Retaliation and Employee Silence in an At-Will Environment

Let us assume that employers and employees respond rationally to the costs and benefits they face, and let us see where those assumptions take us. Discharges of

133. *See supra* notes 90-92 and accompanying text.

134. *See* MICELI & NEAR, *supra* note 58, at 235-36.

135. Of 16 federal health and safety statutes with antiretaliation provisions for private sector employees, only two generated more than 45 claims in 1985; 12 of them generated fewer than five complaints. *See Hearings*, *supra* note 65, at 183-84.

136. In other words, we must assume that the lawyer, in deciding whether to take a case, will discount the likely recovery both by its probability (taking into account the quality of the evidence and the difficulties of proof) and the cost of obtaining it. Of course, probability of success and investment of time in investigation and discovery are related.

137. *See* RAND study, *supra* note 88, at 35-36.

138. That is the prescription of several scholars who have studied the efficacy of state whistleblower protection statutes and have found that they did not result in any increase in claims over the common law. *See* Dworkin & Near, *supra* note 64, at 261-62. They suggest that the statutes' apparently low impact may be due in part to their inadequate remedies; none allows punitive damages and some do not even allow compensatory damages. *Id.*

139. FACT FINDING REPORTS, *supra* note 15, at 113.

productive employees, especially discharges that other employees regard as unfair, have costs.[140] Unfair discharges may bruise employee morale and loyalty; they may lead to lower productivity, greater turnover, or perhaps an interest in unionization; a reputation for unfairly discharging employees may hurt the firm's ability to compete for some of the best prospective employees.[141] Unfortunately, the economic deterrents to unfair discharges may be much weaker than they are often portrayed.[142] This is particularly true in the case of discharges based on protected speech.

Consider first that the speech the law protects often harms the employer for the very reason for which it is protected: It brings information to the public or spreads ideas among the workforce that may threaten the employer's chosen way of doing business. So the employer often stands to gain a great deal from the discharge of an employee speaker. For example, the discharge of a union activist will remove one disruptive voice (for that is, at best, how most nonunion employers view union organizing[143]) and will very likely deter others. Similarly, the discharge of an employee who has complained internally of unsafe working conditions may neutralize her complaints, avert a potentially expensive OSHA investigation, and deter other employees from making similar complaints. Unfortunately, the incremental benefit of a single speech-based discharge—suppressing one speaker and deterring others from speaking in ways that harm the organization—will often outweigh the costs of that discharge.[144]

Unfortunately, the unwieldy procedures and limited remedies for enforcing those protections mean that a retaliatory discharge may be cost-effective even after taking into account the prospect of a legal challenge. Speech protections that are enforced administratively present an almost negligible risk, given the unlikelihood of a prosecution and the extremely limited remedies. Even the prospect of civil litigation may not be an adequate deterrent: The hurdles facing potential plaintiffs—the narrow and uncertain scope of wrongful discharge protections, the difficulty of proving motive, the limited recovery in most cases, the delay, and the array of economic and noneconomic costs of

---

140. *See generally* RICHARD A. POSNER, ECONOMIC ANALYSIS OF LAW 306-07 (4th ed. 1992) (discussing costs and benefits of at-will employment); WEILER, *supra* note 22, at 56-78 (same).

141. *See* POSNER, *supra* note 140, at 306-07. By the same token, due process mechanisms and a reputation for fair treatment may help the firm avoid unionization and compete for skilled workers in the external labor market, particularly with union firms. Due process may also enhance productivity and efficiency within the firm by improving management's ability to monitor supervisors in bureaucratic settings, as well as by fostering employee loyalty, morale, and longevity and by encouraging employee investment in and sharing of firm-specific human capital.

142. For example, the motivating force of reputation depends on prospective employees having better information (and better access to information) about the internal workings of the firm, as well as a more realistic appreciation of their chances of being fired, than they probably have. *See* WEILER, *supra* note 22, at 74-75. *See generally* Willborn, *supra* note 29, at 130-32. Union avoidance and union competition motives obviously depend on a realistic threat of unionization, or on competition from union firms. But unionization is in a seemingly relentless decline, and is hardly a factor in large sectors of the economy, including most of the growing service and information sectors.

The productivity claims on behalf of fairness must also be qualified. Fairness and due process are part of a cluster of practices that characterize the "high-wage, high-performance" participatory workplace. Unfortunately, there are alternative strategies for competition—namely, low-cost, low-wage strategies—that are more familiar and congenial to the culture of management, and perhaps even more profitable, in some quarters. *See* Estlund, *supra* note 11, at 954-62.

143. *See* Estlund, *supra* note 11, at 951.

144. Thus, even some "free market devotees" would concede that the incentives that normally discipline employers and lead them to avoid discharges that are unjustified, will not necessarily be sufficient to deter most discharges for "bad reasons," such as reporting a violation of some law that was enacted precisely to constrain the otherwise rational profit seeking conduct of firms. *See* WEILER, *supra* note 22, at 59 n.28.

both the discharge and the litigation to the employee—should lead employers to steeply discount the expected cost of a wrongful discharge.[145]

Moreover, to the extent that employers can predict that some employees are more likely than others to litigate—the most highly paid, the most assertive, or the most litigious—they may discount the risk selectively. Those employees who are most vulnerable and most in need of the protections of unionization and health and safety laws, for example—unskilled and semiskilled workers in production, maintenance, and service jobs—are least likely to litigate. The cost of discharging these workers is further reduced to the extent that employee turnover is high and the employer counts on little loyalty, morale, or investment in and sharing of skills on the part of employees. In those cases especially, it may be rational for the firm to fire an employee who speaks against the interests of firm management.[146]

Not all employers will act "rationally" in disregard of the law. To various degrees and in different ways, many employers feel constrained to obey the law.[147] But others will be sorely tempted to violate the law by firing a disruptive speaker—particularly if the speaker is not a model employee—where the risks and consequences of detection are very low. Many employers will occupy a comparatively safe middle ground: they will simply communicate, explicitly or otherwise, that certain topics are off limits, letting employees translate this if they choose into a threat of retaliation. Indeed, the veiled threat of retaliatory discharge may be the most cost-effective approach for employers, for it may yield most of the benefits of a discharge—suppression and deterrence of speech—with few of the costs.

The problem is not simply that wrongful discharges go unremedied. I am ultimately concerned less with the potential wrongful discharge claims that are not vindicated than with the potential speech that is not spoken. If we assume that employees are generally aware of what it takes to redress a wrongful discharge, and that they tailor their conduct

---

145. This logic will not hold if employers significantly exaggerate the likelihood of litigation, or are extremely risk-averse. They may take excessive precautions in that case. There is some evidence in the private sector that employers in fact do invest far more in avoiding or defending against wrongful discharge liability than the actual incidence and direct costs of litigation in these cases seems to warrant. But the precautions that employers take do not uniformly favor the protection of employees against unjustified discharge. *See infra* notes 173-75 and accompanying text.

146. It is also possible for an organization to "accidentally" punish speech by discharging the speaker. First, the decisionmaker might discharge an employee based on false information stemming from the employee's protected speech; for example, a coworker or immediate supervisor might mischaracterize (deliberately or accidentally) an employee's statements, as may have happened in *Waters*, or falsely report nonspeech misconduct or poor performance as a way of undermining a dissenting employee. Second, the injury might be accidental from the organization's perspective if the decisionmaker is not acting in the interests of the organization—for example, if the employee's speech criticized the decisionmaker personally but did no harm to, or even aided, the organization as a whole.

These are both problems of agency—of mismatched incentives facing organizations and the agents through which they act—that the organization could avoid by taking "precautions." Even in the absence of liability, wise management has an incentive to take some precautions against "accidental" speech-based discharges—those that do more harm than good for the organization. Internal review and appeals processes, through which management could approve and employees could challenge disciplinary actions, would allow upper management to make more informed and prudent decisions and to avoid "accidental" discharges, including some based on protected speech. *See infra* notes 173-75 and accompanying text.

147. The multiple and conflicting forces that motivate firms, and human actors within firms, are not remotely captured by the simple "rational actor" model of economic literature. On the other hand, instrumental rationality plays a very important role, particularly when the prospects of detection and punishment of rational wrongdoing is very low. For an illuminating discussion of the roles of rationality and moral sensibility in regulated firms, see IAN AYRES & JOHN BRAITHWAITE, RESPONSIVE REGULATION: TRANSCENDING THE DEREGULATION DEBATE 20-35 (1992).

accordingly,[148] then we can comfortably predict that all but the most intrepid employees will be deterred, or "chilled," from speaking out in ways that might provoke the employer's displeasure.[149] Keeping in mind that much of this speech is a "public good" and carries no tangible benefit for the speaker, many employees are likely to be "chilled" from speaking out by even a slight and unspoken threat of discharge. The resulting silence of employees about workplace issues and corporate conduct impoverishes public discourse, hinders the enforcement of workplace and economic regulations, and undermines the formation and reform of institutions for employee involvement in workplace decisionmaking. If I am right about the "unfreedom" of employee speech, the workplace may be less a school for democracy than a training ground for apathy and disengagement.

Of course, some people do speak out. There are whistleblowers who defy fears of retaliation and union activists who brave the often open threat of reprisal. But what does it mean for workplace discourse if the only people who speak out against the employer are those who fail or refuse to succumb to rational fears and economic pressures? The few who do speak out may appear to be (and may sometimes be) idiosyncratic, odd, or a little nutty; sometimes the very qualities that enable them to overcome the fears that silence most employees may isolate them and make them both less appealing and less effective in their articulation of potentially shared concerns. As many union activists have learned, their speech itself may heighten the anxiety and even provoke the hostility of the more typical, less brave employee. The current system of freedom of expression in the at-will workplace—the existing patchwork of speech protections against a background of employer power and discretion—gives a false promise of protection that few employees may be willing to test. It fosters an atmosphere in which workplace debate, criticism of current practices, and employee monitoring of workplace conditions are not normal and ongoing, but exceptional, dramatic, and seemingly irrational.

C. Two Models of Due Process in the Private Sector Workplace

For the vast majority of private sector employees who are employed at will, the wrongful discharge system offers the only hope of a remedy. But due process, as I have defined it, is not wholly absent from the private sector workplace. I will turn next to two very different systems of "due process" in the private sector workplace and discuss how they affect the protection of valuable employee speech.

---

148. This may in fact not be true. It may be that, just as employers seem to have an inflated fear of wrongful discharge litigation, *see infra* notes 173-75 and accompanying text, employees are overly optimistic about their abilities to sue employers successfully for what they believe are wrongful discharges. If so, employees would be deterred from speaking out less than I predict, though they would be more often disappointed with their attempts to mount these legal challenges.

149. Employees as well as employers can take precautions against injury, and are especially likely to do so where injuries are likely to go unremedied, whether because of the standard of liability or other practical hurdles to litigation and recovery. *The most effective precaution employees can take to reduce the risk of discharge based on protected speech is silence.* Economists would term this a decrease in the prospective victim's activity level as opposed to an increase in victim care. Here it means simply less employee speech on matters of public interest.

1. "Industrial Due Process" and the Protection of Employee Speech

Virtually all employees represented by a union are protected by a just cause requirement for discipline and discharge, together with a grievance-arbitration system for enforcing it. The just cause clause has generated a body of arbitral law known as "industrial due process."[150] As the unionized sector shrinks to near ten percent of the private sector workforce, this system may seem to be of increasingly marginal importance.[151] But it remains important at least as a model of how "due process" could work in the private sector to protect employee free speech.

Under a just cause provision, the employer must have a valid basis for discipline or discharge. If an employee "grieves" the decision, the union may take the grievance through several steps of discussion with successively higher management officials, and eventually to arbitration. The arbitrator is an impartial third party with experience in labor relations, and often in the particular collective bargaining relationship, who is chosen jointly by the employer and the union, and whose future employment as an arbitrator depends on a reputation for impartiality and evenhandedness. The hearing, at which the employer bears the burden of proof,[152] resembles a trial, but is less formal. An attorney or other representative for each side presents arguments, documents, and witnesses, but briefing is limited or nonexistent. The arbitrator is typically required to render a decision and some short explanation within a few weeks. The standard remedy for a discharge without "just cause" is reinstatement and backpay. The entire process, from the employer's discharge decision to the arbitrator's ruling, may take as little as two to four months.[153]

How does this process protect employee free speech? Industrial due process typically affords no direct, explicit protection of speech at all. Arbitrators are bound to apply the contract; this generally includes principles of industrial due process that have developed out of the just cause requirement, but there is considerable dispute as to whether it includes external law such as protections of whistleblowers and the like.[154] But it is rare, in any event, that an employer will expressly base a discharge on speech that is protected by external law.[155] More typically, the employer denies that the discharge was based on

---

150. For a general review of the principles of "industrial due process," see generally ELKOURI & ELKOURI, *supra* note 113. As in the public sector, it is the employer's acceptance of substantive constraints on its discretion that triggers procedural protections. *See supra* text at notes 114-15. In both cases I include both the substantive and the procedural elements in the term "due process."

151. According to the Bureau of Labor Statistics, 16.7 million workers belonged to unions in 1994. This figure represented 15.5% of all employees but only 10.9% of private sector employees; the union share of private sector employment thus continued its long-term decline. *Data for 1994 Shows Membership in Unions Held Steady at 16.7 Million*, 9 LAB. REL. WK. (BNA) 143 (Feb. 15, 1995).

152. *See* ELKOURI & ELKOURI, *supra* note 113, at 661-63.

153. For a description of this process, see ARCHIBALD COX ET AL., CASES AND MATERIALS ON LABOR LAW 744-47 (11th ed. 1991).

154. *See* ELKOURI & ELKOURI, *supra* note 113, at 366-84 (describing disparate views). Some external law is actually incorporated into the contract. The protections of the labor laws—for example, protections of union activity and other workplace speech under § 7 of the NLRA—are often expressly part of the contract. Many union contracts also incorporate nondiscrimination clauses that roughly parallel Title VII. Other wrongful discharge doctrines are less likely to be incorporated expressly, and may not be considered by the arbitrator.

155. A cautionary note: as of approximately 1970, many whistleblowers (at least those who went public with their disclosures) appear to have lost in arbitration against their employers' successful claims of "disloyalty." *See* Malin, *supra* note 32, at 288-89. One might expect this to have changed as public and judicial approval of whistleblower claims has grown, and as the duty of loyalty has evolved accordingly. But there are few reported arbitration decisions of this nature,

speech and claims some other cause. In that case, the issue is the purely factual one of whether the employer's reason is just cause and is proven by the evidence. Simply putting the employer to its proof will protect employee speech indirectly by making it more difficult to discharge a workplace critic on pretextual grounds.

In addition, on the purely procedural front the employee may challenge the adequacy of the employer's pre-termination process, including the adequacy of notice, compliance with "progressive discipline" in the form of warnings and suspensions prior to discharge, and equitable treatment vis-à-vis other offenders. These procedural requirements are supplemented by the grievance process itself, the first steps of which give the union employee an opportunity to probe the employer's case and often to settle the dispute prior to arbitration. All of this process enforces norms of fair and equal treatment that make it hard for the employer to seize upon minor infractions or lags in performance to discharge employee dissenters.

The employee may also challenge the substantive justification for discipline: she may contest the reasonableness of the employer's rules, the job-relatedness of alleged misconduct, and the severity of the penalty.[156] Through these substantive limitations on discharge, the just cause requirement inevitably generates some protection for "low level" freedom of speech: speech that is not protected by external law, but that is also not harmful enough to justify discharge. Most complaints about workplace conditions, criticism of supervisors or management or aspects of the workplace regime, and workplace arguments will be "protected" simply because they do not violate reasonable workplace rules of which the employee had notice, or are not serious enough to justify the penalty.[157] Appreciation for the value of free expression can readily creep into the determination of just cause, for example, in deciding whether criticizing or challenging a supervisor is "insubordination," or whether heated discussions, and even some rude or offensive language, are part of the "shop talk" that is acceptable under past practice in the workplace.[158]

The employee protected by a just cause clause, like the tenured civil servant, has a kind of property right in continued employment, the termination of which must be justified by good reasons and preceded by fair procedures. If she has the support of her union, the protection of a just cause clause, and a union that believes her discharge was based on legally protected speech, she is in much the same position as the tenured civil servant with a potential First Amendment claim: the employee may challenge her discharge and demand a prompt hearing before an impartial arbitrator, at which the employer must show just cause. The delay and the cost of the proceeding is minimal, and the burdens of proof and uncertainty fall on the employer.

Industrial due process should deter some retaliatory discharges, and it should offer a more accessible remedy for claims of retaliation. But it should also enhance employee freedom of speech at the most basic level by giving employees a measure of breathing

---

probably because, as noted above, employers will rarely confess to a retaliatory motive so as to "test" its legality under the just cause clause.

156. *See* ELKOURI & ELKOURI, *supra* note 113, at 664-73.

157. It is, for example, generally agreed that off-duty, off-premises conduct cannot be cause for discharge unless it has a substantial adverse effect on the employee's work performance or on the firm. *See id.* at 656-58. This principle will protect some employee speech, as well as employee liberty in general.

158. Of course, just cause protection can protect even harmful speech such as sexual harassment against punishment that is hasty or unsupported by the evidence, or that is not the subject of a reasonable, clear, and fairly enforced workplace policy. But I would contend that, on balance, this consequence of due process can foster, rather than defeat, fair, reasonable, and comprehensive efforts to combat harassment. *See* Estlund, *supra* note 37.

room and confidence that they cannot easily be fired or penalized on manufactured grounds. In large part because of these protections, union employees with a well-functioning grievance apparatus and an effective union should experience much more freedom of expression—including in areas in which all employees are supposedly protected—than do nonunion private sector employees.

There is one major functional difference between constitutional due process and industrial due process that has important implications for the protection of speech: unlike constitutional due process, industrial due process is a collective right. Under a collective bargaining agreement, the union decides whether to carry a grievance through arbitration.[159] This makes the employee's position especially vulnerable if her speech is critical of or simply contrary to union policies or procedures.[160] The union is subject to a duty to fairly represent employees, but that does not guarantee every employee a hearing.[161] Moreover, the duty of fair representation is enforceable only through litigation; an employee who is forced to file suit in order to get a hearing on her discharge carries all the burdens that, I have argued, undermine the practical effectiveness of wrongful discharge remedies.

On the other hand, the presence of an active, effective collective bargaining representative bolsters the employee's position in a number of ways. The union is a repeat player standing in a position of rough equality with the employer in selecting an arbitrator; the arbitrator's future livelihood depends on dealing fairly with both sides. The union also provides representation, either by a union official experienced in handling arbitrations or by an attorney. Moreover, if the arbitrator reinstates the individual, the union remains on the scene to help protect the employee's position.

The union's presence in the workplace also supports employees' freedom of expression in ways that go beyond just cause protection. The presence of a strong institutional voice not only backs up employees' freedom to discuss their shared concerns, but gives them tools for redress and reform in the workplace. Unionization, when it works well, brings several elements of democratization to the workplace beyond the elements of due process and free expression. But given the steady decline of union membership over the last few decades, I am loath to conclude that unionization is the necessary precondition for either effective due process or genuine freedom of expression. I therefore turn briefly to another form of due process in the private sector.

---

159. *See* WEILER, *supra* note 22, at 90-92.

160. That has unfortunately been the case in many workplaces with respect to complaints of sexual harassment. *See* Marion Crain, *Women, Labor Unions, and Hostile Work Environment Sexual Harassment: The Untold Story*, 4 TEX. J. WOMEN & L. (forthcoming 1995). Speech critical of union policies is generally protected under § 7 of the NLRA against retaliatory discharge and against union retaliation. But both § 7 rights and the right to fair representation rely on after-the-fact wrongful discharge-type enforcement proceedings, and I have argued that this sort of protection is inadequate. The question here is whether such speech also enjoys the protection of an independent due process protection against unjustified discipline, such as a just cause hearing can provide. Given the union-controlled nature of the right to a hearing, this cannot be assumed. Moreover, a union's refusal to process a grievance because of union dissidence is generally a breach of the duty of fair representation. *See* Breininger v. Sheet Metal Workers' Local 6, 493 U.S. 67 (1989).

161. The union violates its duty of fair representation only if its conduct is "arbitrary, discriminatory, or in bad faith"; the cost of arbitration or the failure to meet filing deadlines may be an adequate excuse for the union's failing to take even a meritorious case to arbitration. United Steelworkers v. Rawson, 495 U.S. 362, 372 (1990) (quoting Vaca v. Sipes, 386 U.S. 171, 190 (1967)).

2. The Growth and Limitations of "Corporate Due Process"

The expansion of wrongful discharge liability has prompted a proliferation of internal grievance procedures established unilaterally by firm management since the mid-1960's.[162] Such systems are most prevalent among large firms and firms with extensive dealings with government; they can be traced in large part to the enactment of substantive constraints on the power to discipline and discharge, particularly the antidiscrimination mandates beginning with the 1964 Civil Rights Act, but also the antiretaliation mandates that I have discussed here.[163] It appears that many private employers, faced with the threat of wrongful discharge liability, are willing to supply some form of due process. Might this be an answer to the problem of free speech and due process in the workplace?

If due process is conceived of as a kind of precaution against wrongful discharge, it may also be a sensible precaution for employers to take on their own. As noted above, unjustified discharges have costs, including legal consequences. We would expect those costs to lead employers to institute procedures for monitoring and reviewing discharge and disciplinary decisions. The basic economic theory of tort law would lead us to expect employers to add precautions up to the point that additional precautions would cost more than would the discharges those precautions might avoid.

Internal due process mechanisms are well suited to avoiding discharges that, on balance, do not serve the firm's interests. Under these systems, decisionmaking is more centralized and more elaborate, providing some mechanism for employees to challenge, within the firm, what they regard as unfair decisions and for employers to avoid potentially costly mistakes. But "mistakes" in this context are discharges, the expected cost of which exceeds their expected benefits. Unfortunately, many wrongful discharges based on protected speech probably cost less, even considering the prospect of liability, than they gain for the firm.[164] The shape of internal due process systems reflects this limitation.

Most companies' grievance procedures consist of either an informal or a formal "open door" policy: a policy allowing an aggrieved employee to approach anyone in management regarding her complaint.[165] Relatively few private companies have more elaborate procedures, including the right to a hearing of some kind.[166] Even those firms with more elaborate forms of due process almost invariably retain ultimate decisionmaking power within the company; the final decision in almost all corporate due process systems, unlike both constitutional and industrial due process systems, lies with upper management.[167] The threat of wrongful discharge liability has not led companies

162. *See* Lauren B. Edelman, *Legal Environments and Organizational Governance: The Expansion of Due Process in the American Workplace*, 95 AM. J. SOC. 1401 (1990). A recent study showed that private firms' maintenance of internal disciplinary procedures for nonunion employees rose from about 5% in 1960-65 to about 47% in 1985. *See* John R. Sutton et al., *The Legalization of the Workplace*, 99 AM. J. SOC. 944, 955 (1994).

163. *See* Edelman, *supra* note 162, at 1428-31; Sutton et al., *supra* note 162, at 965-67.

164. *See supra* notes 140-46 and accompanying text.

165. *See* J. Hoult Verkerke, *Notice Liability in Employment Discrimination Law*, 81 VA. L. REV. 273, 370-71 (1995).

166. *See* Edelman, *supra* note 162, at 1426-35.

167. Estimates of the extent of this due process vary. A 1985 BNA survey found that, among 218 employers with nonunion workforces, 71% maintained formal procedures for appealing disciplinary actions. In 56% of those 154 companies which maintained formal procedures, the chief executive officer made the final decision. Personnel managers decided in 16% of these companies, while department heads decided in 5%. In 19% of the companies, some other company official made the decision. Only 2%—five employers—provided for a decision by an outside arbitrator. The last five were

to submit nonunion personnel disputes to an independent arbitrator as an added precaution against mistaken discharges.[168]

The continued resistance to outside arbitration may be changing in the wake of the Supreme Court's decision in *Gilmer v. Interstate/Johnson Lane Corp.*,[169] which upheld an employee's pre-hire agreement to submit employment disputes to final and binding arbitration, and foreclosed litigation of an employee's claim under the Age Discrimination in Employment Act.[170] A broad interpretation of *Gilmer* would make arbitration not simply an additional precaution against mistaken wrongful discharges, but a shield against liability. It seems likely that many employers will be willing to give up final control over discharge decisions in exchange for freedom from most wrongful discharge litigation.[171] Whether that is a fair exchange, and one that will vindicate the policies underlying the various wrongful discharge doctrines, is another matter with which I will wrestle below. But *Gilmer* notwithstanding, few corporate due process systems currently provide for review of discharge decisions by an impartial outside decisionmaker.

Nor has the threat of liability (nor any other incentive) led management in most cases to make substantive promises of fair treatment. On the contrary, employers *increase* their exposure to one kind of liability—liability for breach of an implied contract—by

all "nonbusiness" entities—government or nonprofit employers. PERSONNEL POLICIES FORUM, BUREAU OF NATIONAL AFFAIRS, EMPLOYEE DISCIPLINE AND DISCHARGE 10 (1985) [hereinafter BNA SURVEY NO. 139]. Another more recent study, however, found that 17% of nonunion businesses had third-party arbitration systems for manufacturing and production employees, 24% for clerical employees, 21% for professional and technical employees, and 20% for managers. David Lewin, *Grievance Procedures in Nonunion Workplaces: An Empirical Analysis of Usage, Dynamics, and Outcomes*, 66 CHI.-KENT L. REV. 823, 824-25 (1990). On the other hand, in a very recent survey of 305 human resource professionals from various industries, conducted by the Society of Human Resource Management, 92.5% of nonunion employers reported "never" using arbitration to resolve personnel disputes. Less than 1% use arbitration "always" and 6.7% use arbitration "sometimes." Of those who use arbitration, however, 30% use nonbinding arbitration, and 12.2% use an in-house panel. *Survey Finds Half of HR Professionals Favor Arbitration of Employee Complaints*, DAILY LABOR REPORT, Oct. 4, 1994, at d11, *available in* LEXIS, Nexis Library, CURNWS file, at d11.

168. That has been true even though courts may be inclined to give the employer "credit" in some wrongful discharge litigation for the use of outside arbitration. One of the landmark implied contract decisions, Toussaint v. Blue Cross & Blue Shield of Michigan, 292 N.W.2d 880 (Mich. 1980), suggested that employers could avoid litigation by providing for binding arbitration. *Id.* at 897. But as several attorneys for management observed, "not too many employers have adopted the 'velvet glove' suggestion made in *Toussaint*. The obvious reason is a traditional reluctance on the part of management to voluntarily place itself in a situation where its decisions can be reversed or modified by others." BOMPEY ET AL., *supra* note 60, at 379. The authors urge employers to take another look. They conclude, "ADR [alternative dispute resolution] is a reasonable approach to dispute management. It reduces an employer's exposure to and liability for wrongful discharge litigation, while at the same time maintaining a positive employee relations climate." *Id.* at 428.

169. 500 U.S. 20 (1991).

170. The scope of *Gilmer* is unclear. *Gilmer* did not technically involve an employment contract but a securities industry broker's agreement that included an agreement to submit all disputes, including employment-related disputes, to binding arbitration. The application of *Gilmer* to ordinary employment contracts is in doubt, and has generated conflicting decisions. That is because the statutory basis of *Gilmer* is the 1947 Federal Arbitration Act which exempts "employment contracts of transportation workers in interstate commerce." 9 U.S.C. §§ 1-14 (1994). Insofar as those were probably the only workers that Congress was confident it might otherwise regulate in 1947, there is a good argument that the statute was not meant to apply to employment contracts at all. But some post-*Gilmer* decisions have construed the exemption for employment contracts narrowly, opening the door to widespread use of binding arbitration agreements in nonunion employment. *See, e.g.*, Crawford v. West Jersey Health Sys., 847 F. Supp. 1232 (D.N.J. 1993); Williams v. Katten, Muchin & Zavis, 837 F. Supp. 1430 (N.D. Ill. 1993); Hampton v. ITT Corp., 829 F. Supp. 202 (S.D. Tex. 1993); Scott v. Farm Family Life Ins. Co., 827 F. Supp. 76 (D. Mass. 1993); Hull v. NCR Corp., 826 F. Supp. 303 (E.D. Mo. 1993); DiCrisci v. Lyndon Guar. Bank of N.Y., 807 F. Supp. 947 (W.D.N.Y. 1992); Hydrick v. Management Recruiters Int'l, 738 F. Supp. 1434 (N.D. Ga. 1990).

171. Lawyers who advise employers are urging greater use of arbitration agreements, largely in view of the lower cost of adjudication, the greater predictability, and faster resolution, as well as the substitution of arbitrators for juries, whose sympathies tend to run toward employees. *See, e.g.*, BOMPEY ET AL., *supra* note 60, at 377-428.

explicitly limiting their right to fire at will in employee handbooks and the like.[172] Along with the growth of internal corporate grievance *procedures* for challenging discipline and discharge, we have seen a flight from substance. The trend is toward adding to employee handbooks express language affirming the right to discharge at will, and toward removing language that appears to limit the permissible grounds for discharge.[173] A typical corporate due process scheme thus offers nothing like the "just cause" requirement that, in my view, is a necessary element of due process.

Employers seek to minimize liability in a variety of ways, many of which do nothing to protect employees against unjustified discharge. Employers may not simply take more precautions against injury; they may also reduce their "activity level"; that is, they may employ fewer individuals. A RAND Corporation study found that the expansion of wrongful discharge liability—particularly tort liability—was associated with a reduction in employment levels that is quite staggering in relation to the comparatively minimal direct costs of litigation.[174] Even if these findings are exaggerated, it is clear that employees do not gain security against wrongful discharge in direct proportion to the increase in wrongful discharge liability.

This evidence suggests that employers are acutely sensitive—even oversensitive—to the threat of wrongful discharge liability.[175] But neither the desire to avoid liability nor the desire to remain nonunion while attracting and retaining skilled and productive employees is pushing employers toward due process as I have defined it. Corporate due process mechanisms are proliferating, but their prevailing forms are shorn of two crucial

---

172. *See* BOMPEY ET AL., *supra* note 60, at 243-56 (describing risks of handbooks to employers and importance of express disclaimers reaffirming right to fire at will). In fact, employers' fear of implied contract liability seems to be greatly exaggerated, largely by employment relations specialists who might thereby increase the demand for their services. *See* Lauren B. Edelman et al., *Professional Construction of Law: The Inflated Threat of Wrongful Discharge*, 26 LAW & SOC. REV. 47 (1992).

173. A 1984 survey of predominantly large companies found that 71% had taken at least one of the following measures in the previous two years to avoid wrongful discharge liability: removing language from handbooks that could be construed as a promise of job security ("permanent employee" or "tenure") or as a limit on the permissible reasons for discharge ("just cause" required for discharge), adding language affirming the employer's right to terminate employment for any reason and disavowing any oral promises to the contrary, training recruiters to refrain from promises of job security, and using severance agreements to arrange for release of all claims against the company by terminated employees. *See* BNA SURVEY NO. 139, *supra* note 167, at 25-27. Professor Verkerke has found the same pattern among large and small employers in five jurisdictions. J. Hoult Verkerke, *An Empirical Perspective on Indefinite Term Employment Contracts: Resolving the Just Cause Debate*, 1995 WIS. L. REV. (forthcoming). The proclivity toward express at-will clauses was especially pronounced in large companies and in jurisdictions with more pro-employee legal doctrines. *Id.*

174. *See* RAND study, *supra* note 137, at xii-xiii. The study found that, in spite of all the hoopla, wrongful discharge litigation was actually "rare," *id.* at xiii, and its actual direct legal costs (including judgments or settlements and attorney's fees and costs) were small. Even in California, which had the most liberal wrongful discharge regime, the average cost of such litigation per employee was less than $10; the cost per termination was at most $100. *Id.* at 35-36. But the study also found that in jurisdictions with the most costly types of wrongful discharge doctrines—particularly those that sound in tort—indirect costs associated with these doctrines are about 100 times as much as direct litigation and liability costs. *Id.* at 62-63.

175. *See supra* notes 172-73. Employers' striking overinvestment in precautions against wrongful discharge liability requires some explanation. The RAND Study authors suggest that employers may believe that the prevalence and costs of wrongful discharge suits are greater than they in fact are (a belief that the employee relations experts might be fostering, intentionally or otherwise), or that employers are successfully avoiding much greater liability costs, or that employers are highly risk averse. *See* RAND study, *supra* note 137, at 64. There may also be costs to employers (such as loss of reputation) that are not accounted for among the direct costs of litigation.

These findings are still astonishing, and challenge even the most restrained assumptions of economic rationality on the part of employers. They suggest a number of questions: Did the study adequately take account of other economic factors affecting employment levels in states like California? Was the study's focus on differences in common law wrongful discharge doctrines sensible in light of the many nationwide limitations on wrongful discharge such as Title VII? One schooled in econometric analysis and the law of employment would do well to scrutinize this major study.

features: impartial resolution of grievances and substantive guarantees that discipline will be just and fair.

We can assume that these systems deliver something that employees value, for if they did not, they would seem to accomplish few of management's own objectives. But internal grievance systems are unlikely to provide a meaningful check against retaliatory measures. Rather, these systems are more likely to curb overreaching or hasty actions by lower level supervisors, provide for more even-handedness in discipline, and implement more routine systems of employee evaluation, and even forestall some justified discharges. These results may give some limited "breathing room" for employee speech, such as criticism of supervisors and the like. But purely internal corporate due process seems unlikely effectively to support employee freedom of speech in areas in which management feels threatened.

D. A Brief Look Back at the Data

I have sought to explain a gap between law and reality, a gap between the freedom of expression that the law purports to afford employees and the freedom that employees seem to experience, based on the incidence and apprehension of retaliation and the willingness to speak out. I have argued that much of the gap results from an underlying presumption of at-will employment that surrounds and constrains each of its exceptions, including the speech protections at issue here. I have also contended that actual freedom of speech in both the public and private sector workplace depends to a great extent on the presence of independent due process protections in the form of procedural and substantive guarantees that discharges and serious discipline are for just cause.

Unfortunately, I know of no studies examining the relationship between employee freedom of expression and job security or due process rights. We are left to draw inferences from the spotty evidence discussed above. The massive study of federal employees discussed above[176] involved the civil service only; given the lack of a comparison group of at-will employees, it can tell little about the significance of due process rights. Still, the study injects a strong cautionary note, for it suggests a fairly high level of managerial hostility and employee "silence" (failure to report perceived wrongdoing) even in the most legally protected environment. Even with the civil service laws and due process rights backing up the explicit protection of federal whistleblowers, many employees experience subtle forms of retaliation that are not easy to detect or challenge, particularly through a due process regime. At least partly as a result, many who observe wrongdoing choose to remain silent.

These data discourage any expectation that due process will insure complete freedom of expression. But my argument is a comparative one: I contend that employees protected by due process will enjoy much *greater* freedom of expression than purely at-will employees. Unfortunately, that claim is fully consistent with the rather discouraging portrayal of free speech in the federal sector. It may be that more severe reprisals are threatened, feared, or carried out, and that the silence resounds all the more loudly in the absence of due process protections.

Some very indirect evidence to this effect may be found in the data on union talk in the pervasively at-will environment of the nonunion private sector. Recall that nearly eighty

---

176. *See supra* notes 71-79 and accompanying text.

percent believed that employers will fire employees who try to organize a union, and over forty percent of nonunion employees believed that they personally would be fired for engaging in union activity.[177] At least as to union talk, many more employees expect much harsher forms of reprisal than was reported in the federal civil service. The comparison is rough but suggestive: perhaps the difference is partly due to strong due process protections in the latter sector, and their complete absence in the former. On the other hand, there is another obvious difference between the two sectors that probably accounts for at least as much of the apparent difference in levels of retaliation: Market forces in the private sector may drastically increase the incentives to suppress speech that is believed to be economically threatening.

Another suggestive piece of evidence is the higher reporting of OSHA violations and the safer conditions present in union as compared to nonunion workplaces.[178] This evidence offers some confirmation of my strong impression that union employees, who are protected by a just cause clause and who have access to a grievance process, feel much more free than nonunion employees to discuss workplace issues with their coworkers and bring grievances to management. Unfortunately, other differences between nonunion and union shops again confound the picture. It would appear nearly impossible to isolate the influence of industrial due process—as opposed to the other advantages of having an informed agent for the collective body of workers and a collective bargaining relationship with the employer—in fostering greater freedom of speech.

There is currently little empirical evidence for my claim about the fundamental significance of due process in the system of freedom of expression in the workplace. On the other hand, I do not believe that the propositions are counterintuitive, or that they require big inferential leaps, for they follow quite reasonably from an assumption that employee behavior is basically rational. Speaking out on issues of public and collective concern promises little direct benefit to the employee and poses a significant risk, or at least a perceived risk, of direct harm in the form of employer retaliation. Under the existing "wrongful discharge model" of speech protections, such retaliation, even when it is unlawful, may be very hard to redress. Under a due process model, speaking out is less costly because redressing employer retaliation is easier, faster, and cheaper. Recognizing that the proof is incomplete, I hope to have laid the groundwork for more research and analysis of the contours of the existing and the best system of freedom of expression in the workplace.

VI. Securing Free Speech Through Due Process in the Workplace: Some Preliminary Observations on Implementation

I have argued for the recognition of a basic principle of fair treatment and due process to provide a foundation for the system of freedom of expression in the workplace. The proposal is *not* narrowly tailored to meet the free speech problem I have identified; on the contrary, I have argued that the existing narrowly tailored approaches to protecting

177. *See supra* note 85 and accompanying text. The disparity between the two figures seems to reflect employees' belief that their own employer is more fair and just than the typical employer. Whether this reflects an overly optimistic assessment of their own employer or an overly cynical opinion of other employers is not evident from this study.

178. *See supra* note 92 and accompanying text.

valuable speech—which take the form of discrete statutory and common law remedies against particular kinds of retaliatory discharge—have failed to overcome the shadow cast by the basic at-will presumption.

The implications of my analysis obviously reach far beyond the protection of freedom of expression, into parallel issues of "equal protection" in the workplace, and into the ideology and economics of managerial prerogatives that form the background for all workplace regulations and employee rights. So I do not pretend to have offered a complete case for the abandonment of the at-will rule and its replacement with a regime of just cause and due process. Rather, I have sought to inject into the broader debate over at-will and just cause regimes a recognition of some of the less visible costs of the existing at-will rule. Among the significant costs of at-will employment is the undermining of existing legal protections of employee speech and the resultant unfreedom of workplace discourse. But in this final Part, I will offer some preliminary thoughts on how to implement universal due process in the public sector (in Part VI. A) and in the private sector (in Part VI. B), with an eye toward the present objective of supporting freedom of expression.[179]

A. Universalizing Due Process in the Public Sector

Universal due process for discharge is not hard to envision in the public sector; it was indeed envisioned and rejected over twenty years ago in the early public employee due process cases. But the logic is sound: The government is subject to the substantive constitutional constraints of the First Amendment and the Equal Protection Clause, as well as the minimal obligation to act reasonably—not "arbitrarily and capriciously"—in its dealings with citizens. When the government is dealing with its own employees, weighty interests are affected, for one's job is the foundation of economic, psychic, social, and moral well-being, and discharge from employment has particularly devastating consequences. So, in the context of termination of employment, the inherent constitutional constraints on government action should translate into an entitlement protected by the due process clause: All public employees should be entitled, before they are finally discharged, to a hearing before an impartial decisionmaker at which the government must demonstrate a constitutionally valid reason for discharge: a reason that is not arbitrary and is not otherwise unconstitutional.[180]

Under this broad view of due process—admittedly a blast from the Warren Court past—due process would serve as a bulwark for other substantive constitutional protections, including the First Amendment. Speech protected by law, such as speech on matters of public concern that is not unduly disruptive, could not constitute a valid reason

179. Once again, I recognize that due process has costs as well as benefits beyond those I have discussed in depth. But we should keep in mind that the relevant comparison is not with a pure at-will regime but with the current system of modified at-will employment, with a heavy overlay of wrongful discharge liability. The current system, a good deal of which could be supplanted by a universal due process regime, appears to have enormous costs, as well as rather disappointing benefits, at least for freedom of speech.

180. If the discharge was found to be unjustified, the remedy would normally be reinstatement and back pay. There might be an exception to the general just cause and procedural protections for "probationary employees," or those on the job for six months or less. The weight of the individual interests at stake grows with the period of incumbency, and at the very beginning of one's tenure may be outweighed by the government's interest in expeditiously discharging unsatisfactory employees during a "trial period." All public employees have First Amendment rights, of course, and could bring their claim directly to court under the *Waters v. Churchill* standard. *See Waters*, 114 S. Ct. 1878. Of course, very few probationary employees would do so, given their limited investment in the job.

for discharge.[181] Simply requiring the government to prove a nonarbitrary and valid reason for discharge would give added protection to speech of public concern and would effectively protect some speech that, while not deemed important enough to merit First Amendment protection, is not so disruptive as to constitute a legitimate basis for discharge. This would create a buffer zone around the critical core of speech on matters of public concern, and allow some breathing room for employee speech.[182]

What effect would universal due process have on the level of employee speech, the number of wrongful discharges, or the volume of litigation? These are all empirical questions on which I can currently offer only informed speculation. If I am right about the value of due process, it should encourage more employee speech critical of or disagreeable to public employers. As the federal whistleblower data demonstrate, universal due process would not produce complete freedom of expression, but it would surely give added security to otherwise at-will employees against the most powerful forms of retaliation for protected speech.[183] By the same token, due process safeguards should reduce public employers' resort to retaliation. The need to justify discharge would make such retaliation easier to uncover and harder to carry out than it currently is for employers.

What about the volume of litigation? Less retaliation should result in less litigation. But we might see less litigation even without optimistic assumptions about less retaliation. Due process allows employees who are fired, and who challenge their discharges, to peek into the black box of the personnel process and learn something about the employer's justifications for these decisions. This gives them some free discovery if they decide to litigate and in any event educates them about the employer's defense. Some employees who would otherwise not litigate might be encouraged to do so by information they discover in the administrative proceedings. But some who win at the hearing will be satisfied with the outcome and forgo the additional cost, stress, and risks of litigation. Some who lose at the hearing will conclude that their case is weaker than they had thought. It is possible, though hardly certain, that the net effect of a due process regime would be less First Amendment litigation.[184] The litigation that does occur even after a due process hearing should, in any event, be based on a more educated assessment of the facts.

A more modest alternative is also possible: employers might be required to give all public employees at least the minimal pre-termination process called for by *Loudermill*:"[o]ral or written notice of the charges against him, an explanation of the

181. I intend by this formulation to accept as given, for purposes of this due process proposal, existing First Amendment doctrine defining what speech is protected. I remain critical of both the public concern requirement, particularly as applied by the courts, and the too deferential balancing test that follows. But as to the former, I have said my piece, *see* Estlund, *supra* note 50. As to the excessively deferential balancing test, I do not wish to further prolong and complicate this Article with my critique, which would in any event largely echo the critiques of others. *See* Lieberwitz, *supra* note 50; Massaro, *supra* note 6.

182. Though I have criticized the "matters of public concern" limitation on public employees' freedom of speech, *see* Estlund, *supra* note 50, that limitation would be less threatening if it was coupled with a background principle of basic rationality and fairness.

183. The due process hearing would provide a relatively accessible, low-cost forum for the vast majority of now-at-will employees who otherwise would have no realistic remedy. But the Constitution would still afford the employee a right to bring a First Amendment claim to court. Litigation may be an unwieldy and insufficient mechanism for vindicating employee free speech rights in the majority of cases, but it is still a necessary one, particularly for the most important cases, in which the public interest is greatest. So the employee who lost her due process hearing, or who won and sought additional remedies, could still bring a First Amendment lawsuit.

184. This does not mean that a universal due process system would cost the government less overall, for a due process regime has some costs of its own.

employer's evidence, and an opportunity to present his side of the story" *before termination.*[185] Employees who are then in fact discharged, and who claim that their discharge is actually based on protected speech (or some other illegal ground), would be entitled to a full post-termination process of the sort available to tenured civil servants. In the absence of a substantive just cause requirement, the issue at the hearing would be simply whether the discharge resulted from protected speech; the burden of proof would logically rest with the employee.

Such a hybrid procedure would be less costly and would offer some support to free speech rights by providing an inexpensive and relatively prompt hearing on the retaliation claim.[186] But it would leave in place the hurdle of proving motive, and it would not confer the indirect protection of speech—the breathing room—that just cause or its equivalent would. It would also yield some of the same anomalous results as the *Waters* plurality: If the requisite predetermination inquiry or the later hearing disclosed that the employee "had been complaining about the perennial end-of-season slump of the Chicago Cubs, her dismissal, erroneous as it was, would have been perfectly OK."[187]

Just as in the case of the plurality's approach in *Waters*, these complications and anomalies can be traced to the attempt to preserve a sphere of at-will employment—of virtually unfettered employer discretion—in the public sector. I am inclined to view that sphere as an anachronistic holdover from the days of the "rights/privileges distinction" that long kept the Constitution out of the sphere of government employment and benefits. It is hard to reconcile with, and in fact undermines, the full range of substantive constitutional and statutory protections that have arisen in the last thirty years.

The proposed universalization of due process would do more to protect the speech rights of now-at-will public employees than would any of the opinions in *Waters*. But it would do so by reaching far beyond the relatively few cases in which public employees claim they are fired for protected speech. Securing the free speech rights of public employees may not be a sufficient justification for extending due process rights to all. But when we assess the costs and the benefits of such a regime—both of which go beyond the impact on employee speech—we should attempt to take into account the significant cost of silence that I believe attends the present regime and the largely unquantifiable benefits of supporting the freedom of public employees to speak out on matters of concern to them and the public.

B. Universal Just Cause and Free Speech in the Private Sector: Lessons from Industrial and Corporate Due Process

The analogue to these proposals in the private sector—statutory just cause protection—has been debated among labor law scholars for many years.[188] Admittedly,

---

185. Cleveland Bd. of Educ. v. Loudermill, 470 U.S. 532, 546 (1985).

186. It would thus resemble the administrative processes available to enforce most of the statutory antiretaliation provisions discussed above, though with the additional protection and information provided by the informal pre-termination process, and with the employee herself, rather than an administrative agency, in control of her case.

187. *See* Waters v. Churchill, 114 S. Ct. 1878, 1895 (1994) (Scalia, J., concurring).

188. Professor Clyde Summers published his pathbreaking article nearly 20 years ago. Clyde W. Summers, *Individual Protection Against Unjust Dismissal: Time for a Statute*, 62 VA. L. REV. 481 (1976). The problem of unjust discharge and proposals for its redress predate Professor Summers' article. *See, e.g.*, Lawrence E. Blades, *Employment at Will vs. Individual Freedom: On Limiting the Abusive Exercise of Employer Power*, 67 COLUM. L. REV. 1404 (1967); Philip J. Levine, Comment, *Towards A Property Right in Employment*, 22 BUFF. L. REV. 1081 (1973); J. Peter Shapiro & James

employee speech is involved in only a small fraction of the discharges that would be affected by a shift to just cause. Still, I maintain that among the virtues of just cause protection is the important and largely unrecognized benefit of expanding real employee freedom of speech, both that speech which currently enjoys formal protection and some speech that currently does not.[189]

Innumerable questions of forum and procedure would arise under such a proposal: Should it be a state or federal forum?[190] What kind of tribunal: arbitral or administrative? What time limits for a hearing and a decision? How much discovery? While these and other questions must be answered before a proposal can be implemented, I choose to put these questions largely beyond the scope of this Article.[191] But a few observations are in order.

The union experience demonstrates that it is both important and possible to design a process that is expeditious and inexpensive (compared to litigation), with adequate but not extravagant remedies, and with fair and impartial decisionmakers. In two respects, however, the system proposed here would differ from industrial due process. First, any system of universal due process should entertain not only the just cause issue but any argument that the discharge is in fact for reasons that are unlawful; external law should thus be fully in force within the due process proceedings. Moreover, the individual should have full control over her case; no intermediary could decide not to seek a hearing.

But the union experience raises an important concern on the other side. Unions, as potentially powerful collective institutions in the workplace, bring far more than the industrial equivalent of due process to the employees they represent. Would a universal mandate of just cause support employee free speech in the absence of institutions that perform at least some of the functions that unions perform? The short answer is that just

---

F. Tune, Note, *Implied Contract Rights to Job Security*, 26 STAN. L. REV. 335 (1974).

189. There has been little attention in the literature to the role that just cause protection would have in protecting employee freedom of speech. Among the most important problems Professor Summers recognized was retaliation for "whistleblowing," which was rarely actionable at the time unless protected by statute. *See* Summers, *supra* note 188, at 481-83. The problem that loomed largest for Professor Summers in 1976 was the limited scope of existing protections of speech, not the difficulty of enforcing them. *See id.* at 491-99.

190. Given the many federal statutes whose antiretaliation provisions (and antidiscrimination provisions) would be supported by a just cause requirement, together with the national economic interest in reducing wrongful discharge litigation and in expanding employee voice and participation in the workplace, a federal statute would probably be appropriate. I recognize the complicated issues of federalism that such a proposal raises, but I choose to put them beyond the scope of this Article. For a detailed proposal for a federal statute, see Jack Stieber & Michael Murray, *Protection Against Unjust Discharge: The Need for a Federal Statute*, 16 U. MICH. J.L. REF. 319 (1983).

On the other hand, the proposal that has achieved greatest currency nationally is that approved by the Commission on Uniform State Laws as the Model Employment Termination Act ("META"), which no state has yet adopted. Some of the choices made by the drafters of the META illustrate areas of controversy and the political forces that will tend to operate in this area. *See* Theodore J. St. Antoine, *The Making of the Model Employment Termination Act*, 69 WASH. L. REV. 361 (1994). In addition, Montana has adopted its own version of statutory just cause: Wrongful Discharge From Employment Act, MONT. CODE ANN. §§ 39-2-901 to -914 (1991). For assessments of early experiences with the statute, see Leonard Bierman & Stuart A. Youngblood, *Interpreting Montana's Pathbreaking Wrongful Discharge From Employment Act: A Preliminary Analysis*, 53 MONT. L. REV. 53 (1992); Leonard Bierman et al., *Montana's Wrongful Discharge From Employment Act: The Views of the Montana Bar*, 54 MONT. L. REV. 367 (1993).

191. Professor Weiler makes a strong case for an administrative scheme, modeled on the unemployment and workers' compensation systems, that would offer "rough justice and limited relief" in the form of scheduled financial remedies for unjustified discharges; he would keep in place the existing tort scheme for discharges for "bad reasons" that contravene public policy. WEILER, *supra* note 22, at 99-104. Because I am more skeptical about the efficacy of the tort system even within that limited realm, I might be willing to move further toward integration of the existing tort actions into an administrative scheme. But these are disagreements of detail. In the main, I would embrace Professor Weiler's proposed scheme, but I would do so in part because of the role I believe such a scheme would play in reinforcing the protections that the law purports to guarantee already through statutory and common law wrongful discharge law.

cause and an individual right to a hearing should accomplish no less in the private sector than it does in the public sector. But this answer may be too short. It would not be surprising to discover greater depths of resistance in the private sector to the demise of the right to fire employees at will and to an order to reinstate an unjustly fired employee.[192]

A "works council" within the workplace, or even an employee membership organization operating outside the workplace, could perform some of the functions of a union, such as monitoring the performance of decisionmakers, providing experienced representation, and perhaps helping to secure the notoriously vulnerable status of the reinstated employee.[193] At a minimum, there would need to be an "employee bar," consisting of attorneys experienced in and willing to handle discharge cases, to help employees present their cases effectively. In order to attract private attorneys for ordinary employees, an effective just cause regime must include some provision for reasonable attorney's fees.

All this is possible under some form of universal mandate, accompanied by either a system of arbitration or a network of administrative tribunals. But is a one-size-fits-all solution the only or the best way to institute universal due process? The rise of "corporate due process" shows that there are forces both inside and outside private firms that favor the institution of some form of due process. The emerging employer response to *Gilmer* in particular suggests that there may be forms of legal intervention short of a universal, mandatory just cause regime that could dramatically expand the availability of real due process for employees.

The Supreme Court's decision in *Gilmer* has been read by some courts to allow employers to require employees, as a condition of employment, to submit legal disputes, to binding arbitration, subject to certain minimum requirements as to the quality of the arbitration process: the arbitrator must be impartial, the employee must have an adequate opportunity to present her case, adequate remedies must be available in arbitration, etc.[194] A modified *Gilmer* doctrine, including a more substantial set of minimum requirements for the arbitration agreement, could induce employers to give employees genuine due process in exchange for giving up their right to the more elaborate and expensive avenue of civil litigation. Most importantly and most controversially, I would propose that, in exchange for freedom from most civil litigation and all its direct and indirect costs, the employer must give up its power to fire employees at will, and must give a promise of just cause for termination, enforceable through arbitration. This requirement would leave the employer with substantial freedom to define what just cause means through the promulgation of rules and standards of performance. But it would give the employee something valuable in exchange for the rights she has under a variety of wrongful

---

192. To some proponents of employer discretion, that may be a mild comfort; just cause in the private sector is very unlikely to evolve into the equivalent of civil service tenure, if only because we would expect private sector employers to more effectively and vigorously press their need for productive and competitive employees. This observation only underscores the vulnerability of the private sector employee in the absence of a powerful institutional advocate.

193. Commentators have argued that reinstatement is an ineffective remedy outside the union context, because the lone employee is so vulnerable to repeated reprisals. *See, e.g.*, WEILER, *supra* note 22, at 85-86. That is most likely to be the case if reinstatement is long delayed, as it is under all current wrongful discharge doctrines. I believe that prompt reinstatement is crucial in the context of retaliation for protected speech, because of the chilling effect that a discharge has on other employees. Although alternative remedies such as "front pay" ought to be available where reinstatement appears to be inappropriate or impractical, reinstatement ought to be the standard remedy, and the process should be structured to make reinstatement viable.

194. *See* Gilmer v. Interstate/Johnson Lane Corp., 500 U.S. 20, 30-32 (1991).

discharge laws and doctrines to put the employer through the very costly litigation process.[195]

Some of the hardest questions that remain concern the extent to which the due process hearing should substitute for access to the courts. Again, a broad reading of *Gilmer* would allow employers to move very far in the direction of cutting off access to the judicial forum through "binding arbitration," with, presumably, only the very limited judicial review to which arbitration awards are normally subject. In practical political and economic terms, the only prospect for this sort of sweeping reform would be to give employers substantial relief from the threat of large civil verdicts and costly litigation. Such a system would reduce and spread out the cost of windfall judgments and other direct and indirect costs of litigation by largely replacing the current system with a less costly and elaborate, yet more accessible and dependable, system of protection for the typical employee.[196]

In my view, most employee would do well to trade the slim, "lottery-like" prospect of a large wrongful discharge judgment for a genuinely fair and accessible administrative or arbitral process for challenging the fairness of a discharge. But the complete "privatization" of employment law would not serve the public interest, which is deeply implicated in many of the doctrines involved here, including those concerning the protection of free speech. The answer may lie in a bifurcated standard of judicial review: findings of fact and determinations of just cause simpliciter would be subject to very limited review, but conclusions of law—for example, regarding which causes for discharge violate public policy or particular statutes—would be subject to de novo review.[197]

As a historical matter, it seems clear that a good deal of the impetus behind the growth of common law wrongful discharge law, and even of some statutory interventions, has been dissatisfaction with the underlying at-will presumption to which employees are otherwise relegated. This is true not only of the broadest challenges to at-will employment, in the form of the implied covenant of good faith dealing and implied-in-fact contract doctrines, but even of some of the common law public policy exceptions. Perhaps the most amusing illustration is *Wagenseller v. Scottsdale Memorial Hospital*,[198]

195. One problem with the *Gilmer* option is that it will offer no relief to employees who are unlikely to litigate, for the attraction of binding arbitration depends largely on the threat of wrongful discharge liability. There is yet another possible approach, short of a straightforward regulatory command, to expanding due process more broadly: "mandatory self-regulation." *See* AYRES & BRAITHWAITE, *supra* note 147, at 101-32 (discussing merits of "enforced self-regulation"). Under mandatory self-regulation, the law would prescribe minimum standards for due process—for example, as discussed in relation to *Gilmer*—but then allow each employer to create a system which best suits its particular workplace, including a definition of cause for discharge. The law would then supply an administrative mechanism for those workplaces with no adequate system of their own. Mandatory self-regulation takes advantage of voluntary employer initiatives and the diverse motives behind them, recognizes the need for flexibility and variation among workplaces, and potentially increases the effectiveness and economy of regulation. Such an approach would work best in tandem with some form of universal employee representation (perhaps also promoted through mandatory self-regulation), so that employees would have a collective agent to monitor the operation of the due process system. *See id.* at 54-100 (discussing the virtues of "tripartism," or the empowerment of third-party institutions to monitor the interaction of regulators and the regulated firms). On the possible use of "mandatory self-regulation" in the area of workplace sexual harassment, see Anita Bernstein, *Law, Culture, and Harassment*, 142 U. PA. L. REV. 1227, 1292-95 (1994).

196. Similarly, the only way employers will enter a *Gilmer*-type binding arbitration agreement (particularly under the stricter standards I tentatively propose) is if they can expect to foreclose a good part of the litigation to which they might otherwise be subject.

197. For a thorough justification of this dual standard of judicial review of arbitration of individual employment rights, see Martin H. Malin & Robert F. Ladenson, *Privatizing Justice: A Jurisprudential Perspective on Labor and Employment Arbitration from the* Steelworkers Trilogy *to* Gilmer, 44 HASTINGS L.J. 1187 (1993).

198. 710 P.2d 1025 (Ariz. 1985) (en banc).

in which the Arizona Supreme Court found a public policy exception to the at-will rule in the state's indecent exposure statute in order to rescue a nurse who was fired allegedly for refusing to engage in "mooning" and other risqué activities at an employee retreat.[199] Cases such as *Wagenseller* suggest that the oddly shaped and growing body of wrongful discharge doctrine is largely a product of the clash between the at-will rule and developing norms of fairness in the employment arena. In other words, under a background rule of just cause, much of this doctrine would never have come into being.

In fact, the whole law of wrongful discharge would need to be reevaluated if we reversed the crucial background assumption of employer discretion to discharge at will. The background assumption of termination at will is so full of holes that it offers little comfort to employers and induces them to take expensive defensive measures; in its current form it has none of the virtues that its market-oriented champions claim for it. On the other hand, the at-will presumption erodes each of the many exceptions that have developed, betraying the legal promise of protection to those who most need it. The at-will rule leaves the majority of discharged employees adrift and without recourse, looking enviously at those to whom the law promises protection, however incomplete that protection proves to be. Starting over on the basis of a promise of just cause protection could hardly yield a worse system than what we now have.

CONCLUSION

The at-will presumption in employment has been under attack for decades, and has become riddled with exceptions, each of them motivated by concerns of justice and the public good. But the debate over at-will employment has occupied a shrinking terrain. Both sides in the debate have tended to assume that the domain of the at-will presumption retreats with the adoption of each wrongful discharge exception, and that it now is significant only for the cases in which the employer's reason for discharge is not discriminatory, retaliatory, nor otherwise unlawful, but is (or may be) just not good enough to justify discharge. This belief has lent a strongly economic cast to the debate, in which the preferences of the contracting parties and not the public welfare are the dominant concerns. I believe the critics of at-will employment have ceded too much important ground. My basic argument is that the at-will presumption remains important not only in the residual areas where no exceptions apply, but also in weakening each of the many exceptions and the public interests underlying them and in continuing to foster a destructive sense of vulnerability in the workplace.

The present argument concerns the significance of the at-will regime for employee freedom of expression. Just as our freedom of expression as citizens depends largely on the government's obligation to act on rational grounds and to follow fair procedures in its treatment of us, actual freedom of speech for both public and private employees depends on some independent guarantee of fair treatment together with fair procedures for enforcing it. Where there is an effective system of industrial due process, private employees may experience as much freedom of expression as against their employer as do tenured public employees, and more freedom of expression than do at-will public employees. Where there is no such due process, employees, whether public or private, will not experience the freedom of expression that the law purports to afford them.

199. *Id.* at 1038-40.

Fairness helps resolve a multitude of problems. A universal requirement of just cause and fair process would provide crucial support and "breathing room" for the existing free speech rights of public and private employees. It would dissolve the embarrassing paradoxes advertised by Justice Scalia in *Waters*; no longer would the discharge of a public employee for "complaining of the perennial end-of-season slump of the Chicago Cubs"[200] be perfectly lawful. Due process may even offer something to employers: a prompt, low-cost, fair remedy for unjustly discharged employees could supplant at least some of the most costly and least predictable of the wrongful discharge remedies.

This Article is thus part of a larger project on the consequences for the workplace and the society of the prevailing juxtaposition of at-will employment and its various "wrongful discharge" exceptions. The lack of substantive and procedural due process rights affects not just the willingness of employees to speak freely, but other aspects of workplace dynamics as well. In the present legal environment, the at-will employee must claim unlawful discrimination or retaliation of some kind in order to secure a review of her unexplained and unappealable termination. This may encourage some employees to see and to claim discrimination or retaliation where there is only personal favoritism, pique, or sloppiness in evaluation or investigation. Certainly if these employees consult an attorney they will be encouraged to portray their claim in that light. At the same time, the apparent availability of discrimination arguments by some employees may foster resentment by others who may perceive fairness as a special privilege from which they are excluded. Without substantive and procedural due process rights for all employees in the workplace, the net result may be a dynamic of fragmentation and polarization.

Fair treatment should not be or appear to be a special privilege. The time may have come to move from the old rule of unfettered employer discretion, riddled as it now is with exceptions, to a new rule of fair treatment. A requirement of just cause and a fair administrative procedure for enforcing it would do much to realize free speech and other legal rights for those employees for whom litigation is not a real alternative, and it could provide a cheaper, quicker, and less disruptive alternative for some employees who would otherwise choose litigation.

Legally mandated fairness, in the form of a universal due process regime, has costs, of course. I do not claim to have assessed either all of the costs or all of the benefits of a universal just cause regime. But among the benefits of due process, we must count the support of employee freedom of speech. Due process is needed to undergird existing free speech rights in the workplace, public and private, just as due process is necessary in society generally to protect citizens' free speech rights against government overreaching and retaliation.

---

200. Waters v. Churchill, 114 S. Ct. 1878, 1895 (1994) (Scalia, J., concurring).

Acknowledgments

National Labor Relations Board v. *Jones and Laughlin Steel Corp.*, 301 U.S. 1–49 (1937).

Epstein, Richard A. "A Common Law for Labor Relations: A Critique of the New Deal Labor Legislation." *Yale Law Journal* 92 (1983): 1357–1408. Reprinted by permission of The Yale Law Journal Company and Fred B. Rothman and Company.

Getman, Julius G. and Thomas C. Kohler. "The Common Law, Labor Law, and Reality: A Response to Professor Epstein." *Yale Law Journal* 92 (1983): 1415–34. Reprinted by permission of The Yale Law Journal Company and Fred B. Rothman and Company.

National Labor Relations Board v. *Catholic Bishop of Chicago*, 440 U.S. 490–518 (1979).

Trans World Airlines, Inc. v. *Hardison*, 432 U.S. 63–97 (1977).

Gregory, David L. "Government Regulation of Religion Through Labor and Employment Discrimination Laws." *Stetson Law Review* 22 (1992): 27–68. Reprinted with the permission of the Stetson Law Review.

Communications Workers of America v. *Beck*, 487 U.S. 735–780 (1988).

Waters v. *Churchill*, 511 U.S. 661–699 (1994).

Estlund, Cynthia L. "Free Speech and Due Process in the Workplace." *Indiana Law Journal* 71 (1995): 101–51. Copyright 1995 by the Trustees of Indiana University. Reprinted by permission.